Forensic Mental Health
Counseling

Forensic Mental Health
Counseling

Leigh Falls Holman, Ph.D.

University of Memphis

SAN DIEGO

Bassim Hamadeh, CEO and Publisher
Laura Pasquale, Specialist Acquisitions Editor
Amy Smith, Project Editor
Casey Hands, Associate Production Editor
Jess Estrella, Senior Graphic Designer
Sara Schennum, Licensing Associate
Kim Scott/Bumpy Design, Interior Designer
Natalie Piccotti, Senior Marketing Manager
Kassie Graves, Vice President of Editorial
Jamie Giganti, Director of Academic Publishing

3970 Sorrento Valley Blvd., Ste. 500, San Diego, CA 92121

Brief Contents

Table of Contents

Preface

WHY THIS BOOK?

This book is the result of a process I have gone through first as a clinical mental health counselor, then as a counselor educator and researcher. I have counseled children, adolescents, and adults in forensic settings since 1993. I care deeply about this group of people, so having become somewhat of an expert in working with them, I decided to become a counselor educator. However, as a professor I found that little specific information or skills are taught related to forensic counseling.

There are classes that teach students about offender profiles, those that teach about victim profiles, some special topics classes on domestic violence, sex offender treatment, or treatment of substance use disorders (SUDs) without always specifically talking about the mandated nature of counseling for many with SUDs. Generally, even when there is forensic-related coursework, victim and offender are separated in these classes. They are treated as two distinct categories, rather than addressing the complexity of relational entanglements that lead some victims to become offenders, lead some to repeatedly enter victimizing relationships, and yet others emerge from them experiencing traumatic growth. In fact, the relationships between adverse childhood trauma (ACEs) and development of mental illness, addictions, or offending behaviors tend not to be emphasized in the coursework, although professionals understand more and more that there is a connection, and that due to this fact, we really need to utilize trauma-informed interventions in order to be effective.

Also, in partnering with jails and prisons whose staff reported feeling overwhelmed by the numbers and severity of mentally ill offenders in their care, I began to realize that the "counseling" provided, as mandated by the Eighth Amendment, was often provided by people called "counselors" who actually had little to no training in counseling. Counseling is a profession that trains people in the assessment, diagnosis, and treatment of mental health disorders across socioculturally diverse populations. It involves the application of research-informed interventions using counseling skills, which are taught didactically, practiced in labs, evaluated, and practiced in the community and evaluated further. At the end of didactic education and practical training components, counselors can earn licensure at the master's or doctoral degree level.

Counseling is not a skill set that involves advice giving, solely case management, or regurgitating pre-canned workbook lessons to a disinterested group of court-mandated clients. But, if the person "counseling" does not actually have training or skills in counseling, then these other pseudo-counseling activities often become what the correctional counselor engages in. Truthfully, this does not meet the spirit of the Eighth Amendment mandate for appropriate qualified professional care. Some organizations have begun to train their staff in motivational interviewing, which is an improvement utilizing some counseling skills, but it is not the expectation across forensic settings.

I am also very aware that the ethical and legal issues these new counselors in forensic settings would face were some of the most challenging ones any counselor could face in his or her career. There were unique issues related to mandated treatment (whether as a victim or as an offender) that challenged how we deal with limits to confidentiality, informed consent, and our understanding of the principles underlying our foundational ethics. There are questions about who the counselor's client really is; is it the judge? The child protective services worker? The probation officer mandating treatment? Or was it the person sitting in front of the counselor seeking treatment? Documentation and risk assessment are also heightened concerns in forensic settings. Additionally, because the environments are intense, complicated, potentially risky, and often under-resourced, there is a genuine risk of job stress, vicarious trauma, compassion fatigue, and burnout negatively impacting these valuable counselors and potentially compromising their work with clients through impairment, resulting in a competency to practice issue. These are just a few of the unique issues that counselors need to understand before working with forensic populations (victims or offenders).

Over the past 10 years teaching, I also realized that many students were placed in clinical forensic settings working with kids and families involved with child protective services or child advocacy centers, following abuse or neglect; in domestic violence shelters or domestic violence perpetrator programs; in court-mandated addiction treatment programs or sex offender treatment programs. This is not likely to change, given that there are more people with serious mental illnesses placed in jails and prisons in most counties and states in the nation than are placed in county or state mental health institutions. Therefore, more counselors (qualified, trained counselors) are needed to provide appropriate treatments based on a special set of knowledge and skills. I have diligently searched for resources, integrated my knowledge informally into almost every class I taught, but I always knew we needed to have the option of coursework in forensic mental health counseling to meet these needs. However, I had trouble finding any textbook I could use to teach students about counseling in forensic settings with victims and offenders. The population-specific coursework mentioned previously is great, but it does not provide a foundational understanding of the breadth of issues counselors will be faced with in many clinical placements.

APPROACH OF THE TEXT

The approach taken in this text is consistent with the counseling profession's orientation toward viewing human behavior from a strengths-based, holistic, developmental lens. It is **strengths based** by valuing assessment and treatment planning, which identifies and incorporates a client's resources and resilience factors, in addition to maladaptive behavior or risk factors. As a result, I will encourage readers to strive to *understand* the behavior, rather than simply label or categorize it. It is **holistic** by examining contextual factors affecting behavior. Finally, the text is **developmental** by attempting to understand the developmental trajectory of presenting issues and viewing resulting behavior(s) as adaptive within the context it develops, even if maladaptive in new contexts. As part of the developmental approach, the text discusses how interpersonal neurobiology affects and is affected by interpersonal interactions and sociocultural influences. I integrate basic information on developmental neurobiology in order to inform our understanding of common behaviors presented in forensic settings. The text presents this material in a simplistic and concise manner aimed at communicating with someone who does not have or need a more complex understanding of neurobiology.

The counseling interventions recommended are similarly **neuro-developmentally sensitive,** including use of creative, experiential, behavioral, or interpersonal interventions as primary (Briere & Scott, 2015 van der Kolk, 2005; van der Kolk, Roth, Pelcovitz, Sunday, & Spinazzola, 2005). Currently many interventions in forensic settings are cognitive focused or cognitive behavioral focused. Therefore, this is a unique perspective. As such, the text approaches client behavior from a **trauma-informed** perspective. The basic assumption being that people involved in forensic settings who have mental health concerns have frequently experienced relational trauma (Procter, Ayling, Croft, DeGaris, Devine, Dimanic, et al.., 2017).

STRUCTURE OF THE TEXT

Throughout the text, key terms are bolded, as are significant legal cases. Also, in each chapter I discuss specific examples applied to cases based on my 20-plus years' experience as a forensic mental health counselor in order to help the reader understand what the information "looks like" in real life. Case studies are present in each chapter of section II and III. There are also reflection questions that encourage the reader to integrate and apply the material from the chapter. Finally, there are additional resources, including YouTube videos, TedTalks, professional resources, and resources for clients that the reader may be interested in, at the end of each chapter.

The text has three sections. **Section I** provides foundational information applicable to all settings and populations. Chapter 1 defines forensic mental health counseling (FMHC), introduces how adverse childhood experiences (ACEs) affect neurodevelopment, and Bruce Perry's neurosequential model of therapeutics (NMT) (Perry, 2006) is introduced. The chapter discusses overarching historic and systemic issues affecting FMHC. These include serious mental illness and de-institutionalization, criminalization of addictive disorders, mass incarceration and privatization, child welfare and victims' advocacy, and sociocultural contexts within which victimization and offending occur. It introduces broad categories of common mental health concerns addressed in forensic settings and discusses the **cautionary statement for forensic use of the DSM-5**. It introduces the concepts of continuum of severity and corresponding levels of change; some of the unique ethical and legal concerns in forensic counseling settings are discussed in order to frame the text.

Chapter 2 is informed by the fact that this type of work requires you to work with people and in situations that are challenging because of the complex nature of the issues, the competing agendas of those involved, and the difficulty navigating complex systems. As a result, it is common for FMHCs to experience **job stress, vicarious trauma, compassion fatigue, and burnout** (Mathieu, 2012). This topic appears in section I, in order to prepare students for the exposure to chapters on offenders and victims that could result in a negative emotional reaction and to encourage self-care. It is always preferred that self-care is pursued prior to exposure to potentially harmful stimuli; therefore, this is one of the first chapters of the text.

Chapter 3 provides a thorough discussion of common assessment skills needed in documenting a broad picture of the client's **biopsychosocial history, mental status, stage of change, and risk of harm to self and others**. Several assessment models utilized in criminal justice and public health settings are discussed, including the **risk-needs responsivity model**, prevention models from the World Health Organization (WHO) and from the Institute of Medicine (IOM), as well as assessment of risk and resilience factors using the epidemiological triangle and approaches to prevention/intervention. This chapter explains **how assessment of severity is related to placement decisions**. Finally, the chapter discusses the **ACA ethical decision-making model**, documentation, informed consent, competency to assess, and mandated reporting. Specific assessments for a population (e.g., domestic violence perpetrators) are integrated into population-specific chapters in section III.

Section II of the text emphasizes understanding the developmental factors involved in presenting mental health issues and resulting behaviors. This section includes chapters on Child and Adolescent Victims Part I: Foundations (chapter 4) and Child and Adolescent Victims Part II: Mental Health (chapter 5). In chapter 4, a comprehensive explanation of **traumatic neurodevelopment** and Bruce Perry's NMT model is given in language that a lay person should be able to understand. There is a discussion of the historical social and public policy contexts as well as the familial and sociocultural factors that affect the child welfare system. In this chapter, the case study of Enrique is introduced with analysis questions.

Chapter 5 provides the legal definitions and practical examples of different types of **neglect and abuse**, as well as their prevalence rates and risk factors associated with abuse and neglect. There is a detailed discussion of **child sexual abuse** (CSA) and **commercial sexual exploitation of children/human trafficking**, including risks, **STAR Courts** for teen prostitution/sex trafficking cases, sexual abuse accommodation syndrome, and short-term (including sexually reactive behavior) and long-term effects of CSA. It describes the **trauma outcome process assessment model** (TOPA) and the three potential victim outcomes resulting after abuse experiences.

This chapter also discusses the neurodevelopmental impact of trauma as related to behavioral and interpersonal manifestations in victims and resulting diagnostic indications; the legal and ethical considerations as well as the process for **reporting and treating child abuse**; and child abuse prevention and intervention. Developmentally appropriate trauma-informed interventions such as **play therapy** and **activity therapy** are described. This is followed by a detailed discussion of **child advocacy centers**, including issues related to **forensic interviews** and **"false memories," child review teams**, and court-related issues,

mandated reporting requirements, how to manage mandated reporting issues in practice, and understanding what will likely happen after a CPS call so that the counselor can help the client understand what to expect. Finally, confidentiality and privilege when working with minors is discussed. The chapter ends with a case study and application questions.

Juvenile offenders (chapter 6) distinguishes how juvenile and adult criminality are different and discusses determination of competence (*Dusky v. U.S.*, *Kent v. U.S.*, and *McKeiver v. Pennsylvania*). The chapter describes the relationship between experiencing ACEs (e.g., child abuse, neglect, violent households) and development of juvenile offending behaviors, specifically addressing **dually involved** or **crossover youth** and **victim-offender overlap**. Theories of development of offending behaviors (**rational choice theory, deterrence theory, routine activity theory, strain theory, social disorganization theory and cultural transmission of delinquent behavior, social learning theory,** and **trauma process outcome theory**) are reviewed.

The next chapter then reviews important historic policy and case law influences, including due process protections for juveniles; changes in juvenile justice laws from 1992–1997 related to transfer provisions, sentencing authority, confidentiality, victims' rights, and correctional programming; and retributive justice, distributive justice, and restorative justice. Then a discussion of sociocultural influences like **institutionalized racism, racial profiling, and criminalization of poverty** is followed by family system influences (parenting styles related to **delinquent identity development**), common mental health concerns, and a discussion of **sociopathy** and **psychopathy**. Then the text reviews prevention and intervention models; settings (**diversion, problem-solving courts, juvenile detention centers, boot camps, juvenile justice alternative education programs**); and ethical and legal issues (status offenses/minor in possession, felony offenses).

Adult Offenders Part I: Foundations (chapter 7) provides the reader with information leading to his or her ability to analyze developmental issues related to early, middle, and late adulthood offenders. It reviews various theories of cognitive, social, emotional, moral, and spiritual development, and aging counselors may want to consider when working with older offenders. This is followed by a discussion of developmental theories of offending (**Moffit's dual taxonomy, interactional theory, social control theory, integrated cognitive anti-social potential theory**). Current sociocultural contextual issues related to adult offenders, such as differences in prevalence of different types of offending by gender, race/ethnicity, socioeconomic status, and so on, and how these are related to policy and law, are discussed. There are discussions of the **effect of incarceration on families** and the role of **spirituality** in offender treatment. Finally, specific issues related to **aging offenders** and their counseling needs are discussed.

In this chapter, I talk about different interventions used with adult offenders beginning with **crisis intervention training** (CIT) for police officers utilizing the **PREPaRE Model**. The text discusses adult **mental health treatment courts,** including drug court, veterans' courts, mental health treatment courts, and domestic violence courts and interdisciplinary treatment teams commonly part of this model. Probation and parole (or reentry) services and challenges a correctional counselor may experience in working with adult offenders is described. There is a more in-depth discussion of **treatment settings and levels of intensity** as they apply to adult offenders where the chapter describes many of the settings where offenders are placed in the community or in corrections where counselors may work with them. The case study of Enrique: Part II continues at the end of chapter 7.

The final chapter in section II, entitled Adult Offenders: Part II: Mental Health (chapter 8), discusses common mental health concerns and challenges to treating these mental health issues among adult offenders; common issues related to therapeutic intervention forensic mental health counselors experience with adult offenders; and the unique challenges to gaining informed consent in a correctional setting, including mandated counseling, vulnerability of the population, limits to confidentiality, legal rules related to competence, and the importance of documentation as a risk management tool. Finally, advocacy issues are discussed, including appropriate access to care, sexual assault in prison and the Prison Rape Elimination Act (PREA), and placement in administrative segregation for mentally ill or elderly inmates.

Section III includes chapters that are population specific. Each chapter discusses incidence and prevalence data, significant research on the topic, assessment instruments or counseling techniques specific to the population, mental health issues related to the population of interest, and diagnostic information along with recommendations from the literature on treatment interventions most often used. Each chapter provides explanations of intervention methods used with the population highlighted, so that the reader can envision what it "looks like" in actual practice. At the end of each chapter is a case study. Some of the case studies are a continuation of a case study that was first presented in the developmental chapter. Chapter 9 deals with counseling people with **addictive behaviors in forensic settings**. Chapter 10 addresses working with **domestic violence/intimate partner violence** (DV/IPV) **victims**, while chapter 11 addresses working with **DV/IPV offenders**. Chapters 12 and 13 are similarly arranged focusing on counseling **sexual assault survivors** (chapter 12) and **sex offenders** (chapter 13). These chapters are intended to give the reader a good foundation in each population from which to grow through more specialized training. At the end of each chapter additional resources for specialized training are provided.

Acknowledgments

I would like to thank all of the kids and families (and adults with wounded child souls) whom I had the honor to work with over the years who 'braved the wilderness' to share their stories with me, who taught me about resilience, who showed me light when most people would only see darkness. I will never forget them. This textbook is a culmination of over 20 years' of professional experiences walking this journey and trying through my ears, heart, and head to see them, understand their stories while bearing witness to their pain and trying to stay genuine in the process. I have grown tremendously through my professional journey, and for that I thank these broken, but often beautiful, souls. My hope is that this textbook will offer a perspective that is reflective of the complexities of the lives these HUMAN BEINGS shared with me, while also paying attention to the research and common counseling practices that affect the possibility of healing.

I want to thank my mother for raising me to truly see people who others look away from, to wrestle with the complexities of the struggles and joys in humanity, and to keep going when it gets hard. She is and was a 'social justice warrior' before I had ever heard that term. I thank my father for teaching me to think critically about everything. Without this I may only see the simplistic stereotypical picture of those clients who are involved with the legal system with whom I've worked. They are more complex and deserve to have counselors willing to see that complexity and think critically about the statistics and stereotypes and systemic biases that affect their lives. Finally, I want to thank my husband Perry and my children Devin and Payton for giving me the time and space to write, sometimes rather than spending time with them. They are my joy and may hope for a better future for the world.

I want to acknowledge the support I received from my colleagues in the Department of Counseling, Educational Psychology and Research at the University of Memphis, particularly Dr. Richard James, my mentor. His willingness to help me translate my extensive work history into research opportunities has helped me transition into academia in a meaningful way. The work reflected in this text is the synthesis of these two careers (counselor and academic) coming together. Transmitting this knowledge is the reason I became a counselor educator. Finally, I would like to acknowledge my dissertation chair Dr. Richard Watts who helped me have the confidence in myself to believe I was capable of writing a book.

Foundations of Forensic Mental Health Counseling

The Starfish Story: One step towards changing the world

Once upon a time, there was an old man who used to go to the ocean to do his writing. He had a habit of walking on the beach every morning before he began his work.

Early one morning, he was walking along the shore after a big storm had passed and found the vast beach littered with starfish as far as the eye could see, stretching in both directions. Off in the distance, the old man noticed a small boy approaching. As the boy walked, he paused every so often and as he grew closer, the man could see that he was occasionally bending down to pick up an object and throw it into the sea.

The boy came closer still and the man called out, "Good morning! May I ask what it is that you are doing?" The young boy paused, looked up, and replied "Throwing starfish into the ocean. The tide has washed them up onto the beach and they can't return to the sea by themselves. When the sun gets high, they will die, unless I throw them back into the water."

The old man replied, "But there must be tens of thousands of starfish on this beach. I'm afraid you won't really be able to make much of a difference."

The boy bent down, picked up yet another starfish and threw it as far as he could into the ocean. Then he turned, smiled, and said, "It made a difference to that one!"

Foundations of Forensic Mental Health Counseling

Upon completion of this chapter, readers will be able to do the following:

- Identify roles and contexts, which differentiate forensic mental health counseling as a unique field
- Discuss historical, political, and sociocultural contexts influencing forensic mental health counseling
- Discuss common ethical and legal issues in FMHC work

TABLE 1.1 Myths and Myth Busters

Myths	Myth Busters
Forensic mental health counseling is conducted only by people with degrees in psychiatry, psychology, or criminal justice.	**Forensic mental health work often involves social workers or professional counselors in prevention and intervention activities with offenders and victims.**
Forensic mental health counselors (FMHC) focus on assessment and investigation not intervention.	**FMHC work in a variety of settings, including assessment, prevention, and intervention.**
FMHC involves working solely with offenders.	**FMHC work with victims, offenders, and investigators in situations where mental health/illness intersects with the law.**

INTRODUCTION

This textbook discusses a variety of behavioral manifestations of mental health issues, as they intersect with the legal or justice systems. Historically, the mental health professionals interacting with forensic populations are limited to social workers in child welfare agencies, criminal justice professionals working as probation/parole officers, or forensic psychologists specializing in forensic assessments (e.g., competency to stand trial or custody evaluations). However, with increased awareness of the intersections between mental illness, addiction, and trauma and the justice system, more licensed mental health counselors are working in these settings. However, there is little guidance for the role of a forensic mental health counselor focused on counseling outcomes rather than assessment, placement, or casework issues. The content of this textbook is designed to meet this need by providing a foundation for mental health professionals who seek to provide counseling with forensic populations or in forensic settings.

In an editorial for *the British Journal of Psychiatry*, Mullen (2000) defines forensic mental health counseling as "an area of specialization that, in the criminal sphere, involves the assessment and *treatment* of those who are both mentally disordered and whose behavior has led, or could lead, to offending" (p. 307). He discusses common limitations in defining the role of a mental health professional working in forensic settings, such as application of psychology or psychiatry to conducting evaluations for the court. He states that this is "an impoverished vision [that] constrains our specialty to acting exclusively as handmaidens to the courts" (Mullen, 2000, p. 307). Traditional definitions also limit forensic mental health counseling to focusing solely on offenders. Although this is a significant portion of the field, it is not exclusively so. When counselors work with victims of child abuse, survivors of sexual assault, victims of domestic violence or intimate partner violence (DV/IPV), or even with police officers in matters related to their jobs, they are acting as forensic mental health counselors.

Therefore, the definition of **forensic mental health counseling** (FMHC) used in this text is any activity conducted by trained, credentialed, professional mental health counselors in settings that require them to work with an interdisciplinary team, including individuals whose goals may be different from the goals of the counselor for the purpose of behavior change. This may include law enforcement officers, protective services investigators and caseworkers, probation and parole officers, correctional staff, or mental health courts, family courts, or criminal courts. Tasks a FMHC conducts include diagnostic assessments, treatment, providing expert witness testimony or recommendations to the court, client advocacy, and working in interdisciplinary teams.

These roles are unique from other mental health professionals working with forensic populations. Forensic psychologists are hired as evaluators who do not counsel or advocate for the client, and FMHCs do not serve as forensic evaluators because the roles conflict. Similarly, many forensic populations work with caseworkers who often have bachelor's degrees in social work or criminal justice. Caseworkers focus on minimizing systemic barriers to successful rehabilitation, such as referrals for counseling services, helping with transportation to and from counseling, resources for housing, employment, and/or comorbid medical issues. FMHCs, on the other hand, focus on counseling these individuals. FMHCs may have training in a variety of mental health-related fields, such as counseling, marriage and family therapy, clinical or counseling psychology, or social work. The role of a FMHC is the key, not the degree or license the individual holds. The role is to provide counseling services from diagnostic assessment, to treatment planning, to counseling services.

DEVELOPMENTAL ISSUES

This text approaches FMHC from a developmental lens, consistent with the counseling profession. This means that we attempt to understand the developmental trajectory of the client's mental health and behavioral issues, which bring them to counseling. Although each client's story, and therefore, his or her developmental trajectory are unique to that individual, there are some basic underlying neurodevelopmental processes which influence both the client's presenting problems and chosen interventions.

For instance, if we structure FMHC systems to address mental health issues only in such a manner as to help control the person's behavior, then the focus often becomes medication and behavioral interventions (e.g., level systems) and cognitive interventions (e.g., changing maladaptive thinking and making better choices, which is what is prevalent in current FMHC settings. However, if we focus on treating the underlying mental health issues motivating the behavior, be it addiction, posttraumatic stress disorder (PTSD), anxiety, depression, paraphilias, personality disorders, etc., then a variety of evidence-informed interventions may be employed.

For instance, we know from multiple **adverse childhood experiences** (ACE) studies that relational trauma early in life increases a host of problematic mental and physical health issues later in life, including offending behaviors, addiction, and increased risk of continued victimization (Centers for Disease Control and Prevention [CDC], 2015). Additionally, we know from these studies that if someone has experienced one ACE, then he or she is more likely to experience multiple ACEs. The compounding nature of multiple relational traumas frequently results in complex trauma (CDC, 2015; Herman, 1997, 2015; van der Kolk, 2005; van der Kolk et al., 2005). Therefore, a synthesis of the research indicates that FMHC clients likely need a **trauma-informed approach** to intervention, meaning the client's needs, not the systems', are the focus.

Individuals who have complex trauma need to have interventions that are "**neurosequential**" (Perry, 1995, 1997, 2006, 2009) or "bottom-up" (Siegel, 1999). In other words, rather than focusing first on cognitive interventions, which utilize brain regions in the cortex, which develop last in the neurodevelopmental sequence, we need to focus on regions that develop earlier such as the limbic system, the location of sensory non-declarative memory and emotion and the autonomic nervous system (ANS). Dr. Bruce Perry developed the **neurosequential model of therapeutics** (NMT) from extensive psychological work and study at the Child Trauma Academy and their clinical partners in different locations around the United States (Perry, 2006). He bases the NMT on several key principles of neurobiological development, illustrated in **Table 1.2.**

TABLE 1.2 Six Principles Underlying Bruce Perry's Neurosequential Model of Therapeutics

Principle 1	The brain is organized in a hierarchical fashion, such that all incoming sensory input first enters the lower parts of the brain.
Principle 2	Neurons and neural systems are designed to change in a "use-dependent" fashion.
Principle 3	The brain develops in a sequential fashion.
Principle 4	The brain develops most rapidly early in life.
Principle 5	Neural systems can be changed, but some systems are easier to change than others.
Principle 6	The human brain is designed for a different world.

(Perry, 2006, pp. 30–47)

Using the NMT logic, creative interventions that are neurobiologically informed are those that are sensory and/or experiential interventions, such as music, art, animal-assisted therapy (AAT), recreation therapy, meditation, yoga, and so on.

However, since a neurosequential approach accesses sensory memory, emotion, and ANS fear-based reflexes, it can trigger the addictive or acting-out behavior that resulted in the presenting issues in the first place. This is the catch-22. These interventions are ideal because they access the trigger that motivates presenting emotions or behaviors. Therefore, they allow for here-and-now access to the target of the therapeutic intervention. However, they can simultaneously create a situation that results in behavior that is "out of control" and therefore potentially threatens the safety and well-being of the client and the other community members, whether in outpatient, inpatient, residential, or correctional settings. This would result in police, probation, or parole officers in community settings or frontline staff or correctional officers in inpatient, residential, or correctional settings needing to control the acting-out behavior. Therefore, if we are looking at the common symbol of the scales of justice, there might be a need for maintaining safety and peacefulness, resulting in a behavioral control focus on one side and the need for neurosequential trauma-informed intervention resulting in accessing triggers for acting out behaviors on the other side. However, from a neurodevelopmental perspective, to be effective as FMHCs, counselors must approach treatment from the understanding that we need to pursue this balance, rather than seeking one goal (e.g., behavior control for safety) over the other (e.g., neurosequential interventions that may trigger strong emotional reactions and corresponding challenging behaviors). This is a foundational description of NMT, which will be further addressed in subsequent chapters of the text.

CONTEXTUAL ISSUES

When viewing behavior holistically, it is crucial that we attend to contextual issues. Often the context helps us make sense of the behavior or events presented. I will discuss historical and systemic influences in order to help you examine how social norms and legal policy has affected what we consider offending behaviors and how we define victimization. The forensic setting itself is its own context, which has unique norms, rules, and systemic issues. Finally, sociocultural issues such as poverty, race, sexual orientation, religion, gender, and so on provide a third context for making sense of how someone came to be in a forensic counseling setting.

Historic and Systemic Influences

There are a number of trends influencing the rise of forensic mental health counseling as a specialization. The first is a long history this country has had determining how to care for seriously mentally ill (SMI) individuals. It appears that we have gone through a cycle of criminalization of mental illness to placing the SMI in psychiatric institutions to deinstitutionalization of SMI resulting in the closing of psychiatric facilities, to now treating more mentally ill adults in correctional facilities than in county and state psychiatric facilities (Torrey, Kennard, & Eslinger, 2010).

Simultaneously, the country has struggled with what to do with people with addictive disorders. We initially treated them as morally deficient, imprisoning them to providing treatment. The most recent trend, however, is criminalization of drugs and mandatory minimum sentences. Currently, there are 2.2 million people in prison, according to the Sentencing Project (Graziani, Ben-Moshe, Cole, 2017). Mass incarceration contributed to another significant contextual influence, privatization of corrections. The first such company, Corrections Corporation of America, opened in 1983 to meet the needs of increasing numbers of offenders with drug-related charges in prisons following implementation of mandatory sentencing (Mason, 2012). As of 2010, the combined earnings of the two largest private prison corporations was just under $3 billion (Mason, 2012). The latest iteration finds these corporations promoting a "continuum of care," similar to psychiatric hospitals, in order to profit from mild decreases in incarceration rates, following concerns about inequities resulting in mass incarceration of poor and minority individuals and people with mental health problems.

Another major influence in FMHC is the growth of child welfare laws, mandated reporting, and victims' advocacy, including domestic violence/interpersonal violence and sex offender laws. These laws and social movements led to more jobs serving victims of crime as well, including families involved with protective services, kids involved with juvenile justice agencies, child advocacy centers and children's mental health services, domestic violence centers and rape crisis centers, and so on. Additionally, there are more jobs with offenders, including domestic violence batterers programs, sex-offender treatment programs, drug court–mandated addiction treatment, and other mental health court programs. I will discuss each of these in more depth; however, I discuss victim and offender treatment thoroughly throughout the rest of the text.

Serious Mental Illness and Deinstitutionalization

As early as 1694, communities legally imprisoned mentally ill individuals believed to be dangerous (Grob, 1973). However, in 1825 a Congregationalist minister, Reverend Louis Dwight, founded the Disciple Society, which advocated for placement of offenders with mental illness (OMI) in hospitals (Grob, 1966). Because of their efforts, in 1833 Massachusetts built a psychiatric hospital in Worcester, and more than half the admissions in the first year were OMI transferred from jails and prisons (Grob, 1966). Around the same time (1837), social advocate Dorothea Dix began a 30-year project to ensure mentally ill people were taken out of prisons and put into state psychiatric hospitals (Parry, 2006). By 1880, 75 psychiatric hospitals were built and housed 50 million, most of them previously residing in prisons and jails. She argued that prisons were not set up to house OMI and that incarcerating mentally ill people with felons is inhumane (Dix, 1971).

Because of advocates like Dix and the Disciple Society, between the mid-1800s and the 1970s, it was uncommon to imprison mentally ill individuals (Torrey et al., 2015). However, movement to psychiatric institutions did not guarantee adequate treatment, as evidenced by Nellie Bly's 1887 expose, "Ten Days in a Mad-house," written for the *New York World* documenting appalling conditions of a state psychiatric hospital in New York (Bly, 2015). The exposé led to an investigation finding these institutions needed to be reformed. Additionally, forced medical procedures occurred at state institutions for decades. For instance, Indiana became one of the first states enacting compulsory sterilization laws. More than 30 states followed suit. These laws allowed the state to perpetrate involuntary sterilization of people in psychiatric institutions and prisons (Stern, 2005). California performed 20,000 sterilizations at state institutions, more than any other state between 1909 and 1979 (Chavez-Garcia, 2012).

In addition, although controversial, Eantonio Egas Moniz won the Nobel Prize in 1949 for creating a neurological intervention called psychosurgery, or lobotomies (Jansson, 1998). Between 1936 and 1959, doctors performed approximately 50,000 lobotomies in the United States (Johnson, 2018). Between 1940 and 1951, almost 20,000 occurred in the United States, 60% on women. However, these virtually stopped following the discovery of antipsychotic medications (Johnson, 2018). Electroconvulsive therapy (ECT) was another controversial intervention introduced as a treatment for SMI individuals in 1938 (Rudorfer, Henry, & Sackheim, 1997). It became popular in the 1940s, resulting in an estimated 100,000 people receiving ECT each year (Herman, Dorwart, Hoover, & Brody, 1995). Interestingly, even today, only 13 states have laws regulating ECT (Shorter, 2013).

Advocacy efforts continued by citizens who were concerned about the living conditions and frightening treatment of seriously mentally ill persons in psychiatric facilities. In 1946, a shift in public consciousness is reflected in President Truman's signing the National Mental Health Act, which called for establishing the National Institute of Mental Health (NIMH); however, because there was no funding, the NIMH was not completed until 1949 (Pickren & Schneider, 2005). It was one of four institutes charged with conducting and supporting research under the National Institutes of Health (NIH). However, it took the Johnson administration in the 1960s to expand funding for mental health research by calling for research-informed policy approaches to solve social problems. This resulted in research centers on crime and delinquency, minority group mental health problems, urban problems, schizophrenia, child and family mental health, and suicide. During this time, the NIH also established the National Center for Prevention and Control of Alcoholism, which was the first acknowledgment of alcoholism as a mental health disease (Eghigian & Hornstein, 2010).

However, several events occurred in the mid- to late-1950s and early 1960s that paved the way for Johnson's efforts. First, the Mental Health Study Act of 1955 called for "an objective, thorough, nationwide analysis and reevaluation of the human and economic problems of mental health" (Pub. L. 84–182). That year, the number of institutionalized mentally ill individuals was at an all-time high of 560,000 (Eghigian & Hornstein, 2010). The Joint Commission on Mental Illness and Health subsequently published the Action for Mental Health Report in 1961 (Eghigian & Hornstein, 2010). It was a thorough 10-volume series examining the status of mental health/illness in the United States and assessing the resources for meeting these needs, which led to President Kennedy establishing a cabinet-level interagency committee to examine the commission's recommendations in the report (Eghigian & Hornstein, 2010).

The following year, literature influenced public opinion when the bestseller *One Flew Over the Cuckoo's Nest* was published, based on the author's experiences working as a nurse at a veterans' facility, which helped build interest in the community regarding treatment of institutionalized SMI people (Kesey, 1962). Then, as part of Kennedy's New Frontier, the Community Mental Health Centers Construction Act of 1963 (Pub. L. 88–164) passed, resulting in the establishment of community mental health centers, which treated mental health and mental retardation in community settings (Kennedy, 1963). Two years later, Title XIX of the Social Security Act (Pub. L. 89–97) established Medicaid. As a result, psychiatric facilities would not receive payment for SMI, which led to **deinstitutionalization**, moving mentally ill individuals out of psychiatric hospitals into the community (Eghigian & Hornstein, 2010; Moore & Smith, 2005). Additionally, California Governor Ronald Reagan signed the Lanterman-Petris-Short Act in California, significantly limiting involuntarily hospitalization, which exacerbated the issue, resulting in the number of SMI in correctional facilities to double (Torrey, 1997).

Funding shortages compounded this situation. For instance, in 1970 the Alabama state legislature repealed a cigarette tax that funded mental health services. This resulted in firing close to 100 staff members from a state psychiatric institution. They later filed a lawsuit seeking reinstatement stating that the patients would receive inadequate care. They included the name of a 15-year-old boy (Wyatt) whose aunt, one of the suing staff members, placed him there because of his delinquent behavior. Before its' resolution, the lawsuit grew to include patients from additional hospitals and state schools. Because of *Wyatt v. Stickney* (1971), the court ruled that involuntarily committed patients had the right to mental health treatment that would reasonably result in improvement in their mental condition, as a matter of due process. The ruling articulated "three fundamental conditions for 'adequate and effective treatment programs in public mental institutions' including a human psychological and physical environment, qualified staff in numbers sufficient to administer adequate treatment, and individualized treatment plans" (*Wyatt v. Stickney*, 1971). The Supreme Court affirmed these rights in *Olmstead v. L.C.* (1999).

This legal requirement affects the legal and ethical expectations for care in correctional counseling today. Due to deinstitutionalization, in 1972 a California psychiatrist identified a significant increase in the number of mentally ill people entering the San Mateo County Jail, leading him to write a seminal article called "The Criminalization of Mentally Disordered Behavior" (Torrey et al., 2015). He predicted what we now experience, which is the housing and care of more SMI individuals in jails and prisons than in psychiatric facilities in 44 states and most counties across the United States (Torrey, Kennard, Eslinger, Lamb, & Pavle, 2010; Torrey, et al., 2015).

In 1975, a movie version of *One Flew Over the Cuckoo's Nest* encouraged more public advocacy for deinstitutionalizing SMI people. By 1977, there were close to two million SMI patients receiving services at 650 community mental health facilities across the country (Torrey et al., 2015). However, community centers, designed to help people with less severe mental illness, quickly became overwhelmed with the severity and numbers of patients presenting for treatment (Eghigian, & Hornstein, 2010). By the late 70s a U. S. General Accounting Office (GAO) study reported that SMI people who were moved into the community and out of psychiatric facilities were being forced into the criminal justice system (Torrey et al., 2015).

Subsequently, shortly after becoming president in 1977, President Carter signed an executive order creating the President's Commission on Mental Health (PCMH), which emphasized a public health model focusing on prevention as well as early intervention (Grob, 2005). The PCMH's work revealed that there was a growing need for community mental health services. As a result, President Carter signed the Mental Health Systems Act in 1980. The Mental Health Systems Act was an attempt to restructure community mental health agencies in order to build more centers and to improve efficiency and quality of service SMI individuals were receiving.

Although the commission's efforts led to establishing the National Plan for the Chronically Mentally Ill, the intended system of care did not materialize, due to change in presidential policy one year later (Grob, 2005). Shortly after Reagan became president in 1981, he signed the Omnibus Budget Reconciliation Act, which repealed the community health legislation in favor of funding block grants so that states could develop their own systems of treatment for mental illness, in an effort to limit the role of the federal government. By 1985, the amount of federal funding for community mental health was only 11%, shifting the burden of cost to states and local communities (Eghigian, & Hornstein, 2010). This further exacerbated the situation; states were forced to cut over $4 billion in mental health spending over 3 years due to the recession that followed the 2008 housing crisis (Torrey et al., 2015).

According to Torrey (1997), "[D]einstitutionalization has two parts: the moving of the severely mentally ill out of the state institutions and the closing of part or all of those institutions" (p. 13). Between 1955, when deinstitutionalization began, and 1994, state psychiatric hospitals discharged just under a half million mentally ill patients, resulting in a permanent loss of 43,000 psychiatric beds by 2010, a ratio of 14 beds for each 100,000 people (Torrey et al., 2015). As a result, around 200,000 SMI persons with diagnoses such as bipolar disorder and schizophrenia were homeless with little or no psychiatric intervention, and more than 300,000 SMI are now in correctional facilities (Torrey et al., 2015).

Since the 1980s, correctional facilities and law enforcement frequently reported being ill equipped to address the needs of increasing numbers of SMI persons, resulting in poorer outcomes for inmates and parolees (Belcher, 1988; Torrey et al., 2015). In spite of this, the 1990s demonstrated unprecedented increases in SMI in correctional settings. Jails surveyed reported that people with minor charges associated with the lack of mental health treatment resulted in increased arrests, and many, not having financial resources, ended up in prison (Torrey, 1997; Torrey et al., 2015).

A decade later, the Senate Judiciary Committee commissioned the Subcommittee on Human Rights and the Law, which held hearings about mental illness in correctional facilities. According to Torrey and colleagues (2015), there was little public interest and almost no media coverage of the hearings. This is true in spite of the fact that the Treatment Advocacy Center reported that there are over three times the number of SMI in correctional facilities than in hospitals, and in some states incarcerated SMI is as much as 10 times the rate of those hospitalized (Torrey, Kennard, & Eslinger, 2010). Additionally, research indicates that the cost of housing someone with SMI in a correctional facility, in a less-than-optimal treatment milieu, is double what it would cost to provide treatment in the community (Swanson et al., 2013).

Then, when the Affordable Care Act (2010) passed, it mandated insurance companies cover 10 essential benefits including mental health care and addiction treatment. There is a chance that this could increase availability and affordability of mental health treatment in the community. However, currently there are no perceptible differences in the numbers of SMI in correctional facilities. As Torrey and colleagues (2015) report,

> The practice of putting seriously mentally ill persons into prisons and jails was abandoned in the middle of the nineteenth century in the United States. The reasons behind the abandonment of this practice included the fact that it was widely regarded as inhumane and that it also caused multiple problems for those who are mentally ill, for other prisoners, and for the prison and jail officials. In the view of these well-known problems, the re-adoption of this practice in the late twentieth century is incomprehensible. (p. 14)

The historical cycle of criminalization, then institutionalization, and criminalization again of people with mentally disordered behavior illustrates a need for new, creative interventions for OMI. Additionally, competent care by trained mental health counselors is crucial to providing intervention that will more likely result in improved behavior, as required by the Supreme Court (*Olmstead v. L.C.*, 1999; *Wyatt v. Stickney*, 1971).

Criminalization of Addictive Disorders

In addition to deinstitutionalization of SMI individuals, another issue influencing forensic mental health counseling is U.S. policy on alcohol and drugs. Early in our history, society viewed alcoholics and addicts as morally deficient, so the U.S. enacted laws to control access to drugs and to punish people who broke those laws, thus criminalizing addiction (White, 2014). This subsequently resulted in incarceration of increased numbers of people based on the mental illness of addiction, most of whom have comorbid trauma and other mental health issues. Although U.S. policy on addiction is thoroughly discussed later in the text, it is important to note here that the War on Drugs in the 1980s and 1990s stopped treating addictive behaviors as a mental illness and began treating it as a "bad choice" that needed punishment. Prevention efforts utilized scare tactics and categorized addictive disorders as bad choices by bad people. Another important trend during this time was the passage of mandatory minimum sentencing, which resulted in mass incarceration of low-level drug offenders. However, once the opioid crisis reached epidemic levels between 1997–2015, touching more middle class or wealthy White families, the tide again changed toward developing treatment courts to encourage treatment over incarceration (Quinones, 2015).

Criminal behaviors may stem directly from the addiction, such as drunk and disorderly charges or driving while intoxicated, if the addiction is to a substance. It may be that charges are embezzlement or theft if the client has a gambling or shopping addiction. For individuals with sexual addictions, their behaviors may result in charges (e.g, having sex in public), or they may cross the line into downloading child pornography, frequenting prostitutes, pedophilia, rape (sadism), or a host of other illegal paraphilias. Additionally, addictive behaviors often precipitate intimate partner violence, child abuse, and other interpersonal violent behaviors (Burnette et al., 2008; Center for Substance Abuse Treatment, 2003; Chermack et al., 2008).

In these respects, conceptualization of what addiction is and how it is treated by social norms and government policies and laws impacts the criminal justice system, child advocacy clients, rape crisis clients, and community agencies or DV/IPV programs and shelters that provide services to offenders and to victims. A parent's addictive behavior also increases the risk that his or her children will experience abuse or neglect. FMHCs frequently work with children and parents involved with protective services. In these settings, FMHCs must be aware of child protective care plans developed by the Child Protective Services (CPS) worker. These plans often serve as motivation to enter treatment. Generally, if a parent does not successfully complete the plan in a timely manner, which often includes addiction treatment, he or she is at risk of the court terminating his or her parental rights. Kids whose parents are involved with CPS may live at home with the parent, resulting in a FMHC who may work in a program for at-risk youth that offers community-based or even home-based counseling services. A CPS worker may place children in foster care, if he or she deems the home environment a risk to the child's safety, or if the parent enters residential treatment or a correctional facility. A significant controversy is that when parents become prisoners, it may result in the parent's loss of parental rights because the parent is unable to complete the CPS care plan.

Mass Incarceration and Privatization

Another related issue affecting FMHC is mass incarceration that led to privatization of corrections. Deinstitutionalization of persons experiencing serious and persistent mental illness and criminalization of persons dealing with addiction both contributed to mass incarceration. However, Simmons (2007) states that

[i]t is an open secret that the public criminal justice system has essentially given up on rehabilitating convicted criminals ... to be replaced by an ever more punitive system, which incarcerates defendants at an astonishing rate: the United States leads the world by imprisoning 750 people out of every 100,000 citizens, while almost every European country ranges between 100 and 200. (p. 913)

In fact, over the past 40 years, incarceration has grown 500% and spending on corrections has increased 324% (Stullich, Morgan, & Schak, 2016). The concept of a privatized criminal justice system began with the creation of more private security jobs than public police officers; in the 1960s (Forst, 2000). Laband and Sophocleus (1992) it was estimated that spending for the entire criminal justice system was three times less than the amount spent on private-sector security by 1992. Forst (2000) identifies several reasons for the growth in private security, including significant increases in crime in the 1960s that overwhelmed public resources, specialization of services, more private citizens being able to afford private alternatives, and an increasing interest in privatizing all things government.

In the 40 years from 1950–1990, private correctional facilities more than doubled (Torrey et al., 2015), just as more people live in these facilities, under mandatory minimum sentencing. The arguments for privatization include cost savings; however, cost savings in practice generally accompanies problems with safety and inmate care. They offer lower benefits and salary, have less training, and staff in lower numbers. This results in higher turnover, increased injuries to staff and inmates, and substandard care (Mason, 2012). For-profit correctional corporations include companies like Corrections Corporation of America (CCA), Serco, Sodexo, and G4S. According to the Sentencing Project, these companies have profited greatly, while SMI inmates have suffered (Mason, 2012). CCA alone underwent 600 malpractice lawsuits related to treatment of mentally ill inmates over a 5-year period (Forst, 2000).

Interestingly, after the financial crisis of 2008, government began seeking alternatives to incarceration in these settings, like probation, home arrest, diversion programs, and re-entry programs (Graziani, Ben-Moshe, & Cole, 2017; Isaacs, 2016). This move, coupled with sentencing reform over the past decade, resulted in a national average reduction of 3% in incarceration rates, according to the Sentencing Project (Graziani, Ben-Moshe, & Cole, 2017). However, 2.2 million people remain behind bars, making the U.S. the "most incarcerated country in the world" (Gaziani, Ben-Moshe, & Cole, 2017, p. 5).

This trend resulted in private correctional corporations rebranding themselves as having a continuum of care similar to psychiatric hospitals. For instance, one group acquired specialized companies to offer electronic monitoring, reentry, and probation and parole services (Gaziani, Ben-Moshe, & Cole, 2017; Issacs, 2016). Today, almost two-thirds of people in the criminal justice system are on probation or parole (Issacs, 2016). According to the Grassroots Leadership, "[T]he problem with such so-called alternatives is that they only increase the scope of incarceration and become an addition to traditional forms of incarceration instead of an alternative" (Gaziani, Ben-Moshe, & Cole, 2017, p. 12).

Child Welfare and Victims Advocacy

In addition to laws, which led to increased FMHC working with addictions and offending populations, advances in child welfare policy and statutes, as well as victim's advocacy, FMHC increased work with crime victims. Chapter 4 discusses the impact of child welfare laws, including child labor laws and legislation affecting child and adolescent victims of child abuse and neglect and mandated reporting of child abuse and changes in the foster care laws over the years. The first significant child welfare legislation occurred when President Taft established the Children's Bureau (CB) in 1912 (Brown, 2011) to address these issues. However, the complex system providing a social support system for children, as we know it today, really began during President Johnson's War on Poverty in the 1960s (Orleck & Hazirjian, 2011).

Mandated reporting of suspected child abuse and neglect became law in 1967, which led to the **Child Abuse Prevention and Treatment Act of 1974** (CAPTA) (Pub. L. 93–247) and establishing the National Center on Child Abuse and Neglect (NCCAN), which provides minimum standards for defining maltreatment of children and support for prevention and intervention of child abuse. From the 1960s through the 1990s, child protective services went through a number of changes (discussed in chapter 4), resulting in increases in mental health professionals working in government and community agency programs related to child welfare. One of the most significant changes was the establishment of a model for Child Advocacy Centers (CACs) National Child Advocacy Center in 1985, changing the way in which we investigate and treat child abuse and neglect cases. CACs are multidisciplinary response programs, which generally house all elements of the child abuse/neglect investigation and treatment in one child-friendly location. With the growth in numbers of CACs over the past 30-plus years, more counselors are working in forensic settings directly treating children for mental health issues arising out of their abuse and neglect.

In 1986, popular talk-show host Oprah Winfrey (2010) disclosed that she suffered sexual abuse by a relative when she was a child. This was the first in a number of media discussions of sexual assault. As a result of the increased public awareness, child abuse reports spiked in the late 1980s and early 1990s and then decreased 40% between 1992 and 2000 (Finkelhor & Jones, 2004. Both reports of child abuse and reports by adults abused as children, or those sexually assaulted by known perpetrators as adults, became more frequent, resulting in more counselors working with sexual abuse survivors. Additionally, with more reports there were more adult and juvenile offenders entering the justice system because of their perpetrating behaviors. Both of these trends resulted in increases in professional counselors working with both offenders of interpersonal violence, whether physical or sexual, and their victims. (The third section of this book discusses each type of setting and population in detail.)

Concerns about juveniles involved in criminal activity, most of whom were child abuse or neglect victims themselves, became a topic for child advocates in the 1800s (Loerzel, 2010). However, it took many years before the government began addressing juvenile delinquency and youthful offenders as a unique group. In 1961, President Kennedy established a Committee on Juvenile Delinquency and Youth Crime. The group advocated for passage of the 1961 Juvenile Delinquency and Youth Offenses Control Act (Pub. L. 87–274), which created a 3-year federal grant program to research programs designed to prevent or intervene with at-risk youth or juvenile offenders. Similar to child welfare trends, juvenile justice has gone through multiple iterations, discussed in-depth in chapter 6, which led to increases in the numbers of counselors employed in programs for at-risk youth or juvenile justice.

Forensic Mental Health Counseling as a Unique Setting

There are several issues unique to working in forensic settings, which influence the context of FMHC. To be a competent forensic mental health counselor, it is crucial that you train in not only the basic counseling knowledge and skills necessary for all counselors. It is also important to receive training in the unique contexts where forensic work takes place. The forensic context has unique challenges and rewards, for which you need to be prepared. For instance, correctional settings focus on maintaining safety and security of the inmates, the staff, and the community, which often results in an environment that *values external control* of the inmate's behavior. However, a mental health providers' goal is to help offenders learn healthier, more functional ways to cope so that they are less likely to reoffend and to encourage building a support structure to facilitate their continued success post release. This approach *values building internal controls* for behavior and personal responsibility that couples internal control. Additionally, although changing, law enforcement, courts, and corrections often focus on retribution, rather than rehabilitation. This is a particularly important distinction for offenders with mental illness. When offenders' mental health issues directly relate to the reasons they offended, it becomes crucial that they receive treatment that is competent and focuses on rehabilitation, including mental health counseling, to address the underlying mental health issues.

Sociocultural Influences

Throughout this text, each type of setting and population is described in light of sociocultural influences. For instance, it has been well documented that marginalized populations, those with lower socioeconomic status (SES), as well as racial and ethnic minorities, are more likely to be involved with the child welfare system and the justice system (Child Welfare Information Gateway, 2016; National Conference of State Legislatures, 2017). Additionally, gender minorities and those from minority sexual orientations experience increased rates of violent victimization (Federal Bureau of Investigations [FBI], 2017). Even other trends, such as mass incarceration, disproportionately affect minorities, including separating parents from their children, resulting in foster placement (Vagins & McCurdy, 2006). The Sentencing Commission reported to Congress, following in-depth study on mandatory minimum sentencing practices, that Whites were more likely to receive minimum mandatory sentences, and African Americans were more likely receive to more time in prison (Vagins, & McCurdy, 2006). Similarly, these laws have affected women much more than men, resulting in a 400% increase in women incarcerated from 1986–2006 (Vagins & McCurdy, 2006). More than half the women in federal prisons are convicted of drug-related offenses; most of these are African American and Hispanic, an increase of 800% between 1986–2006 (Vagins & McCurdy, 2006).

Further, it is well documented that racial and socioeconomic biases are *inherent* in a system established and powered primarily by White males of privilege; these biases have resulted in, for example, criminalization of certain types of substances and forms of substances primarily used by Chinese (opioids) or Mexican (marijuana) immigrants and African Americans (marijuana or crack cocaine) that disproportionately result in marginalized populations being incarcerated (Cox, 2015; National Association for the Advancement of Colored People [NAACP], n.d.). When the federal Anti-Drug Abuse Act of 1986 imposed mandated sentencing for using crack cocaine, commonly used by lower socioeconomic (SES) groups and minorities, these sentences were lighter than for the use of powder cocaine, commonly used by higher SES groups and Whites (Pub. L. 99–570, 100 STAT.3207). Prior to the law's passage, African Americans' drug sentences were 11% higher on average than their White counterparts were. Four years later the average was 49% higher, according to the American Civil Liberties Union (ACLU) (Vagins & McCurdy, 2006).

Contrast the response to the crack cocaine crisis with the epidemic of heroin addiction that is primarily a middle-class White problem of prescription opiate abuse, considered an epidemic in 2017. At least 24 states and Washington, DC, enacted laws to allow naloxone, a prescription that counters the effects of a heroin overdose, more easily accessed. Additionally, treatment courts, focused on treatment rather than punishment, began proliferating in formerly law-and-order states like Tennessee and Texas, as middle-class Whites began knowing people affected by prescription opioid abuse (Quinones, 2015). This example illustrates how drug addiction among middle-class White people prompted changes in public policy and advocacy, where the crack cocaine crisis in the 80s resulted in minimum mandatory prison sentences and mass incarceration (Torrey et al., 2015). Additionally, mass incarceration creates issues upon reentry, particularly for those with felony convictions, who find it difficult to find work and unable to benefit from social services otherwise available to help with housing and food (Vagins & McCurdy, 2006). Many ex-felons revert to using drugs or committing crimes to survive, continuing the cycle of incarceration.

Having reviewed the systems in which FMHC services have been provided, some common presenting issues are described.

COMMON MENTAL HEALTH CONCERNS

Behaviors that bring clients into forensic settings are often the outward manifestation of mental health issues, hence the term "behavioral health" to describe mental health services. Using the developmental lens, those in the counseling field generally consider all behavior to have been functional in the context it developed. In other words, a behavior came about in an effort to meet an unmet need, or to escape an intolerable situation. Therefore, the behavior "makes sense" if you understand the context. Broadly, we categorize behaviors that bring people to counseling in two groups: internalizing and externalizing behaviors. **Internalizing behaviors** are those that clients employ that involve focusing inside themselves to express or deal with their psychological distress. These often result in anxiety, depression, and other mood disorders, addictive disorders, or dependent personality disorders. The ultimate internalization is psychosis. Psychosis occurs when people respond to internal stimuli (hallucinations) as if based in external reality, and they make up stories or explanations (delusions) to help this experience make sense. **Externalizing behaviors** tend to focus outside attention outside the client in an effort to express or deal with psychological distress. These often include behaviors such as conduct disorder, intermittent explosive disorder, paraphilias, antisocial personality disorder, or borderline personality disorder. The text addresses common mental health issues in forensic settings, at different points.

As noted previously, most people who enter forensic settings, whether as a victim or as an offender, generally have experienced trauma (Ardino, 2012; Jaggi, Mezuk, Watkins, & Jackson, 2016; Sidicich et al., 2014; Smith et al., 2017; Wolff & Shi, 2012). The individual who experiences it defines whether the experience is/is not traumatic. Involvement with the legal system may be considered traumatic. However, the trauma may be something that happened to him or her as a child, such as child abuse or neglect, going into foster care, placement in a psychiatric hospital, witnessing domestic violence, or living in an environment full of crime or in a war zone.

These experiences are adverse childhood experiences (ACEs), which were previously described. There are two common instruments used to identify a history of ACEs. The first is the five question Centers for Disease Control (CDC) version. The second is the World Health Organization (WHO) ACEs, which reflects violent community environments or experiences in war that may be relevant to forensic populations. Trauma could also be something that happened as an adult, such as a sexual assault, being the victim of a hate crime, experiencing intimate partner violence, and so on.

Adverse Childhood Experience (ACE) Questionnaire from the Centers for Disease Control, https://tinyurl.com/y6wyhvrt:

Adverse Childhood Experience International Questionnaire (ACE-IQ) from the World Health Organization, https://tinyurl.com/yxvej5me:

These mental health challenges are discussed in this chapter, highlighting the setting or population where they are most likely to occur. However, it is crucial to understand that any of these behaviors, and often a complex comorbidity of mental health issues, occur across the developmental continuum and across the continuum of victim and offender. As stated earlier, most offenders were also victims, and some victims develop coping strategies, such as addictions, which result in offending behaviors. Finally, as stated in the Diagnostic and Statistical Manual, 5th edition's (DMS-5) cautionary statement for forensic use of DSM-5, diagnostic information is at risk of being misused or misunderstood if someone other than a trained mental health professional uses it. Beyond meeting diagnostic criteria, there are questions of functional impairment and severity of the disorder, which affect what one understands of the diagnosis in relationship to offending behaviors (American Psychiatric Association [APA], 2013). Too frequently, legal professionals distort the use of diagnosis and psychosocial history as an excuse, rather than an explanation, for offender behaviors.

PREVENTION AND INTERVENTION

Throughout the text, prevention and intervention will be discussed as relevant to the focus of the chapter. **Prevention** is any activity with the purpose of stopping a behavior before it begins. Prevention activities of FMHC include working with at-risk youth programs or working with kids and families involved with CPS or foster care. These kids are at greater risk to become victims and to develop mental illness, addictive behaviors, or offending behaviors (CDC, n.da.; Herrenkohl, Hong, Klika, Herrenkohl, & Russo, 2013). Therefore, although there is intervention regarding their victimization, the goal is also to prevent more serious issues as they get older. A key element in prevention is risk assessment, which will be discussed in chapter 3. **Intervention** is an activity undertaken to improve a person's situation or behavior after it becomes known. Most of the text will focus on intervention, as does most of the FMHCs' work.

Continuum of Severity and Corresponding Levels of Intervention

Prevention and intervention strategies occur on a continuum, ranging from identification of high-risk populations in need of information to raise awareness and deter development of problematic behaviors. This might include a minor who has no criminal behavior but who lives in a gang-infested neighborhood whose mom is on probation for possession of an illegal substance and prostitution and whose dad is serving time for assault. Because of the living/residential environment, this minor is at higher risk for developing offending behaviors. Therefore, mentorship may be provided through an at-risk teen program, as part of a grant-funded community agency service.

Early intervention may occur following an initial incident. For example, what if police arrest the same kid, now 17 years old, for driving while under the influence of alcohol. However, she has no record of drinking and driving in the past and no addiction treatment history. Therefore, the court puts her on probation with the requirement that she attend an alcohol and drug psychoeducational class. However, 6 months later, police arrest her for a third DUI, and they find out that she previously had two unsuccessful attempts at addiction, competing demands of conviction/punishment and rehabilitation. Then the recommended intervention level would be more intense. She may go to drug court, which may order her to treatment at a halfway house and residential treatment.

Two years later the hospital emergency room may admit the same person for an overdose. During the process of a police investigation, police find a bag of 200 pills in her possession, and they arrest her for possession of oxycodone with the intent to sell. The level of intervention would likely be even more intense. We would take into consideration her history in determining the best intervention. Elements to consider would include her family history, overdose, use of an illegal substance in addition to alcohol, continued use after intervention, and relapse/recidivism at lower levels of treatment intensity signaling a need for more external controls. As a result, the court may order her to an addictive disorders treatment program in a county prison for an extended period (e.g., 2 years).

After she served her time in the program, she may maintain her sobriety for a year, but then she becomes discouraged with her inability to find a decent paying job, her relationship with her girlfriend turns to violence, and she is at risk of losing her kids to foster care. In response to feeling overwhelmed by multiple stressors, she relapses. Because of a 6-month drug binge, police arrest her as part of a prostitution raid, a "job" she chose in order to make money to buy drugs, which also reinforced her experience of sexual and physical abuse as a child and as an adult. In this situation, the court may send her to a state prison with a substance abuse treatment program for 5 years. This illustrates one example of the continuum of prevention through various levels intervention in which a FMHC may be working, with the consistent goal of stopping decline and preventing the need for more intensive interventions.

SETTINGS

Because they address so many different issues, with different types of clients at different levels of functioning, FMHCs work in a variety of settings. The one thing they have in common is that they work with people who may be involved with the justice system as police officers, victims, or offenders. For instance, FMHCs may train law enforcement in crisis intervention training (CIT) (discussed in chapter 8). They may also work with victims in foster care, children's homes, home-based therapy programs, CACs, rape crisis centers, at-risk youth programs that are grant funded through agencies, outpatient private practice, in-patient hospitals, specialized treatment centers, or residential treatment facilities. FMHCs work with offenders in residential settings, community corrections (probation/parole), and detention, jail, prison, and re-entry settings. Each type of setting is discussed in more detail in the upcoming chapters of the text.

ETHICAL AND LEGAL ISSUES

There are unique legal and ethical concerns in forensic counseling settings. Common ethical dilemmas in FMHC often stem from the following:

- The mandated nature of counseling, (e.g., court mandated for treatment following a third DUI)
- Concerns regarding risk assessment, (e.g., risk of harm to self/others, child abuse)
- The intrusion by investigators or attorneys, which often work at cross-purposes to healing for victims. Legal concerns include risk management issues, documentation, and being court ordered to produce documentation or provide testimony.

Common Ethical Issues

There are six ethical principles that provide a framework for most professional codes of ethics for human services professionals, including autonomy, nonmaleficence, beneficence, justice, fidelity, and veracity, described in Table 1.3 (American Counseling Association [ACA], 2014). These descriptions are not exhaustive, and most organizations have identified procedures and limits for their services to help address these principles. The reader is encouraged to refer to these principles when thinking about one's professional role and particular responsibility to clients.

Mandated counseling can result in ethical dilemmas for counselors regarding who they serve. This might include the police, CPS investigators or caseworkers, a grant, or the court from whom they get referrals or the client with whom they are working. However, this text takes the position that counselors serve clients, not referring entities. Although the FMHC must often work with representatives from these entities as part of a formal or informal interdisciplinary treatment team, the primary concern can be quite different for these people than it is for the counselor. It is the primary ethical responsibility of an FMHC to attend to client welfare (the principles of beneficence and maleficence). When FMHCs focus primarily on the needs or preferences of a referring agency, their ability to build a trusting psychologically safe therapeutic relationship is in jeopardy (the principle of justice).

TABLE 1.3 Ethical Principles Applied to Forensic Counseling

Principle	What does it mean?
Autonomy	The client has the right to control the counseling process.
Nonmaleficence	Counselors should avoid doing harm to the client.
Beneficence	Counselors should attempt to benefit the client.
Justice	Clients should be treated with fairness and equity.
Fidelity	It is the FMHCs professional responsibility to maintain client trust in the professional relationship.
Veracity	Counselors are truthful with the client and with other professionals.

It is important for FMHC to understand that mandated clients generally come to counseling believing they do not have a choice about whether they attend or engage in counseling. Often, this automatically places them in a perceived adversarial relationship, rather than a therapeutic one, with the counselor. Additionally, if the court mandates a client to treatment, a FMHC must ask herself if the client's signature on intake/admissions paperwork is actually autonomous. Are they signing the informed consent to treatment because they want to pursue counseling or because they believe they do not have a choice? If they believe they do not have a choice, is it actually consent? Consider the ethical principle of autonomy. How might this be relevant in this situation? What should a FMHC do to ensure he or she respect a client's autonomy in decision making? (Many standard forms contain a signature line for the FMHC or other helping professional to attest that the form has been offered for signature and perhaps the client was provided an opportunity to have the document read aloud, in the event that the client refuses to sign.)

In addition, in many of these situations, mandated clients do not attend to the rights and responsibilities or the confidentiality limits or consequences articulated in informed consent documents. It is incumbent on the FMHC to ensure the client reads (or is read) the informed consent and that he or she understands both what he or she is consenting to and the potential consequences to the client for certain disclosures or behaviors (e.g., mandated reporting of suspected child abuse). If the FMHC does not do this, then there is a significant risk that the consent is *not informed*. Therefore, it is crucial that FMHC spend the necessary time attending to this task at the outset of the relationship in order to ensure that if/when the client's behavior results in negative consequences, which he or she may experience as unfair, it is still consistent with the information the counselor provided in the beginning of the relationship.

This demonstrates respect for the ethical principle of veracity because the FMHC is attending to the restraints or limits on the relationship in a truthful professional manner with clients. It also demonstrates the principle of justice by creating a situation where the counselor informs the client about what the limits are and what the consequences are for different choices he or she makes during treatment.

FMHCs have to respect the limits and consequences involved in informed consent documents or program expectations in which they work; however, they also have to be honest in representing this information to clients at the outset of the relationship in order to maintain the client's trust and out of respect for the client's autonomy. Presenting the information to the client allows the client to choose, rather than believing there is no choice in whether to engage in treatment. A client may express a belief that he or she does not have a choice because he or she is court ordered to treatment. However, we know that a piece of paper cannot *make* a person engage in treatment, and if they feel coerced, they are more likely to resist rather than engage. Therefore, we must emphasize that, although it may be a choice they do not like (e.g., choose to engage in treatment and be able to stay in the community or choose not to engage in treatment and potentially be sent to jail), they still have a choice, and the choice is theirs to make. Thus, the counselor is demonstrating the ethical principle of respect for client autonomy.

If/when the client violates a boundary, as discussed in the informed consent document, the counselor must follow through with the consequences discussed. By doing so, the FMHC demonstrates the ethical principle of fidelity. Fidelity occurs when the FMHC fulfills his or her responsibility by demonstrating that what he or she said would happen actually does happen, that the FMHC was truthful and therefore is honoring the relationship by following through with consequences. In street vernacular, offenders consider this "keepin' it real." Although perhaps counterintuitive, many offenders respect FMHC who follow through with consequences rather than those who avoid carrying out consequences because they feel pressure to be nice or give the client a break. It demonstrates that the client cannot manipulate the counselor and that the counselor can be trusted to do what he or she says he or she will, even when the outcome is difficult. Of course, a good counselor will also take the opportunity to process the client's reactions to the situation as a here-and-now example of the client's choices resulting in predictable, but perhaps unwanted/disliked, consequences, which is often the therapeutic issue at the core of their treatment.

Another frequent dilemma for FMHCs is the clash between objectives. When working in forensic settings, counselors interact with (in person or through written communication) investigators whose aim it is to determine whether a crime was committed and/or attempt to establish a legal case for prosecution. This is obviously contrary to the personal goals of offending clients. However, even when working with victims, prosecution of a perpetrator may not be the desired outcome for the victim/client. They may want to forget the abuse happened and focus on healing. Rather than take on the objectives of an investigator, the FMHC's role is to "safeguard the integrity of the counselor-client relationship," according to the professional values stated in the ACA Code of Ethics (2014). FMHCs cross ethical and legal lines when they forget their primary focus is on client welfare.

For instance, a Child Protective Services (CPS) worker brings a child in for play therapy stating that she wants you to "find out" if the child has been abused. The caseworker's question is an investigatory one. Counselors are not investigators; they are there to help a client identify and work through psychological distress in whatever way that makes sense for the client. Because of play therapy, the child may process through emotional material that demonstrates clear play themes indicative of experiencing abuse. However, many children enter play therapy and process through material, moving forward with their lives without the counselor understanding in "grown up terms" the events in the child's life that resulted in the distress. The goal for this counselor is to facilitate the child's process of healing, regardless of the precipitating events. It is not to find out what happened to cause the child's distress. When counselors lose sight of their role and acquiesce to investigators, attempting to conduct investigations rather than providing counseling, they are not guarding client welfare, and therefore, their behavior is unethical. In some situations, these external demands from investigators may result in a FMHC breeching confidentiality. **Confidentiality** is the ethical principle that what a client says to a counselor will remain between the client and counselor. Again, readers are encouraged to consider these possibilities before they occur, possibly through discussion with supervisors or through ongoing professional training.

Common Legal Issues

However, there are certain legal exceptions or **limits to confidentiality,** including the legal requirement for FMHC to **report** *suspected* **or known abuse or neglect of a child, elder, or disabled person**. It is important to note that emphasis is placed on suspected because when a FMHC begins to assume they must "know" that abuse or neglect has occurred, they often begin acting as investigators, which violates their code of ethics as well as hinders actual investigatory and prosecutor outcomes. If you suspect, report. If you know, report. Counselors should not investigate as this can create its own complications and risks. There are trained police officers and protective service investigators who have this charge. It is NOT the role of a FMHC!

In some states, FMHCs have a legal **duty to warn** targeted individuals and/or law enforcement when the counselor becomes aware of an eminent threat of harm to a specific person, under the Tarasoff rule (*Tarasoff v. Regents of the University of California*, 1976). Courts apply this rule differently in different states, so it is important for the FMHC to learn the specific statutory requirements that are relevant to the jurisdiction where the counselor practices. Some states protect counselors more if they err on the side of caution and break confidentiality by reporting. Other states provide more protection if the counselor maintains confidentiality, unless they are certain that there is eminent harm (a standard that is sometimes difficult to establish in practice), or that there is an identifiable victim. Texas law is unique in that it is protective of counselor's decisions as long as the counselor follows the standard of practice for the profession and acts in good faith.

A FMHC is also legally bound to break confidentiality when a client indicates an **intent to self-harm**. In these cases, the FMHC may break confidentiality by contacting a crisis response unit to evaluate the client, a hospital, or someone with whom the client has a significant relationship. Regardless of whom the counselor contacts to discuss the situation, the purpose should be solely to develop and carry out a plan to help maintain the client's safety. Forensic counseling necessarily involves offenders and victims; therefore, risk assessment regarding potential self-harm or harm to others is inherent in the work. FMHCs are more likely to conduct risk assessments more often and have to develop safety plans more often than counselors in other settings. Risk assessment and safety planning is discussed in those sections focusing on different populations and settings in the last section of the text.

FMHCs must also be cognizant that a court may subpoena documentation. This leads to the issue of privilege, which is the way the law safeguards a client's ethical right to confidentiality. **Privilege** is a legal principle that belongs to a competent adult client or to the legal guardian of a minor or otherwise incompetent individual, as determined by the courts. The law protects privileged communication between a lawyer and client, health professional (including FMHC and client), priest and parishioner, or spousal communication from disclosure in legal proceedings. Because privilege belongs to the client, he or she may waive privilege. The FMHC may request the court respect the client's privileged communication with the counselor; however, the client's behavior/choices may result in unforeseen dismissal of this right. Specific examples are discussed in future chapters.

Regardless, it is crucial that FMHCs understand that documentation is a legal record of the client's case. Therefore, documentation should meet professional standards regarding inclusion of only necessary documentation of progress based on the client's treatment plan and documentation of risk assessment, consultation, and safety planning. Documentation should focus on behaviorally observable or reported data (e.g., client report, collateral source report) and the FMHC must support any assessment statements with this type of evidence. Documenting one's conceptualization of the case (e.g., hypotheses about assessments of the case that involve a professional or theoretical interpretation) should only occur in process notes. **Process notes** are notes only viewed by the counselor as memory aides. Counselors should never share process notes with anyone else, and therefore, the counselor will never place the notes in the client's file. The FMHC should protect process notes in a locked file drawer in the counselor's office, and no other person should have access to them. One exception is when a counselor who is under supervision and is working under the license of another professional counselor. In this circumstance, the supervisory counselor may have access to the notes because the professional therapeutic relationship with the client extends to the supervisor. Any missteps regarding what the counselor documents, what is excluded from documentation, or where documents (progress or process notes) are maintained may result in harm to the client and/or legal or ethical jeopardy for the counselor.

For FMHCs, regardless of the legal doctrine of privileged communication, they should *expect* courts to subpoena their records and document accordingly. When the court subpoenas counseling records or serves a court order to testify, you must respond. I recommend that FMHC consult their liability insurance and professional association prior to going to court or prior to presenting records to the court. The legal consultation can provide you with your options for maintaining both professional and legal obligations.

The Professional's Responsibility to Stay Informed

However, regardless of the specific situation, FMHCs need to understand the importance of supervision, consultation, and documentation. As stated earlier in this chapter, FMHCs who work under supervision should seek supervision to ensure ethical decision making regarding risk assessment issues. If the FMHC works independently, then he or she should have a network of colleagues whom he or she may consult on such matters. Finally, regardless of the level of supervision or consultation, FMHCs must document all components of the risk assessment, supervision/consultation sought, conclusions drawn, and safety planning or interventions undertaken in the client's chart. This provides legal cover for FMHCs should any problems occur following the assessment. Documenting risk management processes also ensures you are more likely to act in a manner that is consistent with ethical standards (ACA, 2014) and legal requirements.

SUMMARY

This chapter provides a foundation for the reading that follows. Having read and reviewed it, you have learned what a FMHC is, what type of populations he or she works with, and in what contexts. Additionally, you have gained contextual awareness of historical, sociocultural, and forensic influences affecting the work of a FMHC. You have a basic understanding of both prevention and intervention and potential common mental health concerns of forensic clients. Additionally, you can identify ethical principles, which guide your work and how those manifest in forensic counseling situations. Finally, you have a basic understanding of the common legal issues you will encounter as a FMHC.

The rest of section I will provide additional foundational information such as self-care, burnout, and vicarious trauma, which counselors need to be prepared for as a FMHC. This section also provides a basic understanding of assessment of risk and resilience factors. Section II will discuss developmental approaches to understanding FMHC clients. Finally, section III will discuss information on specific populations, issues, and settings.

CHAPTER 1 REFLECTIVE QUESTIONS

1. Describe the roles and contexts that a forensic mental health counselor would work, differentiating this group of professionals from other types of forensic professionals.
2. Describe the developmental trajectory of someone with a high ACE score and how that might impact his or her development of mental illness.
3. Describe the unique challenges for offenders with mental illness in light of deinstitutionalization, mass incarceration, and privatization of corrections.
4. Discuss common ethical and legal issues unique to counselors working in forensic settings.
5. If you were to develop a prevention or early intervention psychoeducational workshop for your community, how would you describe to lay people how adverse childhood experiences affect a person's neurobiology and how trauma-impacted neurobiology may impact that individual's behavior in relationships, in the community, and in school/work settings?

RESOURCES

Child Trauma Academy and NMT: http://childtrauma.org/nmt-model/

Adverse Childhood Experiences: https://www.cdc.gov/violenceprevention/acestudy/index.html

ACES Connection: https://www.acesconnection.com/blog/the-who-18-question-ace-questionaire-1?reply=421545695276935301#421545695276935301

WHO ACE Questionnaire: http://www.who.int/violence_injury_prevention/violence/activities/adverse_childhood_experiences/questionnaire.pdf?ua=1

Ten-Question ACE: https://www.ncjfcj.org/sites/default/files/Finding%20Your%20ACE%20Score.pdf

Adaptations of ACE Questionnaire: https://www.acesconnection.com/g/resource-center/blog/resource-list-extended-aces-surveys

Johns Hopkins ACEs Resource Packet: http://childhealthdata.org/docs/default-source/cahmi/aces-resource-packet_all-pages_12_06-16112336f3c0266255aab2ff00001023b1.pdf?sfvrsn=2

CHAPTER 2

Vicarious Trauma, Job Stress, Burnout, and Self-Care in Forensic Counseling

Upon completion of this chapter, readers will be able to do the following:

- Distinguish between vicarious trauma, compassion fatigue, job stress, and burnout
- Analyze personal and organizational risk and resilience factors contributing to prevention of vicarious trauma, job stress, and burnout
- Design an individualized self-care plan for prevention and ongoing monitoring
- Discuss common ethical and legal issues resulting from impairment

TABLE 2.1 Myths and Myth Busters

Myths	Myth Busters
Experienced counselors do not experience vicarious trauma (VT).	Experienced counselors may be at greater risk of vicarious trauma because they have heard multiple trauma narratives over many years, which may increase their vulnerability to developing VT.
Self-care is not practical in a forensic mental health counseling (FMHC) job.	Self-care must be intentional in any job. Part of planning for self-care is identifying challenges and how to manage self-care in spite of the challenges.
Letting someone know you are in distress from vicarious trauma, job stress, or burnout is disclosing you are not cut out for a FMHC job.	Many counselors (new and experienced) are affected by their client's and by the environments in which they work. Almost half of all counselors experience one or more of these at some point in their career.

INTRODUCTION

Being a forensic mental health counselor is a challenging job—for anyone! These jobs inevitably expose counselors to parts of human behavior that reveal the worst in people. For example, forensic clients typically do not initially want to attend counseling. They will blame you for their choices and behaviors. Court systems will hinder the therapeutic nature of your work. You may feel unsafe at times. There will not be enough resources to meet the demands of the job. You may feel responsible for your client's success or failure in treatment. Although these statements may seem harsh, if you do not prepare for these realities, you are much less likely to navigate them well. This would be detrimental to you personally and increase the chances that you become impaired and are not able to conduct your job in an ethical manner, safeguarding client welfare.

This chapter has been included at the beginning of the text in order to emphasize the importance of evaluating your risk and resilience factors for developing job stress, vicarious trauma, compassion fatigue, and burnout. Additionally, its placement highlights the fact that you need to develop a self-care plan as soon as possible. Please, *do it before you read the other chapters of this book*. Simply reading the material in this book could result in distress for you by triggering uncomfortable thoughts or feelings. Self-care is your responsibility, so take it seriously.

DEVELOPMENTAL ISSUES

This chapter discusses job stress, vicarious trauma, secondary traumatic stress, compassion fatigue, and burnout. These are related phenomena, but they are distinct from one another. Each has a developmental trajectory to consider as you monitor your own thoughts, feelings, and behaviors. Understanding the development of these experiences will raise your awareness and improve your ability to intervene early when you identify a problem.

Each of the concepts discussed in this section arises out of a counselor's intention to be empathic toward clients, which is essential to being a counselor. **Empathy** is being conscious of and sensitive to another person's emotional state, often feeling what he or she is feeling. This is different form **sympathy**, which is feeling sorry for someone else through the emotion of pity. Counselors work at cultivating empathy as a necessary component of their jobs. However, being empathic is a potential risk factor in developing some of the phenomena discussed in this chapter.

Development of Job Stress

Job stress is normal for just about any profession. The term **stress,** according to Selye's (1950) seminal work, is the nonspecific response to physical, chemical, or psychological environmental triggers on the body in response to external demands for change (Szabo, Tache, & Somogyi, 2012). **Distress** is the reaction one has to stress that is unpleasant. According to the Centers for Disease Control (CDC), "**Job stress** can be defined as the harmful physical and emotional responses that occur when the requirements of the job do not match the capabilities, resources, or needs of the worker" (Sauter et al., 2014, p. 6). Stress is distinguished from activities (physical or mental), which a person simply finds challenging. Counseling in forensic settings is definitely challenging work, but it does not have to be stressful, at least not all the time.

Karasek and Theorell (1990) devised a theory explaining the development of job stress called the **job-demand-control model of job stress** (JDCS) (Karasek, 1979). "The model posits that job strain (stress) results when job-decision latitude (control) is not commensurate with the psychological demands imposed by the job" (Sauter & Murphy, 1995, p. 2). Further research indicates low support or isolation (iso-strain) in combination with

FIGURE 2.1 Job stress flowchart

low control in high demand situations increased the predictive value of the model (Sauter & Murphy, 1995; Theorell & Karasek, 1996). Several meta-analytic studies utilizing over 2 decades of research demonstrate support for the JDCS model (De Jonge & Kompier, 1997; Morrison, Payne, & Wall, 2003; van der Doef & Maes, 1999).

Therefore, job stress develops when a counselor perceives his or her job has high external demands, particularly if they come from multiple conflicting sources, with little control over how he or she carries out his or her responsibilities. This experience is further compounded by situations where the counselor has little supervisory or peer support in managing these expectations. Chronic job stress is a precursor to burnout and can result in a counselor being more susceptible to secondary traumatic stress, vicarious trauma, and compassion fatigue (Figley, 1995; Kanno, Kim, & Constance-Huggins, 2016; Kraus, 2005; McCann & Pearlman, 1990, 1993).

Development of Secondary Traumatic Stress or Vicarious Trauma

Secondary traumatic stress (STS) can occur when a counselor over-empathizes with a traumatized client, resulting in the counselor experiencing traumatic stress symptoms similar to those which the client experiences (Molnar et al., 2017; Pearlman & Mac Ian, 1995; Wilson & Lindy, 1994). Herman (1997, 2015) conceptualized it as a form of *traumatic countertransference*. Therefore, if the trajectory continues unchecked, the counselor will exhibit symptoms of posttraumatic stress disorder (PTSD) simply from bearing witness to a client's trauma narrative, or from more frequent exposure to a series of these over time from multiple clients.

When the experience of STS begins affecting counselors' attitudes, feelings, and behaviors toward others, they may develop vicarious trauma. **Vicarious trauma** (VT) is "a process involving a transformation in inner experience of the therapist resulting from empathic engagement with clients' traumatic material" (Adams & Riggs, 2008, p. 26), and it "occurs when a person's beliefs about safety, trust, control, esteem, and intimacy become increasingly negative as a result of being exposed to a client's traumatic experiences" (Adams & Riggs, 2008, p. 415). Vicarious trauma, first defined by McCann and Perlman's research (1990, 1993), therefore negatively affects the way a counselor perceives him- or herself, others, and the world.

This results in suspicion of others and doubts about their own effectiveness as counselors. People suffering with VT may exhibit behaviors such as isolating from others or becoming overly controlling in both personal and professional relationships (McCann & Pearlman, 1990, 1993; Trippany, White Kress, & Wilcoxon, 2004). Over time, this hypervigilance may result in counselors becoming mentally, emotionally, and physically exhausted. As a self-protective defense, they may begin to experience compassion fatigue (Ivicic & Motta, 2017).

Development of Compassion Fatigue

There is a continuum ranging from compassion satisfaction to compassion fatigue, which a counselor may experience toward his or her job. **Compassion satisfaction** "is a sense of reward, efficacy, and competence one feels in one's role as a helping professional" (Molnar et al., 2017, p. 130). **Compassion fatigue** (CF), however, occurs "when [clinical] work ... suffers from the negative impact of trauma experienced by clients, to the point where [counselors] are no longer able to effectively help those seeking their services" (Molnar et al., 2017, p. 130). It is also called the "cost of caring" (Perry, 2014). CF may develop when a counselor exhausts his or her ability to separate his or her work with clients from his or her personal feelings of anxiety, depression, or even traumatic stress reactions (Henson, 2017). It jeopardizes client welfare, because counselors demonstrate less interest in the client's experience and can no longer bear witness to the client's trauma. CF is similar to the burnout cycle, as applied to mental health professionals.

Development of Burnout

Research indicates that job stress, as defined by the job-demand-control-support (JDCS) model, is a precursor to burnout (Bakker, Demerouiti, Taris, Schaufeli, & Schreurs, 2003).

The **Maslach model of burnout** involves a cycle of *emotional exhaustion*, followed by *depersonalization* (pulling away from the client), then a *reduced sense of personal accomplishment* (realization that you are not doing a good job). The feelings of reduced personal accomplishment then motivate the counselor to work harder—rather than resting—and to give more in order to meet the client's needs, which leads to more emotional exhaustion, beginning the cycle again in a downward spiral. When a counselor experiences compassion fatigue over time, by definition, he or she is experiencing emotional exhaustion and depersonalization.

In forensic mental health counseling, the needs of the clients, the system, and society can be overwhelming and impossible to meet in reality. Therefore, we define **burnout** (BO) as the "psychological and emotional exhaustion, associated with feelings of hopelessness and difficulties in dealing with work or in doing ones job effectively" (Turgoose, Glover, Barker, & Maddox, 2017). The burnout prevalence rate for

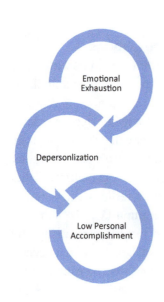

FIGURE 2.2 Emotional exhaustion cycle

mental health workers ranges between 21–67% (Rohland, 2000; Siebert, 2005; Webster & Hacket; 1999). Additionally, a study of British forensic mental health counselors reported 21–48% experienced high levels of emotional exhaustion, which is the first sign of burnout (Oddie & Ousley, 2007).

CONTEXTUAL ISSUES

In the descriptions of job stress, secondary traumatic stress, vicarious trauma, compassion fatigue, and burnout, several contextual factors are identified that may influence the development of these phenomena. Job stress involves high levels of external demands, low decision-making ability, and little support and supervision. Secondary traumatic stress and vicarious trauma involve work that requires empathic engagement with trauma survivors and bearing witness to trauma narratives (McCann & Pearlman, 1990, 1993). These are all organizational contextual factors. Compassion fatigue and burnout indicate individual contextual factors, such as becoming overwhelmed and increasingly emotionally exhausted, disengaging from clients (depersonalization and compassion fatigue), and no longer being an effective counselor (low personal accomplishment). Individual factors are the reason one person may develop burnout while another person working in the same environment may not. Organizational and personal factors each contribute to a counselor's risk of developing stress-related symptoms. However, there are also protective factors, which may promote resilience depending on the context.

ORGANIZATIONAL FACTORS

Although counselors are likely to have more control over personal factors than organizational factors, an extensive review of burnout literature indicates that workplace factors far outweigh personal factors in the development of burnout (Lambert, Hogan, Griffin, & Kelley, 2015; Maslach & Leiter, 2008). Therefore, when interviewing for jobs, this may be something to consider. Additionally, you may be in a position to advocate for organizational changes that are supportive of other counselors, based on the factors discussed next. The literature identifies a variety of organizational factors influencing job stress and burnout, including organizational climate, ethical climate, systemic influences, colleague support, and supervision. Sauter and colleagues (2014) identify several conditions, which contribute to job stress described in Table 2.2:

Organizational structure can negatively influence levels of job stress and burnout for correctional counselors (Lambert, Barton-Bellessa, & Hotan, 2015). Organizational factors such as limited autonomy or input in decision making, poor communication, lack of administrative and supervisory support, and experiences of injustice result in higher levels of job stress among correctional staff (Cieslak, Korczynska, Strelau, & Kaczmarek, 2008; Dollard & Winefield, 1998; Garland, 2004; Griffin, Hogan, & Lambert, 2012; Lambert, Altheimer, & Hogan, 2010; Lambert, Hogan, & Jiang, 2010; Neveu, 2007; Savicki, Cooley, & Gjesvold, 2003). Additionally, studies on correctional staff burnout indicate that role conflict, role ambiguity, work overload, experiencing harassment, and conflict between work and family roles and

TABLE 2.2 Job Conditions Contributing to Stress

Stressful Job Condition	Example
Task design	Large caseloads, few breaks, long hours, tasks that require lower skills than the counselor is trained for.
Management/supervision style	Counselors are not consulted in decision making for the program, poor communication or lack of supervisory support, policies that do not support counselors personally (e.g., family leave) as well as professionally (e.g., scheduled supervision groups).
Interpersonal relationships	Lack of support from coworkers and supervisors resulting in feelings of isolation.
Work roles	Job expectations are ambiguous, multiple stakeholders (e.g., referring agency, program supervisor, and client) exerting conflicting demands on the counselor's time.
Career concerns	Working in grant-funded programs, lacking job security, no room to grow (e.g., professional development, promotion options).
Environmental conditions	Dangerous situations, unpleasant conditions, exposure to trauma.

responsibilities can all increase burnout levels (Lambert & Hogan, 2010; Lambert, Hogan, Jiang, & Jenkins, 2009; Savicki et al., 2003).

Organizational Climate

Organizational climate is how workers perceive their work environments as supportive of their personal and professional goals, value their input and expertise, and engage them in decision making (Arnetz, Lucas, & Arnetz, 2011). It encompasses primarily interpersonal and systemic aspects of a person's work. This is particularly important for counselors who work within systems that often focus on investigating wrongdoing and punishing that behavior when found. Therefore, forensic mental health counselors must negotiate often-competing demands of the justice system's focus on punishment and the counseling profession's focus on helping people cope with their circumstances in a more functional manner. Although both approaches seek to improve potentially unsafe situations, they exhibit *different priorities and values* in their attempts to achieve the end goal. Researchers indicate there are four factors to consider when evaluating organizational climate:

- The social and ethical climate (support)
- Level of employee participation in decision making
- Goal clarity (or job ambiguity)
- Performance feedback from supervisory leadership (Arnetz, Lucas, & Arntetz, 2011; Vogt, Hakanen, Jenny, & Bauer, 2016).

We know that there is a correlation between organizational climate and employee mental and physical health (Arnetz, Lucas, & Arntetz, 2011). Some stress-related behaviors associated with working in a poor organizational climate are increases in distractibility, irritability, and being more prone to make mistakes in one's work (Greenberg, 2006; Hansson, Arnetz, & Anderzen, 2006; Letvak & Buck, 2008; Spielberger, Vagg, & Wasala, 2003; Westman & Eden, 1996). Obviously, these behavioral manifestations can have negative effects on client welfare. In contrast, when counselors are engaged in their work, they experience it as "stimulating, energetic, significant, and meaningful, and are engrossed and concentrate fully" (Vogt, Hakanen, Jenny, & Bauer, 2016, p. 194).

For forensic mental health counselorss, perception of environmental threats can influence their perception of the organizational climate. One example is when correctional counselors and child welfare workers experience an ever-looming threat of violence. These counselors must always function at a heightened level of awareness, which necessarily engages their ANS stress responses. Additionally, child welfare and correctional counseling programs often lack resources and are frequently short staffed, which limits their ability to provide a safe, humane work environment, leading to ethical conflicts regarding client welfare (Lambert, Hogan, Girffin, & Kelley, 2015).

Ethical climate is another organizational factor defined as the culture of valuing professional ethics supported by policies, procedures, and actual practices of an organization. Victor and Cullen (1987) identified three levels of ethical climate:

- *Egoism* (looking out for self/organizational interests)
- *Benevolence* (focusing on social responsibility and colleague support)
- *Principle* (focusing on personal and organizational morality and professional ethical codes)

Organizational culture provides both formal and informal systems focused on behavioral controls and larger organizational values that shape ethical decision making (Detert, Treveno & Sweitzer, 2008; Schein, 2010; Schneider, Salvaggio, & Subirates, 2002; Trevino, Butterfield, & McCabe, 1998). In a review of the literature, Newman, Round, Bhattacharya, and Roy (2017) identify four contributing variables to an organization's ethical climate, including (a) organizational and cultural contexts, (b) organizational practices, (c) leadership and managerial practices, and (d) individual differences. They also identify four outcome categories affected by organizational climate:

1. Work attitudes (organizational commitment, job satisfaction, absences, supervisory trust, commitment to quality, etc.)
2. Ethical intensions, work behaviors and other ethical outcomes
3. Psychological states of individuals (mindfulness, moral distress, empathic concern)
4. Performance outcomes (job performance, client satisfaction, organizational citizenship, safety and quality, team work, etc.)

Support

Even when facing organizational factors that might be beyond individual control, coworker and supervisor support may significantly moderate development of job stress (Karasek, 1982). For FMHC social and peer/colleague support is crucial in creating a work climate that nurtures counselors and the work they do. Although FMHC's work with both victims and offenders, in my experience, finding support among colleagues within a victim-focused agency like a child advocacy center or domestic violence victim's program is easier than finding it in offender counseling settings, such as batterer's intervention programs or prisons. However, there are exceptions to both of these generalizations. For instance, working in foster care is notoriously challenging because of the high caseloads and seemingly insurmountable demands on caseworkers; as a result there is a high rate of burnout.

Any time counselors work in settings with multiple people experiencing burnout, the support is low (Dollard & Winefiled, 1998; Karesek, 1982; Luthans, Norman, Avolio, & Avey, 2008; Spielberger, Vagg, & Wasala, 2003). However, there are some correctional counseling programs, like those associated with mental health courts or drug courts where the personnel perceive their role in the context of a whole system that is focused on rehabilitation, rather than retribution. This seemingly simple distinction has major effects on the workplace climate by valuing the counselor's contributions as essential to the overall mission of the mental health courts. When people feel their work contributes to a greater purpose, generally, they are happier with their jobs, even when there are stressors over which they have little control (Acker, 1999; Kraus, 2005; Senter, Morgan, Serna-McDonald, & Bewley, 2010).

The quality of interpersonal relationships with colleagues or other team members affects staff cohesion, which is an important indicator of levels of support (Choi, 2011; Slattery, 2003). Open communication practices facilitate good interpersonal working relationships. This often leads to counselors who perceive their input regarding decisions is valued, which ultimately affects their experience of job stress.

Supervision

Supervisory support is another moderator in the development of counselor stress (Karasek, 1979; 1982; Karasek & Theorell, 1990; Sauter et al., 2014; Theorell, & Karasek, 1996; van der Doef & Maes, 1999). Supervisors often have control over the number of cases and types of cases assigned to counselors. This is important when we consider that the level of exposure to traumatized clients a counselor works with increases the likelihood that the counselor will experience secondary trauma, for instance. Supervisors are in the position to limit the amount of clinical hours a counselor spends with trauma survivors, the number of trauma clients the counselor is assigned, and the level of trauma experienced by the clients assigned to a particular counselor (Kanno, Kim, & Constance-Huggins, 2016; Wee & Myers, 2002). Additionally, supervisors are in the position to facilitate open communication and staffing of cases between colleagues, which is helpful in decreasing vicarious trauma experiences, decreasing job stress, and helping counselors manage the challenges they experience on the job (Choi, 2011; Slattery, 2003). Further, supervisors provide leadership in the organization either by "backing up" counselors when there is conflict or by undermining counselors who are dealing with challenging client situations on a daily basis.

Systemic Issues

Early research on organizational variables affecting counselors' stress levels found that job stress also increased as participants experienced mounting pressures from societal changes, difficulty negotiating proper boundaries in their relationships with clients, and public criticism regarding their professions (Cherniss, Egnatios, & Wacker, 1976). Similar to the JDCS model, they reported that the lack of control over job expectations further exacerbated the likelihood that they would experience burnout (Cherniss, Egnatios, & Wacker, 1976). Similarly, Farber (1991) identified systemic issues, including social and familial changes and the increased importance placed on individuality, rather than community solutions to societal problems, as increasing job counselor stress and burnout. He theorized that these systemic factors negatively affected counselors' self-perceptions about people (like themselves) who work with troubled clients. He concluded that this led to symptoms of burnout such as exhaustion, cynicism, negative affective states, and a lowered sense of self-efficacy.

PERSONAL FACTORS

As previously stated, we know that different people can work in the same organization and experience different levels of job stress or burnout. We attribute these differences to personal factors. Individual counselors can draw on personal resources, including psychological characteristics associated with resilience, to positively impact stress levels. These include cognitive and affective aspects of personality, such as having a positive worldview and positive sense of self that motivates and facilitates their ability to engage in and achieve work-related goals (Bakker & Demerouti, 2008, 2014; Hobfoll, 2001; van den Heuvel, Demerouti, Schaufeli, & Bakker, 2010; Vogt, Hakanen, Jenny, & Bauer, 2016). Positive self-assessment and positive outlook affect level of motivation to do the work and levels of job satisfaction (Judge, Van Vianen, & De Pater, 2004).

Another personal factor that Antonovsky identified is a **sense of coherence** "a global orientation, in which an individual perceives life as comprehensive, manageable, and meaningful" (Vogt, Hakanen, Jenny, & Bauer, 2016, p. 195). When someone has a high sense of coherence his or her perception of the world is that events are structured and predictable and demands are perceived as challenges that are worthy of investing time and effort. (Consider the alternative: no structure or predictability to demands, with little return on investment of time or effort.) Interestingly, we also know that we can build *psychological capital* through having positive learning experiences in the workplace, which can generalize to more positive personal resources, and then build more resilience to workplace stressors (Kohn & Schooler, 1982; Luthans, Norman, Avolio, & Avey, 2008; Xanthopoulou, Bakker, Demerouti, & Schaufeli, 2007, 2009).

Part of building this sense of coherence may be developing a strong professional identity as a protective factor. Correctional counselors who express higher levels of professional identity based on their attitudes, beliefs, and feelings about their profession are less likely to experience burnout (Senter et al., 2010). Additionally, having a proactive personality, dispositional optimism, positive affect, good self-esteem, and hardiness are indicative of lower levels of burnout (Alarcon, Eschleman, & Bowling, 2009). However, even when a counselor has these positive dispositional attitudes, feelings, and behaviors, working with forensic populations may still increase the likelihood a counselor will experience a higher than average rate of burnout.

For instance, both victim and offender counselors will work with trauma narratives, which is a documented risk for developing burnout (Shapiro, Brown, & Biegel, 2007). Many trauma survivors and offenders come to counseling in crisis and may be suicidal, and work with both of these populations increases burnout risks (Miller, 1998; Ting, Jacobsen, & Sanders, 2011). Additionally, mandated clients present additional risks, and clients in offender programs mandated through mental health courts, those on probation or parole, and those incarcerated are common clients for the FMHC. Substance abuse counselors (Knudsen, Ducharme, & Roman, 2006), sex offender treatment therapists (Kraus, 2005), and correctional counselors (Griffin et al., 2012; Hurst & Hurst, 1997; Senter, Morgan, Serna-McDonald, & Bewley, 2010; Whitehead, 1989) all experience high rates of burnout, also.

Addiction counselors report that a number of systemic issues negatively affect their levels of job stress, including having to interact with the criminal justice system and working with clients who experience significant comorbid physical and mental health issues (Covington, 2007; Ducharme, Mello, Roman, Knudsen & Johnson, 2007; Garner, Knight, & Simpson, 2007; McNulty, Oser, Johnson, Knudsen, & Roman, 2007). These systemic issues are areas to monitor. Finally, counselors working with seriously mental ill clients (Acker, 1999) are at greater risk, and victims and offenders often have multiple serious mental illnesses such as PTSD, chronic depression, and even psychosis. One common stressor in working with forensic populations is the need to appear highly competent, resulting in higher stress, particularly when the counselor is uncertain about how effective he or she actually is in influencing change in the client because the client lacks motivation (Deutsch, 1984; Thériault, & Gazzola, 2006). Discussing these stressors with a supervisor or in peer support can be helpful in managing these feelings.

PREVENTION AND INTERVENTION

Now that you are aware of the risks, what do you do? Counselors need to take responsibility for their own self-care. However, organizations or programs can also address organizational factors and have policies and procedures in place to monitor job stress and to intervene early if difficulties are noted. Prevention starts with increasing awareness of risks and in self-care planning to address risks and increase resiliency. Intervention, if needed, should happen early, and therefore necessitates continuous monitoring.

Prevention

One of the best prevention measures is **self-care planning**. This should include an evaluation of your mental/emotional, physical, and spiritual life. Some potential categories to explore include the following:

- **Personal and professional relationships**: Which relationships are a source of strength for you? Which add stress, and are there ways to address this? Do you feel heard in my relationships? Am you able to set healthy limits, and if not, what can you do about this? Do you have a peer support group you can rely on, and how can you engage them in my self-care plan? How can you access consultation or supervision?

- **Personal capability**: Do you feel challenged to your capability? Is your input valued? Do you feel you contribute to the world, your clients, our mission? Do you need or want to be more involved in the professional organizations representing you? Do you want to pursue a special certification, credentialing, or new degree? How can your personal and professional worlds support you in reaching your capabilities?
- **Physical nurturing**: What are your eating, sleeping, and exercise habits? Would meditation or some other physical form of self-care be helpful for you? How can you realistically plan these into your day?
- **Mental nurturing**: Do you feel supported? Are you attending to your own mental health needs? Do you have a therapist you can see if/when needed, and if not, can you find one? How do you become more present and attend to your mental health? Can you schedule regular mental health breaks from your responsibilities?
- **Spiritual nurturing**: Where do you find support and energy in the world? How do you seek out spiritual nurturing? Do you have any creative outlets? Is prayer or meditation helpful for you, and if so, how can you integrate it into your self-care plan? Is it helpful for you to sit in silence or to go into nature to recenter yourself? What rituals help you feel renewed?

By completing a thorough self-care assessment, counselors can identify individualized targets in each of these categories, for which you can plan individualized prevention activities that will work for you. For instance, for physical health you may notice that when you experience more stress you begin having trouble sleeping. For one person, engaging in physical activity, such as walking 3 miles a day, is helpful; however, for another person it may work better to set aside 20 minutes a day to meditate or read something enjoyable. In other words, like any behavioral plan, you need to identify early signs of stress and prevention activities that are unique to you.

Based on the literature, there are some personal characteristics associated with burnout, which should be part of any self-care plan. These include addressing sleeping and exercise habits (El-Ghorouy, Galper, Sawaqdeh, & Bufka, 2012). Seeking therapy as part of their self-care plan may result in improved levels of job stress (Pope & Tabachnick, 1994). However, there are barriers for professional counselors who want to go to therapy, including stigma of having a mental health issue, issues with insurance coverage, and concerns that a colleague or a client may see them going to therapy and draw conclusions that the counselor is deficient (Bearse, McMinn, Seegobin, & Free, 2013). For this reason, it might be practical to seek services outside the counselor's own clinical community, and/or to seek services in a geographic area removed from the workplace. Similar to seeking therapy, case consultation, supervision, and continuing education provide additional supports helpful in managing stress levels, particularly for female counselors (Rupert & Kent, 2007).

Female counselors should also include action plans for monitoring and managing the multiple roles of counselor, wife, and mother, which research indicates contributes to role conflict and job stress (Cushway & Tyler, 1996; Deutsch, 1984 Rupert & Morgan, 2005). Developing peer-support networks with other female counselors who manage similar roles may be a helpful preventative measure. However, for counselors working in rural areas, there may be additional constraints on accessing support resources (Hargrove & Curtin, 2012; Kee, Johnson, & Hunt, 2002). With the advent of the Internet, however, you have additional potential resources through online support and supervision groups, which could prove helpful, such as the American Counseling Association (ACA) and the International Association of Addiction and Offender Counselors (IAAOC). Connect listservs you can access as a member of these organizations.

Monitoring is a key aspect of self-care. Counselors can monitor physical and emotional symptoms of job stress, so they can intervene as early as possible. *Physical signs* of burnout include feeling exhausted, getting sick more often, increasing headaches or other aches and pains, and changing sleep habits. *Psychological symptoms* include difficulty concentrating, shorter temper, job dissatisfaction, sense of failure and self-doubt, feeling helpless or trapped, isolation, loss of motivation, becoming more cynical, and low morale. *Behavioral signs* of burnout include withdrawing from responsibilities, isolating, procrastinating, using food or addictive behaviors to cope, taking your frustration out on others, being absent from work, and being less conscientious about client welfare. Finally, *spiritual symptoms* include experiencing less joy in the work, no longer finding meaning in the work, and not feeling connected to a higher purpose. Long term, job stress can result in cardiovascular disease, musculoskeletal disorders, psychological disorders, workplace injuries, and other more serious chronic or even life-threatening diseases (Sauter et al., 2014).

The U.S. Centers for Disease Control (CDC) discusses several prevention measures an organization can take to reduce stress in healthcare settings:

- Educating management and employees about job stress
- Reducing organizational sources of stress by changing problematic policies or procedures
- Establishing employee assistance programs for early intervention (Sauter et al., 2014)

Organizations can support workers by developing an organizational climate that has policies and procedures in place that create a safe, humane work environment. Processes that value open, honest communication, and seek feedback on decision making at all levels of the organization can improve climate. In addition, developing an organizational culture that values professional ethics and facilitates and rewards ethical decision making can promote a positive ethical climate. Additionally, organizations should provide prescribed time to staff cases with colleagues and supervisors. This demonstrates that the organization values both the professional development of its workers but also values them as individuals.

Supervisors can create a supportive environment by offering regular case staffing to counselors and by providing timely constructive feedback on job performance. The supervisor is also in a good position to help prevent stressors such as ensuring counselor caseloads are consistent with the counselor's current resources and training. They can help counselors under their supervision understand their roles and responsibilities within the larger mission of the program or organization, which may assist counselors finding meaning and purpose in their work. Supervisors can also promote activities that provide social interaction among workers so that they build personal relationships that can provide more of a team focus and opportunities to offer support to one another.

Finally, counselors should plan for continuing education and professional development. These activities often help counselors recharge and find new purpose in their work. Additionally, counselors who are engaged in professional organizational activities, like the International Association of Addiction and Offender Counseling, are more likely to feel supported and engaged in their work. Finding ways to engage in the profession as a whole will help strengthen your professional identity, a protective factor for burnout, and will help develop additional non-work-related collegial relationships, which a professional counselor can draw on for support.

Intervention

Self-care planning necessitates that counselors identify *a priori* interventions that will be meaningful for the individual counselor. Therefore, counselors should identify interventions that may be helpful to you related to physical health, mental health, support, and spiritual practice. However, when the job becomes so problematic that it negatively affects personal relationships or one's ability to care for clients ethically, then the professional may need to consider taking a break. This may mean a mental health day or week, or it may mean choosing to stop counseling the population you are currently working with.

> For instance, when I burned out working with sex offenders, I quit working in that area and went back to school to study a different type of counseling, so that I could re-specialize with clients who are more functional. Once I took a break from the trauma-heavy work I had done for years, I was able to begin doing some limited work with kids in foster care and with adults who had addiction issues, utilizing my previous expertise in trauma, addictions, and offender counseling. However, given my previous experiences, I decided to be more proactive about my caseload, and to limit the number of hours I spent working with these clients in my private practice.

Organizational interventions focus on supervisory support. Miller and Sprang (2017) describe a supervision model that assists counselors in managing difficult emotional reactions to trauma clients. There are five components to the **components for enhancing clinician engagement and reducing trauma (CE-CERT) model**. These include supervisors helping counselors build skills in the following:

Experiential engagement, which involves helping the counselor learn to "establish, balance, and maintain a connection to a client and the client's experience and to acknowledge and experience the feelings that arise as a result of this engagement" (Miller & Sprang, 2017, p. 155). Skills include intentionality, conscious acknowledgement of the experience, and being nonreactive regarding the emotional experience.

1. **Regulating rumination**, which involves "reducing the cognitive reproduction of distressing experiences through active control of the cognitive processes away from a wandering state to a focused, goal-directed activity" (Miller & Sprang, 2017, p. 156). Skills include acknowledgement of the rumination, focused engagement on the here and now, social engagement to reduce isolation, and consciously transitioning from abstract ruminations to making thoughts action oriented, concrete, experiential, and specific (ACES).

2. **Conscious narrative** is facilitated by the supervisor providing the counselor with "both opportunity and ability to coherently describe a difficult or traumatic experience or memory throughout the therapeutic encounter in a manner that promotes assimilation of the narrative and calming of dysregulated states" (Miller & Sprang, 2017, p. 157). Skills include consciously identifying antecedent narratives the counselor holds about his or her role, examining the counselor's concurrent narrative about his or her skill level in dealing with the situation, and exploring a consolidation narrative so that he or she can find meaning in the emotionally arousing event(s).

3. **Reducing emotional labor** is the next element in which the supervisor and the counselor "develop … an awareness of and reconciliation of differences between expressed and experienced emotions and enhance the skills needed to decrease the perceived burden associated with doing clinical work with clients who have experienced traumatic events" (Miller & Sprang, 2017, p. 159). This includes taking a stance of curiosity, using behavioral strategies to manage reactions, and acquiring empathy with intentionality.

4. **Parasympathetic recovery** is the final element, which describes the "real-time activation of strategies to monitor internal states and to intentionally produce a state of physical, psychological and emotional regulation" (Miller & Sprang, 2017, p. 160). The sympathetic nervous system can become overstimulated during times of stress, putting the body into a chronic "fight-or-flight" mode; therefore, parasympathetic recovery might be necessary to keep bodily processes such as digestion and respiration functioning normally. This includes practicing meditation on a schedule as part of the counselor's professional practice, recognizing supervision as important to self-care, avoiding professional isolation through organizational engagement, scheduling periodic movement breaks, and planning strategic vacations.

If counselors and their supervisors do not intervene effectively, the next intervention level may be an ethical board or licensing board sanctioning the counselor. As discussed next, secondary trauma, compassion fatigue, and burnout can all result in a counselor's developing unethical behavior, which negatively affects client welfare and potentially could result in licensing violations. When this occurs, it is best for the counselor and the supervisor to intervene immediately. However, when intervention does not occur, the counselor could become impaired or professionally incompetent, and that may result in an ethics board or licensing board limiting the counselor's ability to practice.

COMMON MENTAL HEALTH CONCERNS

Stress reactions can result in anxiety and depression or create triggering events for addictive behaviors. Many counselors have preexisting mental health challenges, as do others in the general population. So, just as with any other person, under additional stress, the counselor may experience a worsening of mental health issues.

Depression and Suicidality

Counselors suffering with burnout symptoms experience increased cynicism and a corresponding negative outlook on life. They also experience negative self-appraisal as they begin to demonstrate poorer workplace behaviors. Additionally, key to developing burnout are emotional exhaustion and depersonalization, which mimic the fatigue and isolation that many people with depression experience. Therefore, a significant concern for people with burnout is the development of depression. Additionally, because a counselor experiencing burnout may often feel a lack of meaning in his or her work, he or she may experience an existential crisis and begin to feel suicidal. These are serious mental health concerns that a treating professional must evaluate. The FMHC might want to seek treatment through an insurance provider network or other local source of urgent care, where follow-up referrals can be provided.

Anxiety

As a counselor begins to notice feeling less motivated to engage in professional work, he or she may also experience anxiety about how he or she will continue to support him- or herself and his or her family. It is therefore not uncommon for someone experiencing compassion fatigue or burnout to develop anxiety symptoms, which may be specific to a situation (e.g., a specific phobia) or generalized (e.g., generalized anxiety disorder). Similar to depression symptomology, it is important for the counselor to receive a professional evaluation of symptoms and follow any recommendations stemming from the evaluation.

Posttraumatic Stress Disorder (PTSD)

Vicarious trauma or secondary trauma, by definition, results in posttraumatic stress symptoms. In these situations, counselors develop hypervigilance that can result in controlling behaviors that are detrimental to the client. Additionally, the counselor may evaluate situations as unsafe for clients when that may not be an accurate assessment, due to the counselor's hypervigilance. PTSD also affects sleep patterns due to nightmares. Sleep disruptions may negatively affect the counselor's concentration and judgment necessary for client work.

PTSD is a serious mental health concern requiring evaluation by a professional. If PTSD develops in response to bearing witness to clients' trauma narratives, then the counselor must seek respite from working directly with clients. This is something that the counselor can negotiate with the program or organization with which he or she works. This is a potential risk management issue for the organization, so it is in their best interest to support the counselor in disengaging from direct client contact and finding other suitable work within the organization while he or she seeks treatment for his or her trauma symptoms.

Addictive Behaviors

In an effort to cope with the symptoms of job stress and burnout, many people use alcohol or food to manage their negative emotional states. Others may engage in behaviors like shopping, gambling, or gaming to disconnect from the here-and-now realities of their jobs and the unusual stressors they experience working in a forensic setting, which they do not believe they can share with other people in their lives. These behaviors can develop into addictive disorders. Impaired professionals often come to the attention of licensing boards or ethics boards when an addictive behavior develops, which results in the counselor's judgment being impaired. The counselor may forget to go to appointments or otherwise neglect the client's safety and his or her corresponding risk management responsibilities. In more severe cases, they may engage in a boundary violation, up to and including a sexual relationship with a client. When this occurs, it is important for a trusted colleague or supervisor to address the situation as soon as they become aware. These trusted individuals can then provide a safe space to discuss the challenges and work with the counselor to find addiction-specific treatment, preferably in a program for impaired professionals.

SETTINGS

Forensic settings pose a unique threat to counselors' development of vicarious trauma, compassion fatigue, job stress, and burnout. Forensic mental health counselors work with victims and offenders who have experienced multiple relational traumas. Additionally, because we work with clients who are mandated to counseling, by definition they do not choose or want to be there, including victims. There are also external constraints placed on the way we work that may run counter to what we believe is in the best interest of our clients and their therapeutic goals. These include court systems, correctional facilities, and probation and parole mandates, and child protective care plans. Learning to negotiate each of these potential landmines is crucial to managing stress for a FMHC.

Work with Victims

The most obvious risk in working with crime victims is the counselors' repeated exposure to victim accounts of their traumatic experiences. When bearing witness to trauma, counselors attempt to empathize with victims; however, they simultaneously increase their risks of developing vicarious or secondary trauma. Through this process, they may have difficulty maintaining boundaries. This is particularly true when working with children or working with clients with whom you personally have more risk of experiencing counter-transference reactions.

Counter-transference reactions are any thoughts or feelings that a counselor experiences resulting from his or her own life experiences, rather than resulting directly from the client. Clients may trigger counter-transference reactions. One important use of case consultation and supervision is to help the counselor identify and manage these reactions. In the case of child victims, for instance, the counselor may feel a responsibility to take on a parenting role for the child, when in fact, it is not the counselor's role, and interacting as such could actually damage the therapeutic relationship.

There are unique challenges for counselors in these settings. Domestic violence survivors or sexual abuse survivors, for instance, often experience great difficulty allowing themselves to be vulnerable and to trust in a therapeutic relationship. This makes sense given that they have experienced relational trauma, often perpetrated by a previously trusted person in their lives. As a result, these clients may resist engaging in therapy because they are fearful of being hurt again. Entering into a therapeutic relationship requires vulnerability, which may actually result in worsened symptoms for the client, initially. How the counselor makes sense of these client behaviors can affect his or her stress levels. For instance, if the counselor views these responses as evidence of his or her own inability to do his or her job effectively, he or she may become so frustrated that it increases his or her job stress level. However, if the counselor conceptualizes the client's behavior as a normal part of the process for abuse clients, approaching it with empathy and nonjudgment (toward the client and toward him- or herself), then the counselor is more likely to have a positive attitude about the situation.

Working in systems that are imperfect or biased can also lead to frustrations because the counselor may believe the court system or a managed care provider is not treating the client well. One common example of this is when a domestic violence victim has experienced significant physical abuse and stalking by a perpetrator, but due to overloaded courts, the judge may simply require the offender to wear an ankle bracelet to monitor his whereabouts, rather than placing him in custody. This can result in a significant danger risk for the client, which the counselor may feel responsible to address. Another example would be a court subpoenaing your clinical notes for a child abuse client, in order to share the notes with the defense in preparation for a trial (**subpoena duces tecum**). This is likely to increase the client's PTSD symptoms, thus working at cross-purposes to healing, but the law requires counselors to appear with your records.

Each of these examples provides a potential advocacy route, but these may not be obvious to an inexperienced counselor. This is a great example of a time that consulting with a more experienced counselor or a clinical supervisor may be helpful in determining the best path that respects the court but also advocates for your client's needs. If a counselor is part of a professional organization or carries liability insurance, he or she can often access legal or ethical consultation through these venues. For instance, the American Counseling Association (ACA) has a risk management helpline staffed by an attorney and an ethics line staffed by a professional practice specialist at ACA. A member can access both through the ACA website at www.counseling.org/knowledge-center/ethics.

Depending on the situation, counselors may experience potential safety concerns for themselves as well. One study (Newhill, 2003) found among 1,600 child welfare social workers, 58% had experienced at least one incidence of physical violence during their careers. This is consistent with other studies (American Federation of State, County, and Municipal Employees, 2011; Ringstad, 2005). The highest rates were among those working in the criminal justice system (79%), addiction counselors (76%), and child welfare counselors (75%), all forensic settings. The National Association of Social Workers (NASW) reported among 10,000 social workers surveyed that 44% experienced personal safety issues; however, most were in their first 5 years of service (Whitaker, Weismiller, & Clark, 2006). Males experience higher rates of property damage (42%), threats of attack (64%), and actual physical attacks (39%) than females (Ennis & Douglas, 2007; Newhill, 2003; Spencer & Munch, 2003). This may indicate, once again, the need for continuing education in risk management and de-escalation techniques and for real-time case consultation and clinical supervision resources for forensic mental health professionals to help them learn to navigate potential violence situations more effectively.

Work With Offenders

There are a number of challenges that offender counselors' experience, which may influence stress levels. The most obvious challenge is that offenders are almost exclusively mandated to attend counseling by court order. These clients do not choose to go to counseling on their own, so they are naturally "resistant" to engaging in counseling. This reality presents unique challenges to establishing and maintaining a trusting therapeutic relationship. These clients are naturally suspicious of any counselor whom the courts refer them to see. They often view the counselor as an extension of the system that put them on probation or locked them up. As a result, counselors frequently become a target of externalizing behaviors offenders engage in as a method to avoid responsibility for their thoughts, feelings, and behaviors. As long as they have you to blame, they do not have to take responsibility. This is particularly trying when the counselor is unprepared regarding skills for engaging reluctant clients, such as motivational interviewing techniques (Miller & Rollnick, 2013).

These clients may avoid engaging in counseling through deflecting responsibility or through engaging their counselor the way they engage a victim. Offending clients may attempt to act out their therapeutic issues with the counselor through manipulation using seduction or imitation and flattery or through threats of intimidation and invalidation (Roundy & Horton, 1990). It is not surprising that dealing with these challenges can result in counter-transference reactions. This is particularly true when the counselor has experienced some form of victimization in his or her own life, which the offender's interpersonal maneuvering may trigger. Given that we know from the Adverse Childhood Experiences (ACEs) study that around 46% of U.S. citizens experience one or more ACEs as a child, the likelihood that a counselor has a history of victimization is quite likely (Sacks, Murphey, & Moore, 2014). Counselors who take advantage of case consultation, supervision, and continuing education opportunities are more likely aware of these issues when they arise and are able to identify effective management strategies so that the relationship remains therapeutic.

One clinically perceptive way to address a client's use of the therapeutic relationship to act out offending behaviors is to use interpersonal process comments to identify and make explicit what the counselor is observing and experiencing in the relationship (Teyber & Teyber, 2017). A **process comment** is a therapeutic intervention where the counselor reflects his or her observation of the interpersonal process occurring between the counselor and the client, often a parallel to interpersonal difficulties, which are part of the therapeutic issue the client is in counseling for.

For instance, imagine a male inmate who has a history of interpersonal violence behaviors approaches a female counselor in the prison day room and requests the counselor give him a ballpoint pen to complete therapy homework (which is strictly against the rules at the prison). The counselor states that she can provide the inmate with a pen, but she offers him one that is not a ballpoint pen. The inmate steps closer to the counselor looking down at her and responds in a loud voice that she is preventing him from doing the homework he is supposed to complete for tomorrow's group, using profanity. "Look bitch, if you want me to get this done, then you need to give me the pen. Or are you trying to set me up?" This is clearly intimidation, which is a therapeutic issue for someone incarcerated on a violent felony offense. He has likely used intimidation techniques in the past, an interpersonal maneuver, to engage someone through fear to get what he wants from them. The counselor has a choice to make. She can react out of fear and agree to give him a ballpoint pen or alternatively threaten punishment with a level reduction for his behavior (both counter-transference reactions triggered by the client), or she can choose to react therapeutically.

First, she might respond with a reflection, "It seems you are angry that I can't provide you with a ballpoint pen even though you know it's against the rules." What if he responds, "Yeah I'm pissed! You're setting me up. You're making me get an assignment done, but you refuse to help me out by giving me a pen"? His response clearly overlooks the fact that the counselor offered him a pen, just not the one he wanted. The counselor may then make a process comment: "John, I'm noticing that when I didn't agree to break the rules for you, you decided to step into my personal space and raise your voice, using profanity, to try to intimidate me. I wonder if that's the kind of thing you did with your victims." The counselor, in doing this, is addressing the therapeutic issue of the interpersonal dynamics acted out in vivo. Process comments often result in an offender feeling unbalanced because the therapist is clearly aware of what the offender is attempting to do, but she is not reacting to the client in the manner that he expects or is eliciting through these interpersonal maneuvers. By using process comments, the counselor intervenes therapeutically rather than acting out a counter-transference reaction.

A common challenge that results in stress for offender counselors, particularly for those in correctional settings, is that the system may not be supportive of counseling interventions. There is a prevailing belief that correctional counseling amounts to "hug a thug." They believe the counselor simply sympathizes with the offenders and the offender frequently uses the counselor's sympathies to manipulate him or her. This is a cynical but common view among many who work in the criminal justice system. This comes, in part, from a system established and maintained by people who are educated from a criminal justice perspective combined with the machismo culture in which any show of empathy receives reactions of suspicion and bravado. Often, people who work in these systems as police or correctional officers or frontline staff of a residential treatment center believe that the system should only deal with offenders through external control and punishment, rather than addressing the behavior directly and interacting in such a way as to develop internal controls and responsibility for self.

Some, especially those who are experiencing their own burnout, may not believe that people adjudicated for offending behaviors are capable of change and therefore, the system is wasting precious resources on mental health care. As a result, their interactions with the offending clients may trigger offending behaviors by escalating the offender, rather than working to de-escalate and become more aware of their offending behaviors. Therefore, rather than working toward internalizing responsibility for their thoughts, feelings, and actions, the environment may work at cross-purposes to the therapeutic goals by recreating offending opportunities, which further solidifies these beliefs that offenders cannot change. This clash between external control and therapeutic intervention can create an adversarial environment that is incredibly stressful for the counselor.

These systemic issues are often triggers for counselors developing burnout. Ironically, when a counselor begins to develop burnout symptomology, one of the first signs is exhibition of the same cynical attitudes and behaviors that the frontline personnel (officers or staff) exhibited, which led to the counselor's conflict and stress (compassion fatigue). One way to combat this is to have a strong professional identity that the counselor nurtures through active involvement in professional organizations, such as the International Association for Addiction and Offender Counseling (IAAOC), the National Association for Alcoholism and Drug Abuse Counselors (NAADAC), or the Association for Treatment of Sexual Abusers (ATSA) to name a few. These organizations offer professional consultation and peer support, continuing education, and ethical and legal resources to assist offender counselors in educating non-counseling agencies, systems, and staff about the counselor roles and responsibilities and addressing misperceptions of the field. Additionally, by increasing awareness of non-counseling staff as to the role that counselor's serve, professional relationships can be built where mutual and reciprocal learning about respective roles and challenges exists so as to better work together toward a common goal. This may also help the counselor advocate for clients when needed.

ETHICAL AND LEGAL ISSUES

The impact of vicarious trauma, compassion fatigue, and burnout on counselors can result in serious ethical issues. These stress-related experiences increase the potential for clinical error, anger, and cynicism toward clients, and ultimately risks compromising therapeutic boundaries (Trippany, White-Kress, & Wilcoxon, 2004).

Ethical Issues

According to Section A .1 of the American Counseling Association's (ACA) Code of Ethics (2014), counselors are primarily responsible for "respect[ing] the dignity and promot[ing] the welfare of clients" (p. 4). The values underlying the code of ethics, as described in chapter 1, further enumerate the importance of doing no harm (maleficence) and doing good (beneficence). Therefore, when a counselor begins acting out of his or her own frustration, counter-transference, secondary traumatic stress, or burnout, he or she is at risk of doing harm to the client, thereby undermining the very foundation of the counseling relationship.

Part of your self-care plan should be ongoing monitoring of your stress levels as related to competency to practice effectively and ethically. Section C.2.d of the code of ethics requires that "[c]ounselors continually monitor their effectiveness as professionals and take steps to improve when necessary. Counselors take reasonable steps to seek peer supervision to evaluate their efficacy as counselors' (ACA, 2014, p. 8). Therefore, your self-care plan should include how you will utilize consultation or supervision to monitor your effectiveness and how you will address problems as soon as they become evident.

However, if comprised functioning does occur, we consider the counselor is an **impaired professional**. The code goes on to state in C.2.g,

> Counselors monitor themselves for signs of impairment from their own physical, mental, or emotional problems and refrain from offering or providing professional services when impaired. They seek assistance for problems that reach the level of professional impairment, and if necessary, they limit, suspend, or terminate their professional responsibilities until it is determined that they may safely resume their work. Counselors assist colleagues or supervisors in recognizing their own professional impairment and provide consultation and assistance when warranted with colleagues or supervisors showing signs of impairment and intervene as appropriate to prevent imminent harm to clients. (ACA, 2014, p. 9)

Further, according to the Code of Ethics (ACA, 2014), "[I]f counselors lack the competence to be of professional assistance to clients, they avoid entering or continuing counseling relationships" (p. 6). Therefore, when counselors are impaired due to secondary traumatic stress, compassion fatigue, or burnout, it is prudent that they work with their agencies and supervisors to arrange for a break from their work. This may include taking personal leave to address the counselor's mental health concerns, and it may mean deciding to stop counseling a particular population or stop counseling altogether. Regardless, it is still the counselor's responsibility to facilitate a proper termination of his or her counseling relationships and appropriate referrals for those clients (ACA, 2014, A.11 and C.2.h). However, if a colleague is impaired, it is important to intervene by encouraging him or her to get help, and if necessary, to go to a supervisor or even the licensing board, depending on the situation, to intervene for the sake of client welfare.

Legal Issues

Boundary violations are common among impaired counselors who may develop difficulty discerning where their professional selves and personal selves digress. This can lead to interacting with clients in a manner that is not professional, including developing sexual or romantic relationships, which are particularly harmful for clients (ACA, 2014, Section A.5). This is one of the most often cited issues among state licensing boards for sanctioning a licensee and for either suspending or revoking a counselor's license to practice. Further, if a counselor is not guarding client welfare, then he or she is at risk of negligence in his or her duty to the client. This could result in legal sanctions beyond licensing, depending on how the behavior manifests.

Some guidelines, for maintaining a professional relationship are, as published in the Center for Substance Abuse Treatment (2000) TIP 36, the following:

- Making regular appointment times, specified in advance
- Enforcing set starting and ending times for each session
- Declining to give out a home phone number or address
- Canceling sessions if the client arrives under the influence of alcohol or psychoactive drugs
- Not having contact outside the therapy session
- Having no sexual contact or interactions that could reasonably be interpreted as sexual
- Terminating counseling if threats are made or acts of violence are committed against the counselor
- Establishing and enforcing a clear policy in regard to payment

When counselors have clear standards of practice such as these, which support consistent structure, grounded in the literature or in a professional code of ethics, then they will be more likely to adhere to these standards of practice in order to minimize the potential legal intervention.

SUMMARY

Job stress is inevitable when working in forensic situations. Forensic mental health counselors will bear witness to trauma experienced by clients, whether victims, offenders, or even police/correctional officers. Repeated exposure to trauma narratives can result in secondary traumatic stress and vicarious trauma, which will negatively affect the way some counselors perceive the world and their relationships (personal and professional). If left unattended, counselors may develop compassion fatigue and burnout, possibly resulting in cynicism about the work done, anger toward clients, and a depersonalization or overinvolvement with clients in a manner that is unprofessional and potentially harmful to the client's welfare.

However, planning for self-care and monitoring personal and organizational variables, which cause stress, you are more likely to recognize signs early and intervene. Provisions for colleague support and consultation and administrative and clinical supervision are key elements in self-care planning. These are the people counselors will work with to help identify when the counselor is crossing over boundaries or is disengaging from clients and work.

CHAPTER 2 REFLECTIVE QUESTIONS

1. Distinguish between vicarious trauma, compassion fatigue, job stress and burnout.
2. Think of an organization you have worked or volunteered with that was stressful. Analyze the personal and organizational risk and resilience factors contributing to potential job stress and burnout. What prevention or early intervention activities might have been helpful for these organizations or the individuals impacted?
3. Identify a person, it could be yourself, who has experienced burnout. Utilizing the JDCS model and then the Maslach burnout model, analyze the development and manifestation of job stress and burnout for this person, comparing the two models as they apply to this situation.
4. Analyze your own risk and resilience factors related to potential development of counter-transference, vicarious trauma, and/or compassion fatigue, if you were to work with forensic populations. Design an individualized self-care plan for prevention and ongoing monitoring that you could use to help mediate the risks you've identified.
5. Using the ACA (2014) Code of Ethics, discuss common ethical and legal issues forensic mental health counselors need to be aware of related to job stress and burnout.

RESOURCES

American Counseling Association fact sheet on vicarious trauma: https://www.counseling.org/docs/trauma-disaster/fact-sheet-9---vicarious-trauma.pdf

International Society for Traumatic Stress Studies, vicarious trauma toolkit: http://www.istss.org/public-resources/vicarious-trauma-toolkit.aspx

Stress and Satisfaction Offset Score (SOSS) self-assessment: http://www.workplacementalhealth.org/getattachment/Case-Studies/Pittsburgh-Plate-Glass-Industries-(PPG)-II/fd_ssos.pdf?lang=en-US&ext=.pdf

Professional quality of life elements: Compassion satisfaction and compassion fatigue, burnout, secondary traumatic stress, vicarious trauma and vicarious transformation: https://proqol.org/

ProQOL self-assessment for compassion satisfaction and compassion fatigue: http://www.macmh.org/wp-content/uploads/2016/05/Wkshp22_handout.pdf

American Counseling Association Code of Ethics: https://www.counseling.org/resources/aca-code-of-ethics.pdf

Foundational Assessment

- Identify the components of a biopsychosocial assessment and mental status exam and know what these entail
- Assess the stage of change a client is in and respond based on the stage
- Assess a client's level of risk for committing non-suicidal self-injury, suicide, or harm to others
- Assess individual, family, and community risks and protective factors
- Work through an ethical dilemma using an ethical decision-making model

TABLE 3.1 Myths and Myth Busters

Myths	Myth Busters
Only psychiatrists or psychologists evaluate a client's mental status, including risk of dangerousness.	Evaluating mental status and risk of dangerousness are essential parts of being a forensic mental health counselor.
An assessment is not necessary if a client is court mandated to treatment.	Even when a pretrial assessment, forensic interview, child protective services plan, or a correctional evaluation are provided, you must conduct a forensic mental health assessment so that you can understand the developmental trajectory of the client's presenting issues and best understand the appropriate treatment interventions needed.
Only clinical psychologists can conduct assessments.	Risk assessment is often a significant portion of what you will do as a forensic mental health counselor. The coursework you take as part of your master's degree will prepare you with a foundation for learning to administer, score, and interpret specific measures you may use with the population you work with.

INTRODUCTION

Forensic mental health counselors (FMHC) conduct assessments so that they understand a client's presenting issues and treatment needs. Each type of forensic population is assessed with unique instruments, which will be discussed in future chapters. However, they all involve some common overarching assessment concepts, discussed in this chapter.

DEVELOPMENTAL ISSUES

In order to understand the referral or target behavior, you need to understand the client's history and current circumstances. This includes medical, psychological or mental health, and social history. We call this a *biopsychosocial assessment*. The quality of information gathered directly relates to the quality of the relationship the client has with the counselor; therefore, it is crucial that FMHCs attend to building therapeutic rapport and trust with the client in order to gain the most complete and qualitatively useful assessment they can, early in the relationship. Motivational interviewing techniques are helpful with a forensic counseling population because the system often mandates clients to seek treatment, resulting in lower internal motivation to engage in treatment. Therefore, we will discuss motivational interviewing techniques in relationship to the assessment of stages of change, which is another area of assessment. It is helpful for a FMHC to be genuinely curious about understanding the client's perception of events, examining their thoughts or beliefs and exploring the client's feelings about the events they discuss. Additionally, it is helpful for the counselor to ask the client how he or she is "making sense of" his or her life experiences.

During this phase, FMHCs must scan their own thoughts, feelings, and sensory experiences to identify any material that seems incongruent with the counselor's experience or with other evidence presented. Although it is important to identify incongruence, it is not appropriate to confront discrepancies during the initial assessment phase of the relationship. Doing so would likely result in limiting client trust in the relationship and subsequently limiting the information he or she shares. The counselor's experience of the client may be useful in conceptualizing the client's personality, relationships, interpersonal templates, cognitive schema, and patterns of attitudes, behaviors, or emotions.

Additionally, the counselor must be aware of and critical of any assumptions he or she makes without adequate evidence to support these assumptions. These assumptions are evidence of *implicit bias*, which can incorrectly affect the FMHC's assessment. Counselor bias may present a risk to fully understanding the client's situation. The initial assessment is crucial to developing a foundation for counseling. However, *continuous assessment* is dynamic, occurring throughout the relationship. In this way, as new data (information, experiences with the client, etc.) develop, and the client shares it (verbally or experientially) within the therapeutic relationship, the counselor's assessment and/or conceptualization of the client's situation may change.

Assessing How the Target Behavior Developed

A FMHC conducts a biopsychosocial assessment at the beginning of every relationship. In forensic settings, this assessment involves reviewing referral information and collateral data (e.g., arrest report, forensic interviews, prior psychological assessments, etc.), a clinical interview with the client, interviews with any collateral sources of information (e.g., parent, spouse, probation officer, caseworker, etc.), and potentially administration of formal standardized assessment measures appropriate to the population. A thorough developmental history helps the FMHC understand the developmental trajectory of the target/referral behavior. This provides clues as to what is motivating the behavior; the particular constellation of thoughts, feelings, and actions the client engages in which serve to perpetuate or even escalate the behavior; and ultimately clues as to where the counselor can target interventions in an individualized manner. Some of the information may not be available; however, the counselor should attempt to gather as thorough a history as possible. Counselors document missing data as "no evidence of (insert assessment area) at this time" or "the client did not report (insert assessment area) at this time.' "

Biopsychosocial Assessment

To begin, FMHCs must identify *demographic information*, including age, race/ethnicity, gender (gender identity), religious/spiritual affiliation, sexual orientation, and so on. Then the assessment should identify the *presenting problem* and the *history of the presenting problem*. This is the referral/target behavior, any significant history of the target behavior from the client's perspective, noting any incongruence between the client's perception and collateral source data. Then the FMHCs document their biopsychosocial assessment of the client. The *biological* part of the assessment involves examination of a variety of developmental and medical categories, illustrated in **Figure 3.1**. If there are significant findings, then inquire about the development and course of the problem, interventions attempted, and results of interventions.

The *psychological* part of the assessment covers mental health history, illustrated in **Figure 3.2**. The counselor should note type and severity of symptoms (historically and currently), and assess onset, duration, frequency, and intensity of any significant mental health symptoms. Note if the symptoms are intermittent or chronic in nature. Also, explore the results of interventions attempted previously (e.g., counseling, hospitalization, medication, etc.), whether symptoms are related to a medical condition or associated with substance use. Ask whether client's experience of interventions was successful, and whether the client's experience of treatment providers was positive. In addition, counselors document information on family history and any relevant sociocultural context (e.g., religious beliefs related to hallucinations or conduct disorder within a violent community context), which may impact our understanding of the psychological data documented. Finally, the counselor should assess the client's *social* history (**Figure 3.3**) including any information about the client's relationships, functioning in school and work settings, and functioning in the community.

Interpersonal Process and Mental Status Data

During the assessment, FMHCs note their own observations and experiences of the client. This includes being aware of interpersonal process information and identifying, documenting, and responding to mental status data. *Interpersonal process* information includes the counselor's experience of the client, as well as how the client relates to the counselor, both

- **Pregnancy:** Normal term, prematurity, complications during birth, exposure to teratogens, environmental stressors for parent/family
- **Postnatal and infancy:** Circumstances of birth (normal/breech/cesarean/forceps/induced) and any health problems at birth or during infancy
- **Childhood health status:** Chronic health problems, significant illnesses, surgeries, hospitalizations, lost consciousness, concussion or head injury
- **Developmental delays:** Fine motor skills (grasping, holding a crayon/pencil, playing with small toys), gross motor skills (walking, running, jumping), feeding issues (reflux, allergies, difficulty gaining weight, difficulty chewing, sensitive to textures, etc.), coordination problems, speech problems (delays, articulation issues, etc.), and sensory processing challenges (being overly sensitive to or unusually insensitive to environmental stimuli)
- **Adolescent development:** Whether the client met developmental expectations for adolescence; chronic or significant medical illnesses, accidents, injuries, or hospitalizations; chronic or significant psychiatric illnesses or hospitalizations
- **Adult development:** Whether the client met developmental expectations for adulthood and/or any adult/elder developmental concerns; chronic or significant medical illnesses, accidents, injuries, or hospitalizations; chronic or significant psychiatric illnesses or hospitalizations; cognitive decline; physical decline
- **Current medical:** Medical/vision/dental insurance; medical/vision/dental provider; up-to-date vaccinations and immunizations; last comprehensive physical exam and results; current medications prescribed (taken as prescribed, difficulty getting medications filled); current over-the-counter medications taken daily, weekly, occasionally; illegal or prescription drugs taken off label type, duration, and frequency

FIGURE 3.1 Biological or medical developmental history

generally and in relationship to specific topics or situations. Interpersonal process information may include the following:

- How the client reacts to you
- How he or she communicates his or her concerns (e.g., open and honest, deceptive or vague, or avoiding expression of emotion, etc.)
- How it feels to be in the room with the client. Whether the counselor's experience of the client changes depending on the setting or the topic
- What thoughts, emotions, or behaviors are evoked by the client in the counselor, and the counselor's assessment of whether these thoughts/emotions/behaviors are solicited/evoked in other people and how that might contribute to the client's cognitive distortions, narrative of his or her life, or target behavior.

Examples of this include a client disengaging in session from the counselor in reaction to the counselor providing an insightful reflection or a client coming late to sessions several weeks in a row after being confronted by the counselor about a behavior the client does not want to take responsibility for.

- **Early development social, emotional, or behavioral challenges:** Anxious, avoidant, or disorganized attachment patterns; out-of-home placements; overly compliant or oppositional behavior; openness to having others interpersonally regulate emotional states; ability to self-regulate emotional states; difficult/easy temperament; mood swings that were not developmentally appropriate for age; fears/anxieties; ability to make and keep friends; ability to interact appropriately with adults; ability to resolve conflicts or solve problem situations within appropriate developmental level; psychiatric diagnoses given in childhood
- **Child or adolescent disorders:** Mental health issues diagnosed in childhood or adolescence; treatment (medication, counseling, other); neurodevelopmental disorders (mental retardation, autism spectrum, specific learning disabilities, feeding disorders; speech disorders); behavioral disorders (ADHD, oppositional defiant disorder, reactive attachment disorder, conduct disorder, enuresis/encopresis); and anxiety-related disorders (separation anxiety; selective mutism; PTSD)
- **Psychotic episodes or disorders:** Paranoid/schizoid/schizotypal personality disorders; outpatient counseling; out-of-home placement; psychiatric hospitalization; involvement with the law resulting from psychotic episode(s); specific nature of delusions and/or hallucinations
- **Mood disorders:** Depression, hypomania, mania, bipolar disorder, post-partum depression, hormone related mood issues
- **Anxiety disorders:** Separation anxiety, social anxiety, panic attacks, agoraphobia, generalized anxiety, specific phobias (specify what kind); avoidant/dependent/obsessive-compulsive personality disorders; obsessive compulsive disorders
- **Trauma-related disorders:** History of childhood neglect; history of poverty; history of living in war or other unsafe or violent community situation; history of physical abuse in childhood/adolescence, or adulthood; history of interpersonal violence victimization in adulthood; posttraumatic stress disorder; dissociative disorders; non-suicidal self-injury; borderline/antisocial/histrionic/narcissistic personality disorders
- **Addictive disorders:**
  - **Substance** use history and evidence of maladaptive use of substances (tobacco, caffeine, alcohol, cannabis, hallucinogens, inhalant, sedative/hypnotic/anxiolytic, stimulant, club/synthetic drugs, misuse of prescription or over-the-counter medication)
  - **Behavioral** or process addictions (gambling, Internet gaming, eating disorders, sex addiction, non-suicidal self-injury) and behaviors that may be used in a maladaptive manner (work, shopping/spending with or without hording, exercise, relationships, etc.)
- **Sexual or paraphilic disorders:** Sexual dysfunction; hypersexual arousal disorder (sex addiction, pornography); paraphilias (voyeurism, exhibitionism, frotteurism, masochism, pedophilia, sadism, zoophilia, etc.)
- **Neurocognitive disorders:** Delirium, dementia, related to Alzheimer's disorder

FIGURE 3.2 Psychological or mental health history

Finally, FMHCs document *mental status evaluations* (MSE), illustrated in **Figure 3.4**, as part of the initial biopsychosocial assessment. Parts of the MSE relate directly to diagnostic information or referral behaviors, so the counselor should systematically assess and document

- **Family of origin:** Makeup of family (genogram); significant relationships; out-of-home placements; pets; family culture; familial history of divorce, abuse, psychiatric or chronic medical illnesses, addiction (substance and behavioral/process); socioeconomic status; neighborhood/community safety; significant familial events; client's subjective experience of each caregiver and each sibling and whether their perception was consistent with others' experience of that individual or not; feelings of rejection or abandonment from significant family members
- **Current family:** Makeup of family of choice (genogram); client's experience of significant relationships; pets; family culture; familial history of divorce, abuse, psychiatric or chronic medical illnesses, addiction (substance and behavioral/process); socioeconomic status; neighborhood/community safety; significant familial events
- **Friendships:** Number and level of closeness of friendships; typical description of type of person client is friends with; childhood friendships and socialization (when first best friend, number of friends, bullying, social awkwardness, etc.); adult friendships and socialization historically and currently (note any changes, number, type, and quality of current friendships); relationship of friendships to spiritual practice and/or hobbies or community involvement
- **Romantic relationships and sexual identity:** Onset, quality, duration, and intensity of any romantic relationship or sexual relationship; sexual identity and orientation; level of self-acceptance; level of dysfunction; level of other acceptance; or current distress
- **Vocational history (school/work):**
  - **School:** When did the client begin formal education? How long did he or she go to school?; client's subjective experience of schooling, teachers, peers, subject matter; successful progression, or if not, why; educational, behavioral, or social interventions; significant attitudes and beliefs about school; ability to work with peers; ability to work under an authority figure; ever expelled, failed, or dropped out; level of education
  - **Academic or learning challenges:** When formal education began; type of schooling (public, private, home); any evaluations or interventions for 504, learning disabilities, giftedness, response-to-intervention; ability to be maintained in regular educational environment; best/worst subject; hobbies/extra-curricular activities
  - **Work history:** When began working; work history; challenges and successes related to work; significant attitudes and beliefs about work; ability to work with peers; ability to work under an authority figure; history of being laid off or fired and circumstances; history of under-employment; history of being unable to get a job or a sufficient income to support oneself and/or family; number of jobs working currently; type of work (physical/mental load, stress level, satisfaction; experiences of harassment or bullying by peers/colleagues, customers, superiors; beliefs/attitudes about current place of employment; barriers to vocational success.
- **Legal history:** History of adoptions, emancipation, divorce, custody, arrests, deferred adjudication, mandated treatment, probation, detention/jail time, prison time, parole; current court orders; involvement with protective services (child or adult); current protective services plan; type of criminal charges (misdemeanor, felony and level); restraining orders past or current; property disputes; addiction-related charges; juvenile and/or adult legal involvement;

FIGURE 3.3 Social history

- **Orienting information:**
  - **Orientation:** Time, place, person, situation
  - **Appearance:** Gait, posture, grooming, apparent/actual age, clothing, significant tattoos, injuries, etc.
  - **Speech/language:** Quantity (talkative, spontaneous, expansive, paucity, poverty); rate (fast, slow, normal, pressured); volume/tone (loud, soft, monotone, weak, strong); fluency and rhythm (slurred, clear, hesitant, good/poor articulation, aphasic)
- **Psychological:**
  - **Attitude:** Cooperative, hostile, open, secretive, evasive, suspicious, apathetic, defensive/resistant, fearful
  - **Mood:** Client's subjective experience; alexithymia?
  - **Affect:** Your observations; whether congruence with client's reported mood; congruence with the subject matter discussed
- **Behavioral:**
  - **Psychomotor Activity:** Notable mannerisms/gestures, agitation, retardation, normal; nonverbal and para-verbal expression (excessive/avoidant/normal eye contact, facial expressions, proximity of physical stance; etc.)
  - **Judgment:** Good, poor, situation specific; risk management concerns (risk of harm to self or others); evidence of impulsivity; provide evidence to support assertion
- **Cognition/thinking:**
  - **Attention:** Ability to attend or focus on topic, ability to concentrate, level of distractibility
  - **Level of consciousness:** Alert, drowsy, lethargic, confused, fluctuating, dissociative, hypervigilant, etc.
  - **Subjective assessment of intelligence:** Your subjective assessment of whether the person seems of average, below average, or above average intelligence without formal assessment.
  - **Thought process:** Logical, relevant, organized, flow and coherence of thought, linear, goal directed, circumstantial, tangential, flight of ideas/loose associations, incoherent, evasive, racing, blocking, perseveration, neologisms
  - **Obsessive thinking:** Obsession with a thought, obsession with a person, obsession with behavior, etc.
  - **Cognitive distortions:** Positive or negative filtering, all-or-nothing/polarized thinking, overgeneralization, catastrophizing, mindreading/fortune telling, magnification, control fallacies, emotional reasoning, personalization, paranoid/victim thinking, parental interjects (should and musts)
  - **Delusions:** Erotomanic, grandiose, paranoid, jealous, persecutory, somatic, mixed
  - **Memory:** Gaps, evidence of dissociation, ability to recall recent/past events
  - **Hallucinations:** Current or historical; development and course; type (tactile, olfactory, auditory, visual)
  - **Insight:** Good, poor; situation specific; provide evidence to support assertion of good, poor, etc.

FIGURE 3.4 Mental status examination (MSE)

them at every client meeting. Some examples are tracking impulsivity in judgment for someone who demonstrates interpersonal violence behaviors or tracking level of suicidality for someone who has a history of suicidal thoughts or behaviors. FMHCs often document both interpersonal process data and mental status data in subsequent sessions with the client, as well as in the initial assessment, as these data provide evidence of diagnostic issues and/or progress in treatment.

Developmental Assessment, Interpersonal Neurobiology, ACES, and Epigenetics

Thinking about Perry's (2006) neurosequential model of therapeutics, introduced in chapter 1, we know that it is important to consider emotional development in terms of neurodevelopment. In other words, using a simplification of the process, clients' behaviors are an external manifestation of internal emotional experiences. These emotional experiences are a function of limbic system processes involving physical sensations tied to non-declarative memories, which environmental stimuli trigger. The environmental stimuli are generally similar to sensory and environmental experiences of the client occurring during significant life events, which resulted in non-declarative memories. The biopsychosocial assessment documents data is related to interpersonal relationships, adverse childhood experiences, and environmental contexts, which interrelate to create genetic expression or epigenetics. Additionally, documenting interpersonal process information provides qualitative data, which deepens our understanding of how the client's early interpersonal neurobiology experiences are manifest in his or her interpersonal relationships today.

> **The case of Bob:** Bob is a child who grows up in a home with two parents who are addicted to drugs. Because the parents use their income to purchase drugs, sometimes there is a lack of food for the child. On Maslow's (1943) hierarchy of needs, this is a basic physiological need for survival. Additionally, the parents are not emotionally present for the child because of their addictive behaviors, so the child is placed in dangerous situations where he is sexually abused by other drug users who "crash" at the parents' home after partying. Therefore, the child also experiences a lack of physical and psychological safety or support needed for survival. However, the client also experiences a natural physiological arousal and physical pleasure from the sexual abuse. As a result, through classical conditioning, as a child the client begins to pair the physical sensations he experiences as unsafe (e.g., an environment lacking structure, a sense of danger, a lack of basic food and safety needs being met) with sexual stimulation. However, Bob also dissociated these memories from his present awareness because they are traumatic, and therefore they are experienced as dissociated and non-declarative so he is unable to consciously identify and discuss the events and emotions experienced. However, he has an overwhelming experience of anxiety when in environments in which he feels he lacks control, and he begins to self-medicate with alcohol and marijuana, which is readily available in his home environment.

As Bob enters pre-adolescence, he begins to develop sexually. His experiences of sexual arousal often trigger additional anxiety, leading to substance use to numb these feelings. However, he also begins acting out through indiscriminate sexual contact with multiple male and female peers. This further results in feelings of shame and self-disgust because he believes his behavior is a confirmation of a cognitive distortion that he created the situations where he experienced sexual abuse and therefore deserved the abuse. Again, to self-medicate he turns to drugs and alcohol. Over time, Bob also develops a sex addiction, where he engages in downloading and masturbating to large amounts of pornography with increasingly violent content. Ultimately, his sexual addiction escalates to accessing child pornography reminiscent of his own abuse as a child. As a result, at 16 he is arrested as part of an Internet pornography sting operation and is placed on deferred adjudication and court mandated to treatment for substance use and assessment of pedophilic tendencies.

If we consider Bob's case in relationship to the information shared about developmental history, adverse childhood experiences, interpersonal neurobiology, and epigenetics, we can analyze the data gathered to form a case conceptualization, which reflects our understanding of Bob.

Case conceptualization may be that this client's developmental trajectory of the target behavior reveals a family history of addiction, which indicates a potential genetic predisposition to addiction. However, placed in a situation where he experienced physical and emotional neglect from his drug-addicted parents who were emotionally unavailable, he was in unsafe situations, resulting in sexual abuse. Additionally, his environment did not provide basic needs like food. These are all considered adverse childhood experiences. Bob's experiences of his primary caregivers and other adults involved consistent repeated experiences of abuse and neglect, which resulted in an overactive autonomic nervous system (ANS), creating anxiety when he experienced a lack of control or safety in his environment, thus triggering physical sensations indicating a situation was dangerous. Also, through these interpersonal experiences, he learned to deal with dysregulated emotional states through using substances and sexual stimulation, rather than through reaching out for emotional support or talking about his thoughts and feelings. Therefore, when Bob enters treatment as a mandated client, he necessarily experiences it as dysregulating because entering treatment is an externally controlled event from his perception. The counselor being aware of this is better able to predict potential thoughts, feelings, and sensations the client may have in response to the counselor's interactions with him.

Assessing Stage of Change

As the client interacts with the counselor, he or she assesses the client's stage of change. Like doing MSEs, this is an ongoing process. However, understanding the client's presenting stage of change gives the counselor information about how to respond appropriately so that the client engages in, rather than resists, the therapeutic conversation. For each stage of change, specific *motivational interviewing* interventions inform how the counselor responds to engage the client in treatment in order to encourage an internal locus of control. The *stage of change model* (Prochaska & DiClemente, 1982) is not a linear model in that a client does not progress through the stages in a step-like manner. A client may begin in a higher level of change and regress to a lower level of change. Alternatively, the client may be in one level of change regarding his alcohol use and a different level of change regarding his sexual addiction.

There are five stages of change. The first is *pre-contemplation*, which is when the client indicates he or she does not see a problem with his or her behavior and therefore does not believe he or she needs to change his or her behavior. When the client is in pre-contemplation, the counselor needs to intervene to improve the client's awareness about how the target behavior may relate to negative consequences, preferably consequences the client has said he or she does not want. Counselors often experience clients in this stage as argumentative, resistant, hopeless, or "in denial." The *righting reflex*, which is a natural response, occurs when the client assumes that the counselor knows the "right way" to think, feel, or act; however, this results in a power struggle with the client. Some questions you might ask in order to raise the client's awareness include the following:

1. What would have to happen for you to know this is a problem?
2. What warning signs would let you know that this is a problem?
3. Have you tried to change in the past?
4. Scale the problem:
   a. On a scale of 1–10, how serious is your (fill in the problem behavior)?
   b. Why a (whatever they said) and not a (a higher number)? You ask about a higher number so that they have to argue for why they are at a lower number.
   c. What would it take for you to see your situation as a (choose a lower number on the scale)?
   d. What can I do to help with that?

The next stage is *contemplation*, where the client may be aware of the problem and may be thinking about change in the next 6 months. However, the client might be feeling ambivalent or stuck. The counselor should normalize ambivalence while helping clients explore their concerns. There is a certain level of cognitive dissonance the clients experience, which the counselor can capitalize on. To help the client move to the next stage of change, the counselor will help the client with *decisional balance*, which is weighing the pros and cons of continuing the way they currently are versus weighing the pros and cons of changing the behavior. One way to do this is having the client complete a chart about the benefits and costs of changing *and* the benefits and costs of not changing. Then the counselor can further explore each of these with the client. The counselor can use *readiness rulers* (**Figure 3.5**) to determine how important it is for the client to make the change, how confident the client is in his or her ability to change, and the level of readiness for change.

The counselor wants to help the client move from extrinsic motivation (e.g., "In order to get my kids back, I have to complete treatment") to intrinsic motivation (e.g., "To be the best

Importance

1. On a scale of 1 to 10, how important is it for you to change?
2. Why a (their number) and not a lower number? This makes it necessary for them to argue the strength of importance.
3. What needs to happen to get you to (a higher number)?
4. How can I help with that?

Confidence

1. On a scale of 1 to 10, how confident are you that you can change?
2. Why a (their number) and not a lower number? This makes it necessary for them to argue the strength of importance.
3. What needs to happen to get you to (a higher number)?
4. How can I help with that?

Counselors can build confidence by reviewing past successes, defining small steps that can lead to success, problem solving to address barriers, providing strategies and resources or teaching skills, or attending to the progress and using slips as occasions to further problem solve rather than viewing it as failure.

Readiness

1. On a scale of 1 to 10, how ready are you to change in the next 6 months?
2. Why a (their number) and not a lower number? This makes it necessary for them to argue the strength of importance.
3. What needs to happen to get you to (a higher number)?
4. How can I help with that?

Other open-ended questions the counselor may use include the following:

1. What are your reasons for not changing?
2. What do you want to change at this time?
3. What would keep you from changing at this time?
4. What are the barriers today that keep you from changing? What might help remove that barrier?
5. What things (people, programs, and behaviors) have helped in the past?
6. What would help you now?
7. What do you think you need to learn to be able to make the change?

FIGURE 3.5 Readiness rulers

parent I can be and set a good example, I need to engage in treatment"). During this process, it helps to engage in *values exploration*, identifying what is important to the client, rather than focusing on what is important to the referral agency, court, or the service provider. If the counselor understands the client's value system, a link can be made between family, community, and cultural values to their desire to change, which is a powerful intrinsic motivator.

In order to tip the decisional balance, counselors should accentuate the most salient reasons for change from the client's perspective or words. In addition, counselors should work to reduce the current rewards the client experiences and reinforce the benefits of change. During this process, counselors identify and work with clients to problem solve any potential obstacles. It is important to explore feelings of loss and grief about giving up the behavior or relationships and benefits connected with the behavior. At this point FMHCs dissuade premature decision making while facilitating full exploration of these thoughts and feelings. Therefore, if a client seems to be moving to the next stage more quickly than expected or is "saying all the right things," but the responses seem disingenuous, then the counselor must slow down the process. Otherwise, the client will not fully explore the issues that result in his or her returning to the target behavior and will likely relapse or recidivate. Common reasons clients respond the way they think we want them to is that they want the potential adverse outcomes of their behavior minimized so that they experience less discomfort. Therefore, instead of focusing on beliefs about the court or referral agency's expectations regarding what they need to do, it is crucial to emphasize the client's personal choice and responsibility throughout this process (in other words, you might say, "No one can decide this for you. It's up to you; you can decide to go on drinking or to change").

The next stage is *preparation,* when the client has resolved his ambivalence and made the decision to change. The client is considering changing within the next month and may even have attempted to change. The counselor should reinforce the decision to change and help the client prioritize change opportunities and identify and assist the client in problem solving around obstacles. Rather than making grand gestures, the client should be encouraged to pursue small steps initially, while also identifying and using social supports. During this stage, it is important to explore the client's self-efficacy around change using the *confidence readiness ruler* (**Figure 3.5**). Di Clemente and colleagues (1985) identify five categories of self-efficacy. *Coping self-efficacy* is successfully coping with tempting or triggering events such as the ability to be assertive with friends who want the client to continue the behavior. *Treatment behavior self-efficacy* is the client's ability to engage in or apply treatment interventions like self-monitoring to his or her life outside to help him or her change the behavior. *Recovery self-efficacy* is the client's ability to recover when the client experiences a lapse in old behavior. *Control self-efficacy* is the client's self-confidence in his or her ability to control the behavior in a variety of triggering situations. Finally, *abstinence self-efficacy* involves the client's confidence in his or her ability to abstain in the face of environmental triggers. Clients' levels of self-efficacy can be different in different situations, including when they are experiencing dysregulated emotions, social pressure to engage in the target behavior, physical illness or exhaustion, or withdrawal and craving. It is important to stress that lasting change happens gradually and provide feedback on the changes the client is making.

Part of negotiating a *change plan* includes offering a menu of change options, developing a behavior contract for change, reducing the barriers to action (e.g., anticipating problems, recognizing barriers to action), enlisting social support, and educating the client about treatment. One way to enhance commitment to change is to help the client explore his goals. This includes discussing the following:

- The type and intensity of help the client needs to begin to change
- The timeframe for making changes
- Social support systems
- Identifying specific strategies for change
- How the client will monitor progress toward strategies and goals
- Barriers or problems (legal, financial, or health problems) that have already occurred due to the target behavior

It is important for counselors to recognize when clients are ready to put their plans for behavior change into action. The *action stage* occurs when clients' resistance behaviors (arguing, interrupting, denying) decrease, and they have fewer questions about the problem. They begin putting the strategies for behavior change into place. During this time, the counselor can help clients process how their change plans are working, identify challenges, and problem solve around those challenges. It is crucial that the counselor remain encouraging and hold the hope that the client can change. Part of doing this may be validating the client's efforts, even when the result is not what the client wanted it to be. Finally, the *maintenance stage* is when the behavior has changed and sustaining the changed behavior over time becomes the focus. The counselor works with the client to continue managing potential challenges, identifying when the client is slipping into old behaviors, and finding new strategies for coping, as needed.

CONTEXTUAL ISSUES

The behaviors clients present with develop within complex systems, which should be considered during the assessment process. Identifying elements of risk and protective factors can also provide information on potential areas for intervention (risks) or supports for behavior change (protective factors). First, counselors evaluate the *agent* or the target behavior. One example is a drug of abuse. Risk factors include early age of drug exposure and the potential addictive nature of the drug of choice, whereas protective factors would be delayed onset of use and low addictive or lethality of the drug.

Next, evaluate the risks and protective factors for the *host*, which are individual client characteristics. These include biomedical, personality, and behavioral or attitudinal characteristics. Biomedical includes genetic or physiological vulnerability, age, gender, and race/ethnicity, and personality characteristics. Personality risks include someone who is seeking novelty or risk, is socially alienated and rebellious, has poor impulse control and coping skills, has existing mental health issues, is experiencing high stress, or has specific issues like living with homosexuality, disability and/or racial oppression. However, protective personality factors include having high self-esteem and internal locus of control, being self-disciplined, having the ability to problem solve and think critically, and having a good sense of humor about themselves and about life. Individual attitudes and behaviors increasing risks include social marginalization, early antisocial behavior, belief they are invulnerable, having positive attitudes toward the target behavior (e.g., drugs), being susceptible to peer influence, perceiving the benefits of the target behavior to be more important than the negative consequences of the behavior, and being involved with other risky behaviors.

The final domain to assess for risk and protective factors is the *environmental domain*. This includes family, school/work, community, and other larger environmental factors. Risks within the *family* include family dysfunction, trauma, or major loss. Also, lack of clear behavioral expectations, little supervision, or clear boundaries are risk factors. Inconsistent, permissive, or excessive discipline or a parent or family culture that has low expectations for the client's success in life, or permissive attitudes and behaviors toward the target behavior, are additional risk factors. Families can be protective, however, when there are close nurturing and supportive relationships, high expectations of family members, and parents who are communicative and involved in their children's lives. Additionally, parents spending "quality" time with kids, including consistent praise and low levels of criticism, is protective. Finally, parents who encourage and support responsible decisions, model healthy stress management and coping skills, and share responsibility in home tasks create protection for future drug use.

The *community* is also part of the environmental domain. Within the community, the availability of drugs or frequency of violence or criminal behavior is a risk, whereas age restrictions and cost may be barriers to obtaining drugs or weapons. Unhealthy or ambivalent social norms or those that glamorize substance use or violence are community risk factors. However, having alternatives to engaging in drug use or violence and social support systems are protective factors. Community protective factors might include after-school programs, good work options, mentoring and peer support, and having strong religious connections.

Finally, the *larger society* is also part of the environmental domain. Risk factors include media glamorizing substance use or violent behavior or social institutions and policy makers who clearly do not demonstrate value for a safe supportive community. However, the larger society can also have positive media or institutions that provide community supports and positive educational, drug, mental health, and crime policies and resources. Additionally, a cultural focus on healthy decision making and pro-social behaviors is protective.

COMMON MENTAL HEALTH CONCERNS: RISK ASSESSMENT

In the discussion of biopsychosocial assessment, both mental status exams and common mental health concerns counselors need to assess and document are presented. However, in forensic settings, clients often enter counseling in crisis. Therefore, this section will focus on triage assessment in crises. Utilizing the *triage assessment form* (TAF) (Meyer, 2001; Myer & Conte, 2006; Meyer, Williams, Ottens, & Schmidt, 1992) helps determine the appropriate level of intervention indicated by a client's current affect, cognitions, and behaviors. **Figure 3.6** illustrates the full TAF. Each subscale provides behavioral indicators of severity of symptoms, which the counselor uses to guide his or her assessments from 1 (no impairment) to 10 (severe impairment). There are alternate forms of the TAF used by law enforcement (triage assessment checklist for law enforcement [TACKLE]; James, Meyer, & Moore, 2006; Meyer & Moore, 2006) and by educators (triage assessment system for students in learning environments [TASSLE]; Meyer et al., 2007; Meyer, James, & Moulton, 2011).

TRIAGE ASSESSMENT FORM: CRISIS INTERVENTION ✹
©R.A. Myer, R.C. Williams, A.J. Ottens, & A.E. Schmidt

CRISIS EVENT:
Identify and describe briefly the crisis situation: _____
_____
_____

AFFECTIVE DOMAIN
Identify and describe briefly the affect that is present. (If more than one affect is experienced, rate with #1 being primary, #2 secondary, #3 tertiary.)

ANGER/HOSTILITY: _____
_____
_____

ANXIETY/FEAR: _____
_____
_____

SADNESS/MELANCHOLY: _____
_____
_____

Affective Severity Scale

Circle the number that most closely corresponds with client's reaction to crisis.

1	2	3	4	5	6	7	8	9	10
No Impairment	Minimal Impairment		Low Impairment		Moderate Impairment		Marked Impairment		Severe Impairment
Stable mood with normal variation of affect appropriate to daily functioning.	Affect appropriate to situation. Brief periods during which negative mood is experienced slightly more intensely than situation warrants. Emotions are substantially under client control.		Affect appropriate to situation but increasingly longer periods during which negative mood is experienced slightly more intensely than situation warrants. Client perceives emotions as being substantially under control.		Affect may be incongruent with situation. Extended periods of intense negative moods. Mood is experienced noticeably more intensely than situation warrants. Liability of affect may be present. Effort required to control emotions.		Negative affect experienced at markedly higher level than situation warrants. Affects may be obviously incongruent with situation. Mood swings, if occurring, are pronounced. Onset of negative moods are perceived by client as not being under volitional control.		Decompensation or depersonalization evident.

DOMAIN SEVERITY SCALE SUMMARY

Affective _____

Cognitive _____

Behavioral _____

Total _____

FIGURE 3.6 Triage assessment form

BEHAVIORAL DOMAIN

Identify and describe briefly which behavior is currently being used. (If more than one behavior is utilized, rate with #1 being primary, #2 secondary, #3 tertiary.)

APPROACH: _____
_____
_____

AVOIDANCE: _____
_____
_____

IMMOBILITY:
_____
_____
_____

Behavioral Severity Scale

Circle the number that most closely corresponds with client's reaction to crisis.

1	2	3	4	5	6	7	8	9	10
No Impairment	Minimal Impairment		Low Impairment		Moderate Impairment		Marked Impairment		Severe Impairment
Coping behavior appropriate to crisis event. Client performs those tasks necessary for daily functioning.	Occasional utilization of ineffective coping behaviors. Client performs those tasks a necessary for daily functioning, but does so with noticeable effort.		Occasional utilization of ineffective coping behaviors. Client neglects some tasks necessary for daily functioning is noticeably compromised.		Client displays coping behaviors that may be ineffective and maladaptive. Ability to perform tasks necessary for daily functioning is noticeably compromised.		Client displays coping behaviors that are likely to exacerbate crisis situation. Ability to perform tasks necessary for daily functioning is markedly absent.		Behavior is erratic, unpredictable. Client's behaviors are harmful to self and/or others.

FIGURE 3.6 Triage assessment form (*Continued*)

COGNITIVE DOMAIN

Identify if a transgression, threat, or loss has occurred in the following areas and describe briefly. (If more than one cognitive response occurs, rate with #1 being primary, #2 secondary, #3 tertiary

PHYSICAL (food, water, safety, shelter, etc.):
TRANSGRESSION ___   THREAT ___   LOSS _____

_____
_____
_____

PSYCHOLOGICAL (self-concept, emotional well being, identity, etc.):
TRANSGRESSION ___   THREAT ___   LOSS _____

_____
_____
_____

SOCIAL RELATIONSHIPS (family, friends, co-workers, etc.):
TRANSGRESSION ___   THREAT ___   LOSS _____

_____
_____
_____

MORAL/SPIRITUAL (personal integrity, values, belief system, etc.):
TRANSGRESSION ___   THREAT ___   LOSS _____

_____
_____
_____

Cognitive Severity Scale

Circle the number that most closely corresponds with client's reaction to crisis.

1	2	3	4	5	6	7	8	9	10
No Impairment	Minimal Impairment		Low Impairment		Moderate Impairment		Marked Impairment		Severe Impairment
Concentration intact. Client displays normal problem-solving and decision-making abilities. Client's perception and interpretation of crisis event match with reality of situation.	Client's thoughts may drift to crisis event but focus of thoughts is under volitional control. Problem-solving and decision-making abilities minimally affected. Client's perception and interpretation of crisis event substantially match with reality of situation.		Occasional disturbance of concentration. Client perceives diminished control over thoughts of crisis event. Client experiences recurrent difficulties with problem-solving and decision-making abilities. Client's perception and interpretation of crisis event my differ in some respects with reality of situation.		Frequent disturbance of concentration. Intrusive thoughts of crisis event with limited control. Problem-solving and decision-making abilities adversely affected by obsessiveness, self-doubt, confusion. Client's perception and interpretation of crisis event may differ noticeably with reality of situation.		Client plagued by intrusiveness of thoughts regarding crisis event. The appropriateness of client's problem-solving and decision-making abilities likely adversely affected by obsessiveness, self-doubt, confusion. Client's perception and interpretation of crisis event may differ substantially with reality of situation.		Gross inability to concentrate on anything except crisis event. Client so afflicted by obsessiveness, self-doubt, confusion that problem-solving and decision-making abilities have "shut down." Client's perception and interpretation of crisis event may differ so substantially from reality of situation as to constitute threat to client's welfare.

FIGURE 3.6 Triage assessment form (*Continued*)

The goal with any assessment of risk is to identify risks early, de-escalate the situation when possible, and plan for safety. This, along with documenting your process, data, and outcomes, will minimize your liability and help keep the target of the risk safe. Assessing risk of harm to self or others is an ongoing process, which consistently occurs in forensic mental health counseling settings. It is crucial that any time you assess for risk that you fully document your assessment procedures, results, and planned intervention resulting from the assessment in the client's record. The TAF can help with this. Particularly when you are within your first 3 years of practice, you should always consult with more experienced professionals and document the consultation. The crisis behaviors evaluated with the TAF include risk of suicidality and risk of harm to others, which may need immediate intervention.

Risk of Harm to Self

Forensic mental health clients often present with histories of complex relational trauma. As a result, it is common for them to display a range of self-harm behaviors. These include non-suicidal self-injury, suicidal gestures, suicidal ideation or intent leading to attempted suicide, or other less obvious forms of self-harm like addictions, eating disorders, and engaging in behaviors or relationships that place them at higher risk of victimization. *Non-suicidal self-injury* (NSSI) is the "direct and deliberate destruction of body tissue in the absence of suicidal intent" (Weierich & Nock, 2008, p. 39). Forensic populations experience high rates of victimization during childhood, and being the victim of child abuse increases the likelihood that someone will engage in self-harm behavior (Glassman, Weierich, Hooley, & Nock, 2007; Nock & Kessler, 2006; Nock & Prinstein, 2005; Romans, Martin, Anderson, Herbison, & Mullen, 1995). Specifically, several symptom clusters of PTSD are associated with increased NSSI. These include re-experiencing recurrent intrusive thoughts and images, dissociative avoidance and numbing, and hypervigilance and exaggerated startle response (Asmundson, Stapleton, & Taylor, 2004; Litz & Gray, 2002; Najmi, Wegner, & Nock, 2007; Nock, Joiner, Gordon, Lloyd-Richardson, & Prinstein, 2006).

According to the National Center for PTSD, NSSI has the effect of decreasing stress and tension brought on by hyper-arousal, blocking intrusive thoughts and images, and serving to express distress in a manner that hurts, or even punishes, themselves, rather than hurting others (U.S. Department of Veterans Affairs, n.d.). The DSM-5 provides assessment criteria for NSSI in section three (American Psychiatric Association, 2013). This includes any intentional self-inflicted behavior such as cutting, burning, stabbing, hitting, or excessive rubbing that results in bleeding, bruising, or pain, but only results in no more than moderate physical harm and no suicidal intent. The purpose must be to relieve emotional or cognitive dysregulation and may be an interpersonal strategy aimed at motivating a particular response in another person.

> **The case of Sue:** For instance, Sue is a client who has a history of childhood abuse and parental abandonment. She is in an intense relationship with her girlfriend Janie, but she senses Janie is about to end the relationship. In response, Sue begins to cut her legs with a knife. This act of self-harm

demonstrates how hurt Sue is and acts to punish herself rather than hurting Janie. Sue unconsciously engages in this interpersonal strategy in order to motivate Janie to respond with concern and stay in the relationship. Janie may stay out of fear that her leaving Sue will result in Sue harming herself, which Janie does not want to happen. We consider this behavior suicidal gesturing when used interpersonally to manipulate a relationship.

In NSSI situations where multiple methods are used, it indicates more severe psychopathology. In addition to assessing for NSSI, forensic counselors must assess for suicidality. Lifetime prevalence of attempting suicide at least once is two to five times greater for people who have childhood histories of abuse (Dube et al., 2001), and about 75% of offenders who have severe mental illness (SMI) attempt suicide compared to 15% of those without SMI (Torrey et al., 2015). Suicidality also increases with *malignant alienation*, which describes a process of interpersonal abandonment and isolation, which occurs as a result of provocative, controlling, and demanding behaviors inmates demonstrate leading to decreased sympathy and support (Fry, 2012; Pompili et al., 2003; Watts & Morgan, 1994). However, the strongest predictor of suicidality is having previously attempted (Bostwick, Pabbati, & Geske, 2016). Additional individual risk factors include chronic physical illness, family history of suicide, a chaotic family history, incarceration and trouble with the law, lack of social support and increasing isolation, and access and familiarity with lethal means (e.g., guns, drugs).

When assessing for suicidality, counselors ask questions about the client's prior attempts (Have you ever tried to kill yourself?); current thoughts (With this much stress in your life, I am wondering if you have ever felt like killing yourself. When did you begin thinking about suicide? How often do you have these thoughts?); plan and means to carry out the plan (If you were going to end your life, how would you do it? Do you have access to [whatever their plan indicates, e.g., gun, pills, rope, etc.]? Where is it right now?); and intent (On a scale of 1 to 10, 1 being I've just had fleeting thoughts and 10 being "I'm going to leave here and do it," how close are you to actually carrying out your plan?).

Clients are at low risk when they have fleeting thoughts of suicide but no real plan or past behaviors that indicate they are at increased risk. They have moderate risk when they have thoughts of suicide coupled with a plan that is not clear and self-rate below a 3 on intent, even if they have previously attempted. For those with low to moderate risk, counselors need to evaluate further psychiatric disorders, explore current stressors, and develop safety plans to increase the likelihood they will ask for help if symptoms become worse. The Substance Abuse and Mental Health Services Administration (SAMHSA) has free resources, including screening tools available to assist with suicide assessment at www.integration.samhsa.gov/clinical-practice/suicide-prevention.

Risk of Harm to Others
Counselors often monitor risk of violence in forensic mental health settings. Individuals have an increased risk of violence if they have a history of violent behavior, prior arrests, were young at the time of first arrest, or have addictive behaviors (Buchanan, Binder, Norko, &

Swartz, 2012). Risk of harm to others can occur in the form of neglect or abuse of a child, elder person, or disabled individual. It may also occur in the context of intimate partner violence or an intent to harm others through violence in a mass casualty shooting. Cruelty to animals and fire setting are particularly indicative of violent behavior (Macdonald, 1963). Additionally, individuals who have documented mental illness and have a history of non-compliance with treatment are more likely to perpetrate violence if they have past violent behavior. Personality characteristics indicative of violent behavior include impulsivity or risk taking, oppositional behavior along with victim mentality, low empathy toward past victims, and low concern regarding the consequences of their violent behavior (Buchanan, Binder, Norko, & Swartz, 2012). Finally, environmental factors associated with violence include a family or community that has high rates of violence, permissive attitudes toward violence, and having access to weapons.

Recidivism Risk

Offenders with mental illness have an increased risk of recidivating, due to the complicating factors related to their mental health diagnoses, including trauma-related disorders and addictions (Nestler et al., 2002; Skeem, Emke-Francis, & Louden, 2006). Recidivism risk assessment occurs at a variety of levels in the criminal justice system. During pretrial detention, courts conduct risk assessments to determine if criminals can safely be released pending trial. At sentencing, a judge uses the assessment to determine level of placement (e.g., community supervision or jail). Probation or parole officers use risk assessments to help identify intervention needs as related to the risk level of each offender. They use the assessment to develop an individualized case management plan, which includes specific interventions and consequences targeting potential recidivism risks. In correctional facilities, risk assessments provide information on the security level each inmate should have (e.g., high, medium, low, or minimum). Specifically, correctional officials focus on risks for behavioral problems while incarcerated or those who are at risk of fleeing from custody (James, 2015).

The *risk-needs-responsivity* (RNR) model of risk assessment relies on behavioral research to assess interactions between individual and environmental characteristics leading to criminal thinking (Casey, Warren, & Elek, 2011; Cullen & Jonson, 2010. The RNR model evaluates the *central eight*, major risks and needs. These include history of antisocial behavior, antisocial personality patterns, antisocial cognition, antisocial associates, family/marital situation, school/work history, leisure/recreation, and substance abuse (Andrews & Bonta, 2010). The three principles of the model are as follows:

1. **Risk principle**: The hypothesis is that criminal behavior can be predicted and level of treatment should match the risk level the criminal presents (Cullen & Jonson, 2011).
2. **Needs principle**: Effective treatment must address risk factors (*criminogenic needs*), which correlate with criminal behavior and should ignore any factors not correlated with recidivism (Edward, Lovins, & Lovins, 2010).
3. **Responsivity principle**: This element indicates that each individual offender has specific motivations, preferences, abilities, learning styles, personality, age, gender,

and culture, which should be considered when tailoring an individualized rehabilitation plans (Andrews & Bonta, 2010).

One criticism of RNR is that although the responsivity principle indicates offenders need individualized interventions, RNR states that cognitive behavioral (CBT) and social learning interventions are most effective, leading many to assume that CBT manualized group treatment is one size fits all. Additionally, research indicates that there is a higher risk of recidivism among mentally ill offenders who also have higher rates of trauma, thus needing trauma-informed treatment (Briere & Scott, 2015; Herman, 1997, 2015; Nestler et al., 2002; Perry, 2006; Skeem, Emke-Francis, & Louden, 2006; van der Kolk, Roth, Pelcovitz, Sunday, & Spinazzola, 2005). However, because criminal justice (CJ), rather than trained mental health professionals, conduct many risk assessments, they almost exclusively use RNR and CBT interventions rather than trauma-informed interventions.

A related criticism is that CJ professionals conducting these assessments train to focus on risks more than strengths and supports or dynamic variables like changes in behavior related to treatment interventions, unlike mental health professionals (Gottfredson & Moriarity, 2006). It is long established that institutionalized systemic racism in the criminal justice culture and structures have

> collective[ly] faile[d] ... to provide an appropriate and professional service to people because of their color, culture, or ethnic origin. It can be seen or detected in processes, attitudes and behavior which amount to discrimination through unwitting prejudice, ignorance, thoughtlessness and racist stereotyping which disadvantage minority ethnic people. (Carmichael & Hamilton, 1967, p. 4)

Therefore, RNR measures of recidivism risk have implicit biases affecting the integrity of results because sociocultural context is not often considered. This disproportionately identifies marginalized populations as having more risk than their majority culture counterparts have (Moffat, 2010; Singh & Fazel, 2010; Tonry, 2014). Finally, risk measures primarily use static variables (e.g., history of drug use, criminal history, etc.), which do not change, regardless of intervention. Mental health professionals believe that intervention should, and can, affect risk level. Therefore, mental health professionals are biased toward using dynamic variables (e.g., current affect, thinking, and social supports) to make risk assessments intervention (Cook & Michie, 2010; DeClue & Zavodney, 2014; Skeem & Monahan, 2011).

PREVENTION AND INTERVENTION

When conducting assessments, the goal is to identify factors that will indicate prevention and intervention methods most likely to succeed. Both the resulting consequences of mental health disorders as well as prevention and intervention may be conceptualized from a public health perspective. Prevention and intervention occur on a continuum. There are five principles involved in *public health model,* including the following:

1. **Levels of prevention**. There are two typologies of prevention levels:
   a. *World Health Organization Model* (WHO), which is more simplistic (Kuykendall, 2018).
      i. *Primary prevention* is anything focused on eliminating or avoiding the problem. (e.g., passing and enforcing laws and ordinances to control access to drugs, education campaigns to raising awareness).
      ii. *Secondary prevention* targets individuals who demonstrate early problems with the target behavior (e.g., drug court interventions for people who have charges of driving under the influence).
      iii. *Tertiary prevention* are interventions focused on managing complex chronic behavioral problems in order to improve functioning and quality of life.
   b. *Institute of medicine model* (IOM) (Kuykendall, 2018). This model considers the complex interactions between the risk and protective factors occurring in multiple domains, which contribute to the target behaviors.
      i. *Universal interventions* are strategies that have wide-reaching impact on communities such as education and media campaigns and legislation or administrative policies.
      ii. *Selected interventions* targets high-risk or vulnerable populations by focusing prevention efforts that speak to the unique risk factors of the group.
      iii. *Indicated interventions* target individuals who demonstrate early signs of the target behavior through things like individual counseling.
2. **Epidemiological triangle**: Assessing risk and resilience factors for each of the following:
   a. **Host** (e.g., assessing a person's age, prior exposure, susceptibility, co-occurring disorders, and response to intervention)
   b. **Agent** (e.g., assessing the toxicity or dangerousness of the addictive behavior/substance, susceptibility to being addictive, and ability of the individual to survive or be resilient in spite of risks)
   c. **Environment** (e.g., community resources, cultural values, and support structures)
3. **Approaches to prevention/intervention**
   a. **Passive**: Any prevention or intervention method that happens universally without any additional effort on the part of the targeted person (e.g., anti-lock brakes, air bags, and gunlocks).
   b. **Active**: Require action from one or more people to ensure the activity occurs (e.g., voluntary ignition interlock device added to a car ignition or a gun buyback program).
4. **Multiple program targets:** For example, using education campaigns to raise awareness, drug court intervention, and methadone treatment programs simultaneously for a comprehensive program
5. **Effective strategies**: Using research-informed strategies and conducting systematic formative and summative program evaluation

As a counselor, you should think about these categories as you assess the client and in choosing the appropriate level and type of intervention for the specific client.

SETTINGS

Assessment of risk and protective factors, risk of harm to self, and risk of harm to others will necessarily inform the level of treatment, or setting, recommended for a client. Levels of care range in intensity and restrictiveness from least restrictive (outpatient private practice or community agency setting) to most restrictive (prison). We will eventually discuss the full range of placements; however, it is important to note that the principle of *least restrictive environment* is a guiding concept in choosing level of care in mental health. However, when dealing with forensic populations, people often allow outside forces (e.g., caseload, overloaded dockets, and biases about certain offenses) to influence the placement. Let's look at how settings and risk factors interact.

When evaluating clients as having higher levels of risk, we recommend higher levels of external control over their environments. These are the most restrictive environments. So, we would evaluate a client as being at high risk for harming another person, if he demonstrates high emotional lability, a history of violence, and is currently stating that he intends to "kill" his girlfriend. Therefore, it would be appropriate to recommend a high level of external control, because he is demonstrating that he has low levels of internal control, and the lethality of his behavior is high. Therefore, there would be a recommendation for placement in jail or detention, while he awaits trial.

However, if a juvenile offender with a history of violence goes through counseling, learns ways to regulate his emotions, and demonstrates this ability under stressful situations, then we may evaluate his placement needs at a moderate level. He still has a significant history of violence, but he also has demonstrated behavior indicating improved ability to internally regulate or control his behavior. This indicates that he needs a less restrictive environment than jail, but he may still need intense monitoring. Therefore, we would recommend probation and intensive outpatient treatment or a halfway house program.

Finally, say we have a client who has one incident of violent behavior resulting from fear for her safety. She has a history of victimization and is remorseful for the violence and upset that she even took place in that behavior because she knows what it is like to be a victim. We also believe, based on our assessment, that she is unlikely to be violent unless she feels threatened. Therefore, she has high internal controls and needs less "support" or external control. Therefore, we may recommend intensive counseling services. Placing her in a more restrictive setting is more likely to increase her acting-out behavior because she is more likely to feel unsafe.

ETHICAL AND LEGAL ISSUES

During the assessment phase, there are a number of ethical and legal issues that are common in forensic settings. Since there are so many potential ethical landmines, new counselors need to be aware of who his or her resources are for supervision and consultation. In addition, all counselors working in forensic settings need to continually read professional literature and involve themselves in professional practices, which will ensure they are competent to counsel their unique populations. When ethical concerns arise, counselors should consult the American Counseling Association's Code of Ethics (ACA, 2014; Forester-Miller & Davis, n.d.). The seven steps to the *ACA ethical decision-making model* (2018) are as follows:

1. Identify the problem.
2. Apply the ACA Code of Ethics.
3. Determine the nature and dimensions of the dilemma (implications for principles of autonomy, justice, beneficence, non-maleficence, and fidelity; review of professional literature; and consultation).
4. Generate potential courses of action.
5. Consider the potential consequences of each option and determine a course of action.
6. Evaluate the selected course of action using the tests of justice (is it fair), publicity (what if it were in the press?), and universality (would you recommend this course of action to another counselor?).
7. Implement the course of action.

Although the model has seven steps, it may be important and helpful to add a step prior to the others, to identify your biases as related to the individual(s) involved and the subject matter (e.g., sexual offending). Making biases explicit can help frame the ethical decision-making process in a manner that is more likely to result in reduced bias affecting the decision.

Consistent with the ACA Code of Ethics (2014) section A.1.b, *documentation* of your assessments, both initial and ongoing, is part of attending to client welfare, and it is crucial to maintaining a practice with as little risk as possible. If working in the area of forensic counseling, it is highly likely you may be involved with the court either through providing testimony or having your records subpoenaed. Consultation is also crucial. This is particularly true if working in forensic settings is new or if you are working with a new forensic population (e.g., sex offenders), even if you have experience working with other offenders (e.g., domestic violence offenders). This is a new specialty area, which may affect your *competency* level (Section C.2.a and C.2.b, ACA, 2014, p.8). Although there may be overlap in skills, there is also specialized knowledge and skills, particularly in assessments, in which you must obtain training. If you develop and maintain good habits related to documentation and consultation, you are less likely to have legal issues of your own.

Informed consent is often an issue that FMHCs must address at the beginning of the assessment phase. Clients are often mandated to counseling and therefore often do not perceive that they have a choice in whether they engage in the assessment process or in treatment. According to the ACA Code of Ethics (2014) Section A.2, counselors must "explicitly explain to clients the nature of all services provided" (p. 4) in a developmentally and culturally sensitive manner (A.2.c., p. 4), including "the limits to confidentiality when working with clients who have been mandated for counseling" (A.2.e, p.4). One of the principles our code of ethics is built on is the principle of autonomy; as such we must always seek to ensure that the client perceives he or she has the ability to choose whether he or she engages in assessment or treatment.

Counselors must be *assessment competent* to conduct assessments. Section E of the ACA Code of Ethics (2014) discusses specific issues related to mental health assessments.

When you graduate with your degree, you will have a basic level of competency to complete biopsychosocial assessments and mental status exams. You will also have basic skills in assessing risk of harm to self and others. However, there are a number of specialized assessments discussed later in the text, which require special training to be competent to administer, score, and evaluate. The responsibility is on the counselor to complete the training and continuing education to be competent to conduct specialized assessments.

Finally, ethics and law often intersect for counselors when they assess that there is a risk of abuse or neglect. Mental health professionals are *mandated reporters*, which means that forensic mental health counselors are required by law to report suspected or known abuse or neglect of a child, elderly person, or disabled person (DePanfilis, 2006). A counselor reports these concerns to the state protective services division in which they practice. Counselors can easily access contact information for each state reporting agency on the Child Welfare Information Gateway website. It is important to remember that counselors are not investigators and therefore are not responsible for determining if abuse or neglect has actually occurred. It is the legal mandate that even if a counselor *suspects* abuse or neglect of one of these vulnerable populations, then he or she must report it under penalty of law. There are trained police or protective service workers who can and will triage reports and investigate those consistent with their agency guidelines.

SUMMARY

Regardless of the setting, a thorough assessment provides a foundation for understanding the developmental trajectory of the target/referral behavior, for identifying appropriate interventions, and for determining the least restrictive level of care for your forensic clients. A thorough assessment includes review of collateral data (e.g., psychological evaluations, arrest reports, or school reports), interviews with collateral sources of information (e.g., parents, arresting officers, probation officers, or teachers), conducting a biopsychosocial assessment and mental status exam, and evaluating the client's stage of change (pre-contemplation, contemplation, preparation, action, or maintenance). Mental health practitioners evaluate assessment data within the context that the behavior developed and currently exists. Contextual issues include evaluation of risk and protective factors involving the agent (target behavior), host (client), and environment (family, community, and larger society). Assessment data informs the counselor about the developmental trajectory of the target/referral behavior and indicates potential targets for prevention and/or intervention. There are two public health models for conceptualizing prevention and interventions, including the World

Health Organization (WHO) model (primary, secondary, and tertiary) and the Institutes of Health (IOH) model (universal, indicated, and selected).

Generally, offenders' risk of recidivism occurs at various levels of the justice system by a criminal justice professional. The risk-needs-responsivity model (RNR) (Casey, Warren, & Elek, 2011) is the most commonly used method for assessing recidivism risk. Risks and needs evaluated include history of antisocial behavior, antisocial personality patterns, antisocial cognition, antisocial associates, family/marital situation, school/work history, leisure/recreation, and substance abuse, also known as the "central eight" (Andrews & Bonta, 2010). However, there are several criticisms regarding the RNR model, including the conflict between supporting individualized interventions while also prescribing cognitive and behavioral interventions, which may not be trauma informed (Casey, Warrant, & Elek, 2011). Another criticism is the implicit systematic institutional bias that affects the criminal justice officers' assessments of risk and the use of group characteristics to evaluate individual risk (Casey, Warrant, & Elek, 2011). Finally, RNR is criticized for using primarily static variables rather than dynamic variables in risk assessment (Casey, Warrant, & Elek, 2011).

When clients enter treatment in forensic settings, they are often in crisis. Specifically, counselors must assess risk of harm to self or others. FMHCs can use the triage assessment form to help evaluate and document risk of harm to self or others in a systematic manner. Risk of harm to self may include non-suicidal self-injury, suicidal gestures, or suicide. Counselors evaluate ideation, method/means, access to method, and intent of suicidality to determine the appropriate level of risk and corresponding intervention. Similarly, counselors evaluate ideation, method/means, access to method, and intent of harm to others when determining risk of harm to others. Higher levels of risk indicate a need for more external control or a more restrictive level of intervention (e.g., hospitalization, jail), moderate risk levels indicate a need for moderate levels of external control and restrictiveness of placement (e.g., residential treatment center, half-way house, partial hospitalization program) (Holman, 2017). Finally, the least restrictive setting (e.g., intensive outpatient counseling) is indicated when there is low risk of harm to self or others. One special situation when counselors are legally required as mandated reporters to intervene is when they suspect or know there is risk of abuse to a child, elderly person, or disabled person.

Using the triage assessment form can be helpful in structuring and documenting risk assessment decisions in a systematic manner. In fact, documentation, as well as consultation, are two important parts of ethical and legal risk reduction for the practitioner. Additionally, identifying resources, which you can consult or seek supervision when faced with ethical dilemmas, is important. A variety of ethical and legal concerns are common when working in a forensic setting, such as conflicts between professional ethics and the forensic settings in which you work, when records are subpoenaed, or when a counselor or mental health professional is called to court to testify in a probation hearing. Therefore, following the ACA's Code of Ethics (ACA, 2014) as best practices will help practitioners stay within the ethical and legal boundaries of the profession and help promote the welfare of clients even when working in a system biased against rehabilitation. Common ethical concerns in forensic settings include issues related to informed consent for mandated clients and competency to practice in specialty area and in administering, scoring, and interpreting assessments. To resolve ethical dilemmas, counselors should utilize the ethical decision-making model outlined by the ACA.

CHAPTER 3 REFLECTIVE QUESTIONS

1. Discuss why biological or medical developmental history is important to understand when assessing someone in a forensic setting.
2. What types of psychological or mental health information would you want to assess in an initial intake with a forensic client and why?
3. What social history information would you want to assess in an initial intake with a forensic client and why?
4. Discuss how mental status can inform your work with a forensic client.
5. Discuss how you would assess a client's readiness for change, including the types of questions you would ask or statements you would make. For each stage of change, how would the stage of change inform the interventions you utilize with the client?
6. Discuss the five categories of self-efficacy in relationship to a change you struggled with making in your life.
7. Describe an incident you've observed where someone was in a mental health crisis. Then, discuss how you would utilize the triage assessment form to assess the person, providing behavioral examples that support the scores given in each area (affect, behavior, and cognition). How would the assessment inform your intervention?
8. Utilizing the ACA (2014) Code of Ethics, discuss some of the common ethical and legal issues a counselor will deal with working with forensic populations.

RESOURCES

Pretrail risk assessment instruments: http://www.ncsc.org/Microsites/PJCC/Home/Topics/Risk-Assessment.aspx

National Institute of Corrections, pretrial: https://nicic.gov/pretrial

National study of CPS systems and reform efforts: Review of state CPS policy: https://aspe.hhs.gov/report/national-study-child-protective-services-systems-and-reform-efforts-review-state-cps-policy

Screening questions for routine intake assessment: http://www.dorightbykids.org/how-do-i-recognize-child-abuse-and-neglect/screening-questions-for-routine-intake-assessment

Clinician's handbook of child Bx assessment, child abuse assessment: https://www.sciencedirect.com/science/article/pii/B978012343014450023X

Triage assessment form: Crisis intervention: https://www.wctcca.com/uploads/1/1/2/3/11232275/triage_assessment_form_crisis_intevention.pdf

Practice guide: Assessing harm and risk of harm in child abuse and neglect: https://www.communities.qld.gov.au/resources/childsafety/practice-manual/pg-assess-risk-of-harm.pdf

IMAGE CREDITS

Fig. 3.6: R.A. Myer, et al., https://www.wctcca.com/uploads/1/1/2/3/11232275/triage_asssessment_form_crisis_intevention.pdf. Copyright © 2001 by R.A. Myer, R.C. Williams, A.J. Ottens, and A.E. Schmidt. Reprinted with permission.

SECTION II

General Victim and Offender Information

Poem Title: *"Nothing's Respite" from a Land that Never Was*

Poet: Conan

Facility: Juvenile Detention Center Clearwater, FL

Judge: R. Dwayne Betts

The cause of all these changes in me
Is the ignition point of my family tree.
I wish my sisters could know,
The reason why my reaction is slow
Is because I grew on my very own bough.

...

And just like the child I intended to be,
I'm chained to the abyss, and I'm not sure,
About whether or not I even want to be free.
Because I know no matter how much I try to flee,
All these chains and shackles keep restraining me.

...

I went to purgatory to fix myself, but I fell
All the way down to the last pit of hell.

...

As I was sitting waist deep in ice-cold fire,
My rage flowed into this bright red pyre,

...

My rage was burning inside, like an ember sea.
My heart turned cold as such is the toll,

...

An angel flew down and gave me some mercy,
And sent me a girl who wasn't used to hell city.
I couldn't take her warmth for my own love's forlorn,
Dear God save me, I'm a glitch, I wasn't meant to be born.

...

I can't go back to the light, happiness is just too foreign.
Oh no, I've left them all on their own, all crying

Child and Adolescent Victims

Part I: Foundations

- Understand the elements involved in child maltreatment
- Distinguish between positive stress, tolerable stress, and toxic stress and describe their relationship to adverse childhood experiences and their impact on neurodevelopment
- Understand how public policy and sociocultural values, as well as familial transmission patterns, impact the manifestation of child maltreatment

TABLE 4.1 Myths and Mythbusters

Myths	Mythbusters
Victims and offenders are two distinct categories of people.	**Many people are both victims and offenders of abuse.**
Victims become offenders.	**Offenders are often victims, but victims only sometimes become offenders.**
Mothers are less likely to perpetrate child maltreatment against their own children than men or nonrelatives.	**Mothers are less likely to perpetrate child maltreatment against their own children than men or nonrelatives.**

INTRODUCTION

This chapter discusses maltreatment (abuse and neglect) occurring in childhood or adolescence. As you read this chapter, keep in mind that there is a high correlation between childhood victimization and later development of offending behaviors (Menard, 2012; Rand, 2008; Snyder, 2008; Snyder & Sickmund, 2006, U.S. Department of Justice, 2007).This is not to say that victims necessarily become offenders; however, offenders are usually past victims. Therefore, although we often place victims and offenders in categories, exclusive from one another, in fact, *they are often the same people, who did not have the supports needed to end the cycle of abuse.* Most people who end up victimizing others begin their lives as victims, often involved with child welfare agencies before "graduating" to juvenile justice and even transitioning into adult offender programs. This chapter discusses traumatic neurodevelopment occurring because of adverse childhood experiences (ACEs), which should help frame our understanding of working with victims *and* offenders.

The Child Abuse Prevention and Treatment Act of 2010 (CAPTA) (P.L. 111–320) states a child is any person under the age of 18, unless emancipated, and the definition of *child maltreatment* is

> any recent act or failure to act on the part of a parent or caregiver, which results in death, serious physical or emotional harm, sexual abuse or exploitation, or an act or failure to act which presents an imminent risk of serious harm.

One and a quarter million children experience abuse or neglect annually, which is one in every 58 children in the United States, as cited by the Fourth National Incidence Study of Child Abuse and Neglect (NIS-4) (Sedlak et al., 2010). Most (61%) experienced neglect, and 44% experienced abuse. There is some overlap, as some children are both abused and neglected. Although this reveals that child abuse and neglect are a serious concern, we must also take into account that many people do not report abuse and neglect cases to child protective services (CPS) for investigation. Therefore, these numbers are probably low estimates of the abuse and neglect actually occurring. Child maltreatment is most often reported by school personnel; however, only 20% of those reports were investigated (Sedlak, et al., 2010).

DEVELOPMENTAL ISSUES

Chapter 1 introduced adverse childhood experiences (ACEs), as well as how ACEs effect neurodevelopment. ACEs are the result of stressful experiences in childhood. Even in healthy development, children experience environmental stressors. Some of this is *positive stress*, which includes normal stressors like going to the doctor, meeting strangers, or attending day care for the first time (Middlebrooks & Audage, n.d.). Sometimes children experience more intense stressors that are time limited. We call this *tolerable stress*, which consists of situations like surviving a hurricane, being in a car accident, having parents' divorce, or a grandparent dying (Middlebrooks & Audage, n.d.).

However, when considering childhood experiences like abuse and neglect, particularly if they occur repeatedly, then children in these situations experience *toxic stress*. Additionally, repeated experiences of living in an environment where caretakers are involved in domestic violence, substance abuse, or have severe and persistent mental illness can result in toxic stress. In situations of toxic stress, children do not have the psychological resources to cope effectively, so their autonomic nervous system (ANS) correctly senses an environmental threat. When maltreatment is chronic, the ANS system becomes overly sensitive to environmental cues, resulting in chronically higher levels of stress hormones, like cortisol, and hypervigilance (CDC, 2014 a; Middlebrooks & Audage, n.d; WHO, n.d.). *Hypervigilance* results if a person is living in an environment with chronic threats to his or her health or safety, then the brain becomes more sensitive to environmental threats, which is actually adaptive. However, this overactivation signals a change in brain development in both structure and functioning.

Traumatic Neurodevelopment

Chronic experiences of toxic stress, or ACEs like child abuse and neglect, result in brain circuitry connections being impaired. This can actually result in a retardation of growth of the brain in extreme cases (National Scientific Council on the Developing Child, 2005). Systems of neural pathways between different regions of the brain (circuitry) transmit chemical signals (neurotransmitters) from one area of the brain to another, sending messages that trigger emotional and behavioral reactions in response to stimuli (environmental or internal). These neural pathways develop and strengthen in response to consistent experiences over time, and these same experiences affect how different parts of the brain communicate with each other.

Brain functioning develops hierarchically. The *reptilian brain*, consisting of the brainstem and cerebellum, is evolutionarily the oldest part of the brain. It regulates heartbeat, respiration, temperature, and balance. To be alive, at minimum, this part of the brain has to be working. When someone is on life support, machines are doing the work of the brainstem, thus we say they are "brain dead" because a machine, not the reptilian brain, is controlling basic life functions. Sometimes the autonomic nervous system (ANS) is being activated. When this happens, environmental cues affect the functioning of the reptilian brain. However, when the ANS system activates, it usually does so in response to limbic system cues.

The next part of the brain to develop in mammals is the *limbic brain*. The main areas of the limbic brain are the amygdala, hippocampus, and hypothalamus. The *amygdala* creates sensory experiences related to environmental triggers (e.g., exposure to an enjoyable experience, good feeling, and exposure to a bad experience, bad feeling). *Emotions* are amygdala-created sensory experiences. Emotional experiences are physical sensations, which we label with "feelings words." Once we can speak, people develop the ability to identify the correct feelings word to connect to the sensory experience of the emotion we are attempting to label. However, there are people who have alexithymia, and many abuse victims, addicts, and offenders are among them. *Alexithymia* occurs when someone feels the sensory experience of emotion but does not have the ability to connect the correct feelings word with that experience. Therefore, much of the work by counselors who work with victims of abuse, addicts, and offenders begins with labeling emotions.

The brain encodes these sensory experiences created in the amygdala in the *hippocampus*, which involves the formation of new memories. These are called episodic or autobiographical memories. They are non-declarative. In other words, the physical sensations created in the amygdala, which are associated with experiences, are "remembered" by the body, but the person does not have words to explain or abstract thought to make sense of the memories. By encoding the emotional context created in the amygdala, similar environmental cues (similar sights, smells, sounds, feelings of physical pressure or temperature, etc.) trigger an emotional connection with those environmental cues, and people react behaviorally out of those emotional connections. Pre-verbal children, for instance, have non-declarative memories, which allows them to respond to familiar environmental stimuli in predictable ways.

In addition, when a person, later in development, experiences a traumatic event, he or she may *dissociate* parts of the memory, thereby encoding it as non-declarative; however, the physical sensations or emotional content of the memory is still stored in the body, apart from the conscious knowledge of the event, and similar environmental cues may trigger the emotional reaction. This is what happens when someone has PTSD and has a flashback. For instance, a Veteran jumps and takes cover when a car backfires because the sensory experience of the noise is an environmental cue that triggers his ANS system to react as if his life is in danger. In fact, everyone has non-declarative memories, also called *implicit biases*, which are unconscious value judgments that strongly influence behavior. Implicit bias results from these non-declarative memories because it is the brain's way of making efficient use of life experiences. The text repeatedly refers to implicit biases because they are important for counselors to be aware of how they affect the way a counselor evaluates forensic clients (e.g., offender = bad, victim + good).

Finally, the *neocortex* involves higher levels of functioning like language, abstract thought, imagination, and the ability to control impulses, problem solve and make decisions, sometimes referred to as *executive functioning*. Children or adults considered to have behavioral problems (e.g., children with oppositional or conduct issues, adolescents/adults with criminal offending behaviors) generally receive interventions focused on strengthening executive functioning. This is due to the fact that people deciding on treatment often identify the clients' judgment, problem solving, decision making, and impulse control as the primary problem. However, for individuals experiencing developmental trauma, counselors must consider more trauma-informed neuro-developmentally sensitive interventions, which focus on lower levels of brain function prior to attempting to address executive functioning challenges.

Trauma results in maladaptive neurodevelopment, which in turn results in damaged circuitry between the limbic system and the neocortex. As a result, these parts of the brain are not "talking to one another." This, coupled with the fact that the vast majority of offenders are trauma survivors, indicates that using interventions that primarily focus on executive functioning (e.g., cognitive) are unlikely to be successful long term. A person may be able to repeat the "right" ways to problem solve a stressful situation, because memorizing information is a cognitive function, which the client may be able to do. However, when the emotional content of an amygdala is triggered by a sensory memory (also referred to as a *hot amygdala*) the limbic system neuro-hijacks the neocortex.

In other words, the survival instincts of the ANS system take over, and the client acts out of the sensory memory of feeling unsafe. Because a client experienced chronic trauma or toxic stress, the individual does not have the neural circuitry sending messages (neurotransmitters as electrical signals) from the amygdala to the neocortex (e.g., "This is scary") and the neocortex sending messages to the amygdala ("It's okay; this is not life threatening"). From an evolutionary perspective, if a person is being chased by a lion (this is scary), then it makes sense to shut off cognitive reasoning and just fight, run, or hide (fight/flight/freeze) to stay alive because the situation is life threatening (e.g., "If you stop to think, he will eat you for a snack"). Your brain's response is adaptive because it adjusts to repeated experiences so that it reacts efficiently to environmental stimuli, thus ensuring your survival. In situations of toxic stress, however, these exposures are so frequent, and often occur over such an extended period, that the fight/flight/freeze response becomes the normal state, predisposing victims of abuse to distressing or maladaptive responses to their environments.

Emotion Regulation

As previously described, the neural pathways that connect the limbic system experience of emotion to the neocortex regions involving language development allow individuals to label emotions with feelings words; this describes *feelings recognition*. More complex, but very important, is *emotion regulation*, the ability to self-regulate or manage emotions, particularly challenging ones like anger, fear, loneliness, etc. Emotion regulation develops by building pathways that rely on mirror neurons. *Mirror neurons* (monkey see, monkey do) are special neurons that allow infants to, in effect, sync their neuronal circuitry with their caregiver's neuronal circuitry. Mirror neurons facilitate the transmission of the caregiver's interpersonal regulation of the infants' emotional dysregulation (e.g., crying when hungry or in pain results in the caregiver feeding or soothing the baby), over the first 3 years of life, to the infant's internal regulation of dysregulated emotions. In this manner, the infant develops an internal model of emotion regulation (through developing and strengthening similar neuronal networks to the caregiver's), which the infant can rely on during times of emotion dysregulation. In other words, people go from interpersonal (caregiver) regulation of emotion (baby cries and caregiver sooths) to intrapersonal (self) regulation of emotion.

In order for this process to work effectively, the child must experience at least one consistently (two-thirds of the time) empathically attuned (attempts to care for, soothe, and meet the needs of the infant) caregiver relationship within the first 3 years of life. Conversely, ACEs involving neglect and abuse, by definition are mistuned interpersonal interactions with a caregiver, resulting in impaired neural development and increased vulnerability to mental and physical illnesses. This is why counselors assess risks/vulnerabilities as well as strengths when evaluating clients for treatment.

In addition, childhood abuse and neglect are more impactful because brain circuitry is more vulnerable during early childhood. During this time, brain functioning is in the process of developing, so any experience (good or bad) will have greater impact during this time period than it will later in life. *Plasticity* is the term used to describe the brain's ability to change, so earlier in development, the brain has more plasticity than it does later in life.

"Once the brain has organized (i.e., after age three), experience-dependent modifications of the regulatory system are much less likely than experience-dependent modifications of cortically-mediated functions such as language development" (Perry, 1999).

ACEs result in damaged neural circuitry and increased baseline levels of stress hormones, like cortisol. Elevated levels of stress hormones can suppress immune functioning, leaving the victim vulnerable to a variety of chronic health problems (Center on the Developing Child, 2005). Child abuse and neglect also damage the hippocampus, which can result in lifelong cognitive deficits. Additionally, some children are genetically predisposed to mental illness, addictions, or chronic health conditions (Center for Genetics Education, 2012; Hyman, 1997); however, the interplay between those genetic vulnerabilities and environmental stressors results in situations where the genetic risk is expressed through the person developing mental illness, addictions, or chronic disease. Scientists call this genetic expression *epigenetics*.

Neurosequential Model of Therapeutics

The text introduces the Child Trauma Academy's neurosequential model of therapeutics (NMT) (Perry, 2006) in chapter 1. In review, there are six principles underlying this model. The first principle is that brain organization is hierarchical, such that all incoming sensory input first enters the lower parts of the brain in the limbic system. Next, neurons and neural systems change in a "use-dependent" fashion. In other words, consistent experiences over time change the structure and functioning of the brain. With experience, the neuronal networks or electrical circuitry and the chemical messages between parts of the brain change. The next two principles are that the brain develops in a sequential fashion and that it develops more rapidly early in life. The next NMT principle is that neuronal systems are plastic or can change, but due to age and experiences, some are easier to change than others. Finally, NMT asserts that the brain is designed for "a different world," and more natural, primitive conditions than exist in modern society.

In other words, it is an *evolutionary design* that developed to facilitate survival of mammals, ultimately people. So, the lower levels of the brain, which are the first to develop (reptilian and limbic), are very powerful and will override executive functions in the neocortex, which were developed after survival from life-threatening experiences were common, like being chased by a lion. This is particularly true if sensory memories cue fear for survival, which happens to people who experience trauma.

The *NMT model* indicates that we must identify where the client is neuro-developmentally and respond therapeutically in a manner that speaks to that neurodevelopmental level and then scaffold learning such that we facilitate building and strengthening new neural pathways (open lines of communication) between limbic system structures and executive functions in the neocortex. In counseling, a common phrase is that counselors need to "meet clients where they are." Using the NMT model, we conceptualize this as beginning treatment at the appropriate neurodevelopmental level, beginning with experiencing interventions, moving to verbal interactions and process, then to higher-order cognitive skills and coping strategies, in that sequence.

CONTEXTUAL ISSUES

Understanding child maltreatment and our sociocultural and political responses to child abuse and neglect requires a review of the context within which these occur. Therefore, the next section will discuss some of the history leading to society's recognition of child maltreatment as problematic and discuss political and public health responses to these sociocultural values. It will also discuss some familial and sociocultural contexts within which abuse and neglect happen, as well as how counselors understand transmission patterns of abuse and neglect occurring intergenerationally in families and in certain sociocultural contexts. Finally, the text reviews how a counselor's life experiences and subsequent implicit biases may affect the way they make sense of clients' and the clients' family and community, such that the reader can be more aware and therefore less likely to act out of these biases.

Historical Context of Initiatives in the United States

Understanding the historical foundation for child welfare will help you understand some of the otherwise complicated laws, policies, and practices you may encounter when working with child and adolescent victims. Child welfare events between 1887 and 1949 are summarized in Table 4.2, and the significant child welfare events from 1950–1980 are summarized in Table 4.3. However, events from 1980 until now are discussed next, as they indicate the current laws or policy trends you are most likely to deal with as a forensic mental health counselor today.

TABLE 4.2 Early Child Welfare History (1887–1949)

Date	Event
1887	**Dawes Act of 1887** passed, which resulted in the U.S. government removing very young indigenous children from their homes and placing them in assimilation-model boarding schools so that they would become "Americanized."
1904	The United States established the first juvenile court in the world.
1908	National Child Labor Committee (NCLC) began documenting child labor practices with photographs.
1909	NCLC members Lillian Wald and Florence Kelly developed the idea for the Children's Bureau (CB), which was endorsed by President Roosevelt's White House Conference on Children and Youth. They recommended that the state provide oversight for these institutions, foster family care, and adoption agencies.
1912	First legislation passed legitimizing the federal government's role in protecting child welfare. President Taft later appointed Lothrop as the first director of the federal Children's Bureau (CB).
1916	First child labor law passed.
1916–1918	CB staff inspected 700 factories and mines for child labor violations. CB recruited 11 million volunteers working to reduce child mortality, stating that child advocacy was a patriotic duty, using the slogan "Save 100,000 babies."
1918	**The Children's Year** culminated with the second White House Conference on Children and Youth. Supreme Court ruled the child labor law passed in 1916 unconstitutional.

Date	Event
1921	**Sheppard-Towner Maternity and Infancy Act** passed, providing federal grants with matching funds to help states with health activities for mothers and children, helping over 700,000 pregnant women and over 4 million children between 1921 and 1929.
1926	CB published **Public Aid to Mothers with Dependent Children** summarizing legislation on mothers' aid legislation, which subsequently became the foundation for Aid for Dependent Children (AFDC).
1927	CB began collecting data on child maltreatment, revealing inconsistencies across juvenile court systems.
1928	**Meriam Report**, formally known as the Problem of Indian Administration, published by the Institute for Government Research, now the Brookings Institution, examined the conditions of Indian boarding schools. The report is based on field observations over 7 months, 23 states, and 95 reservations, agencies, hospitals, and schools documenting poor conditions and neglect by the federal government in caring for indigenous populations. President Hoover requested additional funds to provide food and clothing to the children in these schools, resulting in a number of reforms, including closing the boarding schools and improving medical facilities.
1930	Third White House Conference on Children produced the 19-point **Children's Charter** addressing educational, health, welfare, and protection needs of children based on peer-reviewed research of 1,200 child health and development experts.
1930–1940	The Great Depression: The CB continued to focus on infant mortality, health and wellbeing of children with regard to crippling illnesses, nutrition, and growth. They also maintained oversight of child labor, foster care, adoption, and juvenile courts and delinquency.
1933	**National Industrial Recovery Act** passed, setting minimum work age at 16 for full-time employment and 18 for dangerous jobs, but the Supreme Court ruled it unconstitutional in 1935.
1934	**Indian Reorganization Act** signed by President Roosevelt, which reformed American Indian policy on land allotment, education, and healthcare, following publication of the Mariam Report.
1935	Social Security Act established **Aid for Dependent Children** (AFDC).
1936	CB began publishing *The Child: Monthly News Summary*, which compiled research and other news related to child health and welfare.
1938	**Fair Labor Standards Act** passed, setting the minimum age for child labor at 16 for full-time employment and 18 for dangerous jobs. The standards were consistent with the National Industrial Recovery Act of 1933, ruled unconstitutional in 1935. However, the standards were relaxed during World War II (WWII) from 1941 to 1945. This contributed to increases in juvenile delinquency, according to the CB.
1940	Fourth White House Conference on Children, the **Conference on Children in a Democracy**, focused on poverty and equal opportunity.
1941–1945	Child labor laws were relaxed during World War II (WWII), contributing to increases in juvenile delinquency, according to the CB.
1941	CB conference on the Care of Children of Working Mothers to address issues related to women joining the workforce during WWII.
1942	CB published *Standards for Day Care of Children of Working Mothers* and several publications on the physical and emotional needs of children during war. CB established the Emergency Maternity and Infant Care (EMIC) program aid the lowest-ranking soldiers' spouses and children with medical care. EMIC served 1.5 million women and children during the war and was the first medical program ever initiated by the federal government.

TABLE 4.3 Contemporary Child Welfare History (1950–1980)

1950	Fifth White House Conference on Children developed *A Pledge to Children,* a handbook for social workers and parents, providing guidance for helping children have positive emotional and spiritual development (Williams, 1968). The report was cited in 1954 by the Supreme Court because of its discussion of the harmful effects of segregation.
1950–1960	The number of child welfare workers doubled, partially due to the government providing funds to educate them under the Social Security Act's child welfare program.
1953	CB became part of the New Department of Health and Human Services, at which time the focus shifted to funding research-informed practices with "at-risk" youth. One of these groups of interest was juveniles committing crimes.
1961–1967	President Johnson established the War on Poverty
1962	Congress passed the **Public Welfare Amendments Act**, resulting in the federal government matching funds to states on behalf of children in foster care. As part of this legislation, the law required states provide a **care plan** for each child in state custody and for protective services to conduct periodic reviews to determine if continuation of foster care was necessary. It also required state child welfare agencies to facilitate timely **family reunification**.
1963	CB developed language on **mandated reporting**, which requires health professionals to report suspected abuse or neglect.
1964	**Economic Opportunity Act of 1964** passed, creating Medicare and Medicaid, expanding Social Security benefits, establishing Job Corps, and making the **Food Stamp Act** permanent.
1965	Elementary and Secondary Education Act passed, which established the Title I program subsidies still used for school districts with large populations of children living in poverty.
1967	All states had mandated child abuse reporting laws. Because of the War on Poverty, fewer families were dissolving solely due to poverty; however, this led to a 50% increase in the number of children entering childcare and receiving child welfare services. The reasons for placement changed from poverty related to abuse, neglect, and parental instability or substance abuse, which in turn meant more kids were entering with more severe emotional issues.
1970	The CB undertook a nationwide recruitment effort in 1970 to increase adoption of African American and multiple heritage youth, the same year that the White House Conference on Children and Youth held its seventh conference with a focus on racism and poverty.
1972	President Nixon established the first National Action for Foster Children Week to discuss the rights of foster parents and initiate a public information campaign to raise awareness of foster children's needs, encourage foster parent recruitment, and assess the resources and services available to foster families and children in care.
1974	Congress passed the **1974 Child Abuse Prevention and Treatment Act** (CAPTA) (Pub. L. 93-247), which provided federal assistance to states for prevention, identification, and treatment of child abuse and neglect. Congress also established the **National Center on Child Abuse and Neglect** within the CB. Continues to provide minimum standards for child maltreatment definitions and supports states' prevention and intervention activities today.
1975	Congress passed the **Model State Subsidized Adoption Act** and the CB developed models for state laws to subsidize the adoption of children in foster care and facilitate the termination of parental rights as a strategy to increase special needs adoptions. This program continues to provide financial subsidies to foster and adoptive families who care for children who are in state custody or those adopted from the foster care system. These subsidies provide for the child's basic clothing, food, educational, and medical needs.

1977	The Administration on Children, Youth, and Families (ACYF) established to administer child welfare programs.
1966–1978	Number of children in foster care more than doubled, raising concerns for kids stuck in state custody.
1978	The *New York Daily News* published a series of articles in 1978, which brought public attention to the problem of **foster care drift**, the problematic outcomes for children languishing in foster care.
	CB began supporting the National Clearinghouse for Home-Based Services to Children and Families at the University of Iowa's School of Social Work, which generates and evaluates research on home-based prevention aimed at strengthening and preserving families rather than replacing them.
	Congress also enacted the Indian Child Welfare Act (ICWA) (Pub. L. 95–608) to address concerns about placement of indigenous children with non-native families or institutions. Because of the legislation, child welfare agencies were required to determine the child's tribal ancestry and relationship to one or more federally recognized tribes, and it placed the burden for notification to the child's tribe and native parent or custodian on the court. The assumption was that the tribal representative was the best person to lead the out-of-home placement or termination of parental rights. Additionally, if the tribe could not be determined, the court must notify the Bureau of Indian Affairs. The law asserted that tribes, not the U.S. government, have the primary right and responsibility for the welfare of indigenous children. As a result, tribes were able to intervene in court, requesting transfer of these child welfare cases to tribal courts. It also provided guidelines for placement requiring the primary option be in a native community foster home. Further, it requires welfare agencies undertake active, rather than reasonable, steps to reunify the child with his or her parents.

Recent History (1980 to 2018)

Congress passed the *Adoption Assistance and Child Welfare Act of 1980* (Pub. L. 96–272), which required reasonable efforts to reunite children with their families of origin. It also provided alternative permanency outcomes for those who could not reunite with their families, including family care placement and adoption. The number of children in care subsequently decreased significantly in just 4 years, as did the median length of time in care. However, the median stay across the country was 21 months, with some states (Illinois, New York, and DC) as high as 30–35 months (Barbell & Freundlich, 2001). This is significant, because we know that the longer children stay in foster care, the more likely they will have multiple placements, which results in attachment problems and increases the risk for children developing serious mental health issues (Barbell & Freundlich, 2001).

According to testimony before the U.S. House of Representatives in 2000, 21% of kids in care had three or four placements, 8% had five or six placements, and another 8% had seven or more placements. However, permanency is more difficult the longer children remain in care, whether with their families of origin or with adoptive families. Another result of more kids in care was more also reached the age of majority, 18, while in care. To address this concern, in 1983 Congress established the *Independent Living Program* (42 U.S.C. 677) to provide limited services for kids in foster care who reached the age of majority. This legislation supports programs that teach kids who have often spent most of their lives in the foster care system independent living skills, like how to do housework, clean clothes, cook, get a job, manage money, and so on.

From 1983 to 1993, growing concerns that CPS's efforts to maintain children in their homes and communities were insufficient led Congress to establish the *Family Preservation and Family Support Program* (Pub. L. 103–66). As a result "family-centered," "family-focused," and "family-based" models developed to assess the needs of children within the family and community context. The act provided funding for family preservation and community-based family support services to include birthparents, extended family members, and adoptive parents. It also required states to develop and carry out comprehensive planning processes for developing a "meaningful and responsive family support and family preservation strategy" (U.S. Department of Health and Human Services, 1994, as quoted in Barbell & Freundlich, 2001). I discuss these processes in more depth in a later section.

In 1994, Congress enacted the *Multi-Ethnic Placement Act* (MEPA) (Pub. L. 103–382), prohibiting agencies from discriminating based on the placement family's ethnic or cultural heritage. However, it allowed child welfare workers to consider the child's racial and cultural heritage in the context of whether the placement family could meet the child's needs. However, Congress repealed this legislation in 1996, as part of the *Interethnic Placement Act* (Pub. L. 104–188). Additionally, states must pay financial penalties for violating the anti-discrimination requirement, which allowed private citizens to sue the state if they assert discrimination. However, the original MEPA provision required that states actively pursue recruitment of diverse foster and adoptive parents in order to increase the likelihood that children have the opportunity for placement in a similar ethnic/cultural family placement. However, neither of these laws affects the protections for indigenous youth covered by the Indian Child Welfare Act of 1978.

In 1997, Congress reauthorized the FPFSP as part of the Adoption and Safe Families Act (ASFA; Pub. L. 105–89), changing its name to *Promoting Safe and Stable Families*. The law included a requirement for prospective foster and adoptive parents to pass a criminal background check as one effort to ensure child safety in alternative placements. However, there was also a significant change that established a 12-month period in which child welfare workers presented a clear permanency plan at permanency hearings. Additionally, if the court terminated parental rights, ASFA requires agencies to make reasonable efforts (active efforts for indigenous children under the ICWA) to find timely permanent placement for children.

The reauthorization also provided funding for time-limited reunification services and promotion of adoption and support services. Support services included time-limited reunification while kids are in care, for family preservation services following reunification or adoption, and post-adoption services for children and their adoptive families. However, state utilization of funds is varied (Barbell & Freundlich, 2001). After this legislation, community mental agencies contracted with CPS agencies to work with families with open cases on a 1-year timeline where parents either followed their safety plan and were able to reunite with their children or did not follow their safety plan and termination parental of rights occurred. Significant increases in foster care adoptions followed.

However, there were also significant increases in the number of children entering foster care after 1997. Kids reaching the age of majority (18 years old) while they are in foster care has also increased. The term *aging out* is used to describe this group of kids. Often, these kids do not have the resources to live independently because they grew up in the foster care system. These skills include educational or vocational support and personal care skills. Therefore, more of these kids end up homeless or incarcerated (Barbell & Freundlich, 2001). Congress subsequently enacted the *Foster Care Independence Act of 1999* (Pub. L. 106–169). It was an effort to fortify the 1986 Independent Living Program (42 U.S.C. 677) to provide 18–21-year-old kids aging out of foster care with help transitioning to independent living. These kids could agree to stay in foster care beyond the age of majority and receive limited financial support for housing and food and support to complete their high school education or extend support for post-secondary education or vocational training, mentorship for personal and emotional support, counseling, and other supports and services (U. S. Department of Health and Human Services, 2001). In order to facilitate this, there are volunteer boards of community members called *foster care extension review boards*, who meet with these kids, their caseworkers, and an advocate who is someone who aged out of foster care and is living independently. This group provides support and resources to kids that parents would normally provide such as college application funds, help filling out college applications, and identification of appropriate post-secondary training opportunities (e.g., trade school, technical school, college).

Congress also enacted the *Children's Health Insurance Program (CHIP) Act* of 1997. The purpose of CHIP was to expand health insurance coverage for children of parents who were low-income working poor. These families were not eligible for Medicaid, but they also did not have health insurance. The threshold for CHIP is generally at or above 200% of the federal poverty level (FPL) (Dubay & Kenney, 2009). Dubay and Kenney (2009) found that CHIP resulted in 51% of children living at 300% below the FPL were eligible for public coverage in 1997, and this increased to 75% by 2002. Amid partisan politics, Congress reauthorized CHIP in 2009 and in January 2018. However, in that legislation they did not authorize grant funding for over 10,000 clinics across the country where thousands of children receive care. It is unclear how this will affect children's mental health care in the future.

Familial and Sociocultural Context

The sociocultural context of the family influences our understanding of child maltreatment. Current laws primarily use the majority (White, middle class) sociocultural understanding of child welfare and child maltreatment (Lubell, Lofton, & Singer, 2008). In addition, many FMHCs are of majority culture whether in ethnicity, religion, and/or socioeconomic status (SES). Many descriptions of abuse and neglect discussed later in this chapter involve activities that are highly impacted by availability of resources, whether health insurance, finances, or a safe community. Therefore, FMHCs must intentionally explore implicit bias. Also, the *deficit model* used in child welfare agencies emphasizes assessment of risks, rather than protective factors or resiliencies, disproportionately negatively impacted racial and ethnic minorities, those living in poverty, and single mothers (Guilamo-Ramos et al., 2007; Lubell, Lofton, & Singer, 2008; Maiter, Alaggia, & Trocme, 2004). Therefore, ethnic differences exist in relationship to findings of child maltreatment. "African-American, American Indian, and Alaska native children and children of multiple races/ethnicities experience the highest rates of child abuse or neglect" (Pub. L. No. 111–320). So, it is important to take these potential biases into consideration when reviewing the following data about family risk factors related to incidences of child maltreatment (Sedlak et al., 2010),

- Living with a grandparent or married biological parent have the lowest rates of maltreatment.
- Living with an unmarried parent and another non-relative adult have the highest rates of maltreatment, including being eight times more likely to experience neglect and 10 times more likely to experience abuse.
- Biological parents are most likely to perpetrate abuse (64%) and neglect (92%), although rates and severity of abuse vary by perpetrator.
- Non-parents perpetrate 42% of reported sexual abuse.
- Non-parent physical abuse tends to be more severe than parent-perpetrated physical abuse.
- Families with four or more children have higher rates of child abuse and neglect, followed by only children, with the lowest rates from families with two children.
- Unemployed parents and those in lower SES have higher rates of reported abuse and neglect (five times the rate of maltreatment, three times more likely to experience abuse, and seven times more likely to experience neglect).
- Women are most likely to have abuse charges (68%), and 75% of child abuse cases were perpetrated by mothers.
- Men are more likely to abuse nonbiological children.

Perpetrators of child abuse are more likely to have substance use disorders and mental illness and live in rural areas. Additionally, it helps if a counselor understands diverse sociocultural parenting views when working with children and families involved with protective services.

The CDC's Healthy Parenting Cultural Norms Study provides insight into sociocultural parenting differences, which provide clues as to how you might approach child maltreatment issues with these families. They found that most parents, regardless of cultural background, held similar views about what child behaviors were good or bad. However, the strength of how important certain behaviors were differed by ethnicity. African American, Latino, and American Indian fathers believed religious or spiritual foundation was important; however, Asian and White parents thought self-control was most important. In addition, Asian, Latino, and African American fathers thought assertiveness, independence, and accountability for behavior was important. Much of the responses appear to be socially desirable, so information gathered about what constituted parental abuse of a child may not be reliable. However, the study's conclusions indicate some good advice for counselors working with diverse populations, and that is to discuss with parents and kids how different parenting strategies work within their sociocultural values and belief systems (Lubell, Lofton, & Singer, 2008). In doing so, clients are more likely to engage in teaching about their cultural norms, which can be useful in therapeutic intervention. However, it also opens communication around sociocultural beliefs and values so that clients feel more comfortable correcting you or asserting a difference if they believe the counselor is wrong about something or the counselor does not understand their perspective. This helps build trust in the relationship.

However, a serious consideration that FMHCs working with diverse populations must consider is the *intergenerational or transgenerational transmission of trauma and resilience* (Braga, Mello, & Fiks, 2012; Caruth, 2014; Dekel & Goldblatt, 2008). When a person experiences significant trauma, such as going to war, being part of the Holocaust, being abused as a child, or having a child or sibling die young, the person's behaviors, emotional state, and subsequent meaning making or belief system is impacted. As a result, the person may have unresolved grief or posttraumatic stress responses, and the family may become the container that holds this grief or stress response. Therefore, when the historical legacy of separating children from their parents at very young ages is considered, there is significant attachment trauma that entire communities of indigenous people experience, including those who endured slavery, Indian boarding schools, Japanese-American internment camps, Holocaust survivors, or Latin American child refugee camps.

Culturally competent counselors must consider how such profound experiences of loss, and the cover up the majority culture perpetuates about these horrible traumas, affected the belief systems and affect regulation mechanisms utilized by those individuals who experience(d) them. Consider the information discussed previously on interpersonal neurobiology. Think about how mirror neurons of the child "speak to" the parent's neuronal system such that the child takes on similar organizational patterns in neural circuitry as the parent. This is how past trauma for parents transmit to their children, and so on throughout generations. Therefore, the familial and sociocultural influences at work for the children and adolescents must be considered in forensic mental health centers.

Case Study: Enrique Part I

Enrique is a first-generation Mexican-American male who presents for treatment following a referral from victims' services at the local police department. Enrique recently witnessed his mother's rape and murder by a man in the neighborhood. He presents as a well-groomed 8-year-old boy who is quiet and does not make eye contact. When you speak to Enrique, he flinches, indicating an exaggerated startle response. In the 3 months following his mother's death and the perpetrator's arrest, Enrique has lived with his older sister, Eliana, a homemaker; her husband, a construction worker; and their two children (Juan, 2 years old and a baby, Angel). He attends a local elementary school where he has few friends and does not speak unless spoken to. He makes decent grades, but he seems to isolate and often has a "far-off look" as if he is "checked out," according to his sister. She reports prior to the murder that he was a relatively happy child who liked to play soccer and had many friends.

The rape and murder occurred when Enrique's mother, a widow, invited a neighborhood man into the house to help her fix her dishwasher. When the man made sexual advances at his mom and she rebuffed his advances, the man began beating her, resulting in injuries leading to her death. Enrique was present in the house, although they do not know how much of the events he witnessed. Given the brutal nature of the crime, Eliana believes Enrique heard, if not saw, most of what happened. It was Enrique who called 911 and hid in the closet of his mother's bedroom until police found him there.

Case Application Questions

1. Apply the neurosequential model of therapeutics to Enrique's case. How would this model inform your approach to treatment with Enrique and why?
2. Based on historical context, how would Enrique's case have been handled in 1945? 1970? 2018?
3. What familial and sociocultural contextual issues impact the way Enrique's case may be handled by the child welfare system?

SUMMARY

Chapter 4 focuses on foundational issues related to child maltreatment including defining child maltreatment, describing how it impacts otherwise normal brain development, and how counselors can work from a neuro-developmentally informed position with child maltreatment clients. The chapter also reviews information related to historical public policy and socio-cultural contexts within which child maltreatment is treated. As part of the exploration of foundations of child maltreatment, the chapter reviews historical and public policy changes related to child abuse and neglect. Additionally, economic and sociocultural contextual issues were considered, which potentially influence the incidence, prevalence, and development of child abuse and neglect. For example, Child Protective Services identifies higher rates of child abuse and neglect among African American, American Indian, and Alaska native children, as well as those of multiple races/ethnicities. In addition, due to the deficit model used by child welfare agencies to define maltreatment, which emphasizes assessment of risk rather than assessment of protective factors, it disproportionately and negatively affects racial and ethnic minorities, those living in poverty, and single mothers. Finally, the chapter discusses the intergenerational or transgenerational transmission of trauma, which has had long-lasting effects on the entire cultures.

Chapter 5 will build on the information in this chapter to explore common mental health concerns among child maltreatment victims. We will discuss specific definitions, behavioral manifestations of neglect, and the trauma outcome process model, which helps us understand how trauma is processed, which helps explain the different outcomes (healing, chronic victimization, or development of offending behaviors) experienced by victims (Borja & Callahan, 2009; Burton, Rasmussen, Bradshaw, Christopherson, & Huke, 1998; Rasmussen, Burton, & Christopherson, 1992; Rasmussen, 1999, 2001, 2004, 2008). Chapter 5 will also discuss child maltreatment prevention and intervention strategies, the settings within which we assess and treat child maltreatment, and the unique legal and ethical concerns in working with this population.

CHAPTER 4 REFLECTIVE QUESTIONS

1. Discuss the differences between positive stress, tolerable stress, and toxic stress and describe their relationship to adverse childhood experiences and their impact on neurodevelopment.
2. Describe how emotion regulation develops and its relationship to the neurosequential model of therapeutics.
3. Discuss some of the recent legislative and policy changes that affect work in forensic settings.
4. Discuss some of the familial and sociocultural issues that may affect your work with forensic populations.

RESOURCES

Adverse Childhood Experiences: Centers for Disease Control and Prevention: https://www.cdc.gov/violenceprevention/childabuseandneglect/acestudy/index.html

Substance Abuse and Mental Health Services Administration: ACEs: https://www.cdc.gov/violenceprevention/childabuseandneglect/acestudy/index.html

Neurosequential Network: https://www.neurosequential.com/

Child Trauma Academy: http://childtrauma.org/

Association for Play Therapy: https://www.a4pt.org/

Childhelp: https://www.childhelp.org/child-abuse/

Bruce D. Perry, "Social and Emotional Development in Early Childhood" (YouTube Video): https://www.youtube.com/watch?v=vkJwFRAwDNE

John Bradshaw, "The boy who was raised as a dog and other stories from a child psychiatrist's notebook: What traumatized children can teach us about loss, love, and healing": https://www.johnbradshaw.com/

- Healing the shame that binds you
- Homecoming: Reclaiming and championing your inner child
- Bradshaw on the family: A new way of creating solid self-esteem
- Family secrets: The path to self-acceptance and reunion

CHAPTER 5

Child and Adolescent Victims

Part II: Mental Health

- Identify and discuss different types of neglect and abuse, as well as their prevalence rates and risk factors associated with abuse and neglect
- Describe the trauma outcome process assessment model and the three potential victim outcomes resulting after abuse experiences
- Discuss the neurodevelopmental impact of trauma as related to behavioral and interpersonal manifestations in victims and resulting diagnostic indications
- Discuss the legal and ethical considerations as well as the process for reporting and treating child abuse

TABLE 5.1 Myths and Mythbusters

Myths	Mythbusters
Children involved with child welfare most often experience abuse.	**More children involved with child welfare experience neglect than abuse, although some experience both.**
Questioning a child who reports abuse is important so that you can provide details to investigators when you report.	**Only trained forensic child abuse investigators should conduct interviews, usually videotaped at a Child Advocacy Center. Counselors and other untrained adults should focus on reflecting the child's comments, providing emotional support and validation that they are heard, and documenting and reporting information (even if limited) to authorities as soon as possible.**
Any counselor can provide treatment for a child abuse survivor.	**Counselors must be competent to provide services by undergoing trauma-specific training, play therapy training (if working with children), and training in other experiential developmentally appropriate methods of intervention, as well as training in legal and ethical behaviors for counseling professionals.**

INTRODUCTION

Chapter 5 builds on the foundational work in chapter 4, where we discussed the developmental, historical, and sociocultural contexts within which child maltreatment develops and is treated. The chapter begins with a discussion of common mental health concerns related to child victimization. The chapter defines the different types of neglect and abuse and explores childhood sexual abuse in some depth. The chapter explains the trauma outcome process model in order to help the reader understand different potential outcomes resulting from abuse, depending on how the victim processes what happened. The chapter then discusses prevention and intervention methods and settings, including child advocacy centers, courts who typically hear these cases, child protective services, and so on. Then the chapter discusses unique legal and ethical issues that the reader should be aware of if working with child and adolescent victims.

COMMON MENTAL HEALTH CONCERNS

According to both the Centers for Disease Control (CDC) (Middlebrooks & Audage, n.d.) and the World Health Organization (WHO) (n.d.), common effects of child maltreatment include cognitive impairment and developmental delays, particularly when the child has suffered neglect. To compound these cognitive deficits, maltreated children are more likely to perform poorly in academic settings. These children are at higher risk for developing risk-taking behaviors leading to delinquency and addiction. Children who have suffered maltreatment are more likely to develop eating and sleep disorders, posttraumatic stress disorder (PTSD), anxiety, depression, and non-suicidal self-injurious behaviors, and are more likely to attempt suicide (Middlebrooks & Audage, n.d.; WHO, n.d.). As adults, many develop reproductive health issues and experience challenges with establishing close healthy relationships.

Neglect

There is considerable debate about what constitutes neglect because people do not agree about what the minimum requirements are for child care, or what parental behavior indicates neglect, whether the parent's behaviors must be intentional or not, and what impact the actual parental behavior has on the child's health and safety. However, it is important to define neglect, because our definition shapes how we respond to the issue. *Neglect* is legally defined as "at a minimum, any recent act or failure to act on the part of a parent or caretaker which results in death, serious physical or emotional harm, sexual abuse or exploitation or an act or failure to act which presents an imminent risk of serious harm" (Pub. L. No. 111–320). The CDC (2014) indicates that "failing to provide housing, food, clothing, education, and access to medical care" are neglectful because a child's basic needs are not met; however, this can be complicated by poverty and lack of community resources, as well as investigator bias.

The Keeping Children and Families Safe Reauthorization Act of 2003 (P.L. 108–36) mandated the Children's Bureau to collect data on child abuse and neglect in 2005–2006. They found that among the 1.25 million children in the United States experiencing maltreatment, 61% had findings of neglect (Sedlak et al., 2010). A quarter of these children experienced emotional neglect, over one-third (38%) experienced physical neglect, and 47% experienced educational neglect. Although there are more neglect cases than abuse cases, research tends to "neglect" research on neglect (Mennen, Kim, Sang, & Trickett, 2010).

There are three classifications of neglect including mild, moderate, and severe. An example of *mild neglect* is a parent not ensuring that a child is in a car safety seat. Although this behavior puts a child at risk, the consequence is usually a community-based intervention, like receiving a ticket. *Moderate neglect* may result in CPS involvement to help provide access to community support (e.g., this may occur when a parent cannot afford a coat for a child and therefore sends the child to school during winter without a coat or other weather-appropriate clothing). *Severe neglect* occurs when there is severe harm or long-term neglect issues (e.g., due to poverty). For instance, a child may not have insulin medication for diabetes over a long period of time, which results in serious, even life-threatening health consequences. However, the parent may not have health insurance or any money to purchase the insulin. There are differing ideas about what constitutes neglect, be it physical, medical, environmental, emotional, or educational. The caseworkers' socially constructed perceptions influence their view of what is "normal" or "appropriate." Race/ethnicity, gender, and socioeconomic status of the caseworker affects these perceptions and can trigger implicit bias.

Physical neglect (**Table 5.2**) includes parental abandonment, expulsion from the house, shuttling a child, nutritional, and clothing neglect. *Medical neglect* (**Table 5.3**) includes denial and delay in health care. *Inadequate supervision* (**Table 5.4**), also called *failure to protect*, includes leaving a child unsupervised or with inappropriate caregivers or exposing them to environmental hazards. *Environmental neglect* (**Table 5.5**) includes any environmental factors that place a child at risk of being hurt. *Emotional neglect* (**Table 5.6**) often occurs in combination with other forms of abuse and neglect. It includes inadequate nurturing or affection, chronic or extreme spousal abuse, and permitting the child to use alcohol or drugs or engage in other types of maladaptive behaviors. *Educational neglect* (**Table 5.7**) includes failure to enroll a child in a developmentally appropriate school program, including special education services, or provide homeschool for a child. It also includes a parent allowing a child to be absent an average of 5 or more days each month or a month or more during the school year, without a reasonable explanation (e.g., hospitalization).

TABLE 5.2. Physical Neglect

Abandonment	A parent does not arrange for reasonable care and supervision for a child or has not picked up a child within 2 days of when he or she is scheduled to do so.
Expulsion	Refusing to take custody of a child. Refusing to allow a child to stay in the home, or accept custody of a runaway, and not arranging for care with an acceptable provider.
Shuttling	A parent leaving a child with a variety of caregivers for days or weeks at a time as a method to avoid taking care of the child.
Nutritional neglect	The child is malnourished or frequently hungry.
Clothing neglect	The child does not have clothing appropriate to the weather or situation (e.g., school uniform).
Other physical neglect	Inadequate hygiene, driving while intoxicated with a child in the car, leaving a child in a car unattended, and so on.

TABLE 5.3 Medical Neglect (may be affected by lack of health insurance)

Denial of healthcare	Not following through with healthcare as recommended by a competent healthcare provider for physical injury, illness, medical condition, or impairment. *No federal statute when denial is due to a parent's religious beliefs, but states may find against the parents.
Delay of healthcare	Failure to seek healthcare in a timely fashion. Includes not seeking mental healthcare, if needed.

TABLE 5.4 Inadequate Supervision

Lack of appropriate supervision	Leaving a child unsupervised. Length of time considered inappropriate varies by state and is affected by the child's age, developmental stage, and the situation; duration and frequency of time spent unsupervised; the neighborhood safety and resources; available adults if needed.
Exposure to hazards	Exposure or easy access to safety hazards (e.g., poisons, drugs, second-hand smoke, guns or other weapons, rotting food, animal feces, insect infestation, lack of safe water, not using car seats, etc.)
Inappropriate caregivers	Leaving child in the care of an unsafe or incapacitated caregiver (e.g., with a sex offender or with a grandmother who has dementia).
Other	Leaving a child with an appropriate caregiver, but not providing consent for medical treatment or not providing necessary supplies (e.g., asthma medicine). The caregiver does not supervise the child properly. Allowing a child to engage in harmful behaviors that are risky and/or illegal (e.g., letting a child smoke marijuana).

TABLE 5.5 Environmental Neglect

Practical view	The child's neighborhood or home environment is not safe, lacks opportunity and resources. Focuses on parent not attending to care that is reasonable.
Broad view	Considers both neighborhoods that are not safe and the family situation (e.g., providing safe play alternatives for children living in violent neighborhoods).

TABLE 5.6 Emotional Neglect

Inadequate nurturing or affection	A parent frequently failing to attend to a child's needs for affection, emotional support, or attention.
Chronic or extreme spousal abuse	A parent exposing a child to intimate partner violence that is chronic or extreme.
Permitted drug or alcohol abuse	The parent allows or encourages a child to use alcohol or drugs.
Permitting other maladaptive behavior	A parent allows or encourages behavior that is problematic (e.g., being part of a gang or selling drugs). This presupposes the parent is aware of the activity.
Isolation	A parent refusing to allow a child to interact with age-appropriate peers or safe adults (e.g., a non-custodial parent).

TABLE 5.7 Educational Neglect

Chronic truancy that is permitted	A parent allows or encourages a child to be absent from school an average of 5 or more days each month. The parent must be aware of the problem and attempt to stop it.
Failure to enroll or other truancy	A parent allows a child to miss one month of school or more without a good explanation, (e.g., in the hospital), does not register a child for school, does not allow a child to attend school, or does not provide homeschool.
Inattention to special education needs	A parent refuses to allow a child to engage in special educational services recommended by an evaluation without "reasonable" cause.

The primary concerns related to neglect are that the child's caregiver(s) did not meet his or her basic needs for love, safety, and belonging. As a result, the child is at greater risk for developing insecure attachment patterns. The need for attachment is so significant that in infancy, a child can experience *failure to thrive* when a caregiver does not meet the child's attachment needs, resulting in death. Inconsistent care can result in the child developing an insecure (anxious or ambivalent) attachment and having difficulty accessing appropriate social support systems in times of stress, thereby leading to a host of potential mental health issues ranging from anxiety and depression to personality disorders. If the level of neglect involves a complete lack of consistent empathic experience from a caregiver, as previously described, the child may develop psychopathy because he or she will not develop the capacity to empathize.

Physical Abuse

According to the Centers for Disease Control (CDC) *physical abuse* is "the use of intentional physical force, such as hitting, kicking, shaking, burning or other show of force against a child" (CDC, 2014). Most (58%) findings of abuse result from children who experience physical abuse (Sedlak et al., 2010). Physical abuse is often the "easiest" type of maltreatment to substantiate because there is clear physical evidence of bruises or broken bones or a pattern of injuries and illnesses recorded in medical documentation. Initially, physical abuse causes pain and suffering and sometimes death of a child. Children who survive injuries can develop lifelong physical health issues related to the injuries sustained during abuse. Unfortunately, physically abused children can experience cognitive and language deficits, especially when they have suffered a head injury. In addition to other long-lasting effects, physical abuse can affect emotion regulation long term, resulting in a predisposition to emotional disturbance, addictive behaviors, and an increased risk of becoming an abusive parent themselves.

Children who experience physical abuse have emotional challenges like anger, hostility, fear, anxiety, and humiliation. They often experience low self-esteem and have difficulty identifying feelings and regulating emotions. This results in development of behavioral problems for many physically abused children, including aggression toward others or self-injurious behaviors. Because of the hypervigilance they develop, physically abused children often appear to be hyperactive; however, this behavior is actually a reaction to feeling unsafe and unsure of their environment. Therefore, before diagnosing ADHD, it is important to conduct a thorough assessment to determine if the observed behavior is a function of another trauma-based mental health issue like reactive attachment disorder or posttraumatic stress disorder. Diagnosing incorrectly can delay recovery or even worsen symptoms.

Additionally, these kids often find peer and romantic relationships more challenging and frequently experience difficulty dealing with authority figures like police officers, teachers, and bosses. In fact, we often interpret their reactions toward authority figures as oppositional or resistant behavior. However, if viewed within the context of the physical abuse they have endured, they may feel a need to oppose people in positions of power in an unconscious effort to maintain their integrity and identity and to ward off potential threats from powerful people. After all, the person who physically abused them was an adult caregiver (authority figure) who violated his or her trust and harmed them. Consider what was discussed in chapter 4 about the effect of environmental threats on someone who experienced childhood trauma in relationship to this.

Emotional Abuse

Emotional abuse "includes close confinement, verbal or emotional assaults, threats of sexual abuse (without contact) and threats of other maltreatment, terrorizing, [and] administering unprescribed substances" (Sedlak et al., 2010). In addition, the CDC (2014) indicates that name-calling, shaming, and rejection are emotionally abusive. More than a quarter (27%) of the children found to have experienced abuse were emotionally abused (Sedlak et al., 2010). Emotional abuse tends to occur in families when parents experience stress from financial challenges or work-related stress, have addictive behaviors, or relationship conflict or isolation.

Parents who are emotionally abusive may show little or no regard for the child, talk badly about him or her, refuse to touch or comfort a child, or ignore the child's medical needs. When a child cannot rely on a parent to interact in a manner that is supportive and caring, the child does not internalize a sense of self that is self-caring (van der Kolk, 2014). As a result, these kids often display behaviors indicative of feeling unworthy of love. They may neglect their own needs in relationships and neglect self-care through poor hygiene or not seeking medical care when needed. Some develop self-harming behaviors to punish themselves for not being good enough. These behaviors include non-suicidal self-injury, addictive behaviors, and engaging in relationships that are abusive or allow others to mistreat them because they feel they do not deserve support and love (Oddone-Paolucci, Genuis, & Violato, 2001; van der Kolk, 2014).

The effects of emotional abuse are often "silent." They are easy to overlook or confuse with other causes. Research links long-term, emotional abuse to a variety of social, behavioral, and cognitive functioning deficits (WHO, n.d.). These kids struggle with trying to deal with assaults that are abstract and difficult to label. Emotional abuse attacks a child's sense of self and feelings of worthiness. As a result, they often have a low self-image and unstable sense of self (Perry, 1999; van der Kolk, 2014). Emotionally abused people frequently develop insecure attachments, sometimes being overly affectionate or compliant, at other times exhibiting hostile or passive-aggressive behaviors. This makes it difficult to make friends, form intimate romantic relationships, or function in peer groups at school or work.

As a protective measure, emotionally abused people may avoid relationships or detach from relationships, even with their own children (Sedlak et al., 2010). One manifestation of detachment is that they avoid or restrict play activities and do not take risks in school or social situations (Gil, 2006). Additionally, they may make frequent negative self-statements as a way to take control of the negative appraisal of their abilities, looks, personality, and so on (Middlebrooks & Audage, n.d.). The emotional wounds experienced from abuse can lead to development of addictive behaviors or acting out in such a way that the individual develops legal problems (Oddone-Paolucci, Genuis, & Violato, 2001).

Sexual Abuse

Of the 1.25 million abuse and neglect cases, about one third (24%) were found to have experienced sexual abuse (Sedlak et al., 2010). Child sexual abuse (CSA) affects one out of five women and one out of 10 men, although estimates of male victimization may be underreported due to sociocultural factors (Alaggia, 2005; Alaggia & Mishna, 2014; Staller & Nelson-Gardell, 2005; Stoltenborgh, Ijzendoorn, Euser, & Bakermans-Kranenburg; 2011; WHO, 2004). In fact, a review of large studies in 19 countries found the prevalence rate of male sexual abuse to be 22–26% of the population (Finklehor, Ormrod, Turner, & Hamby, 2005). Additionally, victims of CSA are more likely to suffer additional ACEs. A child's ACE score increased when the abuse began earlier in life, was more severe, had lasted longer, and/or happened repeatedly (Ports, Ford, & Merrick, 2017). Although the text discusses child sexual abuse briefly here, chapters 12 and 13 will discuss sexual assault and sexual offending behaviors in depth.

What Is CSA?

Sexual abuse includes behaviors such as "intrusion, child prostitution or involvement in pornography, genital molestation, exposure or voyeurism, providing sexually explicit materials, failure to supervise the child's voluntary sexual activities, [and] attempted or threatened sexual abuse with physical contact" (Sedlak et al., 2010). According to guidelines for medical and legal care for victims of sexual violence published by the World Health Organization (WHO, 1999),

> Child sexual abuse is the involvement of a child in sexual activity that he or she does not fully comprehend, is unable to give informed consent to, or for which the child is not developmentally prepared and cannot give consent, or that violates the laws or social taboos of society. Child sexual abuse is evidenced by this activity between a child and an adult or another child who by age or development is in a relationship of responsibility, trust or power, the activity being intended to gratify or satisfy the needs of the other person. This may include but is not limited to:

> - the inducement or coercion of a child to engage in any unlawful sexual activity;
> - the exploitative use of a child in prostitution or other unlawful sexual practices;
> - the exploitative use of children in pornographic performance and materials. (p. 75)

A recent development is the increased awareness of child sex trafficking, another form of sexual abuse. *Commercial Sexual Exploitation of Children* (*CSEC*) is a term for what is commonly called sex trafficking. The National Human Trafficking Resource Center answers calls (888-373-7888) or texts (233733) 24 hours a day, 7 days a week in 200 languages.

Child sexual abuse tends to differ from adult sexual abuse. Perpetrators tend to manipulate children, rather than use force. They do this through a process called *grooming*. Grooming initially involves establishing a friendship, gaining the child's trust by offering support in the absence of perceived parental support. Perpetrators gradually sexualize the relationship over time, using these techniques. This process occurs over many weeks, months, or even years. Generally, parents consider these perpetrators as trusting adults. Contrary to many beliefs, rarely are they strangers. In fact, a family member perpetrates about one third of all CSA cases (Sedlak et al., 2010; WHO, n.d.). The abuse tends to occur multiple times with increasing levels of invasion. We consider this an escalation of abusive behavior.

Risks of CSA Victimization

Children who lack parental support or whose parents are emotionally or physically unavailable for a variety of reasons (e.g., mental illness, addiction, single-parenthood, working multiple jobs, etc.) are more vulnerable to victimization because perpetrators can more easily gain access and groom a child who needs adult support (WHO, 1999). In general, children not accompanied by an adult are more likely to suffer victimization. Other relational strain such as being in foster or adoptive care or in step families increases risk. Generally, any child or adolescent experiencing social isolation is at greater risk. This includes sex trafficking victims.

According to FBI crime statistics (Motivans & Snyder, 2018), over half of juvenile prostitution arrests are African American children who are victims of sex trafficking. Los Angeles developed a treatment court model, **Succeeding through Achievement and Resilience (STAR) Court**, to adjudicate these cases. STAR Court reports that all the victims from their court are female and over 91% of them are African American or Latino. Children's Bureau (CB) statistics indicate that between 50% and 90% of sex trafficking victims have been in the foster care system. Additionally, 40% of lesbian, gay, bisexual, and transgender (LGBT) youth are homeless, although they are only 7% of the population, and homelessness is a risk factor for sex trafficking (THORN, n.d.). These kids often report they needed to trade sex for food, money, or a place to stay.

Unfortunately, if a child has suffered previous abuse or lives in a violent family or community (e.g., exposure to domestic violence, gangs, war), then the child is at greater risk of sexual victimization. As such, there is a compounding effect caused by suffering multiple relational traumas, which can result in a phenomenon called complex trauma (Herman, 1992; Perry, 1999; National Child Traumatic Stress Network, n.d.). The National Child Traumatic Stress Network (NCTSN) (n.d.) describes *complex trauma* as "exposure to multiple traumatic events, often of an invasive, interpersonal nature, and the wide-ranging, long-term impact of this exposure." Complex trauma is relational trauma, usually perpetrated by a trusted person who interferes with the child's development of secure attachment relationships, thus becoming an ongoing challenge to seeking support and care in times of stress. As a result, the child often will not seek support or disclose additional traumas.

Unlike adults, children are much less likely to disclose immediately following the event (WHO, 1999). The *child sexual abuse accommodation syndrome* explains why children delay or even retract disclosures. Sometimes, although the child may know that he or she did not like or feel comfortable with the grooming or sexual behavior, it may be that the child does not cognitively understand what has happened and therefore cannot articulate it to a safe adult (Alaggia & Mishna, 2014). In addition, children may question who is "safe" to tell, if the perpetrator is considered a safe person (e.g., teacher, coach, priest, parent, etc.). Perpetrators also use their power position to tell a child that the abuse was the child's fault or that the child is "bad." They may also threaten to harm the child or a loved one or pet. Another threat to the child's safety and security occurs when a perpetrator is the economic breadwinner or the emotional support for a mentally or physically ill parent. Therefore, children often feel helpless and trapped in these situations, and they fear that no one will believe them, so they may accommodate the sexual abuse perpetrator (WHO, 1999).

Abuse disclosures often involve more than a single event. They may occur through a combination of observation of suspicious events or behaviors, inquiries, and investigations. Disclosure may happen accidentally as well. For instance, a child who has a physical complaint, exhibits hygiene issues, or demonstrates obsessive hypervigilance or fearful behaviors may trigger an adult to suspect abuse and either report it or ask about it. Another type of accidental disclosure may occur when an adult overhears a child talking to a peer about the abuse, observes the child playing out sexual abuse with dolls, or reads an account of abuse in a child's journal. The individual who first hears an account of abuse from a child is the *outcry witness*. For investigatory and legal reasons, it is important that this person report to protective services rather than asking a third party (e.g., the counselor) to report it for them. The way this person handles the outcry or initial disclosure can make a big difference in how the abuse affects the child both in the short term and over time.

Short-Term Effects of CSA

A child who is sexually aroused or experiences sexual pleasure or other involuntary physical responses during the abuse can complicate the nature of sexual abuse. Sometimes this results in the child believing that he or she "wanted" the abuse to occur, thus blaming themselves and potentially not disclosing (Alaggia, 2005). Experiencing arousal during sexual abuse may lead to demonstration of *sexually reactive behavior*, exhibiting behaviors outside of what is developmentally appropriate. An example is a toddler who rubs her genitals on a non-offending adult's leg to masturbate. Some pre-pubescent children, even toddlers, attempt to have sex with other young children or insert objects into their vagina or anus to experience sexual pleasure. Children who were abused pre-verbally may not be able to acknowledge the abuse or explain why they engage in the behaviors they do.

Developing a trauma-related disorder is higher among children who experience CSA (Middlebrooks & Audage, 2008; Herman, 1992; Perry, 1999; Sedlak et al., 2010; van der Kolk, 2014). The DSM-5 (APA, 2013) changed the way childhood trauma was diagnosed when it moved from a categorical (has or does not have the diagnosis) classification system to a dimensional approach, which focuses on the extent to which a person displays symptoms of a disorder. At that time, the manual moved child and adolescent disorders into the same categories as adult disorders and discussed these as occurring along a continuum. The APA added a chapter on trauma- and stressor-related disorders (APA, 2013), which includes reactive attachment disorder, a trauma-related disorder usually occurring in children who experience repeated relational trauma. The book also included new diagnostic criteria for PTSD, which specifies symptomology for children and adolescents, in an effort to reduce incorrect diagnoses of attention deficit hyperactivity disorder (ADHD), oppositional defiant disorder (ODD), conduct disorder (CD), and a subsequent escalation of symptomology.

For instance, a sexually abused child may develop PTSD and experience hypervigilance, which appears to look like hyperactivity. ADHD is frequently diagnosed among traumatized children and commonly treated with behavioral contingencies, which can exacerbate PTSD symptoms, thus escalating the child's behavior. With the escalation in behavior, the child demonstrates an increase in non-compliant behaviors around adults, because he or she appraises them as potentially threatening. As such, the child receives the diagnosis of ODD. The resulting cognitive and behavioral interventions do not address the overactive (hot) amygdala and neuro-hijacking of the executive functioning (problem solving, impulse control, decision making) by the overstimulated ANS system. Therefore, interventions aimed at control are experienced by the child as potential environmental threats to his or her safety. With inaccurate diagnoses and ineffective intervention, children who experience sexual abuse are more likely to develop long-term negative effects of CSA.

Long-Term Effects of CSA

Because CSA is a relational trauma, often perpetrated by someone the child trusted, there is a significant negative impact on future interpersonal relationships (Dube et al., 2005; Nelson, 2009; Putnam, 2003). Initially, it affects a child's ability to trust others, not knowing whether they are "safe." Also, people who suffer CSA often feel they are different from other people or not as worthy of love and acceptance as others. So, this can negatively impact their friendships, work relationships, and ultimately their romantic relationships. The ACE studies found a strong positive correlation between CSA and teen parenthood when coupled with witnessing intimate partner violence and experiencing physical abuse (Dietz et al., 1999). It also increases the chances of marrying an addict and generally having more experiences of marital conflict (Dube et al., 2005).

When romantic relationships develop into sexual ones, it may trigger a previously dormant awareness of the CSA resulting in sexual difficulties, which negatively impact the relationship. Some CSA survivors believe their worth lays in the sexual gratification they provide others, so in an effort to connect, they may engage in sexual relationships when they really are not interested sexually in the person with whom they want to connect. This can result in sexual assault victimization, if the survivor engages in this behavior with an unsafe person and tries to stop the sexual encounter. Re-victimization is highly correlated with numbing symptoms associated with PTSD (Ullman, Jajdowski, & Filipas, 2009). Whereas flashbacks, intrusive memories, hypervigilance, and avoidance symptoms have higher correlations with substance abuse, which in turn increased revictimization (Ullman, Jaidowski, & Filipas, 2009).

Research documents long-term psychological manifestations of male CSA, including anxiety, depression and suicidality, addictions, and sexual identity issues and sexual dysfunctions (Chen et al., 2010; Cutajar et al., 2010; Dube et al., 2005; Putnam, 2003; Walrath, Ybarra, Sheenan, Holden, & Burns, 2006). These develop because of their inability to connect emotionally with others. Another significant long-term effect of CSA is development of posttraumatic stress disorder (PTSD) (Briere & Runtz, 1987; Seedat & Stein, 2000; van der Kolk, 2014). In an effort to self-regulate dysregulated moods or to cope with intrusive symptoms of PTSD that make it difficult to relax and sleep, a CSA survivor may use addictive substances (e.g., alcohol, drugs, food) or behaviors (e.g., sex, gambling) to numb these feelings and shut out the memories of abuse. Over time, addictions can develop. However, the most-cited long-term effects of CSA are PTSD and sexualized behaviors (Oddone-Paoluc, Genuis, & Violato, 2001).

Trauma Outcome Process Assessment (TOPA) Model

The manner in which the child makes sense out of the abuse can influence his or her outcome. Trauma outcome process assessment (TOPA) is a research-based theoretical model, which helps us understand how trauma is processed (Borja & Callahan, 2009; Burton, Rasmussen, Bradshaw, Christopherson, & Huke, 1998; Rasmussen, Burton, & Christopherson, 1992; Rasmussen, 1999, 2001, 2004, 2008). The model identifies three typical outcomes after a traumatic experience, including internalization of the distress (originally labeled self-victimization), externalization of distress (originally labeled abuse), and/or recovery or integration (Callahan, Borja, Herbert, Maxwell, & Ruggero, 2013). The TOPA model can help us provide structure for conceptualizing child abuse cases.

> I urge you to continue to apply this model as you think about the material in future chapters that deal with specific types of victims and specific types of offending behaviors. Understanding the systemic influence and effects of abuse will help you understand how best to intervene.

The theory indicates that the response to the child's disclosure of abuse interacts with individual factors, family dynamics, and the ecological context, which ultimately determines the outcome. One potential outcome is *recovery*, which happens if the child experienced the disclosure as one where he or she feels believed and supported, and he or she receives developmentally and situationally appropriate intervention, working through the emotions of trauma and coming to acceptance and integration of the trauma experience into his or her life story (Burton et al., 1998).

We call the second potential outcome *self-victimization* (Burton et al., 1998). Avoiding and hiding feelings associated with the trauma, repression of feelings until they build up and "explode," characterizes self-victimization. This person develops "trauma echoes" and internalizes thinking errors (e.g., "It's my fault," "I am bad and deserved to be hurt," "I am unworthy of love," etc.). Due to chronic emotional dysregulation, this victim exhibits deterioration in self-esteem and associated self-destructive behavior.

The third potential outcome is labeled *abuse* (Burton et al., 1998). If the child feels powerless and appraises the offender as powerful, he or she may identify with the offender in an attempt to regain power and control over his or her own victimization. This client also develops trauma echoes, but he or she externalizes thinking errors onto other people who become his or her victims. This client will experience fantasies of getting back at people for hurting him or her, and as a result, identify and groom a victim whom he or she plans to offend. When the client acts out, offending against someone else, he or she feels empowered. However, he or she experiences shame and/or fear of punishment, which results in reactivating those thinking errors that set this cycle in motion previously.

PREVENTION AND INTERVENTION

Prevention efforts generally work to raise awareness of abuse and neglect, provide skills training, and create community culture that is supportive of victims.

- **Awareness campaigns** target a wide array of people in the community or in schools, fostering discussions of abuse and neglect issues, what to do to avoid abuse, and what to do if it happens to you.
- **Skills training** focuses on minimizing victimization (e.g., relationship and sexual communication skills training, refusal skills, self-defense skills, or parent training).
- **Public policy and legislation initiatives** support a community value that abuse and neglect are wrong (e.g., providing safe school and community resources for kids).
- **Foster care placement**

When a young child enters counseling (e.g., 2–8 years old), the most developmentally appropriate intervention is *play therapy* (Gil, 2006). Much play therapy with abused kids is non-directive in order to facilitate the child's feeling empowered and helping the child move through emotional processing. However, when a child becomes stuck in repeatedly acting out the same scenario, then the play is traumatizing, similar to an adult acting out a flashback of a traumatic event. At these times, counselors must intervene with more directive play therapy methods (Gil, 2006). There are several resources for play therapy with traumatized children, including Eliana Gil's work, which involves integrating directive and non-directive play therapy approaches as well as filial play therapy with abused children. In addition, *theraplay* (Booth & Jernberg, 2010) is a well-researched assessment and intervention protocol that requires specialized training through the Theraplay Institute (www.theraplay.org/). Theraplay, developed by Phyllis Booth and Ann Jernberg, is used to help children who have attachment trauma. It is an attachment-based intervention requiring both the child and one or both parents to participate. Theraplay focuses on specific methods to help a child learn to regulate dysregulated emotions and help parents know how to help their children.

Experiential interventions for older kids, adolescents, and adults who survived child abuse and neglect include *activity therapy* (for example, using therapeutic games or ropes courses to help verbal processing of uncomfortable situations and difficult thoughts associated with the child maltreatment). In addition, *sand tray therapy* is a sensory intervention often used with trauma survivors to help them access sensory images or experiences stored in non-declarative memory. This is particularly helpful for clients who are alexithymic. The sensory experience of feeling the sand (beans or rice can be substituted if sand is not practical) is helpful in accessing emotional material and for self-soothing and strengthening healthy neural pathways.

HIGHLIGHT ON SKILLS: SANDTRAY

Counselors prompt clients to "create a picture" in the sand with miniatures, which you make available. The visual and kinesthetic experience of creating a "picture" helps the client communicate about images or associations that are difficult to articulate verbally. Then, the counselor facilitates verbal processing of the tray by asking the client to tell him or her about the picture. Counselors can add process comments or questions to facilitate the client's process, as the client is able to tolerate verbal processing. By doing this, counselors help the client begin to connect limbic system with cognition, thereby building and strengthening (over time) new neural pathways that help the client build his or her capacity for talking about and emotionally processing thoughts, feelings, and events around the trauma. In similar ways, other types of sensory-based interventions can help clients process through trauma and heal. Throughout the book, different forms of sensory interventions like using art, music, drama, and some behavioral interventions will be presented that may be used to help clients begin to self-regulate.

SETTINGS

Settings in which counselors work with children and adolescents who suffer abuse or neglect vary. However, much of the time, counseling interventions with maltreated children occurs in child advocacy centers, which I discuss next. Counselors may also be involved in going to court if they work with kids in care. Some common court situations will be briefly described, along with some of the settings in which therapeutic services are provided for children experiencing abuse and/or neglect.

Child Advocacy Centers

In 1985, the National Children's Advocacy Center (NCAC) developed a new model for responding to child abuse cases, and now there are over 1,000 *child advocacy centers* (CACs) around the United States and in more than 27 countries. CACs are nonprofit organizations, although they may obtain grant funding from the government, which provide all investigatory and treatment needs for child abuse and neglect victims in a child-friendly atmosphere. Prior to CACs, child abuse investigations often required children to have hospital exams (e.g., to determine if there are injuries consistent with sexual abuse) in an adult-oriented facility, be interviewed at a police department with criminals, go to the district attorney's office to discuss their case, and so on, and these experiences can re-traumatize a child who is already traumatized. Additionally, when professionals not specially trained to work with abuse victims gather information, evidence may be useless for a court case. The professionals are aware of how to engage a child who has been abused in order to gain his or her cooperation in the evidence-gathering process while minimizing further traumatizing the child or tainting the evidence gathered.

Due to concerns about children being developmentally vulnerable to suggestion, which can occur and result in *false memories*, specially trained Child Protective Services (CPS) investigators conduct *forensic interviews* with abused children in a child-friendly environment. The interviews are frequently viewed live (video feed or two-way mirror) by police officers trained to work with child abuse victims, often housed at the CAC. They are able to talk to the specially trained forensic interviewer through an earpiece in order to communicate legal information needed to build a child abuse case against a perpetrator. It may be necessary for children to go to a medical facility for exams, and the nurses providing care have special training to work with the CACs and abused children.

CACs also facilitate *child review teams* (CRTs). The team is an interdisciplinary group of police officers, CPS investigators, forensic evaluators, a nurse, mental health professionals, and a representative from the district attorney's office who prosecutes child abuse cases. They review the evidence from child abuse investigations and when possible the criminal history of the alleged perpetrator to discuss and determine whether the case will be prosecuted. For this reason, it is crucial that when a FMHC suspects child abuse that he or she makes the report to CPS providing as much information as he or she has and then allows the CPS worker to facilitate the investigation.

Courts

There are different types of court that FMHCs commonly attend. The first is *family court*. Family courts deal with family-related issues, such as child custody and child abuse and neglect hearings, for children in state custody. As a FMHC, you may have to attend court hearings to testify as a *fact witness*, to provide information about events related to whether a parent who has a care plan is attending or bringing children to counseling sessions, attending parenting education groups, or generally, doing the necessary work to "get better." Counselors may testify as *expert witnesses*, if they are discussing their clinical impressions of a child or adolescent or family dynamics. Some child abuse and neglect cases result in the victims developing delinquent behaviors like truancy, petty theft, and so on. In these cases, counselors may attend *juvenile court*. There are also *treatment courts* like drug court, veterans' court, domestic violence court, mental health court, and special courts for victims of child sex trafficking who are picked up for prostitution, which counselors may be called to attend depending on the client's circumstances.

Child Protective Services (CPS)

When working with children in CPS custody, counselors may meet with kids in a variety of placements in the community. These include emergency foster care placements, which are often facilities housing multiple kids. Long-term foster care placements may be in a person's home or in a children's home, which is a facility that houses groups of kids in a home-like environment with house parents who care for multiple children. Frequently caseworkers place these children in children's homes because the worker determines that separation from sibling groups into different foster homes may cause additional trauma. Placement of sibling groups often occurs in these institutions because individual families often cannot take multiple children at one time. Also, counselors may work with kids in foster care extension when they need independent living skills as they reach 18 years of age and are about to "age out" of the system.

Other Community Settings

Increasingly, counselors provide services in the community in home-based or school-based mental health services. Generally, if counselors are doing this work, it is through an agency that contracts with CPS or juvenile justice to provide services to *at-risk youth*. If a child has significant behavioral issues, which disrupts placement in a foster home or community setting (e.g., children's home), then the worker may place the child in an in-patient psychiatric facility with intense child and adolescent psychiatric care. This often occurs when a child's assessment indicates he or she presents a significant safety risk to him- or herself (e.g., suicidal) or others (e.g., violent behavior). If the child does needs more intense care than a community setting, but he or she does not need around-the-clock medical or psychiatric care, then he or she may go to a residential treatment facility. Many FMHCs work in these facilities, providing counseling in a therapeutic milieu where kids are in therapy groups and individual therapy focusing on the presenting issues (e.g., eating disorders, drug use, sexual acting out, etc.); they have therapeutic community meetings to work on community-based interpersonal functioning and individual and/or family counseling. Specialized services like activity or recreation therapy, art therapy, or music therapy may also be part of the residential program. These programs are very structured, with little independent time allowed the child or adolescent. They often use behavioral interventions like level systems that work on social learning and behavioral contingency plans to motivate changes in destructive behavior.

ETHICAL AND LEGAL ISSUES

There are common legal and ethical issues FMHCs deal with when working with child maltreatment cases, with some discussed throughout the chapter. However, the text also highlights other areas that are helpful for child and adolescent counselors to use with abuse and neglect clients. Additionally, the text discusses ways counselors can deal with these concerns to prevent problems and minimize risk.

Mandated Reporting and Child Maltreatment Investigations

Mandated reporting is the most important legal issue involved in child abuse and neglect, as it relates to FMHC. State laws legally mandate all mental health professionals report *suspected* or known child abuse or neglect to state authorities. Counselors will make a child abuse and/or neglect report via Internet or phone to the state CPS hotline or a police department (Children's Bureau, n.d.). Counselors will need the child's name, gender, date of birth, and address, as well as parent(s) names, dates of birth and address(es) and phone numbers, and other details regarding the child and the incident. It is entirely likely you will not have all of this information, and that is okay. Counselors can make the report with as much information as you have from the child, non-offending parent, and case file. A state-wide system that tracks reports can provide an investigator information about past reports, past investigations and outcomes, and information on the alleged perpetrator, if past reports have been made, including reports on multiple incidents. This can be helpful, particularly in neglect cases, when there are multiple reports from different sources but no single report results in the hotline deeming the report serious enough to open a case, because multiple reports may be the tipping point for the determination to open and investigate a case. When making a report, counselors should ask what the *reference number* is, so you can include it in your documentation.

After making a report, the CPS worker taking the report will determine if it meets the legal definitions for child maltreatment and follow CPS guidelines regarding response. If the worker determines that it meets legal guidelines, then he or she determines the level of response urgency needed. Most states have a differential response system, also called alternative response, multiple response, and dual tracking. These systems vary between states; however, states generally assign a risk level to the case when reported. The level assigned determines whether a case is opened and whether an investigation will occur. Counselors may ask for the level assigned when you make a verbal report. Often the person taking the report can divulge this information at the time of intake.

States implement differential response systems. The Child Welfare Information Gateway (n.d.a) (www.childwelfare.gov/) identifies six differential responses:

1. **Assessment focused**, which focuses on assessing the family's strengths and needs. Substantiation of an alleged incident is not the priority.
2. **Individualized**, indicates CPS will handle each case based on the family's individual needs.
3. **Family centered**, uses a strengths-based, family engagement approach.
4. **Community oriented**, where workers refer families on the assessment track to community services that meet their needs. The worker must coordinate services with community agencies. Community agencies must have availability to provide services. Child protection is viewed as a shared responsibility.

5. **Selective** families have allegations of serious maltreatment cases and therefore CPS does not provide a differential response. This is true when there may be severe harm to a child, such as sexual abuse.

6. **Flexible** is a response track that can be changed depending on continuous assessment of risk and safety concerns. For instance, if a less severe case results in a caregiver refusing an assessment or refusing to follow up on service referrals, then the CPS may conduct an investigation. Alternatively, if the risk seems to have diminished, then the caseworker may close the case.

If a caseworker "screens in" a case for alleged sexual abuse or severe physical abuse or neglect, the initial investigation will usually begin within 24 hours of the report. Otherwise, most states require initial investigation or differential response assessment to begin within 24–72 hours after receiving the referral.

Although differential response systems vary, they focus on similar principles. These include focusing on the safety and wellbeing of a child; promoting family permanency whenever possible; recognizing that CPS agencies and workers have the authority to make decisions regarding removal and out-of-home placement and when to involve courts; and acknowledging that for some families, community services may be a more appropriate intervention. Cases are either *unsubstantiated,* finding a lack of evidence supporting the allegation and closing the case, or *substantiated*, finding evidence that abuse or neglect occurred and needing intervention.

When a family assessment indicates a need for intervention, a caseworker will develop a *safety plan*, which may allow the child to stay in the home as long as the guardian is following the plan. A safety plan outlines community resources that parents can access like completing a substance abuse counseling or a parenting group at a nonprofit agency, taking a child to counseling with a play therapist, cleaning up their home so that they eliminate safety issues, and so on.

When working with a parent or child referred by CPS, counselors should obtain a copy of the safety plan for record-keeping purposes. Although the plan is significant to the parent, it is common for the parent to misunderstand or misrepresent what the plan says, so it helps the counselor to understand what CPS wants to occur. Additionally, be prepared for the case-worker to ask for updates on the case. When a family enters services through CPS, the child's parent/guardian signs a blanket waiver, allowing the CPS worker to communicate freely with any service provider. However, to be consistent with counseling ethics and laws, counselors should ask for a copy of the release for records prior to talking to anyone.

According the CB, an investigation of child abuse includes the following elements:

- Checking agency records to determine prior involvement of the family with CPS
- Visiting the child's home
- Interviewing or observing the victim
- Interviewing or observing other children in the home
- Risk and safety assessments
- Evaluation of the home environment

- Interviews with the child's parents, caregiver, or other adults residing in the child's home
- Checking criminal records and central registry records for all adults in the home
- Medical and mental health evaluations

HIGHLIGHT ON SKILLS: MANDATED REPORTING

When you make an abuse or neglect report, it is helpful to let a child or adolescent (and non-abusive parent) know that you will not ask any questions about the abuse or neglect. Communicate that you will listen to the child or adolescent and facilitate (using non-directive approaches like empathizing, reflecting, and summarizing) the client's processing of his or her thoughts or feelings related to these events. Similarly, tell parents to provide emotional support and comfort, to express they believe the child, and to listen to the child if he or she wants to talk about the abuse. However, it is crucial that you instruct parents *not* to ask the child questions about potential abuse by another person and encourage him or her to follow through with a forensic interview at the CAC. Take time to explain the process regarding reporting abuse or neglect, and when developmentally appropriate, include the victim in the reporting process. Also, if appropriate, facilitate the call to the CAC to make the appointment for a forensic interview. Explain that you are a counselor, that you have made an abuse report (give the reference number for the report), and tell the person at the CAC that you have the parent/guardian present who would like to make an appointment for his or her child. Disclosing abuse and going through a child abuse investigation is scary for the victim and for the parent(s). It is a crisis, which requires you to provide information and facilitate the process, in order to help them assuage anxieties. If you are able to remain calm and professional during this process, victims and non-offending parents are less likely to experience these events as re-traumatizing.

Court-Appointed Guardians and Special Advocates

Counselors working in forensic settings may interact with court-appointed guardians and court-appointed special advocates. Counselors may also be the first person who explains to a child what this person's role is. A judge appoints a *guardian ad litem* (GAL), when a child's parent is unable to act on his or her behalf. This occurs through a court order that is legally binding. The person can be any competent adult. This person acts on behalf of the minor client to evaluate the necessity for guardianship and the appropriateness of a proposed guardian (e.g., a grandparent).

A *court-appointed special advocate* (*CASA*) is a volunteer guardian ad litem who has gone through an application, evaluation, and background check, and completed specialized training with the CASA for Children program. Although not available in all communities, there are almost 90,000 CASAs in the United States, representing over 280,000 children in care. To learn more about volunteering to become a CASA, you can go to their website at casaforchildren.org.

Mandated Treatment, Care Plans, and Informed Consent

Informed consent includes information from the client or client's representative including a parent, CPS caseworker, foster parent, children's home representative, or other legal guardian who has legal rights to make medical decisions for a child. Some abused or neglected adolescents are legally emancipated from this requirement. In any of these cases, however, you need to have a copy of the court order that specifies who is legally able to make medical decisions for a child prior to seeing the child for counseling services.

As previously noted, parents involved with CPS have care plans, which should be requested at the initial counseling session. The plan will help you understand what the client is required to do to retain parental rights, and it will help you explain this to the parent as well.

When a child enters state custody, the CPS worker becomes the legal guardian for the child. However, there are times CPS may mandate the child's parent to counseling or a parenting group, or the parent may bring the child to counseling as part of the plan. The parent signs a blanket waiver with CPS to have access to all information relevant to investigating the case; be sure to have a copy of this waiver in your file prior to speaking to the caseworker. Clients, even when mandated (child or adult/victim or perpetrator), need to be informed about the policies and procedures involved in counseling, information about confidentiality (ethical standard) and privilege (legal standard), and the limits to confidentiality and privilege.

Confidentiality and Privilege

Confidentiality is the ethical standard that a counselor attempts to uphold in order to engender the client's trust in the relationship. When working with minors, counselors may need to explain to the adults who bring them that confidentiality is very important in building a therapeutic relationship. Without children/adolescents feeling like their communication with a counselor is confidential, they are unlikely to share anything of substance. In fact, they may just sit silently biding their time until the session is over. Kids in care often fear they will cause problems for their families or that they will be put in foster care if they talk to a mental health professional. These are real fears, so developing therapeutic rapport is challenging in the best circumstances. It may be helpful to talk to parents or caseworkers about the need for keeping the child's confidence.

However, it is important to be clear with the adults and the kids so that they know that if it is suspected that there is a safety issue, that information will be shared with the responsible adult(s) in their lives. Counselors should ask the adult parent to trust the counselor as a professional to make that judgment call and remind them that if they do not respect this boundary, then bringing a child to see a mental health professional may be a waste of their resources because it is unlikely to result in a productive outcome.

If a non-offending parent or a caseworker brings the child, he or she may ask that the mental health professional find out whether abuse occurred. The parent or caseworker should be reminded that a counselor's role is to facilitate the child's processing of whatever thoughts, feelings, or events the child wants to. They may also need to be reminded that for young children the developmentally appropriate way to facilitate this is through play therapy, which may not involve any discussion of the events played out in session. There have been many times in my career that I have helped a child in foster care process through trauma without being completely sure what happened. At other times, it is helpful to figure out what happened and ask the caseworker if he or she is aware of it (e.g., they may often say that a counselor validated the report). There is no way to predict what might occur in these cases or whether anything will happen that will help substantiate a case of abuse; in any case, work within a therapeutic role.

Privilege is a legal standard that states a court cannot compel a counselor to reveal communication between a client and the counselor. However, privilege can be waived through the responsible party (legal guardian) signing a release of information. The waiver a parent signs when he or she enters into a care plan is a *release of information*. Generally, this means that the counselor is able to discuss assessment of the case and summary of treatment in court or with a caseworker in order to facilitate the services provided for the child-parental reunification.

Counselor Competency

Counselor competency is the final ethical concern discussed for this chapter. Counselors working with children need to have training on many topics, including, but not limited to, the following:

- Child development
- Child counseling techniques
- Play therapy and other experiential modalities of treatment
- Law and ethics related to child abuse and neglect
- Different types of abuse and neglect
- Crisis interventions
- Risk assessment and intervention
- Specialized trauma counseling techniques

Additionally, counselors working with child maltreatment understand how development may affect processing of traumatic experiences and how to engage both children and caregivers in the counseling relationship. Too many counselors assume that they can work with children or that they can work with trauma without specialized training, and this is unethical and potentially harmful to the child and adolescent clients in their care. Finally, narratives of child abuse and neglect and bearing witness to emotional processing of trauma are difficult. As discussed in chapter 2, it is important that counselors remain aware of their limits and have self-care plans in place to improve the odds that competency issues related to vicarious trauma or compassion fatigue do not negatively affect the welfare of their clients.

Given the high rates of child maltreatment, many emerging counselors reading this text and those working with abuse survivors are, in fact, survivors themselves. This can make it much more challenging to maintain boundaries and not become triggered by the client's issues, particularly when the client is a child. This can lead to *counter-transference* as well.

Counselors may develop anger at the abusive parent or frustration with a caseworker, judge, or system that is working too slowly or that they perceive not to have the child/adolescent's best interest in mind. Alternatively, counselors may develop caretaking or parental feelings toward a child whom they are counseling (e.g., children may ask a counselor to take them home and or be their mommy). Counselors should consult with a supervisor or colleague as needed if boundaries are being tested or weakened in these interactions.

Case Study: Jo Bob Part I

Jo Bob is a 12-year-old Caucasian male presenting for treatment with his caseworker at a community mental health center following disclosure that his mother forced him to perform oral sex on her multiple times between the ages of 6 and 12. Additionally, a Child Protective Services investigation revealed that his stepfather also allowed him to watch pornography and challenged him to do what he watched in the movies with his younger sister and brother. Jo Bob has attended 17 schools due to his mother's nomad lifestyle. His mother, he reports, is a prostitute, and his stepfather is a drug dealer and "hustler." In spite of his moving around a lot, Jo Bob has maintained passing grades with a low 'C' average and has scored high on his standardized testing. A psychological evaluation indicates Jo Bob has a 128 IQ ($m = 100$, $sd = 15$). He appears compliant but does not express any interest in talking in counseling. He is currently placed with a foster family who have two older biological children in the home.

Case Application Questions

1. Describe the possible types of child maltreatment Jo Bob may have experienced and explain your reasoning for drawing these conclusions.
2. Discuss the potential short-term and long-term effects of child sexual abuse on Jo Bob.
3. Using the trauma outcome process assessment model, describe potential scenarios if Jo Bob processes the trauma by internalizing the trauma experiences, by externalizing the trauma experiences, and by recovering from and integrating the trauma.
4. Discuss the types of interventions that would be appropriate for a counselor working with Jo Bob. What about Jo Bob's younger siblings?
5. Discuss the process of investigation and criminal prosecution that is likely to occur in a case like Jo Bob's.

SUMMARY

Chapter 5 defines and discusses neglect and abuse, and their subtypes, including physical, medical, inadequate supervision, environmental, and educational. Neglect can range in severity from mild to severe, and child welfare responses should relate to the type and level of severity of the neglect substantiated. Physical, emotional, and sexual abuse often result in children's involvement with child welfare agencies. Physical abuse is easiest to substantiate, among these; however, emotional abuse is more challenging because of its' "silent" effects on the survivor's emotional and interpersonal functioning.

When children or adolescents experience grooming by an experienced or trusted perpetrator, they may develop child sexual abuse accommodation syndrome, resulting in delayed disclosures of abuse or retractions of abuse reports when interviewed by law enforcement or child services workers. Additionally, some children develop sexually reactive behaviors because of their sexual victimization, which further complicates treatment.

The manner in which the client "makes sense" of his or her experience(s) of abuse and neglect can influence his or her outcome. The chapter describes the trauma outcome process assessment (TOPA) model as one way to conceptualize clients' experiences of trauma and resulting behaviors. The model identifies three typical outcomes after a traumatic experience, including internalization of the distress (originally labeled self-victimization), externalization of distress (originally labeled abuse), and/or recovery or integration.

The DSM-5 provides a range of diagnoses. Due to the interpersonal nature of child abuse and neglect, survivors experience increased vulnerability to developing personality disorders. As powerless victims, these kids develop interpersonal strategies to get their physical, emotional, and psychological needs met; however, over time these interpersonal strategies may be maladaptive. They are more likely to develop subsequent relationships with abusive individuals as well. Working with victims who have developed such interpersonal strategies is challenging and takes special knowledge and supervised practice.

Counselors commonly diagnose child abuse survivors with trauma-related disorders, particularly those with complex trauma. These include diagnoses such as reactive attachment disorder and posttraumatic stress disorder. Victims of child abuse, and child sexual abuse in particular, also experience increased psychological symptomology resulting in diagnoses of anxiety, depression and suicidality, addictive disorders, and sexual identity issues and sexual dysfunctions. Additionally, victims commonly receive diagnoses considered behavioral disorders like ADHD, oppositional defiant disorder, and conduct disorder.

However, misdiagnosis is common among child abuse and neglect survivors. Behavioral and interpersonal manifestations of trauma, resulting from an overactive ANS system, may appear to be hyperactivity or defiance, when in fact, these behaviors result from hypervigilance and fears that an authority figure or other significant relationship will hurt the abuse survivor. Misdiagnosis can result in deteriorating behaviors, because these interventions often re-traumatize clients rather than help them.

The chapter also covered the ethical and legal responsibility of counselors related to reporting child maltreatment and the process for reporting and investigations, and the settings and professionals with which maltreated children interact. Assessment and treatment often occur at child advocacy centers, which are child-friendly centers housing forensic interviewing specialists, police who deal with child abuse cases, health professionals, and mental health counselors. Counselor competency is a major concern with these clients. Working with trauma survivors takes specialized knowledge and supervised practice and working with children and adolescents takes additional specialized training. Properly utilized play therapy with children and experiential therapy with adolescents can help to rework and strengthen neurological functioning.

CHAPTER 5 REFLECTIVE QUESTIONS

1. Discuss the different types of neglect and abuse, as well as their prevalence rates and risk factors.
2. Describe the trauma outcome process assessment model and the three potential victim outcomes resulting after abuse experiences.
3. Discuss the neurodevelopmental impact of trauma as related to behavioral and interpersonal manifestations in victims and resulting diagnostic indications.
4. Discuss the legal and ethical considerations as well as the process for reporting and treating child abuse.
5. Consider that you are a counselor working at a community agency or private practice, and a parent brings in her 11-year-old daughter whose journal she recently read, revealing that the girl had been sexually abused by a neighbor. How would you proceed, and how would you discuss "next steps" with the parent?

RESOURCES

Child Welfare information gateway: https://www.childwelfare.gov/

Mandatory reporters of child abuse and neglect fact sheet: https://www.childwelfare.gov/pubPDFs/manda.pdf

Association for Play Therapy: https://www.a4pt.org/

National Children's Alliance: How the CAC model works: http://www.nationalchildrensalliance.org/cac-model/

Sandplay Therapists of America: https://www.sandplay.org/education-training/education-training-overview/

Ethics in child welfare resources: https://www.childwelfare.gov/topics/management/ethical/casework-ethics/

Juvenile Offenders

- ■ Identify differences in offending behaviors, theories of development of offending behavior, and diagnostic issues related to juvenile offenders
- ■ Discuss historical, sociocultural, and family systems contexts in relationship to juvenile delinquency
- ■ Discuss common legal terms and processes in juvenile justice settings and corresponding ethical dilemmas, which are common

TABLE 6.1 Myths and Mythbusters

Myths	Mythbusters
Juvenile offenders are just smaller versions of adult offenders.	Juvenile offenders are developmentally immature in cognition and psychosocial functioning, which requires unique understanding and approaches from adult offenders.
Juvenile offenders and victims of crime are two distinct categories of people.	Juvenile offenders are frequently victims of crime, particularly child abuse and/or neglect.
Juvenile offenders go through the same system of justice as adult offenders, just in a different location.	The process, terminology, and goals of the juvenile justice system are unique from the adult justice system.

INTRODUCTION

> "The child who is not embraced by the village will burn it down to feel its warmth."
>
> African Proverb

When considering the need for attuned empathic caregiving to nurture and grow empathic children, it is important to consider juveniles who become offenders are lacking something that we, as a society, as professional counselors, must provide. The National Alliance on Mental Illness (NAMI) reports that among the two million kids arrested annually in the United States, 70% have mental health diagnoses, which are proximate causes of their arresting behaviors. However, these kids often are unable to access community mental health services.

Further, incarceration can exacerbate their mental health needs. Many do not receive services while detained, they are isolated from support systems, and correctional facilities use solitary confinement for kids with severe mental illness (SMI) as a way to "control" their behaviors more often than they use it with other kids. Additionally, 75% of these kids are re-arrested within 3 years of being locked up in a correctional facility. Therefore, it is crucial to understand the intersection of mental illness, child welfare involvement (victimization), and juvenile offending behavior.

This chapter discusses kids who become involved in illegal behaviors. It also builds on previous chapters to discuss a portion of child and adolescent victims who cross over into the juvenile justice system. Additionally, the chapter covers information about identification and intervention with the approximately 1.4 million kids who enter the juvenile justice system with a mental health disorder (Smith, H. n.d.).

DEVELOPMENTAL ISSUES

Building on previous chapters, this section presents the difference between juvenile delinquency and adult criminality, competency of minors, and dually involved or crossover youth, ending with a review of major theories on how offending behavior develops.

How Are Juvenile Delinquency and Adult Criminality Different?

The Offices of the U.S. Attorneys (2018) defines a *juvenile* as "a person who has not attained his 18th birthday." However, the law treats someone between 18 and 21 as if they are juveniles, if they committed the criminal act prior to their 18th birthday. However, several states consider someone age 16 or 17 the age of majority for delinquent behavior, whereas in Wyoming it is 19. Although it varies by state, courts do not adjudicate a juvenile as a delinquent unless he or she is a minimum of 6 to 10 years old because legally they lack the *mens rea*, or criminal intent to commit a criminal act. The law considers them unable to understand the difference between right and wrong. Whether someone is a juvenile or not makes a difference in the jurisdiction of the case. In other words, if the court determines someone is a juvenile, then the case will go to juvenile court; otherwise, the case will go to an adult court. However, courts are able to determine whether to try someone as a juvenile or adult by considering maturity beyond age. Judges may even emancipate a juvenile in a civil proceeding so that he or she is an adult, which can affect where a criminal case is handled.

Juvenile delinquency is "the violation of a law of the United States committed by a person prior to his eighteenth birthday which would have been a crime if committed by an adult" (18.U.S.C. § 5031). Individual juveniles who engage in delinquent behavior are referred to as *juvenile offenders*. Delinquent behavior is categorized in three ways:

1. Crimes typically committed by minors, which we address in the juvenile court system.
2. Criminal behaviors that are typically outside of "normal" adolescent rebellion and more typical of adults, which are often dealt with in the adult criminal justice system.
3. Status offenses, which are minor offenses like truancy, running away, or violation of drinking laws, the juvenile system also addresses.

Courts consider juvenile delinquents as having performed *delinquent acts* rather than crimes. Courts categorize these acts as a status offense or as a more serious offense. *Status offenses* relate to the juvenile's age. In other words, someone who is a minor can commit a delinquent act associated with truancy from school or breaking a town curfew. Status offenses may result in the parent paying a fine and court costs, particularly if the charge is truancy. *Serious delinquent acts* are the type that an adult might commit such as theft or assault.

Finally, courts *adjudicate* juveniles rather than try them.

Competence

Competence in juvenile cases refers to the developmental capacity of the youth to participate effectively in court proceedings. It is a legal term, based on court's assessment of the juvenile's level of functioning. The legal standard for competence, described in *Dusky v. U.S.* (1960), requires the juvenile to have a rational understanding of the facts and the process as well as the reasonable ability to communicate with his or her lawyer. In 1966, the U.S. Court of appeals solidified our understanding of due process related to determining competency in juvenile cases when they decided *Kent v. U.S.* (383 US 541). Morris Kent was a 16-year-old boy detained and interrogated by police in relationship to several incidences of rape and robbery. Kent acknowledged some involvement, which led the juvenile court to waive jurisdiction, resulting in a criminal trial as an adult. However, upon appeal, the court found that the juvenile court had not "fully investigated" his competency prior to waiving jurisdiction. Full investigation, according to the majority decision, would include a hearing, access to an attorney, or access to his record prior to waiving jurisdiction.

During the 1990s, legal reforms across the country resulted in lowering the age at which kids could be tried as adults in criminal court. Reforms also resulted in an expansion in the types of criminal behavior, which could result in adult court as well as increasing the severity of punishment in juvenile courts (Torbet et al., 1996). One concern growing from this trend is that we base competence assessments on adult standards. Adults are incompetent to stand trial if they cannot understand charges or participate in their legal defense based on mental disorder (e.g., psychotic) or developmental delay (e.g., mental retardation). These predispose that the person is not developing within normal rages intellectually or emotionally. However, there are child and adolescent developmental issues related to normal cognitive, moral, and affective development, which indicate that youth are unable to function at the level an adult can function, even when the youth is a normally developing person.

To put it simply, kids are kids, not adults. For this reason, the law does not allow a minor to enter into a contract (e.g., buy a car) without a parent/guardian's signature. This relates to our understanding of immaturity of judgment, tested by the MacArthur Judgment Evaluation (MacJEN). Additionally, *McKeiver v. Pennsylvania* (403 U.S. 538, 1971) is a Supreme Court case that supports that the requirements of due process in delinquency cases are not the same as those that regulate criminal cases. This allows the juvenile to remain in juvenile court but also be held accountable for behaviors through a legal proceeding that takes into account the person's maturity to understand and participate in an effective defense.

Dually Involved Youth or Crossover Youth

Kids considered *crossover youth* are those involved with the child welfare system who then cross over into being involved in the juvenile justice system, due to delinquency (Coulton, Crampton, Cho, & Park, 2016). In other words, they have experienced parental abuse or neglect severe enough that Child Protective Services became involved. By definition, therefore, they have experienced trauma. As such, they need trauma-informed interventions. Although there exists a well-established correlation between child abuse and neglect and being *at risk* for delinquency, thinking about and responding to this issue as an intersection of two systems is a paradigm shift (Herz, Ryan, & Bilchik, 2010; Maschi, Hatcher, Schwalbe, & Rosata, 2008). However, the currently used term is *dually involved youth* to describe kids who are involved concurrently in both the child welfare system and the juvenile justice system (Coulton, Crampton, Cho, & Park, 2016).

Kids who experience multiple foster care placements are more likely to become involved with juvenile justice (Ryan & Testa, 2005; Shook et al., 2013; Yampolskaya & Chuang, 2012). Among those kids involved with the child welfare system, males are more often involved with juvenile justice as well. Similarly, CPS involved African American youth are at increased risk for delinquency (Maschi, Hatcher, Schqalbe, & Rosato, 2008; Shook et al., 2013; Yampolskaya & Chuang, 2012). Interestingly, those kids who enter the child welfare system *later* in childhood or in adolescence are at *higher* risk for juvenile justice involvement (Cutuli et al., 2016; Jonson-Reid & Barth, 2000; Kolivoski, Shook, Goodkind, & Kim, 2014; Shook et al., 2013; Yampolskaya & Chuang, 2012), prompting consideration of the value of early intervention.

Development of Offending Behaviors

Theories of offending are either state-dependent prior events focusing on situational factors (e.g., prior victimization) or heterogeneity theories focused on individual characteristics, which are predisposing factors of the victims and offenders (e.g., self-control, stress level, mental health issues). However, interaction between these two methods is an alternative way to understand offending behavior (Miethe & Meier, 1994). Some theories are classical theories (people choose to commit crime) and some are positivistic theories (the environment influences behavior).

Rational choice theory is a classical theory, which explains criminal behavior as simply a rational choice to engage in the crime. This led to the belief that society could deter criminals by punishing them, which is called *deterrence theory*. Cohen and Felson (1979) developed *routine activity theory*, a version of choice theory, to explain cycles in crime. They posit that crime results from the interaction between three routine activities, including the availability of "good" victims, the absence of capable guardians (e.g., parents, police), and the presence of motivated offenders. This theory indicates that social changes can increase the opportunities offenders perceive as good opportunities to commit crime. As a result, they emphasize the role of potential victims' lifestyles and behaviors in creating a situation where a crime may take place. This is a popular theory for juvenile offending.

Sociological theories, like *strain theory*, are positivistic theories, which explain delinquent behavior as occurring because the offender becomes frustrated (strained) because the person perceives he or she does not have the opportunity or ability to achieve social or economic success valued in our culture. As a result, people with low education and low SES are at higher risk for committing crime because they feel alienated, hopeless, and frustrated by their circumstances. Merton (1957), the theory's founder, stressed that once social disorganization or inequalities exist, then those feeling strain from their inability to reach success may normalize a culture where it is acceptable to use crime to achieve success, which otherwise eludes them. *Social disorganization theory*, developed by Shaw and Henry, similarly discusses high population heterogeneity (e.g., culturally diverse), causing frustration (strain), which results in crime if the community is unable to organize itself to interact pro-socially. When a cultural norm develops socializing someone to believe criminal behavior is normal, this is also known as *cultural transmission* of delinquent behavior. Psychological theories are similar to sociological theories in that they explain delinquency through interaction between criminals and their environments. For instance, *social learning theory* (Bandura, 1977) explains criminality as kids modeling behaviors they have experienced or witnessed. So, if a boy has witnessed his father (a good model for a boy) beating his mother, then he beats his girlfriend because he is modeling his father's behavior.

This leads us to victim-offender overlap, which is relevant to those crossover or dually involved youth previously discussed. *Victim-offender* overlap is a phenomenon where victims and offenders share similar characteristics and similar violent experiences as both perpetrators and as victims of violence. This is most often the case in interpersonal violence (Lauristen, Sampson, & Laub, 1991). It is strong in disadvantaged communities, although not in middle-class communities (Berg & Loeber, 2011). This is particularly true in communities that have a lot of violence and street crime, like gangs, whereas it is almost nonexistent in safer communities (Berg et al., 2012). Hans von Hentig (1940), the first to acknowledge this phenomenon, wrote about it in *Remarks on the Interaction of Perpetrator and Victim*. In 1976, Hindelang wrote *Criminal Victimization in Eight American Cities*, which discussed how "eye for an eye" mentalities that served as a cultural norm for laws resulted in retaliation for victimization with offending behavior. Additionally, the interaction between some victims and offenders may result in overlap. For instance, a battered adolescent may kill his abuser in an effort to assert his manliness and save his reputation (Katz, 1988). Alternatively, based on his subjective evaluation of harm, he may kill the abuser preemptively because he "knows" another attack is imminent.

Trauma outcome process theory, as described in chapter 4, indicates there are three ways to process trauma, each leading to a different outcome. If the trauma is addressed in a healthy manner (e.g., acknowledged and counseling sought), then the victim is likely to experience healing and traumatic growth. If the trauma victim develops an identity of self-as-victim, then he or she is more likely to engage in behaviors (e.g., getting intoxicated and walking the street at night or going to a fraternity party) or relationships (e.g., dating an abusive person), which increase the likelihood that he or she will become victimized repeatedly. Finally, if the trauma victim develops an identity as self-as-powerful/offender, then the person is more likely to identify with the offender. The victim is, therefore, likely to engage in offending behaviors because the person wants to feel powerful, as he or she perceives the person who offended against him or her.

CONTEXTUAL ISSUES

Similar to previous chapters, this section will discuss the historical influences on juvenile justice policy. Then, sociocultural influences, including trends related to ethnicity, socioeconomic status, and gender. Finally, the text addresses familial influences related to juvenile offending.

Historic Policy and Case Law Influences

Although there is a table on historical events in juvenile justice for additional relevant legislation and case law, this section will discuss some of the more salient historical trends affecting policy and case law. Shifts in policy occurred over the course of many decades until juvenile courts were established based on the principle that intervention through these youth courts should seek treatment in the community or up to 1 year in a residential facility rather than punishment in jail or prison. However, by the 1960s, it became evident that many kids received 1-year sentences to residential facilities, which were effectively the same as an adult prison. This led to concerns about due process protections for juveniles and several court cases, which changed the way juvenile courts functioned. Therefore, during the 1960s and 1970s, legal systems began moving to deinstitutionalize status offenses so they were diverted to agencies outside the juvenile justice system. You may hear someone talk about a kid being on diversion, which means he or she was adjudicated for a status offense classified as a child in need of supervision. However, a court can adjudicate a delinquent on a status offense and order jail time. The decision whether to divert a case or not is left to the district attorney's (DA) discretion. For instance, a juvenile charged with violating underage drinking laws multiple times, a status offense, may find the DA decides to send them to court for adjudication, hoping for a better outcome with court-ordered substance abuse treatment. **Table 6.2** illustrates the differences between the juvenile court and criminal court proceedings.

The courts established that juveniles are entitled to due process rights (*Kent v. U.S.*, 1966; In re *Gault*, 1967). *Due process* means that there are protections under the Constitution that all parties of legal proceedings are entitled to in order to ensure a fair and impartial hearing.

TABLE 6.2 Differences Between Juvenile and Criminal Court Proceedings

Distinctive terminology	Police take juveniles into custody, rather than arresting them. Police transport juveniles to a detention center, rather than booking into a jail. Rather than a criminal indictment, there is a petition filed for delinquency. Juveniles adjudicated as delinquents, rather than convicted of crimes.
Absence of legal guilt	The court finds juveniles to be delinquent, not guilty, of crimes.
Treatment rather than punishment	The stated purpose of the juvenile court system is treatment of the juvenile and protection of the community, not punishment.
Informal, private court proceedings	Hearings are usually non-adversarial and take less than 10 minutes. The court is closed to the public, in most cases.
Separateness from adult offenders	From the time police take juveniles into custody (arrested), to detention, pretrial, and court hearings, to probation or institutional corrections and parole, the system separates them from adults.
Focus on juvenile's psychosocial history	The court attempts to understand the criminal behavior in the context of the juvenile's social history and psychological concerns.
Shorter terms of supervision and incarceration	Most juveniles are under supervision (probation) or in a detention center (jail) or correctional facility (prison) for only 1 to 2 years, on average.

Due process rights are outlined in **Table 6.3**. However, not all of these rights are due a juvenile offender. Due process rights of juveniles were limited to juvenile cases adjudicated exclusively as bench (judge decided) trials, rather than jury trials (*McKeiver v. Pennsylvania*, 1971). This is because the system intends juvenile court hearings to be informal and non-adversarial, which was contrary to a jury trial. In adjudications, courts must use the standard of proof beyond a reasonable doubt, rather than the lower standard required in criminal courts (In re *Winship*, 1970).

TABLE 6.3 Due Process

These are due process rights of adults. Only some of these are due process rights of juveniles.

Constitutional Amendment	Legal Protection
Fifth Amendment	Courts cannot deprive someone of life, liberty, or property without due process.
	Courts cannot compel someone to self-incriminate themselves in criminal trials.
	Courts cannot try someone for a serious crime unless indicted by a grand jury.
Sixth Amendment	Defendants have a right to a speedy and public trial.
	Defendants have a right to an impartial jury.
	Defendants have the right to cross-examine witnesses.
	Defendants have a right to compel favorable witnesses to appear in court.
	Defendants have right to legal counsel.
Seventh Amendment	Defendants have a right to trial by jury in most civil cases.
Eighth Amendment	Protects defendants against excessive bail.
	Protects defendants against cruel and unusual punishments.

In the 1980s and 1990s, there was a rise in gang activity, including drive-by shootings and car-jackings, which increased concerns that the juvenile system was treating juveniles, especially violent ones, too leniently. Juvenile defendants revealed that older gang members actually chose juveniles to commit certain crimes, because they were aware that juveniles would have more lenient punishments than adult offenders committing the same crime would. Therefore, states began passing more punitive laws. Between 1992 and 1997, all but three states changed juvenile justice laws in transfer provisions, sentencing authority, confidentiality, victims' rights, and/or correctional programming, outlined in **Table 6.4**.

Legislators used language about "getting tough on crime" and "adult crime, adult time" to make their point that consequences for juveniles committing crimes needed to be more stringent. This mirrored the increases in mandatory sentencing and longer sentencing and community supervision periods for adult offenders, during the same time. The result is that some juvenile courts no longer hear certain juvenile crimes. They automatically go to criminal courts instead. Other states have concurrent jurisdiction provisions. In these situations, district attorneys are able to decide whether to file in juvenile court or criminal court (Snyder & Sickmund, 2006). In the past 30 years, research indicates that the court sends more offenders that are juvenile to criminal courts for prosecution and sentencing, and more serve time in adult correctional facilities, than they did before these laws passed.

Historically, there have been three approaches to criminal justice. The first is *retributive justice*, which emphasizes punishment (Gade, 2013). The second is *distributive justice*, which emphasizes therapeutic rehabilitation of offenders (Gade, 2013). Finally, more recently, there is a trend toward restorative justice in juvenile cases. *Restorative justice* rather than focusing on blame and punishment is focused on accountability, making amends, and healing (Center for Justice & Reconciliation, 2018; Van Ness & Strong, 2010). Key principles of restorative justice are that "crime causes harm and justice should focus on repairing that harm; the people most affected by the crime should be able to participate in its resolution; and the responsibility of the government is to maintain order and of the community to build peace"

TABLE 6.4 Changes in Juvenile Justice Laws 1992–1997

Area of Change	Description
Transfer provisions	It is easier to waive jurisdiction and transfer juvenile cases to criminal courts in 45 states.
Sentencing authority	Criminal and juvenile courts have expanded sentencing options in 31 states.
Confidentiality	Laws in 47 states relaxed the confidentiality provisions, allowing increased access to records and court hearings.
Victims' rights	Victims have an increased role in juvenile crime and court proceedings in 22 states.
Correctional programming	Some adult and juvenile correctional administrators developed new programs to address the unique needs of juveniles serving time in correctional facilities.

TABLE 6.5 Historical Events in Juvenile Justice

Date	Event
1880–1920	Large numbers of indigent juvenile immigrants attempted to survive through criminal activity, resulting in children in adult jails.
1856	State Industrial School for Girls opened as a placement for abused, neglected, and delinquent girls.
1899	Illinois created the first juvenile court system in the world in response to juvenile justice advocates Jane Addams, Lucy Flower, and Julia Lathrop, which were staffed by volunteers and funded through charity.
1949	Every state had a juvenile court.
1953	Department of Health and Human Services, Children's Bureau (CB) shifted focus to "at-risk" youth.
1954	**Special Juvenile Delinquency Project** developed practice guidelines for social workers in juvenile delinquency settings.
1960–1970	Society deinstitutionalized juvenile offenders and diverted them to community treatment for status offense.
1961	President Kennedy's Committee on Juvenile Delinquency and Youth Crime created a 3-year federal grant program called the **Juvenile Delinquency and Youth Offenses Control Act** (Pub. L. 87–274). **Division of Juvenile Delinquency Service** provided oversight of 1-year placements at state-run residential treatment centers that were more like correctional facilities than residential treatment. *Kent v. U.S* (383 U.S. 541, 1966) established that a juvenile court could not waive jurisdiction, resulting in trying a juvenile case in adult criminal court, without first having a hearing. This was the first indication that courts should afford due process rights to juveniles, just as they do for adults.
1967	**In re *Gault*** (387 U.S. 1, 1967) the U.S. Supreme Court found that juveniles had the right to due process, including a right to an attorney, in the case of 14-year-old Jerry Gault, imprisoned for 7 years for making a lewd phone call.
1968	**Juvenile Delinquency Prevention and Control Act** passed, funding a national juvenile justice planning and advisory system and establishing the **Office of Juvenile Justice and Delinquency Prevention**, which provides technical assistance, training, research and program evaluation, and shares model programs with local and state juvenile justice entities.
1970	**In re *Winship*** the U.S. Supreme Court found that the standard of evidence for adjudication should be "proof beyond a reasonable doubt" (387 U.S. 358, 990 S. Ct. 1068, 1970). Previously, some juvenile courts used the civil court standard of "beyond a preponderance of doubt," which is a lower standard of proof than that required in criminal courts.
1971	In ***McKeiver v. Pennsylvania*** the U.S. Supreme Court found that juveniles should be given only bench trials (decided by a judge), rather than a jury trial, even if requested by the defense attorney.
1973–2004	**Sentencing juveniles to death**: Courts sentenced 338 juveniles to death, aged 15 or 16 (25%) to 17 (75%). States executed 14% (22), but courts reversed or commuted 86% (134) (Cothern, 2000; Streib, 2005).

(Continued)

Date	Event
1974	The **Federal Juvenile Delinquency Act** (Chapter 403 of Title 18, U.S. Code Annotated §§ 5031–42) passed.
1975	The Supreme Court ruled in **Breed v. Jones** that adjudication in a juvenile court is equivalent to trial in an adult court so a juvenile cannot be adjudicated in juvenile court and then transferred to adult criminal court if they are found not responsible because of double jeopardy, under the Fifth Amendment (421 U.S. 519, 95 S.Ct. 1979, 1975). A waiver hearing must occur before or in place of an adjudication hearing.
1980–1999	Significant rise in violent gang activity.
1988	In **Thompson v. Oklahoma** (487 U.S. 815) the U.S. Supreme Court found that executing juvenile offenders under 16 years old violated the Eighth Amendment.
1989	In **Stanford v. Kentucky** (492 U.S. 361) the U.S. Supreme Court found that execution of 16- and 17-year-olds was constitutional.
1992–1997	States began passing more punitive juvenile justice laws, including 47 states that changed juvenile justice laws in transfer provisions, sentencing authority, confidentiality, victims' rights, and/or correctional programming, resulting in more time waivers to adult courts and more juveniles serving time in adult corrections.
2005	In **Roper v. Simmons** (U.S. 125 S.Ct.1183) the Supreme Court ruled that it is cruel and unusual punishment, thus violating the Eighth and 14th Amendments, to impose the death penalty on anyone under 18 years old at the time of the crime, thus eliminating the death penalty for juveniles.

(Center for Justice & Reconciliation, 2018). It is a process, not an event, in which offenders are able to acknowledge harm he or she caused to the victims, unintended victims (e.g., family members), and the community. It also allows victims, unintended victims, and community members to voice their concerns to the offender directly, if they want to. A professional, like a counselor, who helps guide the stakeholders to answer, facilitates the process:

- Who has been hurt?
- What are their needs?
- Whose obligations are these?
- What are the causes?
- Who has a stake in the situation?
- What is the appropriate process to involve stakeholders in an effort to address causes and put things right? (Zehr, 2005)

This is different from the criminal justice focus, which is what laws were broken; who did it; and what consequences should offenders have for their actions? (Zehr, 2002). Dr. Carolyn Boyes-Watson (2014) of the Center for Restorative Justice describes the process as

[a] growing social movement to institutionalize peaceful approaches to harm, problem-solving and violations of legal and human rights. ... Rather than privileging the law, professionals and the state, restorative resolutions engage those who are harmed, wrongdoers and their affected communities in search of solutions that promote repair, reconciliation, and rebuilding of relationships. Restorative justice seeks to build partnerships to reestablish

mutual responsibility for constructive responses to wrongdoing within our communities. Restorative approaches seek a balanced approach to the needs of the victim, wrongdoer, and community through processes that preserve the safety and dignity of all. The process can include victim and offender dialogue, victim impact panels, family group conferencing, community and school conferencing, peacemaking circles, reparative boards, truth/reconciliation commissions, restorative community service, restitution, victim support and services, and reintegration services.

Sociocultural Influences

Although laws were adjusted to ensure fair treatment of juveniles, inequities in the justice system continued. In fact, there is systemic bias called *institutionalized racism*, which results from a history of bias ingrained in the justice system built by majority culture (White, male, middle or upper class). Some consider the criminal justice system to be the *in*justice system for this reason. Just as the "baked-in" bias against minorities is real, so is the bias against other minority groups. Counselors must therefore view all information, statistics, studies, and so on that deal with crime and criminals with a critical eye. To this day, although there are protections under the law, the outcomes are different for minorities, women, and lower SES citizens (Elliot, 2007).

The Legal and Policy Subcommittee of a joint collaboration of the child welfare and juvenile justice systems of Santa Clara County, CA, created the following guiding language, which is helpful in changing our perception related to sociocultural influences affecting delinquent youth:

> Paradigm shift begins with an acknowledgement of the context in which we are operating. The environment that we, and the families that are the focus of our work, exist in is profoundly unequal. It should come as no surprise that the greater the level of inequity prevalent in a society, the greater the level of poverty and violence. We cannot fully understand and grapple with the challenges faced by the youth we serve without acknowledging the uncomfortable realities that shape our environment.
>
> At a minimum, we must fully acknowledge that the system induced trauma, past and present, shape the way youth and families respond to system involvement. We must acknowledge that historically, systems have perceived, characterized, and talked about families they serve through a deficient lens. Just as importantly, we must acknowledge that discrimination and oppression actively work in small and large ways to create and perpetuate the problems presented to us in the work that we do. In order to create informed and effective practices that move us closer to the outcomes we seek, we must shift our paradigm and consider every issue we discuss through this broader, more holistic lens. (Santa Clara County, 2013, p. 15)

One example of institutionalized racism affecting juveniles and adults is *racial profiling*, which occurs when law enforcement targets someone based on ethnicity, often humiliating and frightening them. Although it is unconstitutional, due to the law requiring equal protection for all citizens, and ineffective, it continues to occur, resulting in alienating entire communities from law enforcement. Racial profiling results in more minorities being arrested, as well as being more likely to be imprisoned for the same crimes committed by White counterparts who are not arrested, fined, or imprisoned (Dolan & Carr, n.d.).

In fact, racial disparity in arrest rates among juveniles grew by 24% over the 10-year period between 2003 and 2013 (Royner, 2016). Arrest rates for Black youth were 129% higher than White youth, and once adjudicated, courts were 19% more likely to incarcerate Black youth. During the same time, the rate of juvenile incarceration fell by 51% overall, which is good. However, under the federal Juvenile Justice and Delinquency Prevention Act of 1988, states are required to address racial disparities in incarceration rates, and since these rates only fell 43% for Blacks and 28% for American Indians, the rate of racial disparity was effectively increased (Royner, 2016). In 2013, American Indian's had incarceration rates that were three times higher than Whites, and Black juveniles rates were four times higher (Royner, 2016). Additionally, Hispanic youth were 61% more likely to be incarcerated than Whites.

Additionally, according to the Brookings Institute, the highest rates of incarceration exist among those who live in poverty (Kearney & Harris, 2014). In fact, poor people of color are much more likely to be arrested and incarcerated for minor offenses (Dolan & Carr, n.d.). Similar to concerns raised in the previous chapter on child abuse and neglect, individuals living in poverty may experience the system deeming their survival choices as criminal. This leads to what is termed the *criminalization of poverty*. Additionally, once arrested, many languish in jail because they cannot afford bail (Tolan, 2017). Additionally, due to over-burdened court dockets, many have multiple continuations, resulting in their cases taking years to resolve, unless they plead guilty. For some poor individuals, pleading guilty is the best way to have resolution, rather than staying locked up in jail. However, once they have a criminal record, it can affect their future educational and employment opportunities. Bail is a business, which brings in $14 billion dollars annually and has its own trade organization, the American Bail Coalition (ABC) (Greenwald, 2017). Their lobbying efforts result in perpetuating the race and class stratification in this country. However, increasingly, due to improved public awareness, legislators across the country are passing laws to disallow locking anyone up for a misdemeanor offense, which is a first step toward addressing the poverty impact on involvement with the justice system.

Family System Influences

The primary family influence on juvenile delinquency is the parent-child relationship. Research indicates that high levels of parental support relate to low levels of delinquency, including responsiveness, acceptance, affection, support, sensitivity, and communication (Hoeve et al., 2009). Another parental relationship quality related to delinquency is the level of control or demands parents place on the child. *Authoritative* parent style is child oriented, using inductive discipline techniques, like guiding behavior, simulating responsible behavior, and so on. This style is linked with low levels of delinquency, whereas an *authoritarian* parenting style correlates with high levels of delinquency. Authoritarian parenting includes adult-oriented parenting that is coercive, restrictive, and uses harsh punishments and withholding affection. Authoritarian control may involve two distinct types of control, *behavioral control* (attempts to regulate a child's behavior through rule setting and monitoring behavior) and *psychological control* (withholding affection, encouraging dependency through guilt). Behavioral control correlates with externalizing problems (e.g., antisocial behavior). Psychological control correlates with internalizing problems (e.g., anxiety, depression).

Family structure influences parenting. For instance, two parents raising their biological children demonstrate higher levels of monitoring, supervision, and attachment with children than all other family structures. Kids growing up in these families also exhibit lower levels of delinquency (Parks, 2013). More conflict in a family is associated with single mother and blended families, and increased familial conflict correlates with increases in delinquent behaviors. However, the single most important characteristic of family structure, which lowers delinquency rates, is having a father in the home (Comanor & Phillips, 2002).

However, exposure to parents who are involved with illegal activity themselves or are permissive of the child's involvement in illegal activity are more likely to raise kids who perpetrate crimes. Through social modeling and desire to "fit in" to a family or community, many kids will develop *delinquent identities*, a belief that one's own identity, who he or she is, necessarily correlates with delinquent behavior. In some communities, violence, drug use, or other illegal behavior is a way to integrate the child into the community or family norm of criminal behavior. Therefore, to be part of the family or community, the child participates in similar behavior in order to connect with important attachment figures.

When we take all of the contextual information and our understanding of interpersonal neurobiology into account, family influence is probably one of the most important factors impacting rates of delinquency. Those parenting styles and family identities that describe behaviors considered abuse or neglect are discussed in chapter 3. As previously discussed, ACEs resulting from abuse and neglect increase risk for developing delinquency.

COMMON MENTAL HEALTH CONCERNS

Experiences of relational trauma, living in unsupportive families and communities, being part of one or more marginalized groups (e.g., poor, person of color) result in high levels of stress on the individual and the systems in which they live. With increased stress, mental illness often develops. Among delinquent youth, the high numbers of mentally ill juvenile offenders involved with the justice system is a crisis. According to a study conducted by the National Center for Mental Health and Juvenile Justice (NCMHJJ) and the Council of Juvenile Correctional Administrators (CJCA), 70.4% of youth in the juvenile justice system have one or more mental health diagnoses, and 60% had a substance use disorder (SUD) (Shufelt & Cocozza, 2006). Additionally, 79% had a comorbid diagnosis and over 60% had three or more mental health disorders. However, female juvenile offenders have higher rates (80%) of mental illness than males (67%), due to high rates of internalizing behaviors like anxiety and mood disorders (Shufelt & Cocozza, 2006). However, when comparing externalizing behaviors like SUDs and violence, males and females appear similar in rates of mental illness. Additionally, having a relational trauma history results in more complex mental health profiles. Between 20% and 27% of these kids have severe levels of mental illness (Cocozza & Skowyra, 2000; Shufelt & Cocozza, 2006). Therefore, there is a significant need among kids involved with the justice system to have mental health treatment.

Criminal behavior is necessarily antisocial because by definition the criminal is breaking social norms and rules. However, diagnostically, we conceptualize antisocial behavior among youth differently than it is for adults. Among adolescents, some level of rebellious behavior is developmentally appropriate. This is different from sociopathy, another criminal or sociological term that describes antisocial behavior. For a kid who is a *sociopath*, caregivers or the community may have contributed to the belief that criminal behavior is normal or desirable. Another typical diagnosis for adolescent offenders is a substance use disorder or a behavioral addiction like Internet gaming disorder, gambling use disorder, or sexual addiction, which can lead to illegal, dangerous, or violent behavior.

Rebellion from family and community norms is part of an adolescent's process of establishing a separate identity from parents. One way systemic biases manifest is when a police officer, district attorney, or judge makes decisions unconsciously based on how they relate to or understand a kid's rule-breaking behavior. These people are in positions to make decisions regarding who they arrest, adjudicate, and how they decide sentences. As a result, if they identify with the youth (e.g., "All kids drink alcohol and make stupid decisions, but we don't want to ruin the boy's life"), then the consequences are likely to be less than if they do not identify with the kid (e.g., "Unfortunately, he's a kid whose parents are screwed up, living in foster care or a drug-infested home and community, so it makes sense he'll end up in jail").

Common diagnostic categories for juvenile behavior that we consider antisocial include attention deficit hyperactivity disorder (26.5%, resulting in impulsivity), oppositional defiant disorder (noncompliant behavior), and conduct disorder (intentionally harming a person or animal or destroying property). Approximately 70% of females and 60% of males incarcerated meet the criteria for conduct disorder (Odgers, Burnette, Chauhan, Moretti, & Reppucci, 2050). True antisocial personality disorder (APD), considered conduct disorder grown up, however, is the only personality disorder that requires the person to be at least 18 years old. APD is a diagnosis similar to the criminal term psychopathy. Someone who is a *psychopath* does not have the capacity for empathy. In other words, he or she did not receive empathically attuned caregiving on a consistent basis in the first 3 years of life, so he or she did not internalize the ability to empathize.

Many kids growing up in chaotic families or communities, as well as those with addictive disorders (50%), develop mood disorders as well. Comorbidity rates are 30% for females and 20% for males. There are kids in the system who have major depression (30.4%) or bipolar disorder (17.3%) (Odgers et al., 2005). Some drugs, like hallucinogens, can actually trigger a psychotic episode. For those juveniles who have a genetic predisposition to psychosis (e.g., a schizophrenic grandparent), they may develop a psychotic disorder (e.g., schizophrenia, schizophreniform, schizoaffective disorder, etc.).

Being part of the system can result in anxiety and trauma for kids, so these are additional diagnoses to consider. Anxiety rates for incarcerated youth is 30% compared to 4.1% of kids in the community (Odgers et al., 2005). Although 90% of kids incarcerated in the United States endorsed at least one traumatic event, doctors only gave between 12% and 14% a PTSD diagnosis (Odgers et al., 2005). However, when using a standardized psychiatric diagnostic interview, 48.9% of females and 32.3% of males met the diagnostic criteria for PTSD (Odgers et al., 2005). Considering the high rates of mental illness among juvenile delinquent youth, it is crucial that we work on effective prevention campaigns and develop research-informed interventions to meet the needs of these kids.

PREVENTION AND INTERVENTION

Prevention necessitates that we evaluate kids based on individual and family risk factors. Some individual risk factors are low intelligence, impulsiveness, aggression, lack of empathy, substance use, and restlessness (Bartol & Bartol, 2009; Farrington, 2002; Graham & Bowling, 1995; Kirk & Sampson, 2013; Viding, 2004; Walklate, 2003; Weigel, 2012). If a kid demonstrates aggression, then peer rejection is a compounding factor that increases the risk of developing criminal behavior (Bartol & Bartol, 2009; Monea & Thomas, 2011). Developmental history sometimes reveals these kids experienced language delays, poor emotional self-regulation, and, for some, cruelty to animals (Bartol & Bartol, 2009). Family factors, previously described, include family structure, having a father in the home, parental supervision, and abuse or neglect, as well as witnessing domestic violence (Graham & Bowling, 1995; Viding, 2004). Additionally, adolescents who have a sibling involved in criminal behavior are more likely to become criminals as well (Bartol & Bartol, 2009).

Given the strong link between family and community violence and delinquency, the primary prevention or early intervention method is preventing or intervening in situations of neglect or abuse. The National Institute of Justice provides a current list and description of evidence-informed practices and programs for both prevention and intervention at Crime-Solutions.gov. Some evidence-informed practices are diversion programs, treatment courts, mentoring programs, and school-based bullying prevention and dating and sexual violence prevention programs (National Institute of Justice, n.d.). The Substance Abuse and Mental Health Services Administration (SAMHSA) encourages collaboration between community-based mental health providers and the criminal justice system (SAMHSA, n.d.). SAMHSA uses the *sequential intercept model*, which uses five intercept points where criminal justice officials connect juveniles with mental health issues with community mental health resources. Intercept 1 is community and law enforcement interaction. At this point, the system directs kids into early diversion programs and/or teen court programs. Intercept 2 is arrest and initial detention or court hearing for adult offenders. Intercept 3 is jails or specialty courts. Jail diversion programs divert people with mental health concerns to treatment courts. There are a variety of treatment courts, including drug court, trafficking court, juvenile treatment courts, and others primarily used with adults. Intercept 4 is re-entry from jails and prisons into the community. SAMHSA's offender reentry program enhances and expands substance use and mental health treatment for adult offenders returning to their families.

Generally, juvenile offender mental health programs almost exclusively utilize manualized cognitive behavioral interventions. Although a multitude of studies indicate they are evidence-based practice, in fact the setting for these studies in controlled settings (e.g., prison or psychiatric facility) and the time for the study is usually time limited. Longitudinal data indicates that the positive effects noted are lost over time.

Finally, research suggests that juvenile offenders whose families are engaged in their treatment are more likely to have positive outcomes (Garfinkel, 2010; McCartin, n.d.). Counselors can work with parents on parenting and communication skills to improve expectations and disciplinary interventions. It is important to understand that there are barriers to family involvement. For instance, two-thirds of parents take time off work without pay to support their child through the system (McCartin, n.d.). One in five families has to take out a loan to pay for court costs, and one in three report they choose between basic necessities and making court payments (McCartin, n.d.). Also, lack of transportation is a barrier for many juvenile justice-involved families. For these reasons, only 32% of families follow through with these services, which facilitate a smooth transition to the community post-release (McCartin, n.d.). Barriers such as inability to take time off work, lack of access to transportation, and lack of funds to pay court costs can leave families feeling powerless and frustrated by the system (McCartin, n.d.).

However, the involvement of family members cannot be overvalued. Supportive family involvement helps reduce anxiety for youth in the system. It also reinforces the importance of treatment, including using psychotropic medication appropriately and attending counseling. Parents can serve as advocates for children and help articulate concerns and needs that the child may be unable to do independently. Additionally, parents involved with incarcerated juveniles are more likely to help their kids' transition home successfully (Garfinkel, 2010). Families benefit from being involved because they are aware of what is happening to their children, which is often a source of anxiety for parents or siblings. They are in a position to ask questions and learn about both the expectations for them and for their child, as well as the process for making informed decisions about interventions. Families often feel valued as important resources when they are connected and involved with the child's recovery. Families provide important historical information and insights into a kid's personality for juvenile justice staff. Finally, having parents involved emphasizes a shared responsibility for success post release.

SETTINGS

Juvenile courts adjudicated 42% of the kids who had petitions before the court (Hockenberry & Puzzanchera, 2017). For status offenses, 56% received formal probation as the most restrictive court order. Only 6% resulted in out-of-home placement (Hockenberry & Puzzanchera, 2017). The court dismissed 76% of status offense cases and 15% resulted in informal probation, and 9% in voluntary dispositions (Hockenberry & Puzzanchera, 2017). *Diversion* from formal juvenile court processing is available for some minor juvenile delinquent behavior. *Problem-solving courts* are called teen courts, youth courts, or peer courts. The purpose of these settings is to provide an alternative disposition for juveniles committing minor offenses. Volunteers usually staff them, although they usually function in cooperation with local juvenile courts and detention centers. Kids usually admit guilt or plead no contest, in order to take advantage of these venues. Sentencing based on restorative justice or restitution principles involves the juvenile taking responsibility for and attempting to make amends to victims and the community for his or her illegal act. Community service is a common form of restitution. However, if the teen's crime involved alcohol or drugs, then psychoeducation on substance use and abuse is a minimal requirement.

There are also juvenile *justice drug treatment courts* for kids who have behaviors indicating problematic alcohol or drug use. According to the Office of Juvenile Justice and Delinquency Prevention (OJJDP) (2016), these courts "are designed for youth with substance use disorders who come into contact with the juvenile justice system" (p. 5). Over one million 12- to 17-year-olds has a substance use disorder, and substance abuse during adolescence is particularly damaging because the brain is still developing. It can alter brain maturation, especially related to emotion regulation, cognition, and executive functioning (e.g., problem solving, impulse control, decision making). Problem substance use in adolescence also significantly increases the likelihood of long-term addictive disorders. Treatment courts are comprised of multidisciplinary treatment teams, which include attorneys, caseworkers, mental health professionals, and a judge who acts as treatment team leader. Kids generally come before the treatment team more often than they would in juvenile court.

Juvenile detention centers are secure facilities, similar to jails, for minors who the court determines need more external controls or supports than can be provided in the community. Juveniles may be in detention while they await an initial hearing, or they may be taken into custody for a period of time following sentencing. At times, kids go to detention because they violate probation orders. Probation necessarily implies that a juvenile is trusted to follow through with certain behaviors (e.g., going to school, not hanging out with delinquent peers, not drinking or using drugs) with little external controls. However, when the juvenile demonstrates that he or she is unable or unwilling to abide by probation orders, then the juvenile is communicating to the court that he or she needs additional support, or external controls, to help him or her stay within legal behavior. Detention centers provide mental health counseling services and educational services. This may be a setting in which counselors may work as forensic mental health counselors helping kids with adjusting to the facility, making better choices, and managing emotions.

Some juvenile detention centers also house *boot camps*, which are military-style programs. Some are organized based on level of supervision needed (Peters, Thomas, & Zamberlan, 1997).

For instance, when I worked in Texas, we had level-four boot camps that were basically day programs. The juveniles attended the boot camp during the day. They had their meals, mental health counseling, schooling, and exercise programs for 8 hours during the day and then returned home to sleep. There was a level-five boot camp, where the juveniles slept at the detention center in cells. The goals of juvenile boot camps are to deter criminal behavior and incapacitate or control the juvenile from being involved in risky behavior, rehabilitation, punishment, and controlling cost (Peters, Thomas, & Zamberlan, 1997).

Juvenile justice alternative education programs (JJAEP) are a less restrictive form of intervention. However, the aim is still to reduce delinquent behavior and increase offender accountability. Kids may be sent to JJAEP (or JJ for short) after being expelled from school for disciplinary reasons. In order to maintain their academics and also attend to the behavioral issues, JJAEP is an alternative educational placement. These programs have several goals, including increasing accountability for choices, recovering course credits (since many juvenile delinquents have academic problems), improving social skills and prosocial behavior, developing leadership skills, and reducing delinquency behaviors. Generally, these programs are community-based programs through the juvenile probation system, which provide academic interventions based on self-paced instruction, smaller classrooms, and level systems to manage behavior. Therefore, there are educational and probation professionals on site who address counseling needs, behavior modification, and character building.

ETHICAL AND LEGAL ISSUES

Courts may find a juvenile delinquent for a variety of different behaviors. *Status offenses* are age-related offenses, which are illegal for adults. Status offenses include truancy, running away, curfew violations, and violating underage drinking laws. *Minor in possession*, also referred to as PAULA, possession of alcohol under the legal age, is a misdemeanor offense. Punishment for this crime generally involves a fine and community service. Juvenile courts can deal with *felony offenses*, or the court may waive jurisdiction to criminal courts.

Of the 40 largest urban counties, approximately 7,000 juveniles have felonies, nearly two-thirds with violent felony offenses, like assault and battery, sex crimes, or murder (Rainville & Smith, 2003). Most (55%) have jurisdiction waived to adult courts. Forty percent of these were within 1 year of majority. A little over half (52%) were released prior to trial, although those charged with violent felonies were released less often (45%), with murder charges resulting in detention pending trial most often (90%). Among those adjudicated, 66% reach findings of guilt.

The court may issue a subpoena for counselors to attend court and may subpoena their records through a *subpoena duces tecum*, which means subpoena for production of evidence. It is a court order requiring counselors to bring a physical copy of their records to court at the specified time and place. The only records counselors would bring to court are assessments, diagnostic information, treatment plans and updates, progress notes made after each session or communication, and treatment summaries or termination summaries. When attending court, counselors should not bring memory aids or process notes, which you keep in a separate location from the file.

This often presents an ethical dilemma for counselors who are concerned about the client's ethical right to *confidentiality* and legal right of privilege. The client may waive the *right of privilege*, and in the case of a juvenile, the parent or legal guardian may waive this right. If the client or a representative waives the right of privilege, then the counselor must provide the documentation to the court. Counselors should consult their liability insurance risk management office or an ethics advisor and the ACA ethics consultation line regarding options counselors have when taking the records to court. Given that juvenile and family courts are most interested in treatment and rehabilitation, judges are often amenable to receiving treatment summary and answering questions, which would not harm the client's progress in treatment. However, counselors must attend the hearing with available records and ask the court for this leeway because counselors believe it is in the client's best interest.

The court may subpoena a counselor as a *fact witness*, which is sometimes a clinical professional who has personal knowledge of events pertaining to the case (e.g., he or she is treating or has assessed a defendant or someone on probation). The court may also call counselors to testify as an *expert witness*, which is a witness who is "qualified as an expert by knowledge, skill, experience, training, or education" (Federal Rules of Evidence, Article VII Rule 702). The court may allow an expert witness in order to explain to the court scientific or specialized knowledge (e.g., the neurobiological effect of trauma on acting-out behaviors).

Finally, counselors may attend less formal *probation hearings*. These hearings usually provide the judge with information from the probation officer, parent, juvenile, and treatment provider(s), which helps the judge understand whether the juvenile is following the probation orders. If not, then the judge may provide some information or engage the juvenile in question and answer to help him or her understand the requirements and the consequences for following or not following the order. Sometimes, the judge orders the juvenile to be detained overnight or for a weekend or go to a more restrictive placement (e.g., level-four boot camp).

> In my experience, judges are different in the level of formality/informality in their courts. You will likely come before the same few judges, so you will learn their idiosyncrasies. However, the probation officers are usually a good source of information if the judge has particular "pet peeves." For instance, a judge may require you come to court in a tie or in dress shoes, admonish people for reading while waiting to appear before him if sitting in court, or may prefer everyone to stand before the bench and jump in with information or be formally called on to provide information.

With mandated clients, informed consent is always a concern. It is important to gain both the parent or legal guardian's consent and the juvenile's *assent* on the documentation. Given that the adolescent may defer to a counselor because of the mandated nature or due to the power differential that naturally exists between adults and minors, it is crucial that counselors take time to explain the informed consent and limits to confidentiality thoroughly, prior to the assent.

I like to meet with the parent or legal guardian first to go through the consent at length, and then I do the same with the adolescent. I actually read it line by line, checking for understanding. When I ask whether the parent or juvenile understands the provision in the informed consent, and they say yes, I then ask that they explain it to me in their words. If I am concerned that they still may not fully understand or if I have experience that a particular line is troublesome in practice, I will provide a scenario that helps translate the jargon of an informed consent document into a real-life situation. Generally, this generates more conversation. Although this process can be time consuming, I found it invaluable to establishing a genuine trusting relationship with the client and the parent/legal guardian. Another complicating matter is that many mandated treatment programs or court orders really limit confidentiality of the client.

Sometimes it is so significantly limited that maintaining confidentiality is your discretion, in effect. For instance, a community-based juvenile sex offender treatment program I ran had very limited confidentiality. We were clear with clients from the beginning that being in a community setting, rather than detention, was a privilege, and that community safety was our first concern. As a result, they had very little confidentiality. The treatment team or I (as program director) determined if their parent, probation officer, or another involved agency/school official needed to be informed about something that may indicate needed supervision enhancements in order to "keep them safe from offending again and ending up in jail." I always discussed any recommendation I made during probation hearings to place them in a more restrictive environment as their "behavior communicating to us that they need more support to stay safe from committing another crime that may end up in a prison sentence." Although they still did not like these restrictions or recommendations, they were never surprised about the outcome of a probation violation, and they believed I had their best interest in mind whenever I made a determination to limit confidentiality.

Case Study: Leroy Part I

Leroy is the youngest of five children in a middle-class family on the south side of Chicago. His parents own several successful small businesses. He reports coming from a strong family unit where expectations were high and tolerance for misbehavior low. He reports that his father is the head of the family, "as the Bible says it should be." He reports that when his mother or the children "get out of line," his dad "yanked them back in line." The family is active in the Olive Branch AME church, and he participates actively in the choir. Leroy is in middle school; his parents decided to bus him to an all-White school on the north side of Chicago. They perceived this as an honor to be able to send their child to a school that was at the forefront of education. Leroy reports knowing that the expectations were that he perform well academically and socially in order to be an example of a socially and academically responsible Black man.

However, they did not ask Leroy his feelings about this "experiment." Most of Leroy's friends were attending a different school, and he had been a popular young man at that school and done well academically. However, he knew not to question his parent's authority on this matter. As a student at the school, he experienced racist taunts and even physical assaults from White kids who met him and a few other Black friends at the door of the school daily to threaten them and tell them they didn't belong.

The White kids who bullied Leroy and his friends were removed at some point during the school year because of their behavior; however, one day the bus driver brought the boys to a White neighborhood and told them to get off the bus. There were White people waiting with baseball bats taunting the boys. He reports knowing that he needed to either run or get beaten. Faster than some of the other boys, he ran, even though he knew that this meant sacrificing a friend. He reports ongoing shame and guilt at what happened to the boy who ended up in a coma and permanently brain damaged from the beating he received that day.

Although he never reported to his parents what happened, out of fear that they would disapprove, he began declining in academic achievement, began getting involved with a local street gang that vowed to protect him, and began doing drugs and drinking. Within a year, the police arrested him for simple assault and drug possession and he headed for his first stay at a juvenile detention facility. His parents and older siblings expressed shame and disappointment at his behavior, not understanding what was motivating it. Currently, Leroy is incarcerated in a juvenile detention facility about 1 hour outside of Chicago. He is in a mandatory substance abuse counseling program and gang intervention program for juvenile delinquents.

Case Application Questions

1. Analyze Leroy's case, applying developmental and contextual issues that may impact the way you approach your work with Leroy.
2. Discuss Leroy's case in light of potential mental health issues that may be the focus of treatment.
3. If you were able to make a recommendation to the court, what setting would you recommend for Leroy and why?
4. Discuss how you would gain consent/assent from Leroy and his parents for work with him in a counseling setting.

SUMMARY

Chapter 6 discusses juvenile offenders, including dually involved or crossover youth, which are those involved in both the child welfare system due to abuse or neglect and also involved in the juvenile justice system, due to delinquency. There are several theories regarding how offending behaviors develop, including those framing the behavior as a rational choice to engage in a crime; sociological theories, which explain the behavior in relationship to the sociocultural context in which it develops; and trauma outcome process theory, previously discussed in chapter 5 and expanded on in this chapter. However, regardless of how the behavior developed, it is important to understand that juvenile offenders are not "mini-adult" offenders.

There are three ways to categorize delinquent behavior, including status offenses related to the age of the offender (e.g., truancy), which results in juvenile courts identifying the minor as a juvenile delinquent, rather than a criminal, who committed a delinquent act, rather than a crime. However, there are also serious delinquent acts, similar to criminal behavior perpetrated by adult offenders, such as theft or assault. Courts address these behaviors in one of two ways: The juvenile court adjudicates them as delinquent acts, or adult criminal court or treatment courts prosecute them as criminal acts. However, the juvenile court must "waive" the right to adjudicate the case and send it to criminal court.

In addition to considering the type of behavior, competence of the juvenile must be considered when determining how to address these behaviors. Three landmark cases related to juvenile competency are discussed in the chapter. *Dusky v. U.S.* (1960) established that juveniles must understand the case facts and the court process and be able to aid their attorney. *Kent v. U.S.* (383 US 541, 1989) addressed due process related to the requirement that the court fully investigate a juvenile's competence before the court waives jurisdiction. Full investigation includes a hearing, access to an attorney, or access to his record. Finally, in *McKeiver v. Pennsylvania* (403 U.S. 538, 1971), the Supreme Court supported the requirements of due process in delinquency cases is not the same as those that regulate criminal cases.

Contextual issues influencing juvenile delinquency and its treatment in society include the concept of retributive justice, emphasizing punishment; the second is distributive justice, emphasizing therapeutic rehabilitation; and more recently a third movement is restorative justice, focusing on accountability, making amends, and healing for all concerned parties including the community. In addition, sociocultural and familial influences affect different societal approaches to juvenile justice. These include institutionalized racism and the criminalization of poverty, as well as family influences like parenting styles and multigenerational transmission of criminal behavior.

In addition to the complex systems juvenile offending behavior develops, we know these kids commonly experience a variety of mental health issues, which necessitates trained mental health professionals providing intervention services. In fact, between 60% and 70% of kids in the juvenile justice system have one or more mental health disorders, including mood disorders, substance use disorders, and comorbid mental health issues, which increases the complexity of these cases. When we consider the increased likelihood that these kids have experienced victimization, family and community violence, and a variety of sociocultural insults like living in poverty and the trauma of oppression, it begins to illustrate why we need specially trained mental health professionals to work with juveniles in the justice system.

SAMHSA uses the sequential intercept model, which identifies five intercept points where criminal justice officials connect juveniles with mental health issues with community mental health resources. Evidence-informed practices include diversion programs, treatment courts, mentoring programs, and school-based bullying prevention and dating and sexual violence prevention programs. However, most juvenile offender mental health programs almost exclusively utilize manualized cognitive behavioral interventions. Although these are considered evidence-based practices, the studies establishing the evidence generally involve small numbers of offenders in controlled settings for limited time periods, which explains high relapse and recidivism rates among participants when they are no longer in controlled settings (e.g., prison, residential treatment) over the long term. Trauma-informed care and integration of psycho-neurobiology into treatment approaches is more complicated and requires more training; however, increasingly it is the preferred treatment method. Additionally, research indicates engaging the juvenile's family in treatment improves outcomes.

CHAPTER 6 REFLECTIVE QUESTIONS

1. Compare juvenile delinquency and adult criminality.
2. Discuss the legal precedents informing determination of competence as it relates to juvenile delinquency.
3. Utilizing the information from previous chapters of the text, how would you describe what dually involved or crossover youth are, if you were advocating for early intervention services with an 11-year-old in foster care who exhibits aggressive behavior toward peers?
4. Compare different developmental theories of offending behavior as they relate to a juvenile offender.
5. Describe the legal precedents that inform due process as it applies to juvenile offenders.
6. Compare retributive, distributive, and restorative justice. Which is most consistent with your thinking about intervention with juvenile offenders and why?
7. Discuss the common mental health issues your clients may be challenged with if you are working with juvenile offenders in the community.
8. Compare the different types of settings forensic mental health counselors may work in, if counseling juvenile offenders.
9. Discuss the common ethical and legal issues you may deal with as a counselor of juvenile offenders.

RESOURCES

Coalition for Juvenile Justice: http://www.juvjustice.org/about-us

Office of Juvenile Justice and Delinquency Prevention: https://www.ojjdp.gov/

Restorative Practices International: https://www.rpiassn.org/

Responding to a subpoena from the American Counseling Association: https://www.counseling.org/docs/default-source/ethics/ethics-columns/ethics_october_2015_subpoena.pdf?sfvrsn=ea22522c_4

National Council of Juvenile and Family Court Judges: http://www.ncjfcj.org/

Child Delinquency bulletin from the U.S. Department of Justice, Office of Juvenile Justice and Delinquency Prevention: https://www.ncjrs.gov/pdffiles1/ojjdp/193410.pdf

Adult Offenders

Part I: Foundations

- Analyze developmental, historical, sociocultural, and familial contexts within which adult offenders' criminal behavior and treatment occurs
- Evaluate levels of restrictiveness of care for clients and make recommendations of appropriate level of care
- Discuss common ethical and legal issues FMHC working with adult offenders encounter

TABLE 7.1 Myths and Mythbusters

Myths	Mythbusters
Adult offenders make rational choices when deciding to break the law.	**Adult offenders' behavior develops within a number of developmental, sociocultural, historical, and familial contexts, all of which affect the manifestation of offending behavior.**
FMHCs only work with adult offenders in prisons.	**FMHCs work with adult offenders in a continuum of mental health programs in settings ranging from community based to correctional facilities.**
Informed consent is not an issue with offenders mandated to treatment because they have to go.	**FMHCs have an ethical obligation to ensure adult offenders with whom they work make informed treatment decisions and do not experience coercion to participate in mental health counseling programs.**

INTRODUCTION

According to the Department of Justice (DOJ) (Carson, 2018), there are 2.2 million adults incarcerated in jails or prisons (Graziani, Ben-Mosche, Cole, 2017) and 1.5 million incarcerated in state or federal prisons serving over 1 year in prison (Carson, 2018). This amounts to 459 people per 100,000. Additionally, due to de-institutionalization of seriously mentally ill (SMI) adults, around 300,000 people with diagnoses such as bipolar disorder and schizophrenia are incarcerated (Torrey et al., 2015). When you add in those on community supervision or in city or county jails, the number of mentally ill people incarcerated rises to a daily average of 500,000. In fact, the rate of seriously mentally ill people in correctional facilities is as much as 10 times the rate of those hospitalized (Torrey, Kennard, Eslinger, Lamb, & Pavle, 2010). In addition to SMI individuals, people with substance use disorders are highly represented in correctional settings. In fact, the War on Drugs in the 1980s and 90s increased incarceration rates among addicts by treating drug use as a "bad choice" needing punishment, rather than a mental health disorder needing treatment (White, 2014). Although most state prisoners (54%) have violent felony convictions, drug offenders are found more often in federal prisons (47%) (Stullich, Morgan, & Schak, 2016).

There are increased costs associated with high rates of incarceration among SMI and addicted adults. As the rate of adult incarceration has increased 500% over the past 40 years, corresponding correctional spending increased 324% (Stullich, Morgan, & Schak, 2016). Prison healthcare costs alone total around $8 billion annually, and mental illness is a significant reason for these costs, according to the Urban Institute (Schaenman, Davis, Jordan, & Chakraborty, 2013; Schiff et al., 2014). In fact, the cost of incarcerating someone with a serious mental illness is twice as much as it would cost to provide treatment in a mental health facility, if there were beds and financial support to do so (Swanson et al., 2013). In order to cut costs, states contract with private companies to provide this care (Spenser, 2017). Those companies view mental health care in prisons as a business from which they seek to profit financially. As a result, there are significant ethical and legal issues regarding the provisions for mental healthcare for adult offenders in correctional institutions (Spenser, 2017). The Southern Poverty Law Center Mississippi Youth Justice Project sued the state for not spending necessary resources on mental health care in 2010. *Braggs v. Dunn* (2017) ended after a 7-week trial adjudicated a class action lawsuit, which challenged the Alabama Department of Corrections' mental health care system, ending in the judge asserting that the state's mental health care system in corrections violated the Eighth Amendment's prohibition against cruel and unusual punishment because it was "grossly inadequate." Additionally, in 2018 lawsuits resulted in court admonishments of correctional facilities in Colorado and Illinois for inadequate treatment of mental illness among inmates.

It is important to note, however, that in 1976 the Supreme Court affirmed that correctional facilities were constitutionally mandated, under the Eighth Amendment, to provide appropriate health care (including mental health care), and when correctional officials display "deliberate indifference" to an inmate's healthcare needs, they are violating the constitution (*Estelle v. Gamble*), 1976. However, mental health professionals do not run correctional facilities

(Morgan et al., 2012). Many correctional settings report not having the financial resources to provide mental health care (Torrey et al., 2015). Additionally, correctional officers and probation officers are not trained as mental health providers, and the primary goal in corrections is maintaining safety, security, and order, not providing healthcare. Therefore, although jails and prisons are constitutionally obligated to provide mental health care to those in need, the services across correctional facilities vary tremendously. Many correctional facilities either outsource mental health services to corporations or hire people with bachelor's degrees in social work or criminal justice who have virtually no training in assessment, diagnosis, and treatment of mentally ill individuals, particularly those with complex trauma histories and comorbid substance use disorders, resulting in care that relies on medication management rather than counseling. As a result, during one 5-year period, one correctional corporation alone had 600 malpractice lawsuits related to treatment of mentally ill inmates (Forst, 2000).

Due to social concerns about high rates of imprisonment in this country, there is a movement to release or not imprison more individuals. As a result, these corporations are now seeking to provide similar mental health services for probation, parole, and re-entry centers. Many private correctional healthcare companies are suffering from the incorrect belief that counseling conducted from a manual is easy (Milkman & Wanberg, 2007). This likely stems from the experience that correctional counseling is simply a combination of casework and manualized (e.g., workbook) interventions, rather than attending to the therapeutic relationship. The therapeutic relationship being the only intervention that a variety of research has consistently demonstrated is efficacious over time with any mental health issue (Ardito & Rabellino, 2011; Stargell, 2017). Unfortunately, because of this trend, many nonprofit community mental health agencies that historically provided this care are now losing funding.

As a result, many mentally ill people in correctional facilities, or even people in outpatient services (e.g., batterers intervention programs), are "counseled" by people who are not competent to provide mental health services. This raises a number of ethical and legal concerns. The primary one being that these offenders are not receiving the care they need. Additionally, given that they tend to have very complex mental health histories, lack of competent care often results in worsening of symptoms and less willingness to engage in treatment, as compared to having received services from a trained counselor. These are issues you will likely face if you work for a correctional facility or work for a private correctional healthcare company.

DEVELOPMENTAL ISSUES

Chapters 4 and 5 discussed child and adolescent victims, and chapter 6 discussed adolescent offenders. In chapters 7 and 8, we discuss the next stage of development, adulthood. For the purposes of this text, *early adulthood* is anyone from the age of majority until 35 years old. *Middle adulthood* ranges from 35 until 65. Finally, *late adulthood* includes anyone over age 65. Often, we can understand abnormal development better when we first understand normal developmental patterns. You may have expected to learn about these in the child and adolescent section of the text; however, I intentionally decided to discuss development in the adult section because we often assume that adults have progressed normally through developmental stages. When we make these assumptions, however, we often fail to analyze the client's behavior within the developmental context. By doing so, we often fail to choose interventions that are appropriate to the developmental level from which they are working. Therefore, first described are adult development concepts in order to provide a framework for understanding the population of focus. Then, some major developmental theories of offending behavior will be discussed. Applying these developmental theories can help conceptualize clients and inform selection of developmentally appropriate interventions.

Theories of Human Development

Human development theorists tend to organize their conceptualizations of development under the following headings: biological, cognitive, moral, social, psychological, and spiritual. *Biological development* includes physiological and neurobiological processes and changes. There are three major theories of biological development, including *simple deterioration theory* (we age as our physiological and neurobiological structures deteriorate); *non-programmed aging theory*, passive aging or nonadaptive aging (aging results from our inability to resist physiological and neurobiological deterioration); and *programmed aging*, active aging, adaptive aging, or aging by design (aging is an adaptation resulting from evolution). Regardless of developmental approach, everyone experiences normal physiological and neurobiological changes. Biological and neurodevelopmental considerations are particularly important when considering older offenders.

Piaget's *cognitive developmental theory* can be used to primarily explain a child's cognitive development. However, not all people go through these stages and reach formal operations, so when thinking about cognitive interventions with adult offenders, it is sometimes helpful to identify what level of cognitive development the person is functioning within, in order to inform the choice of approach. There are four cognitive developmental stages: sensorimotor, preoperational, concrete operational, and formal operational, described in **Table 7.2**. It is important to remember that some clients have experienced past trauma, which they may re-experience at the same developmental stage the person was in when they experienced the trauma. Therefore, developmentally appropriate interventions are those that reflect the developmental level at which these memories were encoded (e.g., sand tray interventions, which are sensory, for someone who experienced childhood sexual abuse). We may also have clients who prefer workbook exercises focused on disputing cognitive distortions, because they have a sense of mastery for cognitively concrete tasks. However, the same clients may exhibit difficulty thinking abstractly regarding how to apply these principles in practice when they are emotionally dysregulated because they function cognitively at a concrete operational level, not a formal operational level.

Kohlberg's stages of moral development evolved as an adaptation of psychological theory and Piaget's cognitive stages (Kohlberg & Hersh, 1977). The model hypothesizes that ethical behavior develops from one's ability to reason morally. He structured the theory using three levels of morality, pre-conventional, conventional, and post-conventional, with two stages under each. Level one, pre-conventional, involves the first stage, obedience and punishment orientation (how can I avoid punishment?) and the second stage, self-interest orientation

---

TABLE 7.2 **Piaget's Stages of Cognitive Development**

Age	Stage	Description
Birth–2 years	Sensorimotor	Understands the world through his or her senses and actions
2–7 years	Preoperational	Understands the world through language and mental images
7–12 years	Concrete operational	Understands the world through logical and categorical thinking
12 and above	Formal operational	Understands the world through hypothetical, abstract thought and scientific reasoning

---

(what's in it for me?). The second level is conventional with stage three being conformity (adhering to social norms, good/bad split) and stage four, authority (law and order). Finally, level three, post-conventional, involves stage-five social contract orientation (mutual respect for different views) and stage-six universal ethical principles (justice is more important than laws). However, Gilligan found Kohlberg's theory gender biased (Gilligan, 1982, 1987). As a result, she developed a moral developmental stage theory based on the ethic of care (Gilligan, 1982, 1987). Gilligan's theory suggests individuals move from pre-conventional (goal: survival), transitioning from self-focused needs to responsibility for others, leading to conventional (goal: self-sacrifice is goodness), then transitioning from seeking "goodness" to seeking truth in the post-conventional stage (goal: do no harm/nonviolence).

Social development considers the changing relationships and roles that adults adapt to in order to make their way through the world. For instance, how would a 65-year-old successful businessperson adapt to imprisonment for embezzling money from his company, particularly if he never had legal issues prior to this point in his life? This change in life circumstances would affect his family and social relationships, his sense of self, and his role in society. One of the best-known social development theories is *Erikson's stages of social development* (Erikson, 1963), described in **Table 7.3**. Each stage presents a psychosocial crisis, which the person must successfully work through in order to move to the next developmental level. For each stage, there is a personal characteristic or virtue, which a person can develop when successfully negotiating the stage. However, people adapt, even when they are not able to master a particular stage. For instance, a 3-year-old girl, who witnesses domestic violence, may often feel scared, and then an older sibling sexually abuses her so that she develops difficulty successfully negotiating the autonomy versus shame stage of development. She will likely go on to attempt to have intimate relationships as a young adult; however, these early challenges in social development will likely manifest within the relationship(s) she has as an adult. She may enter into a relationship with a partner who is also abusive because she did not successfully negotiate the autonomy versus shame stage of development.

Psychological development includes emotional/affective experiences and the way we construct meaning from these experiences. One psychological theory, particularly helpful in understanding human behavior and particularly when working with adult offenders, is *Maslow's hierarchy of needs*, which explains that people are motivated to meet certain basic needs. Without meeting psychological needs at the lowest level, they are not able to move up the

TABLE 7.3 Erikson's Stages of Social Development

Age	Stage	Virtue	Description
Birth–18 months	Trust vs. mistrust	Hope	The infant experiences attuned caregiving and feels love, therefore developing trust, security, and basic optimism. If not, then he or she is insecure in his or her attachments and mistrusts others.
18 months–4 years	Autonomy vs. shame	Will	Feeling of pride associated with his or her ability to have a sense of agency and control in affecting his or her environment. He or she experiences pride and joy. However, if the child does not have success in impacting his or her environment, then he or she is more likely to feel shame.
4–6 years	Initiative vs. guilt	Purpose	The play age. A healthy child learns to play, actively using imagination and fantasy. Develops an ability to cooperate with others, how to lead, as well as follow. However, if guilt immobilizes him or her, he or she stays on the outside of group play, acting fearful. He or she depends on adults, and his or her play skills and imagination do not develop.
Elementary-school age 6–11	Industry vs. inferiority	Competence	Children learn to relate to peers, follow stated and unstated rules, and begin applying self-discipline and self-regulation of emotion. Successful children are trusting, can work alone or in groups, and can initiate activities. However, those who are not successful resolving this stage, experience shame and guilt, feeling defeated and inferior.
Middle-school age 12–14 or later	Identity vs. role confusion	Fidelity	This is when an adolescent exhibits "normal" delinquency behaviors in order to "try on" different roles and begin establishing his or her identity separate from his or her parents. This is also the stage in which kids examine their sexual identities, religious/spiritual identities, and racial/ethnic identities. If they are successful, they develop a sense of self as an individual who can stand on his or her own. However, if they are not successful, they may experience feelings of inferiority, which hinder their development of relationships and ability to initiate setting and attaining goals.
High school through young adulthood 15–25 or later	Intimacy vs. isolation	Love	Someone who successfully negotiates this stage can enter into healthy intimate relationships, which enables him or her to engage in enduring friendships and romantic partnerships. Someone who is not successful experiences feelings of loneliness, inferiority, and isolation.
Adulthood 25 to 65	Generativity vs. self-absorption	Care	Someone who successfully negotiates this stage is able to exhibit prosocial behaviors and seeks to influence his or her community and family in a positive manner. This is when people marry, start families, establish careers and a place within their communities through putting in effort and contributions. If a person is unable to invest him- or herself in something bigger, as a way to contribute to society, then he or she is likely to fall into self-absorption.
Over 65	Integrity vs. despair	Wisdom	This person has a firm sense of who he or she is and how his or her identity "fits" with his or her family, social networks, and community. This results in a feeling of integrity. However, if any of the earlier stages are still unresolved, then he or she may feel despair or disgust toward him- or herself or others.

hierarchy toward higher psychological functioning. The most basic are physiological needs like food and shelter, next is safety and security, then love and belonging, self-esteem, and finally self-actualization (Maslow, 1968/1999).

Additionally, each major theory of counseling explains a different view of psychological development, including how abnormal development occurs, and suggests methods for intervention. There are five major categories of psychological theories; the first are psychanalytic and contemporary psychodynamic theories such as relational psychoanalysis (object-relations), Adlerian/individual psychology, and psychodynamic. The second category includes humanistic theories like person centered, existential, and Gestalt. The third category includes behavioral and cognitive theories, which include cognitive behavioral, rational emotive behavioral therapy, and dialectical behavior therapy. The fourth group of theories includes family systems theories, including Bowenian systems, strategic, and structural theories. Finally, the fourth group of theories are postmodern theories, such as feminist, relational-cultural, constructivist, and narrative-type theories. Most clinicians conceptualize primarily from one theory and integrate concepts or techniques from a variety of theories in practice.

TABLE 7.4 Fowler's Stages of Faith Development

Age	Stage	Description
3–7	Stage 1 Intuitive-projective	Characterized by intuitive images of good and evil. Fantasy and reality are the same. Reality is what they are told.
School age	Stage 2 Mythic-literal	Characterized by strong beliefs in justice and reciprocity. Deities are usually anthropomorphic. Literal interpretation of religious stories. God is a parent figure. The community helps define the content and object of faith. Reality is what you are taught in your spiritual community.
Adolescence	Stage 3 Synthetic-conventional	Characterized by conformity. Increase in abstract thinking. Challenging and analyzing teachings. Identification with a group of believers outside of spiritual practice and community you grow up in.
25–40	Stage 4 Individuative-reflective	You internalize faith as your own, not as something someone taught you. You have analyzed your beliefs in relationship to teaching and come to your own understanding of personal spirituality. Ultimate truth is not understood. To be in this stage, you must critically evaluate faith, so many people never get to this stage.
40–60	Stage 5 Paradoxical-consolidative (Conjunctive)	You recognize the validity of others' beliefs. You function beyond theological formulas and continue to analyze and critically evaluate faith. Belief that you are responsible for determining what your spiritual beliefs are and do not answer to a church or religious doctrine to tell you what to believe.
60 and older	Stage 6 Universalizing	Enlightenment. Rarely achieved. You have a feeling of being one with God/the universe. Invest in a larger cause without being concerned with the personal cost. (e.g., Ghandi)

Finally, using *Fowler's stages of spiritual development* (**Table 7.4**) suggests faith is a holistic orientation concerned with how individuals relate to the universe (Fowler, 1991). Many of our adult clients, particularly as they get older, struggle with how their lives of crime make sense in terms of spirituality and faith. This is particularly true for those serving long sentences in prison or those who struggle with having hope for their futures. Therefore, even if you are not a spiritual person, it is helpful to understand these stages in order to structure your conceptualization of existential and spiritual issues with which your clients may struggle.

Developmental Theories of Offending

There are a number of theories explaining the developmental trajectory of offending behavior; however, this section discusses only those major theories, which may have relevance. First is *Moffit's dual taxonomy*, which proposed two distinct categories of offending.

- *Adolescent-limited (ALs) offending*: criminal delinquency limited to teenage development and rebellious nonviolent offenses resulting from negative peer influence, which they grow out of as they age (Moffit, 1993).
- *Life-course persistent (LCPs) offenders*: early-age delinquency that persists into adulthood, committing a range of criminal acts, including violence because they are antisocial, enjoy criminal behavior, and are unconcerned with consequences. Development of LCPs increase with cognitive deficits, impulsivity, poor emotion regulation, parent-child conflict, and living in chaotic impoverished families and communities.

Interactional theory, developed by Thornberry and Krohn (2005), is distinctive because it emphasizes reciprocal causation, which indicates that the child's antisocial behavior elicits coercive responses from parents and rejection from peers, therefore resulting in more behavior that is antisocial. Thornberry (2005) expanded the theory to explain the intergenerational transmission of antisocial behavior, suggesting that the parent's prosocial or antisocial bonding, family structure, number and intensity of stressors, and parenting styles contribute to the child's prosocial or antisocial behavior.

However, *social control theory* suggests that a person's values, beliefs, and relationships lead to either prosocial or antisocial behavior. Morality is a social construction that allows groups of people to have order in society. Sykes and Matza (1957) identified five common techniques offenders use allowing them to commit crimes, which he called neutralization. The five techniques of *neutralization* are denial of responsibility (I couldn't help it), denial of injury (no one was hurt), denial of victim (he deserved it), condemnation of the condemners (they don't have any right to judge me), and appeal to higher loyalties (e.g., gang leader, mafia boss, grandmother relying on your drug sales to pay the bills). The phenomenon of *drift* is an extension of the theory, which allows people to drift into and out of conventional behavior. Drift rests on four observations. First, criminals express guilt over criminal acts. Second, they often respect people who abide by the law. Third, there is a line between who is "okay" to victimize (a rival gang member) and who is off limits (my mom's friend). Finally, criminals can conform if/when they need.

Integrated cognitive antisocial potential theory (ICAP) is a newer theory developed by Farrington (1995, 2003, 2005) to explain antisocial behavior exhibited by working-class males. The model developed from studying risk factors related to criminal behavior. The theory posits that every person has an *antisocial potential* (AP), which is his or her potential to commit antisocial or criminal acts. *Cognitive processes* or decision-making determines whether the potential activates offending behavior. ICAP indicates people exist on a continuum from low to high AP based on three factors, including desire for material gain, status among peers, and excitement and sexual satisfaction. The higher on the continuum a person is, the more likely the person is to commit crimes. However, if a person can legitimately satisfy personal desires, then he or she less likely to engage in criminal behavior.

Theorists developed these models in the context of a criminal justice focus, rather than a psychological focus, like the previous set of developmental theories. Although we generally do not refer to these theories in a counseling setting, given the overlap with criminal justice/forensic settings, it may be important to be aware of other ways of conceptualizing the development of presenting issues among this population. Next, we will discuss sociocultural influences that may affect offending behavior.

SOCIOCULTURAL CONTEXT

It is important for counselors to understand the perspective of their clients, who are often members of minority groups who have lived lives of marginalization spanning their lifetimes and many generations prior. The sociocultural context influences their perception of counseling, counselors, and the "justice" system, which historically treats minorities and the poor unjustly. For instance, one contextual issue when reading or hearing about adult offenders is how we use statistics to make policy decisions. This is significant when it comes to sociocultural issues like gender and ethnicity because statistics can create the perception that Black or Hispanic men commit more crime than Whites or women. Additionally, it is important that you understand that people sometimes manipulate statistical information in order to make a particular political argument. Considering that there is a legacy of majority culture within the foundation of the justice system, it is easy for those in power to view data solely from that lens, particularly if they are from the majority culture. Therefore, it is important to critically evaluate the sociocultural data to fully understand the implications.

For instance, what if I told you there are twice as many White women serving time in prison than Black or Hispanic women (Carson, 2018). Similarly, young Black males (18–19 years) are 11.8 times more likely to serve time than White males at the same age (Carson, 2018).You might logically conclude that there are more Black and Hispanic people than there are White people committing crimes. By default, you conclude that there is no racial disparity in female prisons. However if you analyze the data within the historical and sociocultural contexts affecting it, you may understand the information differently. Based on this context, you may understand that there is a bias in the system, which disproportionately negatively affects minorities.

Convictions of adults for drug offenses are one example of disparities along racial/ethnic, gender, and SES lines. For instance, although drug offenses account for only 15% of state prisoners, women are more likely (25%) to have drug offenses as their most serious crime than men (14%), according to the justice department (Carson, 2018). Similarly, more females (56%) than males (47%) serve federal time for drug offenses (Carson, 2018). This is also a sociocultural issue because the United States has made drugs illegal and provided increasingly harsh sentencing for those drugs associated with ethnic minorities. For instance, the original outlawing of street opioids was a response to increasing Chinese immigrants, and laws against marijuana was a response to Mexican immigration and African American use (History Channel, 2000).

Racial and gender inequities are further compounded by the passage of the Anti-Drug Abuse Act of 1986. This law resulted in judges loosing discretion in sentencing because the law mandated long sentences (10 years) for possession of even small amounts (individual use) of crack cocaine, commonly used by lower SES groups and minorities, whereas powder cocaine used by higher SES White people was not sentenced as harshly (Pub. L. 99–570, 100 STAT.3207). As a result, racial disparities in drug sentencing rose to 49% longer sentences for Blacks than Whites following the law, up from 11% before the law passed (Vagins & McCurdy, 2006). Furthermore, when you compare these laws to the legal policies related to the current opioid epidemic, the differences are striking. We attribute the current epidemic primarily to the rise of prescription opioids for pain, a function of pharmaceutical corporations' marketing efforts (Quinones, 2015). The public outrage regarding this epidemic resulted from large numbers of deaths among White middle-class and wealthy individuals. The legislative response was to provide easier access to naloxone, a prescription countering the effects of heroin overdose, and to fund more treatment courts to divert these "offenders" to treatment, rather than prison. Contrast this with the crack cocaine crisis in the 1980s, primarily associated with low SES Black teens and adults, which resulted in mandatory minimum prison sentences and subsequent mass incarceration of Black males (Vagins & McCurdy, 2006). Thus, there is an interaction between changing legal definitions and the resulting incarcerations, independent of any actual changes in inmate behavior.

Although incarceration rates have risen dramatically over the past 30 years, the rate of female offender growth far exceeds the male offender population growth, something that often goes unacknowledged (Glaze & Maruschak, 2010). In fact, although there is a decreasing trend in imprisonment (1% state and 4% federal), rates of women sentenced to more than 1 year in state or federal facilities is increasing. Most women experience incarceration for nonviolent crimes. In fact, more than half (59%) of the women serving time in federal prisons are there for drug-related offenses (McConnell, 2017). A higher percentage of women (24%) are serving time for drug offenses in state prisons than males (15%) (Carson, 2016). Similarly, property offenses (e.g., theft) result in a higher percentage of females being imprisoned (28%) than males (19%) (Carson, 2016). However, among violent criminals, 54% are male and 37% female (Carson, 2016). In addition, when women commit violent offenses, it is often in self-defense. For instance, almost half (42%) of the women convicted of murder killed a spouse or significant other because of domestic violence (McConnell, 2017).

Additionally, although most female offenders experience addiction and trauma-related disorders, they have substandard care compared to male offender programs (Aday & Krabill, 2011; McConnell, 2017). Incarcerated women are actually more likely to receive psychotropic medications as the primary or sole intervention for mental illness, which may reflect a gender bias in the system (Auehahn & Leonard, 2000). Even though most female offenders have significant trauma histories, they are unlikely to receive trauma-informed treatment, according to the National Council on Crime and Delinquency (2006).

To compound the marginalization of minority populations, the long-term effects of incarceration disproportionately negatively affect their ability to successfully contribute to society and begin/perpetuate a cycle of incarceration within their families. For instance, consider re-entry for individuals with felony convictions. Acknowledging a felony on a job application is disqualifying for many employers. However, lying about a felony conviction can result in being fired if found out, regardless of your work quality. Because of changes in social welfare laws, it is also more difficult for someone with a criminal record to access social services that help with housing, food, and transportation (Berman, 2005; Vagins & McCurdy, 2006). When someone is leaving jail/prison, offenders often have no resources. Because of the boundaries preventing survival, much less successful reintegration into society, they often believe they have no choice other than returning to drugs or criminal behavior to survive, thus perpetuating this cycle of crime and incarceration.

The long-term effects of incarceration on families are significant. Some incarcerates are the primary or sole provider for their families. When incarcerated, their families suffer economically. Consider the research discussed previously indicating that not having a father in the home and not having an intact family structure contributes to increases in juvenile delinquency (Steward, 2014). Similarly, having a mother incarcerated is also considered to be a factor that contributes to children becoming criminals (McConnell, 2017). Additionally, children who have a parent incarcerated may not have a caregiver at home, and therefore they more often end up in foster care. While it might not have a direct impact on the incarcerated individual, this further increases their risk of developing mental illness, addictions, and future delinquency among his or her children (McConnell, 2017).

Another sociocultural issue to consider is that of religion and/or spirituality. Many addiction treatment programs, which courts often mandate drug offenders to attend, are in religious facilities or model 12-step programs exclusively, which requires that the individual relinquish his or her power to a higher authority. For someone who is atheist or agnostic, this requirement is prohibitive. If they refuse to attend a religious-based or 12-step based treatment model, then the response is often that they are not "working the program" or that they are treatment resistant. In addition to not promoting choice or individual accountability, this type of report to courts can result in incarceration or having parole denied or probation/parole revoked. Therefore, consistent with the ACA Code of Ethics (2014), it is incumbent on counselors to advocate for these clients to receive culturally competent care. Taken together, it is obvious that the justice system disproportionately affects each of these marginalized groups compared to those of majority culture. Some may perceive our system, therefore, as the *in***justice system**, rather than the justice system. Additionally, sometimes these identities (race/gender/religion/age) intersect multiple times to create a more complex sociocultural picture. Culturally competent forensic mental health counselors must be aware of these complex sociocultural and familial contexts in order to provide quality mental health care.

TYPES OF ADULT OFFENDERS

Beyond the developmental, historical, and sociocultural contexts discussed, the criminal justice system further categorizes adult offenders based on their age in relationship to their criminal activity. We categorize adult offenders in one of three groups:

■ *Adult-onset* or *late-blooming offenders* are first-time offenders characterized by participating in similar law-breaking activity as non-offending adolescents do, with criminal involvement evolving in adulthood, however having persistent serious criminal offending behaviors as adults (Thornberry & Matsuda, 2011).

■ *Career* or *habitual offenders*' criminal behavior, alternatively, begins in adolescence and continues throughout adulthood.

■ *Aging offenders* are the result of two phenomenon: the general aging of America and mass incarceration and mandated sentencing. The latter group we will discuss in more depth.

A growing concern among those working with adult offenders is that elderly inmates are the fastest growing group in most state prison systems, and these inmates have age-related health issues (Aday & Krabill, 2011; Compalbert, Pennequin, Ferrand, & Vandevyvere, & Geffray, 2016). Additionally, due to the stress and trauma most offenders experience over their life course, they age an average of 10 times faster than non-offenders (Aday & Krabill, 2011).

Also, due to longer mandatory sentences over the past 30 years, there are more people over age 50 serving time than ever before. In fact, this group comprises 8.4% of arrests, a number that doubled over ten years (Aday & Krabill, 2011).

Aging results in a variety of physical and mental health issues, to which correctional facilities and probation and parole organizations increasingly must attend, including functional impairments that make it difficult for elderly inmates to navigate the physical structures or demands of the correctional facilities within which they live. Due to legal mandates, these facilities need updating to accommodate physical disabilities (ADA, 1990; *Estelle v. Gamble*, 1976). However, these modifications present an additional cost to correctional management. Another costly result of aging inmates is that they also develop serious illnesses as they age, resulting in needed programming that reflects palliative care, hospice, and end-of-life planning (Sanders, Stensland, & Juraco, 2018). In addition, staff need specialized training in how to competently deal with the safety, health, and aging offenders.

Aging brings unique mental health issues, as well. Being in correctional settings is challenging for everyone; however, these stressors compound the experiences of aging offenders. Simply coping with living as an elderly person in a correctional setting is challenging for some offenders. The way older people make sense of their criminal behavior may also change as they age, which has implications for mental health treatment (Sparkes & Day, 2016). Re-storying their offending careers in the context of their life as a whole may be a worthy counseling goal. A common mental health stressor for many aging offenders is a loss of all family and social support outside the correctional setting, resulting in loneliness, despair, and depression. Additionally, common geriatric issues such as dementia, Alzheimer's, age-related depression and suicide, and the effects of chronic substance abuse on mental and cognitive functioning are more common in this population (Aday & Krabill, 2011; Compalbert et al., 2016; Gates, Staples-Horne, Walker, & Turney, 2017).

Chronic illness, common for older adults, often affects self-concept and mood. As physical stature and abilities weaken over time, many aging offenders become targets for physical or sexual victimization. Although this may further compound trauma experiences relevant to counseling, they are generally reluctant to talk about these incidents for fear of protective placement in administrative segregation (solitary confinement). Due to the combined increases in victimization among older offenders, declining health, and mental health concerns about death and dying, particularly if incarcerated, aging offenders may develop anxiety disorders like panic attacks. Mental health counselors in these settings must understand the unique needs of aging offenders when carrying out assessment, monitoring, and intervention services.

These additional needs add to the overall healthcare costs for the government entities caring for aging offenders. Because of the challenges to housing aging offenders, some correctional facilities have *compassionate and early release programs*. Under these policies, correctional settings may release aging offenders, especially if ill, allowing for their return to the community. However, these individuals also face more difficulties upon re-entry. Often imprisoned for longer periods, they have less ability to gain full employment. Like all offenders, they experience challenges finding housing. In addition, family and community support is often lacking because they have not been able to maintain relationships they had prior to incarceration. As a result, because of healthcare needs, lack of housing or employment, they may recidivate just so they can have a social safety net to meet their basic needs.

SETTINGS

Forensic mental health counselors (FMHC) may work with adult offenders in a variety of settings. Each setting involves its' own group of professionals with whom FMHCs must interact and coordinate services. Each professional involved with the offender has his or her own goals related to the offender's outcomes. Although all will agree that reducing recidivism is the primary goal, the means by which each professional discipline intervenes are often different. Sometimes these methods are complimentary and at other times they conflict. Next, I will briefly describe different contexts within which you may provide professional services to adult offenders. The *level of care* (or level of restrictiveness of the setting) in clinical terms is based on an assessment of risks of harm to self and/or others and the need for supervision or whether to monitor medication or to ensure participation in therapeutic counseling. Alternatively, criminal justice settings determine *level of restrictiveness* by the court's determination of risk of harm to others, almost exclusively.

Crisis Intervention Training

We can think of crisis intervention training (CIT) as a community based intervention. Through CIT, counselors may train police officers in methods for identifying, triaging, and de-escalating community members with mental illness. The first CIT program began in the 1980s in Memphis, Tennessee, in response to a hostage situation involving a mentally ill

TABLE 7.5 PREPaRE Model

P	Prevent and prepare for psychological trauma.
R	Reaffirm physical health and perceptions of security and safety.
E	Evaluate psychological trauma risk.
P a R	Provide and respond to psychological needs
E	Examine the effectiveness of crisis prevention and intervention.

citizen, resulting in the torture and murder of one police officer and injuries to other officers and the deaths of several citizens when a tactical unit entered the home. It is frequently referred to as the Memphis model.

CIT utilizes the **PREPaRE Model** (**Table 7.5**) to structure training in order to improve police officers' effectiveness in diverting the mentally ill away from jail and into community treatment, as well as to reduce injuries to both officers and citizens. Officers are taught how to identify citizens with mental health issues, use the triage assessment form to continuously assess dangerousness to self or others, learn de-escalation techniques (including a role playing practicum), and ultimately divert mentally ill citizens to community-based treatment, rather than jails.

Individual studies indicate effectiveness of the program; however, it has many non-standardized iterations around the country, and a recent meta-analytic study demonstrates null effects on both CITs arrests of persons with mental illness and on police officer safety (Taheri, 2016). The study does not assess reduction in citizen injuries or deaths.

Adult Mental Health Treatment Courts

One of the first decisions made in many larger jurisdictions for mentally ill offenders, when police do arrest them, is whether to send them to the criminal courts or refer them to a mental health treatment court. Mental health treatment courts identify individuals with mental illness and divert the defendant to mental health treatment, rather than punishment. *Drug treatment courts*, which were the first treatment courts, are most common. There are over 3,100 drug courts in the United States today (U.S. Department of Justice, 2018). Some believe these courts provide the best possible alternative for individuals arrested for drug-related offenses. However, some, like Physicians for Human Rights, assert that drug courts do not provide appropriate levels or types of treatment to individuals with substance use disorders (SUDs) and are mandating treatment for people who do not need therapeutic interventions (e.g., one-time DUI who does not meet SUDs diagnostic criteria). They assert that people who have no medical background make treatment decisions, which at times violates their human rights. In a 2017 study, they found that problems resulted from the following:

1. Lack of funding for treatment
2. Treatment plans mandated by the court that did not reflect scientific evidence

3. Requiring treatment providers to be quasi-probation officers or requiring probation officers with no training to act as mental health clinicians
4. A lack of ancillary services like housing and employment that support treatment
5. Treatment courts referring offenders to treatment programs, which do not employ scientifically informed treatment practices (e.g., exclusively using 12-step programs). (Mollmann, 2017)

Increasingly, jurisdictions across the country have established *veterans' treatment courts* to meet the needs of an increasing veteran population who have mental health and substance use issues related to their military service, resulting in involvement with the law. *Mental health treatment courts* aim to deal with the massive increases in mentally ill offenders in the system because of de-institutionalization and de-funding of community mental health programs. More recently, some jurisdictions have established *domestic violence treatment courts*, although they are controversial due to the concerns for victims' rights and safety in courts that value family reunification.

Treatment courts act as *interdisciplinary treatment teams*. The judge is the team leader, but there are also treatment professionals representing treatment programs receiving referrals from the court, specially trained probation officers who function as caseworkers, and legal professionals who choose to be involved with mental health treatment courts. The treatment team meets weekly to review progress of those individuals adjudicated in the treatment court and to debate and decide what interventions are necessary to motivate the offender toward recovery and reduce recidivism risks. Treatment professionals present information about the client's progress in treatment, whether he or she is attending and participating in treatment, the overall quality of his or her participation, and results of any objective assessments (e.g., random urine screens, results on psychological testing, etc.). They also make recommendations to the team about how to help the client be successful in his or her program. The court often provides incentives to the offender (e.g., deferred adjudication, having a record expunged, or the threat of a weekend stay in jail) that treatment professionals rely on to motivate a client to engage in treatment.

Generally, the treatment team respects the treatment professional's opinion and work to facilitate treatment. Caseworkers assist with housing, employment opportunities, providing bus passes to get to treatment, or addressing other practical needs that often act as barriers to successful treatment participation. The team discusses the offender's needs and decides together how to proceed with feedback or further intervention with the offender. Treatment team meetings occur prior to offenders presenting themselves to the court for feedback from the treatment team and potentially for changes in "level of care" by the judge (treatment team leader).

Probation or Parole and Re-entry

Probation and parole (or re-entry) services are all community-based services. Someone who was sentenced to *probation* may have spent time in jail prior to adjudication, but they serve their sentences within the community. However, someone on *parole* served jail or prison time, was released before his or her sentence was complete, and is re-entering society as a convicted criminal still under the court's supervision. The challenges for offenders in the community are significant. Probation and/or parole orders often require employment of the offender; however, finding employment with a criminal conviction is extremely challenging because many employers systematically reject any applicant with a criminal history. This leads many offenders to falsify information on job applications in order to gain employment. Lying on a job application may get them in the door, but their probation/parole office must verify ongoing employment, so this process may ultimately reveal the offender's status to employers.

For female offenders, often the primary caregiver for children, the lack of childcare that is affordable or available during shift work serves as a barrier to employment. Another barrier is transportation. If a person does not have access to a working automobile or money for alternative transportation (e.g., bus or subway), then he or she may not be able to go to a job even when he or she becomes employed. Further, the stigma associated with domestic violence or sexual offending behaviors further challenges the offender's ability to find housing, employment, appropriate social support, and quality mental health treatment. Ultimately, inability to find steady or well-paying employment results in difficulties paying for basic needs like food, housing, medical/mental health care and medicine, and treatment that are all necessary to support offenders in their efforts to abide by the law.

Housing is a significant challenge for offenders, particularly those re-entering society after incarceration. Convicted criminals cannot benefit from public housing, which limits their ability to find housing at times. Due to their criminal behaviors, family support in providing housing may also be limited. Some offenders, like sex offenders or domestic violence offenders, have additional restrictions on their housing options based on risks to community safety. Some offenders find a place to live at a halfway house that provides additional structure to offenders re-entering society or who are unable to stay in their homes due to sexual or violent behavior toward others living there. However, even halfway houses find themselves situated in communities that present considerable risks for recidivism or relapse into addictive behaviors, which results in probation or parole violations and trips to jail or prison.

Probation and parole orders for offenders with mental illness and addiction issues often requires the offender to participate in treatment for his or her mental illness or addictive behavior. Additionally, mental health counselors often intervene with offending behaviors that the justice system does not always consider as stemming from mental health problems, like domestic violence behaviors. People convicted of sexual offending behaviors are another group that the justice system requires treatment for, but may not view these offenders as mentally ill.

Grant funding may pay for counseling or other supportive services, but this is less likely for offenders than it is for victims of crime. Society perceives offenders as responsible for the choices they made and the resulting consequences of those choices. Therefore, these grant-funding organizations often do not consider the fact that many offenders became involved with the law because of their mental health or addiction issues, most of the time. Therefore, offenders are usually required to pay for their own mental health needs. Additionally, many of these people require psychiatric medications and monitoring by a psychiatric doctor or nurse practitioner, which are expensive. For someone who struggles to pay for basic food and shelter needs, these services often go neglected. This is one of the most significant reasons that offenders with mental illness have much higher rates of recidivism than those without mental illness, which results in their being incarcerated.

Continuum of Treatment Intensity

Court orders often mandate mental health treatment for offenders. This is particularly true for those with mental illness because of their increased risks of recidivism (Torrey et al., 2015; Wilson, Draineb, Hadley, Metraux, & Evans, 2011). Because of their mental health needs, they tend to cost the system more when incarcerated than non-mentally ill offenders do. Although the cost of community-based treatment (including assistance with housing, employment, childcare, payment for medication and counseling) is less, society more frequently supports incarceration of mentally ill offenders rather than supporting them in the community. There are different levels of restriction in community treatment ranging from highly restrictive, like hospitalization or residential facilities, to less restrictive (e.g., partial hospital, intensive outpatient, and halfway houses), to the least restrictive (e.g., community agency, private practice, or increasingly re-entry centers specializing as a one-stop-shop for probation and parole needs).

Highly Restrictive

Correctional facilities are the most restrictive level of care and the most expensive care available, although they are not always the best quality of care for mentally ill offenders. Intended as short-term placement options for people awaiting trial or for people, *jails* frequently house mentally ill offenders for a variety of reasons. Increases in people with SMI entering the judicial system because of lack of community-based care results in high numbers of people with significant disorders held pretrial because they cannot afford bail or cannot negotiate release due to the effects of their mental illness. Jails generally do not have facilities or funding for mental health treatment. Some jails are beginning to pursue grant funding or negotiate with mental health professionals who volunteer services to provide basic levels of treatment. However, due to limitations of the setting, clinicians frequently experience significant ethical and liability concerns when providing services in jail settings.

Some prisons, state or federal, function with specialized treatment units that focus on addictive disorders and others focus on sexual offending behaviors, etc. Others have mental health units for inmates with diagnoses, within larger prisons that house all offenders. These units must provide competent, appropriate, mental health care under the Eighth Amendment of the Constitution (*Estelle v. Gamble, 1976*). However, how and who determines what "competent" and "appropriate" consists of is vague. With the privatization of prisons, increasing numbers of lawsuits assert that these prisons do not provide adequate mental health care and therefore violate the offenders' constitutional rights (Bauer, 2016; Fazel, Hayes, Bartellas, Clerici, & Trestmant, 2016; Thompson & Eldridge, 2018). Providing specialized mental health care in prisons also has unique challenges. Some prisons have "counselors" who are not trained in counseling, do not have supervised clinical counseling practice, nor have any professional credentials, such a government-regulated counseling license. Additionally, these individuals do not work under the guidance of professional standards of practice or codes of ethics. However, frequently, because they have the title of "counselor," they believe they possess equal skills and treatment authority as someone with a counseling degree and license.

Like jails, prisons are not set up to function as mental health facilities. So, issues of informed consent, confidentiality, and privilege are challenging. Additionally, correctional officers or administrators may override treatment professionals regarding placement level and types of treatment offered. There is a significant lack of culturally competent care including a lack of non-religiously based mental health services (Freshman, n.d.; Kapoor, Dike, Burns, & Carvalho, 2013; page & Travis, 2009). Negotiation between correctional staff who focus on structure and security, and treatment staff who focus on helping inmates develop internal self-regulatory controls, can be problematic and result in strain on the system and confusion among those providing services to offenders with mental illness.

Medical or psychiatric hospitalization is generally reserved for individuals in crisis. A mental health professional must assess them as posing a significant imminent risk to himself or herself or another person. This can result from not taking antipsychotic medication for someone with a psychotic disorder to threats or behaviors indicating intent to self-harm or commit suicide. Increased risk occurs when someone has a history of major depression and history of suicidality. Hospitalization can also result from assessment findings that suggest that the person presents imminent risk to another person if not hospitalized (e.g., a parent who may present risk to a child in his or her care if the parent is off medication or is using illicit substances). Generally, hospitalization is reserved for crisis stabilization or "treat 'em and street 'em." The goal is to help the client establish therapeutic levels of medication, reduce crisis-related mental health symptoms, and reduce risk of danger to self or others. Once accomplished, the expectation is that the person is "stepped down" to a less restrictive level of service.

Residential treatment centers (RTCs) maintain a very restrictive environment without the medical focus. Individuals in RTCs are generally in locked facilities, just as psychiatric hospitals, but the focus is on therapeutic intervention (counseling, therapeutic milieu, and medication maintenance), rather than medical intervention or crisis stabilization. The goal of an RTC is to provide an environment where the individual experiences therapeutic care in multiple venues (group, individual, the therapeutic community) to address long-standing pervasive behavioral manifestations of mental health issues. A number of mental health problems are best addressed in RTCs, including pervasive addictive disorders in which the person experiences frequent relapse, severe abuse, or trauma-related disorders (e.g., PTSD, dissociative disorders, borderline personality disorder), or personality disorders. Additionally, clinicians recommend RTC settings when there is an ongoing risk for de-compensation or need for significant intervention to de-escalate the person when the person becomes emotionally (and behaviorally) dysregulated so as to hopefully prevent escalation to the point of needing hospitalization or to the point that the person engages in harm to self or others.

Less Restrictive

There are several less restrictive options for treatment than in-patient hospitalization or RTCs. These include hospital programs that operate based on a *continuum of care*, which is a range of mental health intervention services that are offered at varying levels of care. This includes psychiatric hospitals that offer step-down services like *partial hospitalization* (PHP) and/or *intensive outpatient services* (IOP). PHP services provide an intensity level of care between residential or inpatient hospitalization and IOP services. PHP typically requires 20 hours or more of therapeutic services. The assessment indicates the client does not require 24-hour care but still requires intense services beyond what outpatient counseling would offer. Generally, psychiatric monitoring is still available, and often the services still occur at the hospital location. IOP is the least restrictive environment before community-based treatment. This level of care typically requires 6 to 9 hours of service per week or more, but less than 20 hours. These services usually occur after work or school hours, either in the evening and/or on weekends. Individuals usually live at home and attend PHP or IOP, although they may stay in treatment-specific halfway houses. PHP and IOP, like psychiatric hospitalization, tend to be expensive and insurance pays or clients private pay, if they can afford it.

Halfway houses are community-based residential facilities where offenders with mental illness are able to secure housing and meals while they work in the community. Residents generally adhere to "house rules" regarding the therapeutic community. The programs require at least 5 hours of treatment-related services each week. A halfway house emphasizes recovery, responsibility, and improved independent functioning within the community. Individuals living in these environments expect to work their way back to living on their own in the community while maintaining therapeutic gains from treatment interventions.

Least Restrictive Outpatient Services

Outpatient services are the least restrictive environment in which offenders may obtain mental health treatment. Unfortunately, this is often an option only for offenders of majority ethnicity or those who have significant financial or family resources, which enable them to follow through with community-based treatment. Outpatient services allow offenders to live in their homes and maintain their lifestyles, work schedules, and other activities of normal living. Ideally, individuals treated in outpatient settings are at lowest risk for recidivism and/or relapse. However, in reality these placements often reflect gender (in the case of domestic violence offenders), socioeconomic, and ethnic biases inherent in the justice system.

There are structured psycho-educationally based interventions or manualized treatment interventions, which require little therapeutic skill, which many courts order offenders to attend. These include batterers' intervention programs, anger management programs, and substance abuse education programs. Agencies frequently have contracts with courts to provide prescriptive (e.g., 10 sessions using a standardized curriculum) interventions for a set fee, which the offenders are court ordered to pay or they could be in violation of probation/parole orders.

Therapeutic counseling skills are necessary for individual or family counseling or process group counseling, often ordered by some courts. These services usually take place in community agencies and are less often specifically outlined as probationary requirements, in court orders. Courts generally do not understand the individualized and unstructured interventions used in therapeutic counseling settings, nor can costs be as easily predicted as "canned" interventions. However, therapeutic services like individual, group, or family counseling may be grant funded. Grants may subsidize or pay full fees for counseling services, which make these services affordable for clients. Agencies also often offer children's groups or childcare, simultaneously as part of their mission to serve the community and ensure a parent's success in treatment. Higher-income clients may pay for therapeutic counseling services out of pocket or use insurance to fund their mental health treatment, which may be provided in agencies or private practice settings.

Specialized treatment is court ordered when they specifically identify the offense with a mental health or behavioral health disorder, such as sex offender treatment. Many states further regulate sex offender treatment because the community perceives these offenders as needing specialized intervention. Some states require specialized training and even require mental health service providers to hold specific professional licenses to work with sex offenders. In Texas, specially licensed and trained sex offender treatment providers treat civilly committed sex offenders, considered the most at-risk for reoffending in community settings. This is an example of least-restrictive environment, with a highly dangerous group of offenders.

Case Study: Enrique Part II

Enrique is a 28 year-old first generation Mexican-American male incarcerated following a third arrest for possession of narcotics with intent to sell. Enrique's history is discussed in chapter 4. Enrique became involved with a street gang, the Latin Kings, when he was 11 years old. He found comfort and protection from older men in the group who he looked up to. He began running drugs for the gang shortly after becoming involved with them. He was smart, didn't talk much, and was well liked by the older gang members. Additionally, the gang liked him because he didn't "use the product."

Within a year, he was running his own crew and began running prostitutes as well. Enrique had a head for business and knew not to "rat out" his fellow gang members. He was first arrested at 16, when he got into a brutal street fight with the son of the man who murdered his mother. The fight resulted in the other boy being in a coma for 2 weeks and resulted in sustained head injuries and lifetime disability. Due to the history between the boys, the court had mercy on Enrique and sent him to a juvenile facility where he could get therapy. However, he did not engage in therapy, manipulated and used his intelligence to "get over" on the staff so that they thought he was a changed person. Within days of release, he was running drugs and prostitutes for the gang again.

He was arrested again at 19, 22, and again at 28 for possession of a large amount of narcotics with intent to sell. Currently, he is incarcerated in Joliet State Penitentiary and aligns himself with the Latin Kings. Enrique enjoys listening to music and drawing and appears to be a very talented artist. His sister, Eliana, provides him with art supplies. Eliana, and sometimes one of her children, visits Enrique at least once per month when allowed by the prison. Her husband, Enrique's adoptive father, does not communicate with Enrique. Enriquee is serving a 10-year mandatory term with no possibility of early release. He is not interested in becoming involved with treatment, but he is interested in taking an art class offered by a visiting art professor who is part of a junior college educational program. As part of participation in the educational program, Enrique must also attend counseling at least weekly. Following his initial assessment, Enrique is found to have a high IQ, but he also suffers from posttraumatic stress disorder and depression. He reports that other than going to play therapy following his mother's murder, he doesn't really remember ever going to any counseling or seeing a doctor for a mental health issue other than that.

Case Application Questions

1. Analyze Enrique's case (using both part I and part II), applying biological, cognitive, social, moral, psychological, and spiritual developmental models. How would this analysis inform your approach to treatment?
2. Describe Enrique's case using one of the developmental theories of offending.
3. Discuss how CIT officers might have interacted with Enrique as a young child following his mother's murder that may have diverted him to treatment rather than escalating his behavior toward criminality.
4. What setting would you recommend for Enrique as a juvenile offender versus as an adult offender? Explain your reasoning.

SUMMARY

This chapter addresses the various contexts within which forensic mental health counselors (FMHC) work with adult offenders, particularly those with documented mental illness. We first described several developmental theories related to normal human development and development of criminality, as well as the sociocultural contexts involved in adult criminal behavior and the criminalization of that behavior. Additionally, the chapter discusses the trend toward increasing numbers of elderly offenders and the impact this trend has on offenders and the facilities and programs working to address their needs. The reader is encouraged to consider these contexts in assessment and diagnosis of adult offenders, as well as in development and evaluation of individualized treatment and population-specific treatment programs housed in community agencies and correctional settings. Additionally, the chapter describes different levels of care as related to different settings in which counselors work, including CIT training with police officers, mental health courts, psychiatric hospitals, correctional facilities, residential treatment centers, partial hospitalization programs, and intensive outpatient and regular outpatient settings.

CHAPTER 7 REFLECTIVE QUESTIONS

1. Discuss current trends for offenders experiencing mental illness and how these trends can inform your advocacy role as a forensic mental health counselor.

2. Analyze yourself using one of each type of developmental theory (biological, cognitive, moral, social, and spiritual).
3. Compare different models of offending behavior. Which one makes the most sense to you and why?
4. Discuss the sociocultural influences on adult offending. How would these inform your work in a community corrections setting?
5. Describe the role of treatment courts for adult offenders. What are the strengths and challenges of this approach to prevention/intervention?
6. Discuss the challenges experienced by adults in community corrections settings (probation, parole, re-entry) and how this knowledge will inform your approach to working with adult offenders.
7. Compare different levels of treatment intensity applied to adult offenders and how it relates to different risk levels.

RESOURCES

Aging Inmates: The Marshall Project: https://www.themarshallproject.org/records/251-aging-inmates

Treatment Advocacy Center: Focus on mental illness to reduce mass incarceration http://www.treatmentadvocacycenter.org/component/content/article/2883

Prison Policy Initiative: https://www.prisonpolicy.org/research/mental_health/

AVID Prison Project: http://www.avidprisonproject.org/

Crisis Intervention Training (CIT) International: http://www.citinternational.org/

National Prison Rape Elimination Act Resource Center: https://www.prearesourcecenter.org/about/prison-rape-elimination-act-prea

"The Impact of an Aging Inmate Population on the Federal Bureau of Prisons": https://oig.justice.gov/reports/2015/e1505.pdf

"Aging Behind Bars: Trends and Implications of Graying Prisoners in the Federal Prison System": https://www.urban.org/sites/default/files/publication/33801/413222-Aging-Behind-Bars-Trends-and-Implications-of-Graying-Prisoners-in-the-Federal-Prison-System.PDF

Human Rights Watch: "Old Behind Bars: The Aging Prison Population in the U.S.": https://www.hrw.org/sites/default/files/reports/usprisons0112webwcover_0.pdf

Adult Offenders

Part II: Mental Health

Upon completion of this chapter, readers will be able to do the following:

- ■ Discuss common mental health concerns and challenges to treating these mental health issues among adult offenders
- ■ Analyze common issues related to therapeutic intervention forensic mental health counselors experience with adult offenders
- ■ Discuss the unique challenges to gaining informed consent in a correctional setting, including mandated counseling, vulnerability of the population, and limits to confidentiality
- ■ Discuss the importance of documentation as a risk management tool

TABLE 8.1 Myths and Myth Busters

Myths	Myth Busters
All adult offenders are psychopaths.	**Many adult offenders are victims of trauma suffering from mental illness and/or addictions, which lead to their criminality.**
Mental illness is not common among correctional populations.	**Offenders commonly have diagnosed mental illnesses like mood disorders, anxiety, PTSD, psychosis, paraphilias, and personality disorders.**
Offenders do not have the right to mental health treatment.	**Appropriate, competent, mental health treatment is guaranteed under the Eighth Amendment of the Constitution.**
Researchers can freely conduct studies on prisoners without special provisions.	**Prisoners are considered a vulnerable population requiring special oversight by institutional review boards when conducting human research.**

INTRODUCTION

Throughout the text, I have provided information about adverse childhood experiences (ACEs), and in section III, I will discuss treatment for past trauma. However, it is important to reiterate that ACEs are common among offender populations. In fact, among state prisoners with mental health, diagnoses were more than twice as likely as those without a mental health disorder to report past physical or sexual abuse (James & Glaze, 2006). Jail inmates with mental illness were three times more likely to have been abused (James & Glaze, 2006). However, given the reduced rates of reporting past abuse and the numbers of offenders who do not classify their early abuse experiences as abuse, this number is likely low. These experiences result in development of mood disorders, trauma-related disorders, and addictive behaviors (Aday & Krbill, 2011; Herman, 1997, 2015). As previously discussed, addiction is common among offender populations. Underlying addictive disorders motivate criminal behavior for a large percentage of offenders (e.g., stealing to get money for drugs, vehicular manslaughter while drunk, selling drugs). For others, the addiction may not be a direct part of their offending behavior, but it may be an underlying mental health issue, which needs treatment. Therefore, this chapter builds on the foundation provided in chapter 7 to discuss the specific issues forensic mental health counselors address when working with mentally ill or addicted adult offenders.

COMMON MENTAL HEALTH CONCERNS

For the purpose of this section, *offenders with mental illness* (OMI) are defined as those offenders currently suffering from diagnosable mental health symptoms or receiving treatment for mental health issues from a mental health professional (James & Glaze, 2006). *Non-specific psychological distress*, on the other hand, includes reports of nervousness, hopelessness, restlessness, being fidgety, depression, feeling things take a lot of effort, and feelings of worthlessness, without acknowledgement of an underlying diagnosis (Bronson & Berzofsky, 2017).

According to the Department of Justice (DOJ), more jail inmates (26%) than federal prisoners (14%) report non-specific psychological distress (Bronson & Berzofsky, 2017). Similarly, a higher percentage of jail inmates report a history of seeking mental health care (44%) than federal prisoners (37%). However, among the estimates of offenders with diagnosable mental illness, the rates are much higher (James & Glaze, 2006). Most state prisoners (56%) and county or city jail inmates (64%) have diagnosable mental illness. Federal prisoners were consistent in having lower rates of diagnoses (45%), but it was still higher than those reporting psychological distress. When thinking critically about this information, different conclusions may be drawn. One explanation is that federal prisoners may be higher functioning than state or local inmates may. Additionally, incarcerated offenders are unwilling to acknowledge mental health issues or are less aware of mental health issues they have (Morgan et al., 2012). Regardless of the rates of mental illness within correction settings, state inmates with mental illness received longer sentences than those without, and only one third received mental health treatment while in prison (James & Glaze, 2006). Additionally, more state and local inmates who have mental health issues had three or more previous incarcerations than those without mental health diagnoses (James & Glaze, 2006).

Mood Disorders

Mood disorders include dysthymia, major depression, and bipolar disorder. These are very common among offender populations; therefore, forensic mental health counselors frequently work with individuals with mood disorders. According to the most recently available statistics from the DOJ, about one third of state and federal inmates report symptoms consistent with a mood disorder (Bronson & Berzofsky, 2017; James & Glaze, 2006). However, almost half of local inmates housed in jails reported depressive or manic symptoms. Given that jail is the entry point for offenders into the system, it is likely that these inmates experience a crisis, which stresses their resources more than those who have some resolution (are to prison) around their crime. Additionally, jails are frequently overcrowded and have less resources than prisons, which may result in increased stress and subsequent problems with active mental illness.

Although mood disorders are common, only 6% of federal prisoners and 12–13% of state and local prisoners report past suicide attempts (James & Glaze, 2006). Among those who are suicidal or have externalizing behavioral manifestations of mood disorders, they are more likely to go into solitary confinement, which further exacerbates these symptoms. According to the World Health Organization (WHO) (2007), pretrial detainees attempt suicide at 7.5 times the rate of sentenced prisoners. Jails often house vulnerable populations alongside violent predators. Jails are notoriously overcrowded and often have few mental health resources and ineffective policies or procedures for identifying or managing suicidal inmates. Drug offenders often experience withdrawal in jail, and people with existing major depression or bipolar disorder may not have access to their medications.

Medication management is the most used intervention for depression. However, increasing socialization on the unit can be helpful, which is why isolation of an inmate in a secure unit is contraindicated. Individuals with mood disorders are at higher risk for suicidal behavior, and isolation can further exacerbate suicidality. Mental health professionals provide information and guidance to correctional staff regarding identifying and assessing individuals at risk for suicidality. Also, providing supportive psychotherapy helps the inmate process through the range of emotions and feelings of isolations, which are common for someone in this setting. One intervention that has demonstrated success in improving symptoms of depression is animal-assisted therapy (AAT). Research suggests, just having a dog on the unit improves the mood of inmates and staff alike (Cooke & Farrington, 2016; Dell & Poole, 2016; Holman, Wilkerson, Ellmo, & Skirius, in press; Mimms, Waddell, & Holton, 2017).

Anxiety Disorders

Given that anxiety disorders are one of the most commonly diagnosed categories of mental illness, it makes sense that many offenders experience anxiety symptoms (Kupfer, 2015). In fact, anxiety disorders are among the most commonly diagnosed mental illnesses in prisons (Steadman & Veysey, 1997). Being in a correctional facility can create or exacerbate anxiety symptoms. Signs and symptoms of generalized anxiety disorder include feeling restless, irritable, or agitated; experiencing muscle tension and sleep problems; feeling fatigued; having difficulty concentrating, and experiencing excessive worry (APA, 2013). Many people in jail experience these symptoms; however, for individuals with existing anxiety disorders, a correctional environment can make these symptoms worse (Metzner & Fellner, 2010; Reinhardt & Rogers, 1998). Anxiety disorders are highly amenable to behavioral interventions like progressive muscle relaxation, visualizations, and sensory interventions like sand tray and animal-assisted therapy. Additionally, encouraging socialization by going to scheduled activities helps alleviate anxiety for many inmates.

Another common anxiety disorder, which can mimic a heart attack, is panic disorder. When someone has panic disorder, they experience repeated panic attacks that cause extreme fear and all the associated physiological responses for fear like sweating, shortness of breath, accelerated heartbeat, pounding heart, palpitations, and feelings of impending doom. Situations of feeling out of control or having intense worry make panic attacks more likely to occur. Again, it is easy to see how anyone in a correctional setting can have these experiences, so if they are predisposed to anxiety, it makes sense that they may have panic attacks.

Although medication can be very helpful for people with anxiety disorders, these prescriptions are less likely in a correctional facility because there is a high risk for abuse. Even if the person prescribed the medicine does not want it, it is common for inmates to "cheek" (hide it in their cheek and not swallow) the medication and then sell or trade it later on the unit for something they want.

Posttraumatic Stress Disorder (PTSD)

Previously categorized as an anxiety disorder, PTSD is also one of the more common mental health diagnoses among inmates (Steadman & Veysey, 1997). Although not everyone who experiences trauma develops PTSD, it is common among inmates who have multiple experiences resulting in complex trauma. To have a diagnosis of PTSD, symptoms must last more than a month and the symptoms must adversely affect functioning. There are different types of symptoms involved in PTSD including re-experiencing symptoms (flashbacks, nightmares, intrusive thoughts), avoidance symptoms (avoiding physical or sensory triggers or thoughts or feelings that trigger the trauma memory), arousal and reactivity symptoms (exaggerated startle response, agitation, hypervigilance, difficulty sleeping, or angry outbursts), and cognition and mood symptoms (dissociation, thought distortions, depression). To satisfy a diagnosis of PTSD, the offender must have at least one each of the re-experiencing and avoidance symptoms and two symptoms from the other two categories.

It is complicated to treat PTSD in a correctional setting because of the threatening nature of the environment (Sarteschi, 2013). The prevalence rate of PTSD among state inmates ranges between 22%–30%; also, 15%–19% of individuals in community corrections met the diagnostic criteria for major depression (Sarteschi, 2013). However, rates of trauma exposure among incarcerated men range from 62.4%–100% (Wolf, Chugo, Shi, Huening, & Frueh, 2015; Wolf, Huening, Shi, & Frueh, 2014). Given that offenders are less willing to disclose mental health issues in a correctional setting, and the fact that they are not always aware of mental health symptoms due to chronic detachment or dissociation, it is possible the rates of PTSD are lower than actual rates of PTSD (Akyuz, Kugu, Sar, & Dogan, 2009; Altinatas & Mustafa, 2018).

Hyperarousal or hypervigilance is another common manifestation of PTSD among offender populations, which can result in the offender acting out of fear, leading to verbally or behaviorally aggressive interactions with peers or staff. Hypervigilance is the experience of having heightened sensitivity to sensory environmental triggers (sights, sounds, smells, noises). When a sensory trigger activates a nondeclarative memory of past trauma, the ANS system responds, and the offender reacts in fight, flight, or freeze mode to the fear associated with the trigger. Given that violent offenders exhibit aggressive behavior, it is likely they will demonstrate considerable anger. Angry and irritable outbursts are the most commonly identified PTSD symptom among this population (Akyuz, Kugu, Sar, & Dogan, 2009).

Correctional settings are triggering environments (for prisoners and for staff). They are loud and institutionally cold in the way they look. Although guards theoretically control the unit, there are underlying interpersonal networks of people or gangs, which have considerable power and who outnumber guards. Offenders do not always know which of their peers are potentially violent and which are not, although offenders circulate this information on the unit in an "unofficial" orientation to prison. In fact, for staff and counselors it is probably a good thing to be on guard as well because these are threatening environments and populations, by definition.

It is helpful for counselors in forensic settings to provide psychoeducation to non-mental health professionals, formally or informally, on the manifestations of PTSD. A good model for this is crisis intervention training (CIT), which we have used to train police officers, border patrol agents, and an Army forward surgical team deployed in Afghanistan. A full description of the CIT model is provided in the interventions section of this chapter. The purpose of CIT is to de-escalate potentially dangerous situations in order to reduce risks of harm to the offender and to community members (fellow prisoners if incarcerated). Secondly, it should result in diverting the offender to mental health treatment when appropriate.

There are trauma-informed treatment practices, which are helpful for some offenders. But the first rule of trauma therapy is to establish safety. In a correctional setting, you cannot guarantee safety. If you help a client access trauma memories and experiences on a prison unit, you will likely put him or her in a more vulnerable position to be victimized. Therefore, in correctional settings, using the types of techniques we teach in CIT is the preferred intervention. However, you can provide psychoeducation on trauma, help the client learn skills to manage the symptoms of trauma being triggered in the prison environment, and act as a sounding board that reflects back his or her thoughts, feelings, and experiences so that he or she feels heard, which will help ameliorate his or her trauma symptoms so that he or she can function in this setting.

Addictive Disorders

The most common crime committed among mentally ill offenders is a drug offense (48%), so it makes sense that many offenders have substance use disorders (SUDs) (Steadman &

Veysey, 1997). According to the DOJ, 50.8% of state and 53.4% of local prisoners had an alcohol use disorder (James & Glaze 2006). This is about twice the rate of federal prisoners (25.1%). Interestingly, the rates of drug use disorders were much more similar. They report that 61.9% of state and 63.3% of local prisoners had a drug use disorder compared to 53.2% of federal prisoners (James & Glaze, 2006). Almost 75% of state prisoners reporting mental illness also reported a co-occurring substance use disorder (James & Glaze, 2006; Kim, Becker-Cohen, & Serakos, 2015). Comorbidity of SUDs with major depressive disorder ranges from 12.3% to 20% for any person with a SUD (Currie et al., 2005; Volkow, n.d.); however, for drug users, the rate of comorbidity is over 40%. Additionally, the rate of comorbidity between anxiety disorders and SUDs is just under 20% for all SUDs and 30% for drug users (Volkow, n.d.). There is an entire chapter on addictive disorders in the next section of the text; therefore, manifestations of addictive disorders among offender populations will not be discussed in this section.

Psychotic Disorders

Psychotic disorders are considerably less common among incarcerated offenders. Most police jurisdictions have CIT training, which teaches them how to engage an actively psychotic person safely and divert them to mental health treatment (psychiatric facility or hospital), rather than placing them in jail. Additionally, mental health courts are more common, particularly in medium to large cities. These courts, discussed in the interventions section, are concerned primarily with treatment rather than punishment for these offenders. However, according to the DOJ, 11.8% of state and 17.5% of jail inmates reported or were observed to have active delusions, and a corresponding 7.9% of state and 13.7% jail inmates experience hallucinations (James & Glaze, 2006). Federal prisoners, however, tended to have less psychosis. Only 7.8% experienced delusions and 4.8% experienced hallucinations.

Paraphilias

Paraphilias are sexually deviant behaviors, which are diagnosable. Individuals with paraphilias experience intense sexual arousal and obsessive thoughts about the objects of sexual arousal. These can be fantasies or situations of sexually deviant behavior like *frotteurism* (sexual arousal from rubbing against someone in a crowded place), *voyeurism* (e.g., peeping Tom), and *exhibitionism* (e.g., flashing). Sexual interests can be objects like shoes, underwear, and so on, called *sexual fetishism*. The behaviors can also be acts of abuse like rape (diagnosed as *sadism*), child molestation (diagnosed as *pedophilia*), or downloading child pornography. Although all of these behaviors are sex crimes, many offenders with paraphilias plead down to a lesser, non-sexual offense and courts sentence them like any other offender. Therefore, they may be in the general population of offenders, even if counselors do not work specifically with sex offenders. Additionally, someone may have a sexual offending history, but his or her *instant offense*, the current offense for which the person is serving time, is not a sex offense. Therefore, it is crucial that counselors maintain awareness as they work with offenders as any attempt to manipulate or flatter them, or attempt to cross boundaries of any kind, can be a function of their underlying sexual disorder. These are attempts to *groom* you to participate in something devious. Paraphilias will be discussed at length in a later chapter on sex offenders.

Personality Disorders

Personality disorders are the most common disorders diagnosed among offender populations, particularly the dramatic cluster including narcissistic, antisocial, histrionic, and borderline (Timmerman & Emmelkamp, 2001). Diagnostic criteria should be demonstrated in multiple settings over the course of years. Historically, mental health providers believed personality disorders were untreatable; however, newer research indicates otherwise. It is important to remember that people can have characteristics/features of multiple personality disorders or even meet diagnostic criteria for more than one. Personality disorders are consistent long-standing patterns of interpersonal strategies people use to get their psychological needs met (American Psychological Association, 2013). Because these are interpersonal strategies, it is almost guaranteed that mental health professionals in forensic settings will experience offenders with acting out their personality disorder(s) with them in the context of the therapeutic relationship. This can be an opportunity for therapeutic interpersonal interventions.

Among these, *antisocial personality disorder* (APD) is the most common personality disorder diagnosed among offender populations (Steadman & Veysey, 1997). This makes sense, given that criminal behavior often dovetails with the diagnostic criteria for APD, including "a pervasive pattern of disregard for and violation of the rights of others, occurring since age 15" (APA, 2013, p. 659). Many people who receive an APD diagnosis have a history of conduct disorder as a child or adolescent. Because APD is such a stigmatizing label, the diagnosis cannot be given to anyone under 18. Men are diagnosed with APD more often than women; however, this may in part be a function of our socialization to believe women are less likely to engage in antisocial behaviors (APA, 2013).

Characteristics of APD include deceitfulness, impulsivity, reckless disregard for safety of self or others, consistent irresponsibility, and lack of remorse. These are similar traits for psychopathy, although the two are different. Psychopathy is a term used in criminal settings and assessed using the Hare psychopathy checklist-revised (PCL-R), along with other measures. Although not an exclusive explanation, one psychological conceptualization of APD is that these individuals experienced little, if any, attuned empathic caregiving as children and often experience repeated trauma. As a result, they believe the only way to get their psychological needs met is to take what they perceive they need from others. They often rationalize their behavior because of their past victimization; therefore, it is important for counselors to take care not to collude with these offenders that their past hurts are an excuse for their criminal behaviors; rather, they are an explanation for them.

Narcissistic personality disorder (NPD) or narcissistic features frequently coexist with APD. NPD includes "a pervasive pattern of grandiosity (in fantasy or behavior), need for admiration, and lack of empathy, beginning by early adulthood and present in a variety of contexts" (APA, 2013, p. 669). People challenged with NPD demonstrate a grandiose sense of self-importance and perceive themselves as "special." They experience obsessive thoughts of power and success, beauty, and/or intelligence. As such, they require constant admiration and praise. Since they are special, they feel and act entitled, as if the rules do not or should not apply to them the way they do with other people. They exploit others in relationships and lack empathy for doing so. To others they may appear arrogant.

A common psychological conceptualization of NPD is that the individual is overcompensating for deep underlying feelings of inferiority stemming from past trauma. They are overly sensitive to any perceived negative appraisal from another person, so mental health professionals should consider this when working with offenders who need be held accountable for their actions. Additionally, narcissistic people can be very charming and charismatic, so they may use these skills to try to befriend mental health professionals. Any time an offender interacts with a counselor as if he or she is his or her friend, counselors need to be aware that they are probably using an interpersonal strategy to manipulate them to get something they want, usually something not allowed. Counselors should not collude with them around their defenses. The therapeutic response is to maintain a professional boundary and process the interaction as evidence of their therapeutic issue.

Histrionic personality disorder (HPD) is "a pervasive pattern of excessive emotionality and attention seeking beginning by early adulthood and present in a variety of contexts" (APA, 2013, p. 667). These people need to be the center of attention at all times, and not being in the limelight results in intense feelings of anxiety or irritability. Behavior of someone with HPD can be sexually inappropriate, through attempts to seduce or provoke others into some inappropriate interchange (verbal or physical). If working in prison, mental health professionals are more likely than not to experience this, and the person's gender or the gender of the offender does not matter. It is important for mental health professionals to set boundaries, report this behavior, and process the interaction. In correctional settings, it is less common than community settings to have an HPD client's physical appearance (dress, hair, etc.) in a manner that draws attention to him- or herself. Most of what the person does is dramatic, almost theatrical. Emotions may shift suddenly and seem to lack depth. They are also easily suggestible, as if no depth to their sense of self. These clients can be particularly draining to work with, as they want a lot of attention. They will attempt to monopolize group or community meetings in therapeutic milieus and attempt to overstep boundaries and go over time in individual sessions. Once again, maintaining boundaries and processing the behavior as evidence of the therapeutic issue is key.

The final personality disorder in this cluster is *borderline personality disorder* (BPD). BPD is "a pervasive pattern of instability of interpersonal relationships, self-image, and affects, and marked impulsivity, beginning by early adulthood and present in a variety of contexts" (APA, 2013, p. 663). BPD is more often diagnosed in women than men; however, like APD, this may be a function of socialization. Additionally, BPD has diagnostic criteria similar to bipolar disorder. Someone can have both diagnoses; however, many clinicians or doctors do not conduct proper differential diagnoses to assess whether the client clearly meets both sets of diagnostic criteria. Interestingly, both disorders involve emotional instability and mood swings and doctors often prescribe mood stabilizers for both disorders. Like HPD, BPD clients are notoriously exhausting to work with because they demand so much attention (Kreisman & Straus, 2004, 2010). This may be due to both sets of clients having underlying shallow senses of selves, so they need constant interpersonal feedback to verify they "exist" psychologically. They often have identities that are fused with a caregiver (enmeshed boundaries, lack of separate identity), lover, and often a counselor.

The motivation for BPD behavior is frantic feelings that the person is at risk of abandonment or rejection. They may be imagining the rejection, but because they are often challenging interpersonally to be in relationship with, they often elicit feelings in others resulting in rejection or abandonment, thus reinforcing their pathological beliefs of themselves as unworthy (Teyber & Teyber, 2017). Simple disagreements with loved ones can result in attempts to reengage the other person in the relationship. Counselors being unavailable are notoriously challenging times for the BPD client. In order to reconnect with people they believe are abandoning them, they demonstrate unstable behavior that can include non-suicidal self-injury or suicide attempts. Due to the lack of a stable sense of self, internally, they exhibit external behaviors that are unstable, including demonstrations of extreme affect, mood, and behavior. Once again, boundaries are crucial. However, BPD clients also need to engage in processing the interpersonal interactions and underlying thoughts and feelings they experienced prior, during, and after an episode of instability in order to gain awareness of patterns. Dialectical behavior therapy was the first systematic easy-to-follow therapeutic intervention, which demonstrated success with BPD clients.

PREVENTION AND INTERVENTION

Forensic mental health providers use both prevention and intervention techniques in their work with adult offenders. Although the prevention efforts tend to occur before individuals become involved with the justice system, we will review some prevention methods that counselors may use in their work. Then common issues in mental health intervention will be discussed.

Prevention

As discussed in the previous chapter, we use *crisis intervention training* in many police jurisdictions as a prevention method. Mental health professionals train police officers to identify when an offender is demonstrating behavior consistent with the manifestations of their mental illness and either ground them in here-and-now reality for those who are dissociative or de-escalate those who are aggressive. The ultimate aim is to de-escalate the situation in order to minimize potential injuries to the office and to community members, as well as helping officers triage situations in order to identify when it is more appropriate to divert a citizen to community mental health treatment than arresting them.

Other common community resources are *mobile crisis units* (*MCU*). Community members can call an MCU number to have a mental health professional come to the community location to assess an individual in crisis. These situations often involve the person having made threats of harm to oneself or another person. The counselor may give the person referrals for community resources or send them to a psychiatric facility.

Interventions

When discussing interventions, unique treatment issues need to be addressed, which complicate offender treatment. These include challenges engaging in a therapeutic relationship and what it means to be in a therapeutic relationship; problems with emotional dysregulation; and other complicating factors like gang membership and work-crime interaction. Then there are the actual interventions. This section covers treating criminality, psychiatric rehabilitation, manualized and cognitive behavioral therapies (CBT), and trauma-informed interventions.

As you read this section, remember that there are two simultaneous overarching goals when working with offenders: providing an appropriate intervention and reducing recidivism. The first is to provide therapeutic intervention for the client, based on assessed needs. Doing this may or may not easily support the second goal, which is to address the criminal behavior in an effort to reduce risk of recidivism. Why would therapeutic intervention *not* support recidivism risk reduction?

I have worked with a subsection of offender clients over the years whose personal goals do not align with reduction in recidivism. They do not *want* to be incarcerated; however, they tend to be *okay* with being incarcerated. These clients fall into two categories, one of which is those who grew up "in the system." In other words, they lived in foster care, maybe even aged out of foster care, and have been in and out of jail. They will tell you plainly that they do not know how to live outside of a system. They know as long as they are locked up, they have a bed to sleep in, clothes to wear, and food to eat. The second category are those who enjoy their roles in the criminal justice system. They live by a street code. They have a sense of integrity around adhering to the street code, and their identities are intertwined with committing crime and being part of a criminal organization (e.g., mafia, gangs).

This is consistent with research on behavioral or environmental elements of recidivism risk, which can change with intervention. Andrews and colleagues (1990) identified the *big four*, which are a history of antisocial behavior, antisocial personality patterns, antisocial cognition, and antisocial associates. Then they added four more elements to those to become the *central eight* including family and/or marital relationship, school and/or work, leisure and/or recreation, and substance abuse (Andrews & Dowden, 2006). Those clients with goals inconsistent with reducing recidivism tended to want to work on the second set of the central eight; however, they were not interested in working on the big four.

Treatment Issues: Problems Trusting and Engaging in Relationships

We know that the therapeutic relationship is the only intervention, which research consistently demonstrates, that is effective in motivating change for counseling clients (Stargell, 2017; Teyber & Teyber, 2017). Based on Carl Rogers's (1957) work, there are three conditions necessary in building a trusting therapeutic relationship that can motivate change: accurate empathy, genuineness, and treating the client with respect and unconditional positive regard. This can feel like a tall order when working with criminals, but the importance of the therapeutic relationship in doing any therapeutic work cannot be overstated. One challenge is that offenders typically have long and complicated histories with multiple relational traumas, often beginning as children and continuing into adulthood. Relational traumas teach people to avoid trusting others because trusting someone else, letting down your guard, results in being hurt. Therefore, this is a hurdle to deal with from the outset, and even after trust is initially established, it is tenuous and needs intentional attention throughout the counseling relationship. Finding things in their lives (currently or historically) that you can express genuine empathy for, and acknowledging these events, thoughts, and feelings, helps build a connection (*accurate empathy*). Again, this does not mean *excusing* the behavior; rather, it means that empathizing with these experiences and how they affected the client's life trajectory, how they *explain* the criminal behavior (*genuineness*).

Additionally, from the offenders' perspective, they are mandated to treatment or choose treatment because they are being punished for something they did that is perceived as wrong by their treatment provider. Therefore, their belief, maybe rightly so, is that they are being judged. It takes time to communicate and demonstrate counselors may judge their behavior as wrong, but that is different from judging who they are as a person. Counselors must do this through consistent interactions, with them and with others on the unit or in the program because they are watching. Approaching them as equal human beings who deserve respect and compassion, which is not always easy, is crucial to building a therapeutic relationship (*respect and unconditional positive regard*). Working through relationship ruptures when a counselor's behavior communicates that they are being judged as a person. These are often the most powerful therapeutic moments, which can really change cognitive distortions through honest open dialogue.

Treatment Issues: Problems With Emotional Dysregulation

If our offending clients could appropriately self-regulate emotions, they probably would not be in offender treatment programs because many people working with offenders become frustrated when a client does not self-regulate appropriately (e.g., talks it out rather than punching someone, uses progressive muscle relaxation rather than using drugs). It is a simple, but not easy, concept. If they could, they would. As previously explained in earlier chapters, their life experiences in relationship to their genetic vulnerabilities resulted in neurological dysfunction. They do not have effective wiring between the limbic and executive function areas of the brain. That is why they need services from a mental health professional. Therapeutic intervention is designed to use interpersonal neurobiology to help our emotionally dysregulated clients move from interpersonal or outside (e.g., drugs, violence) regulation of emotion to internal self-regulation of emotion (talking, progressive muscle relaxation, petting a dog, etc.).

Treatment Issues: Environmental Complications

The offenders you work with may not have social support systems like those that you experience. For some, their social support systems help them externally regulate uncomfortable emotions. Your clients may consider a criminal organization (gang, mafia) their family, so there is a *gang-criminality interaction*.

Take a client I once had in prison, Alfonso (pseudonym), orphaned at 9 years old when his mother was raped and murdered. CPS placed him with family members who did not care for him, but who did take the government check sent to them to care for him. He was living on the street by the age of 10. An older gang member in the neighborhood allowed him to sleep on his couch, gave him food, and put him to work selling drugs and pimping prostitutes, which brought him a good deal of money. He had financial and psychological security thanks to a gang member who most of society (maybe even his counselor) thinks of only in negative terms. However, this is the only "family" he had. While doing his third 10-year stint in prison, I was his counselor. He liked to read. He asked me the types of books we read in school, and he ordered those to read. He was very bright and learned a lot about psychology. He liked to verbally spar with me about the psychology behind crime. He always attempted to look neat and clean and kept his hair in cornrows. One day he had a court date that could have resulted in release. On that day, he took his hair out of cornrows, wore pants that sagged, and a wrinkled shirt. He was not released, and when we discussed it later, I asked why he chose to go to court like that. He said, "Because I'm a thug." We had many subsequent conversations about what "being a thug" meant to him, meant about him. He was clear that his "people" (the gang) had his loyalty and going to court looking like anyone other than the stereotyped "thug" would be disrespectful, judgmental, of those people who cared for him and whom he cared for. His loyalty to a group that encouraged criminal behavior made sense, given his history, even if I knew (as did he) that he was capable of an education, decent work, and a solid law-abiding life.

Similarly, for some criminals there is an interaction between their work and their criminal behavior (*work-criminality interaction*)

An example might be a 45-year-old second-generation Italian man who owns an Italian restaurant. That seems like a good legitimate business. However, his business serves as a social meeting place for a group of men engaged in organized crime. When he is released, in order to make money to feed, clothe, and house his family, he intends to continue running this restaurant. He will necessarily be interacting with criminals who will discuss, maybe even plan or carry out, criminal activities in the restaurant. It will be difficult, if not impossible for this man to disengage from this arrangement because his work relies on criminals. It is a source of survival. Although he is unlikely to want to change the criminal behavior, he may want to learn better ways to interact with his wife and kids. He may be willing to learn different ways to handle anger. So, you work with him on what you can, what he is willing to do.

The final complicating factor I want to discuss is the *splintered treatment* offenders often experience. When a correctional assessment or a community corrections (e.g., probation/parole) officer evaluates an offender's risks and needs and identifies services to minimize risk and address needs (responsivity), they send the offender to one or more treatment programs. They may go to one treatment program for substance addiction and another for anger management, for instance. However, both substance abuse and angry outbursts are symptoms of the same problem. The treatment received is splintered, as if you can treat one problem in one group/program, treat a different problem in another group/program, give medication for a comorbid diagnosis of depression, and not even acknowledge the underlying trauma and insecure attachment that underlies both. Mental health professionals know from years of research that concurrent treatment (in the same group or program) is the best way to treat multiple disorders. The disorders interact with one another in an individually unique pattern, which requires an adept mental health professional or team of professionals working together to adequately treat the complexity of the offenders' presenting issues. However, mental health professionals do not run the criminal justice system, so the criminal justice system either is not aware of this knowledge or chooses to dismiss it.

Approaches to Intervention and Treatment

There are several approaches commonly used in treating adult offending behaviors. Some stem from criminal justice literature and others from mental health disciplines. There are institutions that use one form of intervention approach exclusively, while others integrate several approaches into their treatment systems. Treating criminality, psychiatric rehabilitation, and cognitive behavioral manualized treatment protocols are typical of correctional facilities. Increasingly, however, culturally competent care and trauma-informed care are gaining more traction in these systems due to the high recidivism rates occurring with these "evidenced-based practices." Additionally, due to increased awareness of the unique challenges faced by mentally ill offenders, more jurisdictions have established re-entry clinics that coordinate all the services a parolee may need in one location. For jurisdictions with few resources, like rural areas, they often outsource care to community agencies or engage providers located in other areas of the state through telehealth. The chapters in section III of the text will discuss specific interventions for offenders with addictive disorders, domestic violence offenders, and sex offenders.

ETHICAL AND LEGAL ISSUES

The intersection of the law with mental illness presents complex challenges that speak to both legal standards governing treatment of mentally ill individuals involved with the justice system and ethical standards guiding the obligations of mental health professionals working within these systems. Compounding these challenges, different states use different, laypersons' terminology to label mental health issues (Kim, Becker-Cohen, & Serakos, 2015). However, these terms do often not reflect the clinical definition of mental illness provided by the American Psychiatric Association's Diagnostic and Statistical Manual (5th ed.) (2013), nor do they reflect the complex interaction between comorbid disorders commonly found among mentally ill offenders, making it difficult to classify prisoners with mental illness and to identify them for mental health intervention programming (Kim, Becker-Cohen, & Serakos, 2015). Additionally, nebulous definitions of mental illness or counselor/counseling allow non-trained non-licensed "counselors" (e.g., correctional officers) access to jobs providing mental health care to some of the most challenging mentally ill individuals in our communities. Next, I will discuss some of the common legal and ethical issues professional mental health counselors must be aware of when working in forensic settings.

Competence

To be found guilty of a crime in the United States, an individual must meet two elements, including a criminal act (actus reus) and mental culpability (mens rea) indicating that the individual purposefully, knowingly, recklessly, or negligently engages in the criminal behavior, thus indicating his or her responsibility for the crime. However, we consider some individuals incompetent to possess mental culpability for criminal actions under the law. Mental illness is considered a mitigating factor, which both the U.S. Supreme Court (*Peny v. Lynaugh*, 1989) and the Fifth Circuit Court of Appeals (*Bigby v. Dretke*, 2005) assert must be considered in judicial matters or the court is in violation of the Eighth Amendment. We previously discussed competence as related to juvenile offenders. Here, we review legal competence as it applies to adults involved with the justice system. Although competency evaluations are usually conducted by forensic mental health evaluators or forensic psychologists, forensic mental health counselors should understand these legal principles as foundational knowledge.

There are four types of tests used to determine a defendant's competence, including the M'Naghten rule, the irresistible impulse test, model penal code test, and the Durham rule (Allen, 1962). The *M'Naghten rule* limits the insanity defense to individuals considered unable to distinguish right from wrong. It states that a defendant is not responsible for his or her actions, even if breaking the law, if

> at the time of committing the act, the accused was laboring under such a defect of reason, from disease of the mind, as not to know the nature and quality of the act he was doing or if he did know it, that he did not know what he was doing was wrong (*Queen v. M'Naghten*, 1843, 8 Eng.. Rep. 718).

Although most states adopted this rule, modifications and expansions evolved over the years so that there are jurisdictional differences from place to place. One such modification is the *irresistible impulse test*, which evolved out of criticism that the M'Naghten rule was too broad because the standard resulted in an inability to determine if the individual could or could not have controlled his or her actions based on mental illness, thus resulting in increased changes of malingering (Spirer, 1943). This rule is used in some jurisdictions as a variation of the M'Naghten rule and in others it is considered a separate test of culpability. Defendants using this test must present evidence that proves not only the existence of mental illness, but that the mental illness resulted in the individual's inability to control his or her behavior such that he or she broke the law. *Forensic evaluators*, mental health professionals providing a competency evaluation who are not involved in the individual's mental health treatment, are crucial in assessing and providing expert witness testimony regarding whether the individual is culpable under this test.

The *model penal code rule* (MPCR) provides a standard for legal incompetence/insanity that is an integration of both the M'Naghten rule and the irresistible impulse test. The MPCR asserts that a mentally ill defendant is not responsible for his or her criminal behavior if he or she lacks "substantial capacity either to appreciate the criminality of his conduct or to conform his conduct to the requirements of the law" (American Law Institute, 1962, sec. 4.01(1)). It considers, therefore, both the cognitive capacity (M'Naghten) and volitional capacity (irresistible impulse) in determining competence.

These standards were used regularly until the 1950s when the case of *Durham v. U.S.* (214 F.2d 862) established the *Durham rule*. This rule expanded the allowances made for mental illness. The court's intention was to allow for a mental health professional, through expert witness testimony, to educate a jury about the practical and functional impairments commonly attributed to a defendant's mental illness (e.g., psychosocial history, sociocultural oppression, etc.) on the defendant's behavior. It articulates that a defendant is not guilty by reason of insanity if the jury accepts the expert's characterization of the defendant's mental illness such that they believe he or she is not responsible for his or her actions. However, the rule lacks a standard by which to evaluate such expert testimony.

Advocacy

Once in the system, many offenders with mental illness rely on mental health professionals for advocacy. Counselors have an ethical obligation to provide care that is helpful to clients and to address any problems in care systems through advocacy. However, this discussion occurs within the legal section because in forensic settings, it is crucial that counselors understand legal rights and responsibilities relevant to offenders in correctional settings. These legal issues often inform our advocacy efforts in settings, which often negatively affect this group of offenders' mental health care.

Appropriate Access to Care

One area of advocacy that seems to be a constant struggle when working in correctional settings is access to care. As previously discussed, the Eighth Amendment to the Constitution entitles mentally ill offenders who are incarcerated the right to appropriate care. In 1976 *Estelle v. Gamble* (1976) expanded on this when it explained that correctional facilities not only are constitutionally mandated to provide appropriate mental and physical health care, they are violating the inmate's constitutional rights when correctional officials display "deliberate indifference" to an inmate's healthcare needs. Unfortunately, for a variety of reasons, correctional facilities often do not provide appropriate mental health care in practice. The standards of care in correctional settings reflect a focus on control and maintenance of safety and security, not on providing mental health care.

Some do not provide care at all by failing to identify or acknowledge an offender's mental illness. Others identify mentally ill offenders and place them in a special housing unit. However, they do not appropriately train correctional staff about working with mentally ill offenders, at times resulting in abusive behavior by correctional officers toward the mentally ill such as mocking them, making fun of their symptoms, accusing them of malingering when they are not qualified to make that determination, and manipulating or victimizing them because they are mentally ill. Some facilities provide "counselors" for mentally ill inmates to talk to; however, this text asserts that these lay "counselors" do not have appropriate training to provide mental health care, thus the facility is not actually offering appropriate mental health care. Often these "counselors" are correctional officers trained in criminal justice, not mental health counselors who have or are in a graduate-level educational program developing the following competencies:

1. Education and supervised practice assessing and diagnosing mental illness
2. Training in basic and advanced counseling skills, including supervised practice
3. Specialized training in addictions counseling working with comorbid disorders, trauma, and crisis counseling;
4. Specialized training in working with people from diverse backgrounds
5. An understanding of standards of care established by a professional organization, like the American Counseling Association, and how to apply these standards when laws and ethics conflict or when other ethical dilemmas present themselves
6. Seven hundred hours of supervised practice prior to graduation and 2,000 or more post-graduate supervised practice hours
7. Working toward or possessing national certification as a National Certified Counseling and state licensure, preferably at the independent practice level

Offenders with mental illness have complex histories. They often have multiple mental health disorders, addictive behaviors, and complicated trauma histories. Working appropriately with these clients requires significant didactic information, skills training, and practice. Counselors may find themselves advocating for prisoners who experience abuse by correctional staff, whether intentional or not, because of their lack of understanding or total disregard for mental illness with which some offenders struggle.

Sexual Assault in Corrections

Another advocacy concern for counselors working in prisons is working with vulnerable populations who are mentally ill or physically disabled or targeted for sexual assault. The *Prison Rape Elimination Act* of 2003 (PREA) (Pub. Law 108–79) is an example of legislation that evolved out of the need for increased safety for individuals in custody. Notably, this legislation passed with unanimous support from both parties in Congress. This legislation acknowledges the power differentials that correctional staff or inmates with more physical or social power can abuse through sexually assaulting another inmate. Mentally ill, elderly, and transgender offenders experience more vulnerability to sexual assault in correctional facilities by other prisoners. The purpose of PREA was to "provide for the analysis of the incidence and effects of prison rape in Federal, State, and local institutions and to provide information, resources, recommendations and funding to protect individuals from prison rape" (PREA, 2003). According to the National Center for Transgender Equality (n.d.), PREA includes specific provisions directed at protecting transgender prisoners. Whether you work voluntarily, as an intern, or in a paid position at a correctional facility, you will attend PREA training annually, in compliance with standards established by the National Prison Rape Elimination Commission in 2012.

Although correctional facilities report statistics on prison sexual assault in juvenile and adult male and female facilities, the Justice Department acknowledges that inmates generally underreport sexual assaults while in custody, particularly males. Challenges to gathering information on prison sexual assault include "low response rates resulting from embarrassment or fear of reprisal, challenges verifying victims' self-reports, and lack of common terminology to describe sexual abuse" (Kaufman, 2010). However, it is notable that "staff sexual misconduct was most prevalent in detention centers (7.4%) and training or long-term secure facilities (7.3%)" (Bureau of Justice Statistics, 2017). Sexual assault perpetrated by staff is less than half than at non-state facilities and treatment centers, which mental health professionals usually run and staff.

Placement in Administrative Segregation

Correctional counselors also may need to advocate for mentally ill and elderly inmates who, due to higher risk of assault, are often unduly placed in administrative segregation. There is a risk of administrative segregation, also called solitary confinement, special housing, or special needs units, for mentally ill and for older adult offenders. The Mandela rules define this type of confinement as "confinement for twenty-two hours or more per day without meaningful human contact" (Bedard, Metzger, & Williams, 2017, 931). Administrative segregation presents increased challenges for providing mental health care to both populations because of the lack of access mental health providers have to the inmates in these housing units. Segregated offenders are also, by definition, isolated from others. This results in higher levels of mental distress, which further compounds the mental health needs mentally ill and aging offenders already have. Legal challenges to this practice include extent and level of restrictions, deprivation, reasonableness of the placement, indeterminate length of segregation, and claims of constitutional violations of the First, Fourth, Eighth, and 14th Amendments.

Informed Consent

Under the ACA Code of Ethics (2014), it is the counselor's responsibility to ensure that informed consent occurs prior to beginning a counseling relationship. Counselors consider several issues when ensuring informed consent with adult offenders. Court-mandated counseling results in clients who feel coerced into treatment, and for some they are civilly committed to treatment. Also, unique issues exist with privilege, confidentiality, and limits to confidentiality when counselors work in these settings.

Freely Consenting to Treatment

This can be uniquely challenging when working with adult offenders, because it is common for offenders to express a belief that they have "no choice" to attend sessions. Often they have court orders mandating that they seek treatment or face consequences that result in a loss of certain rights or privileges, including jail time. Counselors must take the time in the beginning of the relationship to talk about whether the client wants to engage in counseling. It is their choice, not yours, not their probation officer's, not the correctional officer's, and not the courts. Think back to our discussion of ethical principles in the first chapter. To be consistent with these principles, it is crucial that you help clients see that they have power to make the decision themselves and that you respect the decision they make. They actually have a choice to make; it may be a choice they do not like, but it is a choice that is theirs to make. To be consistent with the standards of ethical care for counselors, these clients must decide to go into treatment believing that it is their choice to do so, rather than feeling coerced to participate.

A relatively recent change in laws presents another challenge for counselors working with sex offenders, specifically. Civil commitment laws now exist in 20 states under the Adam Walsh Child Protection and Safety Act of 2006 (42 USC 16971). These laws vary from state to state; however, they all require facilities that offer sex offender treatment to the inmate/resident. The offender has the right to refuse treatment, and some do, but the counselor must have the client sign that he or she refuses treatment, which acknowledges awareness that treatment is available and that the offender does not wish to partake of treatment. Courts document numerous cases related to these laws, including constitutional challenges involving due process, ex post facto, and double jeopardy clauses. However, the U.S. Supreme Court upheld civil commitment of sexually violent predators as constitutional in three separate cases, including *Kansas v. Hendricks* (1997), *Kansas v. Crane* (2002), and *U.S. v. Comstock* (2010).

Privilege

Part of informed consent with offenders involves discussing privilege, confidentiality, and limits to confidentiality. The text provided definitions for these terms in previous chapters. Privilege, the legal right to confidential communications between a counselor and client, belongs to the adult offender, and only that person can waive privilege. However, once the offender or the person's defense attorney uses his or her relationship with the counselor to make a legal argument, the court may legally perceive this to be a waiver of privilege and request records and testimony from the counselor. This is one reason that providing counseling pretrial for offenders who have sexual assault or domestic violence can be challenging. Offenders' attorneys sometimes send the offender to counseling prior to the court hearing so that they may argue that the offender is seeking help on his or her own. However, this could result in the counselor being subpoenaed or having his or her records subpoenaed. To guard against this in community settings, it helps to explain these facts to the client during the informed consent process. Additionally, counselors may want to add language about the costs to the client if the counselor must answer a subpoena (e.g., travel, time, food, copying costs, etc.). This frequently dissuades attorneys and clients trying to use the counselor to manipulate the court.

Confidentiality and Limits

Confidentiality is the ethical standard respecting the client's right to privacy. Discussing confidentiality and the limits to confidentiality are important parts of the informed consent process, as well. All counselors should abide by legal limits to confidentiality, which the client must have information about, including mandated reporting of suspected or known child, elder, or disabled person abuse or neglect; risk of harm to self; or imminent danger of harming another identifiable person. However, often there are additional confidentiality limits unique to working in forensic settings.

For instance, when counselors work in forensic settings, like correctional facilities, or with forensic clients in clinical settings, like a drug court or domestic violence treatment program, they agree to provide information to the court about random urine screening, other assessment findings, as well as frequency and quality of participation in treatment. Additionally, sometimes there are limits to confidentiality expected in certain correctional facilities or when working on contracts with probation or parole. One of these may be mandated reporting of disclosure of additional criminal behavior, which if it does not meet the three standard categories would not be disclosed by a counselor. If there are special exceptions to confidentiality that the counselor or treatment program or facility has, then these must be explicitly stated as limits to confidentiality in the informed consent agreement. Additionally, since many offenders lack literacy skills, counselors must verbally review and discuss all elements of the consent form in order to ensure that consent is informed.

In correctional settings, it is particularly challenging to ensure confidentiality beyond these explicit mandates, however. People designing these facilities focus on security, not counseling, when designing these facilities, even when they house mental health units or treatment programs. For instance, informal counseling may take place while an inmate is on lockdown and the counselor is standing in front of the cell. Other guards and inmates will hear everything said during these sessions. Group counseling is the norm in correctional counseling, so counselors cannot ensure confidentiality in group counseling. By participating in group counseling, an inmate may use what he or she learns in group to manipulate another inmate to do something he or she does not want to do. Some facilities may require guards to be within earshot of any interactions between a counselor and client, which increases safety but simultaneously ensures that nothing is confidential. Both the counselor and the inmate must be aware of risks of limited confidentiality. In order to establish and maintain trust with this population, it is crucial that counselors make explicit the limits that exist. Although most, if not all, prisoners already are aware of these issues, the fact that these issues are acknowledged explicitly can communicate to the inmate that the mental health professional can be trusted to be honest and forthright. In a prison setting, this goes a long way toward establishing trust.

Research in Prisons

Informed consent is also a consideration when counselors conduct research in prisons. The National Commission for the Protection of Human Subjects of Biomedical and Behavioral Research (NCPHSBBR) in 1976 published a report and recommendations on research involving prisoners. In these recommendations, they state that respect for prisoners as human beings and justice are the two primary ethical considerations that should guide research in prisons. *Respect for prisoners* includes the expectation that researchers tailor research to the individual setting, considering the unique challenges and concerns involved at the particular facility and the inmates. They recommend ongoing communication and cooperation between the facility and the researchers, as creating research that respects the inmates as human beings and minimizes possibility for exploitation in research. In addition, U.S. government funding for research usually requires adherence to federal requirements for protection of human subjects (Title 34, Code of Federal Regulations, Part 97, Protection of Human Subjects).

The principle of *justice* includes attempts to ensure that researchers and the facility share the benefits of the research and the burdens of said researcher. Distributive justice expands on this by attending to the responsibilities, as well as the needs, of all parties involved by the research. This is particularly complicated when one considers the frontline correctional officers, prison counselors, the inmates, the unit managers, the prison administrators, and the researchers. However, to be compliant with expectations for ethical human research with this vulnerable population, counseling researchers must attend to these principles and practices in designing and carrying out research in correctional settings.

Documentation as Risk Management

Counselors in forensic settings, particularly those working with adult offenders, experience vulnerability to litigation. As a result, it is crucial that counselors not only follow the laws governing their work and their work sites, but they must also diligently attend to professional standards of practice outlined in codes of ethics. When ethical conflicts arise, counselors must seek consultation and/or supervision and apply an ethical decision-making model to the situation, prior to making a decision or taking action. Additionally, it is crucial that the counselor effectively, clearly, and concisely document counseling sessions, other communications, conflicts, consultation sought, and actions taken. These steps will help ensure that even if a counselor is sued, which anyone can do for any reason, he or she is not successfully sued. An extra layer of protection is provided to counselors if they are members of professional organizations like the American Counseling Association. These organizations adhere to codes of ethics and competencies of these organizations and maintain liability insurance through a reputable carrier.

> ### Case Study: Andrea Yates

The case of Andrea Yates always comes to mind when we talk about psychotic offenders. Andrea was the youngest of five children, her mother a German immigrant. She graduated from high school as the valedictorian, attended University of Texas School of Nursing, and worked from 1986–1994 as a registered nurse at M.D. Anderson Cancer Center. Andrea Yates married a NASA engineer and was a stay-at-home mother in an upscale area of Houston. In 2001, she drowned all five of her children in a bathtub during a psychotic episode.

Andrea had a long history of mental health issues, beginning with bulimia and suicidal depression in adolescence. A forensic examiner reviewed her entire 600-page psychiatric history and found that she exhibited manic and depressive episodes as early as high school, began having hallucinations shortly after the birth of her first child, and had thoughts of hurting him in 1994, which she disclosed to a fellow nurse, Debbie Holmes. She received a diagnosis of major depression with psychotic features, with schizophrenia needing to be ruled out. During her treatment, her counselor called CPS, who declined to investigate the case.

Following the birth of her third child, her depression recurred, and she attempted an overdose to kill herself. This was the first of several suicide attempts over the following years, each of which resulted in psychiatric hospitalizations and changes in medication. When medicated with Haldol, her condition dramatically improved. Her psychiatrist said she was one of the five sickest patients she had ever seen and instructed Andrea and her husband Rusty not to have any more children because psychosis was likely to recur.

However, her husband wanted to have more children, so she stopped taking the Haldol in March 2000, gave birth to her daughter in November when she went back on her medication, and seemed stable, according to her husband. However, in March 2001 she stopped taking the Haldol when her father died. She reportedly self-mutilated and read the Bible constantly (typical of many psychotic patients I have worked with), and then became catatonic and stopped feeding her baby. Her husband stated, "She wasn't herself" in news reports. During a routine doctor's visit, her doctor determined that she filled a bathtub to drown herself and requested a court order civilly committing her to Austin State Hospital but rescinded the request after Andrea agreed to be voluntarily admitted.

Admitted to Devereaux in Galveston County, Texas, twice during the spring, her doctors prescribed an antipsychotic cocktail. The records indicate she was catatonic, hallucinating and on suicide watch, but she was required to attend alcohol and drug therapy groups (the hospital's specialty), although she had no substance abuse history. The hospital discharged her on April 13th because her insurance company did not authorize more days. However, she was readmitted on May 4th for 10 days and discharged to the day treatment program. In June, her psychiatrist Mohammed Saeed discontinued her antipsychotic medication and significantly reduced the dosages of two antidepressants (Effexor and Remeron) because he saw no signs of psychosis.

Two days before the murders, her nurse friends Debbie and Mike Holmes discussed their concern for Andrea and a possible murder suicide after Mike saw Andrea in the grocery store "looking like a caged animal." People suffering long-term psychosis often have a wide-eyed fearful look, appear disheveled, and have poor hygiene. As a result, Debbie went to Andrea's home, but Andrea would not let Debbie in.

On June 19, 2001, and about 2 weeks after her medication was discontinued, she drowned her five children. Her doctor told Rusty to provide around-the-clock supervision. However, Rusty announced at a family gathering that he began leaving her alone with the children in order to ensure she did not become dependent on him and his mother for her "maternal responsibilities." That morning Rusty went to work and her mother-in-law arrived about an hour later to help care for the kids. During that time, Andrea drowned the children, hearing voices telling her that is what she had to do, even though she said she did not want to, in order to save them from Satan. After drowning them, she laid them in her bed and called the police repeatedly saying she needed an officer but would not say why. And she called her husband to come home immediately. In jail, she disclosed to a jail psychiatrist that "[i]t was the seventh deadly sin. My children weren't righteous. They stumbled because I was evil. The way I was raising them, they could never be saved. They were doomed to perish in the fires of hell."

In March 2002, a jury found Andrea guilty of killing her children, after the jury denied her insanity defense, and the judge sentenced her to life in prison with eligibility for parole in 40 years. The *insanity defense* is when a criminal case is excused because the defendant's actions are found to be due to a mental defect or psychiatric illness. This is different from *competency to stand trial*, which is when a mental illness prevents a defendant from assisting counsel in his or her case. At the time of the trial, Andrea had been taking antipsychotic medication in prison for about a year and received counseling for depression because of her grief related to drowning her children.

A prosecution expert witness, Dr. Park Dietz, admitted to making a false statement under oath, after an author writing about the case reported an inaccuracy. On appeal, the court found that his testimony was material to the jury's decision not to approve the insanity defense. She was re-tried, found guilty "by reason of insanity," and committed to a state mental health hospital. *Civil commitment* is a process where a person can be court ordered to a psychiatric facility and required to take medication, even without their consent. When people are committed for criminal acts, hospitals are required to provide mental health treatment.

In 2004 Rusty filed for divorce, stating that he and Yates had not lived together as a married couple since June 19, 2001. The divorce was granted in 2005. He remarried, had one child, and his wife divorced him in 2015. During the interim, he attempted to blame the doctors and her medications entirely for the events.

Case Application Questions

1. The Andrea Yates case illustrates that the complex nature of psychosis and comorbid mental illnesses can result in criminal behavior. In addition, there are a number of cautionary tales embedded in this case. If you review her psych-social history, what are the clues indicating the serious high-risk nature of her mental illness?
2. There are obvious mistakes made by mental health professionals and systems (CPS, psychiatrist, psychiatric hospital, and insurance company) and by her family. Analyze how you believe these errors may have happened and discuss how you might intervene as a mental health professional to advocate for the client's needs.
3. Discuss the ethical and legal issues relevant to the Andrea Yates case.

SUMMARY

Chapter 8 builds on the foundation of chapter 7 by moving from contexts of adult offender treatment to a discussion of the mental health disorders and treatment modalities used for prevention and intervention. This includes a discussion of the prevalence and characteristic manifestations of mood disorders like dysthymia, major depression, and bipolar disorder, as well as the common methods for intervention in offender counseling settings. You similarly learned about the prevalence, characteristic manifestations, and common treatment interventions for anxiety disorders, posttraumatic stress disorder, addictive disorders, psychosis, paraphilias, and personality disorders in correctional settings. Then the chapter discussed CIT and mobile crisis units as methods for prevention or de-escalation among adults in legal situations. Then we built on earlier chapters' discussions of common intervention methods like CBT manualized treatment, trauma-informed interventions, and motivational interviewing, and then the chapter discussed common treatment issues forensic mental health providers experience with adult offenders, such as the offenders experiencing difficulties trusting and engaging in relationships, problems with chronic emotional dysregulation, and environmental complications (e.g., gang-criminality interaction, work-criminality interaction, or treatment). Finally, we discussed those legal and ethical issues salient in working with adult offenders that forensic mental health counselors must diligently address and monitor, such as assessing competence, client advocacy for access to appropriate care, the Prison Rape Elimination Act of 2003 and issues related to sexual assault in corrections, and placement in administrative segregation. Additionally, the chapter discussed issues related to the unique challenges experienced in adult corrections related to informed consent for mental health treatment, including autonomy, privilege, confidentiality, and associated limits, as well as issues related to conducting research with prisoners, a vulnerable research population. Finally, we discussed documentation of risk management issues.

You previously completed section I of the text, which addressed foundational issues in forensic mental health counseling, undergirding all work in forensic settings. Now, you have completed section II, which addresses the developmental trajectory of victimization and offending that forensic mental health counselor's address in their work. You will move into section III of the text, which will address counseling work with specific forensic populations, including addictions, domestic violence victims, domestic violence perpetrators, sexual assault victims, and sex offenders.

CHAPTER 8 REFLECTIVE QUESTIONS

1. Describe the prevalence and risks for developing mood disorders among adult offenders and how this would inform your work with adult inmates.
2. Discuss the unique challenges for mental health professionals treating anxiety within a correctional setting.
3. Analyze the challenges a mental health professional needs to consider when treating an adult offender with PTSD in a correctional facility.
4. Compare common personality disorders exhibited by adult offenders and how you would approach working with them as a forensic mental health counselor.
5. Discuss treatment issues you can expect to encounter as a forensic mental health counselor working with adult offenders and how you would address these therapeutically.
6. Compare the different models for determining competency for adult offenders.

7. Discuss common issues experienced by adult inmates that may result in your need to advocate for an inmate/client and how you would address these concerns therapeutically.

8. Discuss the unique challenges to gaining informed consent in a correctional setting, including mandated counseling, vulnerability of the population, and limits to confidentiality.

9. Discuss the importance of documentation as a risk management tool.

RESOURCES

National Alliance for Mental Illness (NAMI), "Jailing People with Mental Illness": https://www.nami.org/Learn-More/Public-Policy/Jailing-People-with-Mental-Illness

National Resource Center on Justice Involved Women, "Using Trauma-Informed Practices to Enhance Safety and Security in Women's Correctional Facilities": https://www.bja.gov/publications/nrcjiw-usingtraumainformedpractices.pdf

Institute for Health and Recovery, "Why Trauma Matters: A Training Curriculum for Corrections Personnel Working With Female Offenders": http://www.healthrecovery.org/images/products/25_inside.pdf

Developing a trauma-informed approach to rehabilitative group work in prisons: https://www.wcmt.org.uk/sites/default/files/report-documents/Allcock%20A%20Report%202015%20FINAL.pdf

SAMHSA guidelines for successful transition of people with mental or substance use disorders from jail and prison: Implementation guide: https://www.ct.gov/opm/lib/opm/cjppd/cjcjpac/samhsa_guidelines_for_successful_transition...from_jail_and_prison.pdf

Substance abuse treatment for adults in the criminal justice system: TIP 44: https://store.samhsa.gov/product/TIP-44-Substance-Abuse-Treatment-for-Adults-in-the-Criminal-Justice-System/SMA13-4056

National Institute of Corrections: Corrections and mental health, trauma-informed correctional care: https://community.nicic.gov/blogs/mentalhealth/archive/2013/09/09/trauma-informed-correctional-care-promising-for-prisoners-and-facilities.aspx

Southern Poverty Law Center: Violations on mental health staffing in prison: https://www.splcenter.org/news/2018/09/18/splc-alabama%E2%80%99s-prison-system-violated-court-order-increase-mental-health-staffing

Human Rights Watch, "Ill-Equipped: U.S. Prisons and Offenders with Mental Illness": https://www.hrw.org/reports/2003/usa1003/usa1003.pdf

Center for Prisoner Health and Human Rights: Incarceration and mental health: http://www.prisonerhealth.org/news-and-events/news/incarceration-and-mental-health/

National PREA Resource Center: https://www.prearesourcecenter.org/about/prison-rape-elimination-act-prea

National Institute of Justice: Challenges of conducting research in prisons: https://www.nij.gov/journals/269/pages/research-in-prisons.aspx

International Journal for Crime, Justice and Social Democracy, "The Craft of Doing Qualitative Research in Prisons": file:///C:/Users/lfalls/Downloads/207-1-825-1-10-20150316.pdf

U. S. Department of Health & Human Services Office for Human Research Protections: Prisoner research FAQs: https://www.hhs.gov/ohrp/regulations-and-policy/guidance/faq/prisoner-research/index.html

Institute of Medicine: *Ethical Considerations for Research Involving Prisoners*: https://www.ncbi.nlm.nih.gov/books/NBK19882/pdf/Bookshelf_NBK19882.pdf

Institute of Medicine: *Ethical Considerations for Research Involving Prisoners* (brief): https://www.nap.edu/resource/11692/Prisoners.pdf

Specific Settings and Populations

Autobiography in Five Chapters

By Portia Nelson

I

I walk down the street.
There is a deep hole in the sidewalk.
I fall in.
I am lost …
I am hopeless.
It isn't my fault.
It takes forever to find a way out.

II

I walk down the same street.
There is a deep hole in the sidewalk.
I pretend I don't see it.
I fall in again.
I can't believe I'm in the same place.
But it isn't my fault.
It still takes a long time to get out.

III

I walk down the same street
There is a deep hole in the sidewalk.
I see it is there.
I still fall in … it's a habit.
My eyes are open; I know where I am;
It is my fault.
I get out immediately.

IV

I walk down the same street.
There is a deep hole in the sidewalk.
I walk around it.

V

I walk down another street.

Counseling People With Addictive Behaviors in Forensic Settings

Leigh F. Holman, Frances Ellmo, and Leigh Pitre

Upon completion of this chapter, readers will be able to do the following:

■ Identify screening assessment measures commonly used with addiction populations
■ Diagnose substance use disorders
■ Describe common interventions and settings for addictive behaviors

TABLE 9.1 Myths and Myth Busters

Myths	Myth Busters
Addicts choose to be addicted.	**Addiction results from a complex interrelationship of** contextual **and neurobiological factors.**
Ten to 14 days of in-patient treatment is sufficient to help someone on the road to recovery.	**Due to the neurobiological, familial, and sociocultural contexts, as well as interplay between trauma and other mental health disorders with addictive disorders, addiction requires a complex, comprehensive, long-term treatment process to** sustain **someone in recovery.**
An addict must want treatment for intervention to be successful.	**The process of trying to change addictive behaviors may be scary, so most addicts resist changing the behavior initially, but with the use of motivational interviewing, we can help** engage **them in treatment.**

INTRODUCTION

This chapter focuses on counseling offenders with addictive behaviors. As previously established, many offenders become involved with drug courts, DUI/DWI court-mandated care, and/or correctional facilities. This chapter provides a broad overview of assessment, diagnosis, treatment interventions, and settings common to treatment of addictive behaviors.

ASSESSMENT

There are over 100 screening and assessment instruments available to screen or assess a client for substance use disorders. *Screening* involves the counselor examining certain behaviors or experiences that tend to correlate with potential problem substance use. We screen clients within general mental health or medical settings to determine if there is a need for further targeted assessment. *Assessment* is comprehensive and uses multiple methods to assess the client's current life situation. Counselors conduct clinical interviews, evaluate collateral data (e.g., urine screen, family interview, past records, etc.), and administer a substance-specific, standardized, psychometrically sound formal assessment measure.

ASAM Criteria and Standards of Care

The American Society for Addiction Medicine (ASAM) criteria are widely used as a comprehensive guide for assessment and placement (American Society of Addiction Medicine's Practice Improvement and Performance Measurement Action Group & Standards and Outcomes of Care Expert Panel, n.d.). There are six dimensions that a treatment provider needs to assess under the criteria:

TABLE 9.2 ASAM Six Dimensions

Dimension	Category	Counselor task
Dimension 1	Acute intoxication and/or withdrawal potential	Explore the client's past and current experiences of substance use and withdrawal.
Dimension 2	Biomedical conditions and complications	Explore the client's health history and current physical condition.
Dimension 3	Emotional, behavioral, or cognitive conditions and complications	Explore the client's thoughts, emotions, and mental health issues.
Dimension 4	Readiness to change	Explore the client's motivation for change using the stages of change model.
Dimension 5	Relapse, continued use, or continued problem potential	Explore an individual's unique relationship with relapse or continued use and related functional impairments (family, community, school/work, etc.).
Dimension 6	Recovery/living environment	Explore the client's living situation including the neighborhood, people, places, and things in the living environment as related to potential for support or barriers to recovery.

The counselor gathers and evaluates information addressing each of the six dimensions utilizing a variety of methods to ensure the assessment data clearly support any potential diagnosis and the level of care recommendation. According the ASAM standards of care, standard 1.1 involves comprehensive assessment, including documentation of the following:

- Physical exam
- Mental status exam
- Medical and psychiatric history
- Detailed past and present substance use history, including withdrawal potential
- History of pathological pursuit of reward or relief through use of the addictive behavior
- Mental health and addiction treatment history, including response to treatment and use of prescribed medications as interventions.
- Client's stage of change, readiness to engage in treatment, and potential for recovery (continued use, social/family situation, recovery environment that supports or impedes use)

Screening Instruments

The setting and client characteristics (e.g., gender, age, pregnancy, etc.) inform the screening instrument used by a counselor. There are several screening instruments commonly used. The most-often used is the **CAGE** (Ewing, 1984):

Have you ever felt you ought to cut down on your drinking/drug use?

Have people annoyed you by criticizing your drinking/drug use?

Have you ever felt bad or guilty about your drinking/drug use?

Have you ever had a drink/used drugs first think in the morning (eye opener) to steady your nerves?

These questions can be asked sequentially or you may gather the information during a clinical interview based on information the client is reporting to you. Each "yes" gives the client 1 point toward the total score, and two points indicate a need for further evaluation. Other screening instruments for **adults** who are not pregnant include the following:

- The Alcohol Use Disorders Identification Test (**AUDIT**) (Saunders, Aasland, Babor, De La Fuente, & Grant, 1993): 10 multiple-choice questions used to assess alcohol-related issues.
- Alcohol Dependence Scale (**ADS**) (Doyle & Donovan, 2009): 29 multiple-choice questions used to assess for severity of alcohol dependence
- Michigan Assessment—Screening Test for Alcohol and Drugs (**MAST-AD**) (Westermeyer, Yargic, & Thuras, 2004): 25 multiple-choice items used to assess for severity of alcohol and drug addictions and for levels of client insight related to their substance use

- Drug Abuse Screening Test (**DAST**) (Skinner, 1982): 28 yes-or-no questions used to screen for abuse of substances other than alcohol

There are also specific screening tools for **pregnant women**:

- **TWEAK** (Russell et al., 1994) consists of five items Tolerance, Worry, Eye-Opener, Amnesia, Cut Down. Two points are given for positive response to questions about tolerance (three or more drinks) or worry about their drinking, and the other three questions receive 1 point for a positive answer. The cutoff score is 2, indicating need for further assessment.
- **T-ACE** (Sokol, Martier, & Ager, 1989) has four questions, Tolerance, Annoyance, Cut Down, Eye Opener. The first, tolerance (two or more drinks) receives 2 points, and the other three (annoyed by criticism about drinking, need to cut down, and eye opener) receive 1 point each. It also has a 2-point cutoff score.

Similarly, there are specific screening tools for **adolescents**:

- Center for Adolescent Substance Abuse Research (**CRAFFT**) (Knight, Sherrit, Shrier, Harris, & Chang, 2002): Six yes-or-no screening questions to determine if further substance use evaluation is needed
- Problem Oriented Screening Instrument for Teenagers (**POSIT**) (Center for Addiction and Mental Health, 2009): 139 yes-or-no items used to assess for substance abuse and co-occurring disorders; it has a subscale to evaluate aggressive behavior and delinquency
- Teen Addiction Severity Index (**T-ASI**) (Kaminer, Bukstein, & Tarter, 1991): Semi-structured interview adapted from the adult version of the ASI
- **Prototype screening/triage form** (Dembo, 1990): For use in juvenile detention centers, interview with multiple choice and open-ended questions designed to assess for substance use treatment needs in juvenile detention settings

Additional measures, copies of screening instruments, including specific drug screening tools, and other information is available for free on the National Institute of Drug Abuse website (NIDA, 2018). Once you determine the client needs further targeted evaluation, you should administer standardized assessment instruments in order to gather more specific information about the client's use.

Standardized Assessment Instruments

You should assess the client holistically. First, assess the client's psychosocial history and stage of change, which were thoroughly described in chapter 3. Through the clinical interview, identify any personality characteristics, potentially comorbid mental health issues, and substance abuse issues indicated by the screening as problematic. I recommend always assessing past trauma as well, given the evidence supporting a high correlation between addictive behaviors and trauma. Then choose psychometrically sound instruments you want to use to evaluate the constellation of issues you believe need further evaluation.

There are several potential tests that can provide information about a client's personality characteristics, trauma history, symptoms of posttraumatic stress, and mood and anxiety disorders. Many counselors refer out to psychologists to conduct a complete psychological assessment and utilize the psychologist's report recommendations to inform treatment. However, addiction-specific assessments may be conducted on site by the counselor. Common addiction assessments include the following:

- **Substance Abuse Subtle Screening Inventory** (SASSI) (Miller, 1997): 95 multiple-choice questions used to identify the probability of a substance use disorder; contains subscales to assess for client defensiveness and involvement with the judicial system
- **Adult Substance Use Survey, revised** (ASUS-R) (Wanberg, 2004): 96 items used to assess a client's alcohol and drug involvement; contains subscales to assess for antisocial and criminal conduct

Although standardized tests are helpful in providing information, counselors are advised by test authors never to use test results alone to formulate a diagnosis. Even when a client is in a program that specifically addresses addiction issues, it is important to conduct a thorough assessment (e.g., evaluating all the life domains, potential complicating factors, and strengths for the individual client). All formal assessment measures must be considered by a counselor in the context of other information gathered from the client and collaterally. Some assessment measures, like the SASSI, can be utilized at different points during treatment to assess changes during treatment. Additionally, it is common for clients in recovery to submit to random drug/alcohol screening by providing urine samples for analysis. This data is also often useful during the treatment process.

DIAGNOSIS

When diagnosing any mental health disorder, you must utilize multiple data points to support the diagnosis. I recommend going through each criterion for the diagnostic category (e.g., alcohol use disorder) and evaluating all the data gathered in light of the specific criterion to determine if the client meets the criterion. Then move to the next, and so on, until you go through all of the criteria for a given diagnosis. This process can be documented in the client's chart so that the evidence supporting your diagnosis is easily accessible and identifiable.

Each diagnosis contains specific criteria, which the client must meet to receive a diagnosis. The specific substance is identified in the diagnosis, and, given that many individuals are addicted to multiple substances, a client may have multiple diagnoses. The reader should consult the DSM-5 (APA, 2013) for specific information on diagnostic criteria, specifiers, prevalence rates, risk and prognostic factors, culture-related diagnostic issues, gender-related diagnostic issues, diagnostic markers, functional consequences of each substance of abuse, differential diagnostic information, and comorbidity. There are differences among these features depending on the substance, so reading all of the information available in the DSM is crucial for you to be competent in diagnosing these disorders. Substance-related diagnoses include the following:

- Alcohol-related disorders
- Cannabis-related disorders
- Hallucinogen-related disorders
- Inhalant-related disorders
- Opioid-related disorders
- Sedative-, hypnotic-, or anxiolytic-related disorders
- Stimulant-related disorders
- Tobacco-related disorders

Finally, given that there are new chemically manufactured substances of abuse produced periodically, there is a diagnostic category for other known or other unknown substance-related disorders that capture substances that people may use/abuse. Substance use disorders (SUDs) are diagnosed on a continuum of severity in the DSM-5; therefore, it is crucial that once a SUD diagnosis is given, the counselor follows instructions in the DSM-5 for identifying level of severity (APA, 2013). Level of severity, in turn, informs the level of treatment chosen for a client. More severe disorders tend to need more external support, a more restrictive placement, and more intense level of services.

Although less likely to receive treatment in addiction treatment programs that provide recovery services to forensic populations, some behavioral/process addictions (BPA) may be present in forensic populations (e.g., gambling disorder, which may result in stealing money to pay debts or involvement in other criminal activity to facilitate gambling behaviors). Another potential BPA, which may result in legal involvement, is sex addiction (e.g., an addiction that may result in downloading child pornography, solicitation of a minor for sex, engaging in sexual activity in public places, or the presence of a paraphilia-like exhibitionism, voyeurism, frotteurism, pedophilia, or rape/sadism).

TREATMENT

We will discuss several common treatment methods used in addiction treatment programs. Treatment providers vary in how they choose interventions, even when a program prescribes certain interventions for clients with a particular presenting substance abuse problem. The ASAM guiding principles (Mee-Lee, 1990) require that treatment be individualized to the person's needs based on a comprehensive evaluation of multiple sources of data, rather than a one-size-fits-all program. Treatment also should consider continuum-of-care services at different levels of intensity as clients move from higher risk, when they need more intense services, to lower risk, when they need less intensive services, or vice versa. Providers may use individual treatment methods, although group and family therapies are more common.

Group Interventions

A client may be involved in support groups or group interventions, such as the following:

- Twelve-step groups and other support groups like Rational Recovery, which are led by lay people

- Twelve-step facilitated groups led by a clinician who structures the group around the 12-step model
- Group therapy led by a clinician, which may be process oriented or topic oriented (e.g., addictive thinking, emotion regulation, etc.)
- Psychoeducational groups

(Note: Chapter 8 specifically discusses ethical issues related to group interventions).

Support Groups

There are several different supporting, or fellowship, programs in which individuals dealing with addiction can become immersed. The first, and most common/popular, fellowship program is the 12-step recovery program. The 12 steps were initially created by the founders of Alcoholics Anonymous (AA), Bill Wilson and Dr. Bob Smith. While the 12 steps were originally created for AA, the steps have also been incorporated into other 12-step programs, such as Narcotics Anonymous, Cocaine Anonymous, Sex and Love Addiction Anonymous, Marijuana Anonymous, Gamblers Anonymous, Al-Non, and Al-Teen. This list is not comprehensive, as there are 12-step programs for almost any addiction. The main components of the 12-step program are total abstinence from the addictive substance or behavior, surrendering to your addiction, handing the addiction over to a higher power, identifying what is at the core of the addiction, and service to other individuals who are seeking recovery. There are 12 steps total that an individual may go through on a continuous basis; the 12-steps are never fully completed and finished (Alcoholics Anonymous, 2001).

In a 12-step program, an individual dealing with addiction will receive fellowship and support from other individuals who have achieved sobriety/clean time. An individual will obtain a sponsor who will help him or her through the 12-step process and be a support for the individual in recovery when he or she experiences cravings or urges to use, as well as if relapse occurs. The 12-step program is a spiritually based program in which the individual's higher power is the main force behind the recovery process. Overall, the 12-step program maintains that no one is truly "cured" from their addictions, but that recovery is a lifelong process that needs to be taken a day at a time, sometimes 1 hour at a time, sometimes 1 minute at a time, and sometimes 1 second at a time (Alcoholics Anonymous, 2001). AA meeting locations can be found on the national websites for each of the different 12-step programs via an online search by zip code.

The next program that will be discussed is the Rational Recovery program. The Rational Recovery program was developed by Jack and Lois Trimpey in 1985 (Trimpey, 1989). They branched out of the traditional 12-step program to include the notion that addiction is mainly psychological and can be overcame through discussion and utilization of cognitive behavioral therapy. They combined the group and fellowship portion of AA with the mind-set that addiction is a psychological disease that views self-intoxication as innocent acts initiated by innocent individuals. Unlike your traditional 12-step programs, Rational Recovery offers a secular, nonspiritual route to recovery. It is a family-centered recovery program that focuses on family values. It focuses on the family member who is dealing with addiction and the importance of him or her receiving support from the family, with the support provided by the family in a way that the family believes is best fit to provide to the individual. Often times, this means no support from the family at all. Rational Recovery articulates that persons dealing with addiction are not victims to a disease, but are "traitors" to their families, and they must re-earn respect in the family system. Nonetheless, Rational Recovery, like the 12 steps, believes in total abstinence from the addictive substance and/or behavior (Trimpey, 1989).

The third program that will be discussed is Celebrate Recovery. Celebrate Recovery is a Christian-based recovery program that incorporates biblical meaning with the traditional 12 steps that were created for AA. Unlike the traditional 12-step program that has 12 traditions, there are eight traditions in Celebrate Recovery that focus on God and a biblical message. This recovery program emphasized Jesus' and God's important role in the recovery progress, and that sobriety can only be achieved through them. Also, like AA, Celebrate Recovery focuses on service to other members of the program and individuals seeking to enter into a sober/clean lifestyle (Celebrate Recovery, n.d.).

The fourth program that will be discussed is Refuge Recovery. Refuge Recovery is a Buddhist-orientated recovery program. Refuge Recovery utilizes meditation and mindfulness-based approaches to recovery. This program has four truths, which are addiction creates suffering, the cause of addiction is repetitive craving, recovery is possible, and the path to recovery is available (Refuge Recovery, n.d.).

Psychoeducational Groups

There are several purposes of holding a psychoeducation group focused on addiction, such as to provide group members with knowledge about the medical, behavioral, and psychological consequences of using and abusing illicit substances (SAMSHA, 2005). Another major purpose of the psychoeducation group is to help move clients along the previously mentioned stages of change and into a recovery-ready and oriented process (Martin, Giannandrea, Rogers, & Johnson, 1996; Pfeiffer, Feuerlein, Brenk-Schulte, 1991). Group facilitators' goals would be to provide group members with information that they can use in order to begin to establish, and eventually maintain, more productive choices in their lives (SAMSHA, 2005).

Family Interventions

The family system plays a huge role in both the addiction and recovery process. Families often facilitate the addictive behavior in order to maintain homeostasis in the family system. So, they can ultimately have an adverse impact on a client's ability to be successful in recovery. This often occurs if the family does not have the tools to provide and maintain a healthier environment that is more supportive of the client's recovery efforts and behaviors. Individuals can play several different family roles whenever there is an addict in the family:

- **Addict.** You will find that the person with the addiction becomes the center of the family; the family's level of functioning totally revolves around the person dealing with addiction, which causes the addiction to become the center of the family's focus. The family will unknowingly take on the following roles to help keep the balance in the family.

- **Hero**. The hero is the family member who wants to make sure the outward appearance of the family is acceptable to others outside of the family unit, as well as the appearance of each individual member of the family within the family system. The hero will attempt to present things in a positive manner, as if no problems exist. The hero tends to be a perfectionist. Some underlying feelings the hero may experience are fear, guilt, and shame (Baker, 2017).
- **Mascot**. The mascot's role in the family system is to attempt to keep the family's balance by obtaining a "jokester" role. He or she attempts to bring humor to the family to take the attention off of the person who is dealing with addiction. The humor utilized is often harmful to the family. The underlying feelings of the mascot are embarrassment, shame, and anger.
- **Lost child**. The lost child is the family member who ultimately stays silent and out of the way and he or she is careful not to create additional problems for the family. The lost child will never discuss or mention the substance abuse or possibility of recovery. The lost child often gives up his or her own personal needs and aspirations in order to avoid any discussion about the family member who is addicted. A lost child's underlying feelings include guilt, loneliness, neglect, and anger (Baker, 2017).
- **Scapegoat**. The scapegoat is the family member who draws attention away from the existing problem in the family. He or she will often rebel and divert the family's attention away from the person who is addicted and his or her need for recovery. Underlying feelings that accompany the scapegoat role are shame, guilt, and feeling empty.
- **Caretaker/enabler**. The caretaker attempts to keep the balance in the family by keeping all of the family members, especially the addict, "happy." He or she will avoid his or her own personal needs in order to maintain that balance. He or she often enables the addict by giving him or her money or other items of value and make excuses for their behaviors. He or she unconsciously helps the person maintain his or her addiction as a result of these behaviors. Underlying feelings that accompany the caretaker role are fear, helplessness, and inadequacy (Baker, 2017).

Healthy family systems demonstrate a sense of self-worth; engage in clear, direct, honest communication; adhere to flexible rules that change in appropriate ways so as to adjust to immediate needs of family members or situations; express openness to community and those outside of the immediate family unit; and identify individual goals and plans that are supported, not directed or discouraged, by other family members. However, addicted families often demonstrate different dynamics from those mentioned, including the following:

- Substance use/addiction is the center of the family life.
- Denial of the substance use/addiction is often the crux of the family dysfunction.
- There is blaming others, secrecy, covering up, emphasis on loyalty bonds, and behaviors that support and enable addictive behaviors.
- They do not talk about private family issues outside of the family.
- They do not directly communicate honest feelings or thoughts, often out of fear.

Family roles often lead to codependency between members where one member of the family makes decisions based on another family member's needs, almost exclusively. This often leads to resentment and displacement of responsibility onto someone else who is perceived to "control" family decisions and actions. People exhibiting characteristics of codependency demonstrate care-taking behaviors with the person dealing with addiction, with the counselor, and with other people: low-self-worth, thus subjugating their needs to the needs of others; repression of thoughts and feelings out of fear; appearing rigid and controlled; poor communication patterns that involve blaming, shaming, advice giving, threatening, and generally indirect or passive aggressive communication styles; anxiety; controlling behaviors; denial of problems; dependency on others for happiness; poor boundaries; lack of trust; and anger.

Family therapy is often beneficial to families dealing with dysfunction. Family therapy is multifaceted but often involves providing education about the addiction/disease, as well as education and practicing of effective communication skills, identifying ways to rebuild trust within the family, learning and identifying behaviors that are helpful and unhelpful, and identifying and reinforcing the needs of everyone within the system (SAMSHA, 2005). Counselors use different family therapy techniques, including the following:

- **Structural** (e.g., joining with each family member, unbalancing, reframing the problem, enactment-like family sculpting, or boundary-making activities)
- **Strategic** (e.g., reframing the problem, communication tracking and restructuring, **paradoxical intention**)
- **Intergenerational** (e.g., genogram analysis, normalizing the family's challenges, describing family members' reactions rather than acting them out, and encouraging use of "I" statements)

Regardless of the approach, or whether work is done solely with the individual or the family as a whole, family systems issues must be addressed in order for the client's recovery to be successful.

Interpersonal/Relational Interventions

The primary interpersonal/relational intervention used in addiction treatment is motivational interviewing (MI) (Miller & Rollnick, 2013), which was described in detail in chapter 3. MI focuses on the relationship as a catalyst for change. The relationship is the therapeutic intervention. The goals of MI are to help clients resolve ambivalence about changing, reduce resistant behaviors, and engage the client in self-motivated change behaviors. It is a directive, client-centered style of interaction that helps clients explore ambivalence about changing through which the ambivalence can be resolved, allowing the client to move forward with planning for and changing problematic behaviors. MI involves five general principles:

1. Express empathy through active reflective listening.
2. Develop discrepancy between the client's stated values/goals and his or her current behavior through exploration of values/goals and both the benefits and negative consequences of the current behavior, as well as the change behavior.

3. Avoid arguing and direct confrontation of the client's problematic thought patterns or behaviors.
4. Roll with resistance by finding a less resistant path to engage the client in treatment.
5. Support clients' self-efficacy or belief in themselves that they are capable of changing and maintaining changed behaviors over time.

MI is a trans-theoretical intervention that can be used across theories in conjunction with other methods of intervention.

Cognitive Behavioral Interventions

Cognitive behavioral therapy (CBT) interventions are considered promising practice in the treatment of addictions; however, the studies establishing CBT as evidence based tend to be situated in controlled settings, like a treatment hospital or residential facility. They also tend to be only short-term interventions that, upon follow up, show little sustained improvement over other intervention approaches. However, CBT continues to be the primary intervention method utilized in addiction treatment programs.

Common cognitive components include identifying cognitive distortions, which support addictive behaviors, such as rationalization, denial, and projection of responsibility for feelings/thoughts/behaviors onto others. After identifying these cognitive distortions, then the client learns to restructure his or her cognitions to be more functional, accurate, and honest, thus supporting recovery behaviors. Psychoeducation is a cognitive intervention used in almost all treatment programs. Additionally, there are cognitive models of relapse prevention used to structure treatment for addiction clients.

Behavioral interventions include pairing aversive stimuli (e.g., Antabuse, which causes vomiting when paired with alcohol) with the target behavior (e.g., drinking alcohol). Covert sensitization may involve the client discussing or writing in depth about the negative consequences of his or her behaviors, then when triggered to use or craving the addictive substance/behavior the client will read or listen to a recording of the negative consequences. This is a more subtle use of aversive pairing utilizing classical conditioning.

Group psychotherapy and therapeutic milieus are commonly used as behavioral interventions that focus on social modeling and in vivo behavior analysis and redirection. Additionally, therapeutic milieus often have level systems based on behavioral evidence of improvement toward treatment goals. With clearly defined improved behaviors, the client can move to a higher level that provides more privileges than were available to them at a lower level. Additional behavioral interventions include learning progressive muscle relaxation, meditation, and/or mindfulness exercises used to improve healthy coping in triggering situations. Physical exercise and nutrition changes are also considered behavioral interventions supportive of recovery. Finally, skills training is a behavioral intervention where clients learn assertive communication skills, time-management skills, anger/emotional arousal management skills, social/relationship skills, and so on and practice these skills through repeated rehearsals in order to improve their ability to react to environmental triggers in a healthier way.

Trauma-Informed Interventions

As discussed throughout sections I and II of this text, adverse childhood experiences (ACEs) and other trauma is common among forensic populations, and this is particularly true of those exhibiting addictive behaviors. It is not uncommon for a person to self-medicate trauma symptoms with addictive substances or behaviors. Additionally, due to the lifestyle and functional consequences of living as an addict, additional experiences of trauma are common. Many people with trauma, particularly those with complex trauma histories involving multiple trauma experiences over the course of their lives, develop PTSD.

Further, research indicates offenders, in particular, have high rates of co-occurring PTSD and SUD (Najavits, 2002). The combination of these two disorders can be complex and difficult to treat. Treatment protocols that work for these disorders separately may not work well together. For example, benzodiazepines are often a recommended course of treatment for a client with PTSD; however, this is not usually advisable when the client suffers from drug addiction. Some providers attempt to treat PTSD and SUDs sequentially. For instance, some programs require the client to be sober for a period of time prior to beginning treatment of PTSD symptoms. The challenge is that the use of substances is often a coping mechanism for PTSD symptoms. Therefore, when the client abstains from substance use, PTSD symptoms often become a major trigger for relapse. Similarly, attempting to treat the PTSD prior to addressing the substance use disorder is problematic. Doing so may prove impossible if the client believes he or she is "successfully" managing his or her PTSD symptoms with a substance. This may prevent the client from accessing and processing trauma issues while he or she is actively using.

Trauma-informed cognitive behavior therapy (TF-CBT) (Positive Psychology Program, 2018) focuses on addressing PTSD symptoms, as well as other behavioral or mental health issues arising from trauma experiences, like addictive disorders. The goal is to provide psychoeducation to the client and members of the person's support system about trauma and PTSD and help them identify and cope with thoughts, emotions, and behaviors that are problematic. This can be particularly effective with adolescents with addictive issues. The PRACTICE acronym encompasses the therapeutic elements of TF-CBT:

- **P**sychoeducation and parenting skills
- **R**elaxation
- **A**ffective expression and regulation
- **C**ognitive coping
- **T**rauma narrative development and processing
- **I**n vivo gradual exposure
- **C**onjoint parent-child sessions
- **E**nhancement of safety and future development

Although utilized more often with abuse survivors, TF-CBT can be effective in treating trauma-based addictive behaviors in conjunction with other traditional addiction interventions.

Seeking Safety is an integrated treatment model designed to help with co-occurring substance abuse and PTSD. Seeking Safety is a semi-structured cognitive behavioral treatment manual that targets PTSD symptoms and substance abuse symptoms concurrently. It presents 25 different coping skill session topics to choose from and can be utilized in both individual therapy and group therapy modalities. The main goal of Seeking Safety is to help re-establish a pattern of safe coping skills for participants. The semi-structured flexibility of the session topics makes it ideal for forensic settings so providers can select the most relevant and necessary topics for the particular client population. Most importantly, it has been shown to significantly improve mental health outcomes, including PTSD and SUD symptoms in forensic populations (Barrett et al., 2015; Lynch, Heath, Mathews, & Cepeda, 2012; Najavits, 2002).

Dialectical behavior therapy (DBT) (Linehan, 1993) DBT is another cognitive behavioral therapy emphasizing group skills training in mindfulness, emotion regulation, distress tolerance, and interpersonal effectiveness, as well as individual psychotherapy. There are five functions and five corresponding modes of DBT training.

Dr. Linehan's theory is that behaviors like addictions evolve as a coping mechanism that provide temporary relief from emotional dysregulation or stress. Although they work in the short term, they provoke functional impairments over time. Through teaching behavioral skills like mindfulness, distress tolerance, emotion regulation, and interpersonal effectiveness, clients learn and integrate improved coping methods without relying on addictive or other self-defeating behaviors.

Experiential/Somatic Interventions

Experiential/somatic interventions are also trauma-informed interventions. There are several different experiential and somatic interventions one can utilize when treating individuals dealing with addiction. As stated earlier in this chapter, counselors should only use experiential interventions after psychoeducation is provided and the individual has progressed along the stages of change and has experienced several months in sobriety. Experiential and somatic interventions are not traditional talk-therapy approaches; they move the individuals out of their cognitive thought processes and help them begin to connect in a more holistic way, for example, connecting mind, body, and soul. Traditional talk therapy is effective, but you want the individual to begin to make connections physiologically, emotionally, and psychologically so that he or she can sustain a prolonged recovery process. Experiential interventions can include a range of strategies, including utilizing music to help begin identifying emotions and make emotional connections in general to mindfulness and meditation to connect spiritually;

TABLE 9.3

Functions		Modes
01	Enhance clients' capabilities	DBT skills training
02	Improve clients' motivation	Individual psychotherapy
03	Assure generalization to clients' natural environment	In-the-moment coaching
04	Structure the environment	Case management
05	Enhance therapists' capabilities and support their motivation	DBT consultation team

family of origin work, such as healing your wounded inner child; asking for help and trust-based exercises; acupuncture; sweat lodges/saunas; yoga; breathwork; grounding techniques; triggering an individual and working through the trigger in the moment; and eye movement desensitization and reprocessing (EMDR). This by all means is not a comprehensive list of experiential and somatic techniques; therefore, consider the benefit of using various techniques as a part of the therapeutic recovery process.

The goal of experiential and somatic interventions is to help the individual heal on a deeper level. Many times individuals with addiction(s) have deep-rooted trauma that help stem the addiction. Experiential and somatic techniques, as previously mentioned, help to begin the healing process so that individuals can begin and sustain their recovery. Nonetheless, therapists want to ensure that the individual has a relapse prevention plan, is somewhat stabilized in his or her recovery process, and has a sustainable support network before he or she begins experiential work. Experiential work can be extremely helpful, but it can also be triggering as well due to having someone connect with his or her body and the spiritual parts of themselves, as well as because the interventions may hit on trauma from the past.

Pharmacologic Interventions

In the past, many substance abuse treatment protocols suggested individuals avoid the use of any medication or chemical intervention. However, current research (reference needed) suggests some psychopharmacologic interventions may be beneficial on their own or as a

TABLE 9.4 Pharmacologic Interventions

Medication	Also known as	How it works:	FDA Approval	Disorders treated
Buproprion	Wellbutrin	Causes unpleasant aversion symptoms (nausea, headache, etc.)	1989	Alcohol use disorder, nicotine use disorder
Disulfiram	Antabus, Antabuse	Causes unpleasant aversion symptoms (nausea, headache, etc.)	1951	Alcohol use disorder
Acamprosate	Campral	Decreases intensity of cravings; eases withdrawal symptoms	2004	Alcohol use disorder
Methadone	Dolophine, Methadose	Blocks pleasurable effects of opioids in the brain and eases withdrawal symptoms	2002	Opioid use disorder
Buprenor-phine	Subutex, Suboxone (with Naloxone)	Blocks some of the pleasurable effects of opioids and eases withdrawal symptoms	2002	Opioid use disorder
Naltrexone	Vivitrol	Blocks pleasurable effects of alcohol and drugs in the brain and reduces cravings	1984	Opioid use disorder, alcohol use disorder

(Center for Substance Abuse Treatment, 2009; Connery, 2015; Douaihy, Kelly, & Sullivan, 2013)

part of a larger treatment plan, including therapy. In forensic settings, psychopharmacologic management of medical or mental disorders is often the first or only treatment option. The following medications are commonly used in the treatment of substance use disorders.

In addition to the medications common in treating addiction, many clients have comorbid mental health issues for which they receive psychotropic medication(s). It is important for you to know what medications the client takes and to become familiar with the typical use of these medications, typical dosages, potential side effects, and potential withdrawal issues. If you work with clients who use psychopharmacologic interventions, you will necessarily need to consult with the client's medical doctor/prescriber during treatment. Ideally, the prescriber will be trained with an addictionology specialty. Although these are rare, with the advent of tele-health, access to specialists is becoming easier.

SETTINGS

Treatment settings vary based on the client's risk for relapse, as assessed using the six dimensions described. Higher-risk clients need services that are more intensive and a more restrictive environment to be successful. Most treatment programs use the **ASAM criteria** (Mee-Lee, 1990) classification of different levels of intensity of services. From least to most restrictive the levels are as follows:

- **Level .5** is an **outpatient prevention** setting focused on prevention, early intervention, and psychoeducation and screening for more serious addiction issues. A lot of folks are required to do this after a first DUI ticket.
- **Level 1** is **outpatient treatment**. These folks are likely to complete detox and treatment with little supervision. They require less than 9 hours per week of intervention for an adult or 6 for an adolescent.
- **Level 2** is **intensive outpatient** (**IOP**) or **partial hospitalization** (**PHP**). This level of treatment is often a step down from more intensive in-patient services at a hospital. These individuals need to be more closely monitored than outpatient clients but not hospitalized. IOP adults receive 9 hours of treatment and adolescents receive 6 hours. IOP does not exceed 20 hours per week, whereas, PHP is over 20 hours per week.
- **Level 3** is treatment in a **residential setting**. This is recommended when there is impairment in multiple life dimensions, which need stabilization. Counselors should consider housing and support in the living situation. These specific issues are the reason many people "stepping down" from prison treatment programs or may go to "residential settings." Adolescents are more likely to be in residential treatment. Residential settings provide 24-hour care with trained staff and structured clinical services provided by clinically trained staff like counselors, psychiatric nurses, and doctors.
- **Level 4**, **medically managed intensive inpatient**, is the most intensive level of service. This is usually completed in a medical hospital, even if the client will then be transported to a step-down psychiatric hospital facility once he or she is no

longer in need of this level of medical management. Clients served in these settings are likely to experience severe withdrawal and/or are currently demonstrating acute intoxication. Medical management of withdrawal is the focus of treatment, not counseling. This level of care provides both 24-hour nursing care and daily physician care.

There are more sublevels under some of these, like 3.1, low-intensity residential, 3.5, high-intensity residential, and 3.7, medically monitored intensive inpatient services, usually provided in a psychiatric hospital. An Internet search on ASAM criteria levels of intensity will result in more information about each.

Some programs are strictly DUI/DWI programs, which provide psychoeducation about substance use and drinking and driving. There are drug treatment court referral programs, which tend to be either outpatient or residential/halfway house–based treatment programs. Additionally, parents involved with protective services because of their use may obtain treatment through outpatient, halfway/residential treatment, or hospitalization programs. Finally, correctional facilities house many persons who are addicted to illicit substances and offer various types of programming, ranging from psychoeducation to specialized substance use treatment units.

Case Study: Susan

Susan is a 25-year-old African American lesbian female who is mandated to treatment through drug court after being charged with a second driving under the influence (DUI). She has a bachelor's degree in journalism and currently works for a small community newspaper. The DUI was reported by her newspaper's police blotter, and as such, she is now having to undergo random urine screening at work since she travels to sites to report on stories, which potentially opens her employer up for liability.

She reported that she has been experiencing lack of motivation, loss of interest, and passive suicidal ideation for the past 2 weeks. After further assessment you also find out that she has been experiencing rapid heartbeat, racing and grandiose thoughts, and nights where she is not able to sleep and feels like "[she] can get anything done." She expressed that she has been experiencing all of the previously mentioned for as long as she can remember. She reported that she has had three past suicide attempts, with the last one being at the age of 21; she also reported that she has been cutting since the age of 13, which began after experiencing a sexual assault from her mother's boyfriend. She stated that she told her mother about the sexual assault, but the mother took the boyfriend's side, and Susan was sent to live with her grandmother.

During her first session she discloses to you that she has been abusing substances since the sexual assault. She reported she first began smoking marijuana and drinking after the sexual assault to help her cope with the flashbacks and shame associated with the assault; she expressed that she blamed herself because "[she] should not have been wearing what [she] was." Susan then disclosed that she "graduated" from marijuana to cocaine at the age of 18, which she has been using, in conjunction with alcohol, ever since. She stated that she originally began by snorting the cocaine, but it messed up her nasal cavities, so she began shooting up. You, the therapist, notice that she is high at the time of her assessment.

Case Application Questions

1. Describe a comprehensive assessment process that you would conduct to analyze Susan's situation. Be specific about the types of instruments you might choose and why. Also, discuss specific questions you would ask and how the answers may inform your treatment approach.
2. If you had to give Susan a preliminary diagnosis based solely on the information from the case, what diagnosis would you give her? Support your diagnosis with evidence from the case. Are there additional diagnostic categories you would want to explore further? What questions would you ask, or what additional collateral sources would you want to use to assess these categories?
3. What treatment modalities would you recommend for Susan, if you were designing a comprehensive treatment program with no limits on resources? Discuss your reasoning.

SUMMARY

In this chapter, you learned the various aspects of assessment for addictive disorders, including conducting a biopsychosocial assessment, assessing the six dimensions of the ASAM criteria, and use of multiple methods of assessment to inform diagnoses and treatment planning. The chapter discussed common short screening instruments, as well as some of the more in-depth assessment measures commonly used with adult and juvenile clients. Additionally, you learned how to diagnose substance use disorders and how to obtain information about prevalence, development and course, differential diagnosis, and common comorbid diagnoses. The chapter also discussed how the assessment of risk level informs level of care, including restrictiveness of the setting and intensity of services, based on risk of relapse. Finally, you learned about both treatment settings and treatment interventions commonly used in addiction settings.

CHAPTER 9 REFLECTIVE QUESTIONS

1. Discuss the six ASAM dimensions and the counselor's task for each one.
2. If you were working with a pregnant woman mandated by drug court for treatment, describe what a comprehensive assessment would look like.
3. Compare group interventions used with addictions populations and the unique uses for each in a comprehensive treatment program.
4. Describe common addictive family dynamics and how these would inform your family interventions.
5. Discuss the role of interpersonal/relational interventions as they relate to motivational interviewing with addiction populations.

6. Compare cognitive behavioral, trauma-informed, and experiential/somatic interventions. Specifically discuss how each type of intervention relates to previous chapters' discussions of ACEs, interpersonal neurobiology, and emotion regulation.
7. Describe the continuum of addiction counseling services available under the ASAM criteria.

RESOURCES

Department of Health and Human Services, Substance Abuse and Mental Health Services Administration, "Emerging Issues in Behavioral Health and the Criminal Justice System": https://www.samhsa.gov/criminal-juvenile-justice/behavioral-health-criminal-justice

Newsweek, "The Case for Treating Drug Addicts in Prison": https://www.newsweek.com/case-treating-drug-addicts-prison-73561

American Society of Addiction Medicine Treatment Criteria: https://www.asam.org/resources/the-asam-criteria/about

American Society of Addiction Medicine Screening and Assessment Tools: https://www.asam.org/education/live-online-cme/fundamentals-of-addiction-medicine/additional-resources/screening-assessment-for-substance-use-disorders/screening-assessment-tools

National Institute on Drug Abuse (NIDA): Chart of evidence-based screening tools and assessments for adults and adolescents: https://www.drugabuse.gov/nidamed-medical-health-professionals/tool-resources-your-practice/screening-assessment-drug-testing-resources/chart-evidence-based-screening-tools

SAMHSA trauma-informed care and trauma-specific interventions: https://www.samhsa.gov/nctic/trauma-interventions

National Institute of Corrections: Corrections and mental health trauma-informed correctional care: Promising for prisoners and facilities: https://community.nicic.gov/blogs/mentalhealth/archive/2013/09/09/trauma-informed-correctional-care-promising-for-prisoners-and-facilities.aspx

Residential Substance Abuse Treatment (RSAT), "Training and Technical Assistance Tool: Trauma Informed Approaches in Correctional Settings": http://www.rsat-tta.com/Files/Trainings/Trauma_Informed_Manual

12 steps and 12 traditions: http://www.portlandeyeopener.com/AA-12-Steps-12-Traditions.pdf

Rational Recovery: https://rational.org/index.php?id=1

Celebrate Recovery: https://www.celebraterecovery.com/

John Bradshaw, author of addiction resources dealing with family systems: https://www.johnbradshaw.com/

International Somatic Movement Education and Therapy Association: https://ismeta.org/about-ismeta

Domestic Violence/Intimate Partner Violence Victims

Leigh F. Holman and Amanda Russell

Upon completion of this chapter, readers will be able to do the following:

- Define domestic violence/intimate partner violence (DV/IPV) and discuss the different manifestations of DV/IPV
- Screen clients for potential IPV victimization
- Understand both the diagnostic issues and corresponding prevention and intervention activities that forensic mental health counselors may participate in with IPV victims

TABLE 10.1 Myths and Myth Busters

Myths	Myth Busters
DV/IPV is private and should not be discussed or acknowledged outside of the family.	**DV/IPV is a community health problem that leads to increased incidences of child abuse, medical and work-related costs, and ongoing social impacts of victimization.**
DV/IPV only happens in heterosexual relationships.	**Homosexual couples experience DV/IPV as well.**
Couple's counseling is an appropriate IPV intervention if this is the first time someone is a victim	**Couple's counseling may place victims in danger, even if the victim states he or she wants couple's counseling.**

INTRODUCTION

Domestic violence includes any abusive behavior perpetrated by one family/household member or romantic partner against another. It includes any physical, sexual, emotional, or psychological abuse. Victims may be a partner, a child, or someone who is disabled, elderly, or in the care of the perpetrator. Siblings can also abuse one another. Child abuse risks, types, mental health consequences, reporting procedures, and intervention were discussed extensively in section II of this text, so we will focus in this chapter on intimate partner violence.

Intimate partner violence (IPV) includes any aggressive or violent physical, psychological, or sexual behavior or threats between romantic partners, whether heterosexual or homosexual, ranging on a continuum from one episode to multiple episodes increasing in severity or changing in severity, over time. The Family Violence Prevention and Services Act (FVPSA) provides treatment guidelines and funds for shelter and treatment of IPV victims of all sexual orientations (National LGBTQ Institute on IPV, 2018). There are four types of IPV:

- **Sexual violence**: Rape, sexual coercion, and unwanted sexual contact
- **Stalking**: A pattern of harassing or threatening behavior, which results in fear or concerns for one's safety
- **Physical violence**: Aggressive physical behaviors ranging from slapping and pushing to chocking, suffocating, burning, or assault with a weapon
- **Psychological violence**: Verbal aggression intended to control the victim, which includes insulting or humiliating comments

According to the Centers for Disease Control (CDC, 2017), a quarter of the women in the United States experience severe physical IPV, 10% experience stalking, and 16% are sexually assaulted by an intimate partner. One in seven men also experience IPV, 2% experience stalking, and 7% are sexually assaulted by a partner. Additionally, 12% of girls and 7% of boys who date report experiencing physical violence and 16% of girls and 5% of boys who date report sexual assault perpetrated by a partner in the previous year (Kann et al., 2016). Bisexual men and women experience a higher lifetime prevalence of IPV than heterosexual men and women. Studies indicate 3.6% of lesbian women, 26.9% of gay men, and between 31.1% and 50% of transgender individuals experience IPV (Goldberg & Meyer, 2013; Langenderfer-Magruder, Whitfield, Walls, Kattari, & Ramos, 2014; Messinger, 2011).

Rates of IPV vary by ethnicity. Almost half of the women and a quarter of men in multiracial households experienced partner violence (Hart & Klein, 2013). The next largest group of victims are Native American women, 39% of whom are victims of IPV. Black women experienced IPV at a rate of 29.2%, as did 23.3% of Black men. White women experienced IPV at a lower rate of 26.8% and White men at 15.5% . Finally, 20.5% of women and 15.5% of men in Hispanic households experienced IPV. For women, pregnancy is a particularly vulnerable time for abuse to happen. In fact, research indicates that 2.4–6.6% of pregnant women experience IPV, most of these young, low-income Latinas. Women with disabilities also reported higher incidences of victimization (28.5 % with a disability versus 15.4% without a disability). Additionally, both active duty military and veterans were more likely than non-military families to experience IPV (39% of female veterans and 30–44% of active duty females).

IPV results in numerous adverse health outcomes, including physical injuries needing various levels of medical treatment, as well as chronic cardiovascular, gastrointestinal, reproductive, musculoskeletal, and nervous system problems (Black, 2011; Cooper & Smith, 2011). Victims may develop psychological disorders (e.g., mood disorders, PTSD), as a result of these experiences (Warshaw, Brashler, & Gil, 2009). Additionally, 40% of women murdered in the United States are murdered subsequent to IPV (Cooper & Smith, 2011). IPV costs society over $4 billion in medical costs and almost $2 billion in productivity losses (CDC, 2003).

ASSESSMENT

When working with any client, counselors should screen for the possibility of domestic violence victimization by asking direct, nonjudgmental questions about IPV. During a biopsychosocial assessment and mental status exam, treatment providers need to be aware of behaviors that indicate abuse and then specifically assess for abuse in more depth, if indicated. Indicators of abuse, which are also part of the *power and control wheel*, are described in Table 10.2.

Victims are more likely to have trauma histories, demonstrate anxiety or depression, experience suicidal ideation, experience sleep disorders, have chronic pain, and use substances to manage emotions or stress (CDC, 2003; Cerulli, Talbot, Tang, & Chaudron, 2011; Fedovskiy, Higgins, & Paranjape, 2008; Follette, Polunsy, Bechtle, & Naugle, 1996). Using the acronym **RADAR** can help you remember the steps in assessing for IPV. **R**outinely screen for IPV; **a**sk direct questions; **d**ocument findings; **a**ssess safety of victim and children; and **r**eview intervention options and refer.

Although victims may not volunteer information about IPV, they often will acknowledge victimization if asked directly. Always ask these questions when the client is alone, as you may not know who the perpetrator of abuse is. Assessing IPV in the presence of the perpetrator can increase the risk for abuse experienced by the victim. Some examples of questions you can ask are the following:

- Are you in a relationship with someone who has physically threatened or hurt you? Have you ever been in such a relationship?
- Has your partner ever destroyed things you care about? Threatened or abused your children? Forced you to have sex or engage in sex you were not comfortable with?
- We all fight at home. What happens when you disagree or fight with your partner?
- Do you ever feel afraid of your partner?
- Are you ever afraid to go home?
- Has your partner ever prevented you from leaving the house, seeing friends, getting a job, or continuing your education?
- You mentioned that your partner uses drugs/alcohol. How does your partner act when drinking or on drugs? Is your partner ever verbally or physically abusive?
- Do you have guns in your home? Has your partner ever threatened to use them when angry with you?

TABLE 10.2 **Indicators of Abuse**

Type of abuse	Behavioral examples
Economic abuse	Victim is given an allowance to live on or is forced to ask for money.
	Prevents victim from getting or keeping a job.
	Controls the victim's access to money.
	Keeps information about family finances from the victim.
Emotional abuse	Making humiliating comments that result in the victim feeling poorly about him- or herself.
	Gaslighting or trying to make the victims feel like they are crazy, that something that was said or done was not reality.
	Trying to make the victim feel guilty or responsible for the abuse.
	Name-calling in private or public.
Isolation	Controls victim's time, movements, and activities.
	Limits any activity outside the home.
	Uses jealousy as a justification for behavior or expectations.
Uses children	Makes the victim feel guilty about children or parenting.
	Sends messages to the victim through the children.
	Uses visitation to harass the victim.
	Threatens to take children.
Denial and Blame	Minimizes acknowledgement of or effect of abuse on the victim.
	Denies abuse has occurred.
	Shifts responsibility of the abuse to the victim.
Coercion and Threats	Threatens harm.
	Threatens to leave, commit suicide, or report the victim to protective services.
	Coerces the victim to drop legal charges.
	Reproductive coercion: Coercion to conceive, carry, or abort a child, as a means of control.
Intimidation	Abuses pets.
	Destroys property, especially personal or important items belonging to the victim.
	Displays weapons.
	Uses physical stature, posture, voice tone or volume, and/or facial/nonverbal expressions to evoke fear in the victim.
Male privilege	Controls major decisions.
	Acts like a master and treats the victim like a slave.
	Defines male and female roles in the relationship.

IPV victims often experience psychological barriers to disclosing abuse, including lack of understanding about physical symptoms being caused by stress or injuries stemming from the abuse, belief that injuries are not severe enough to be considered abuse, religious beliefs about their role in the relationship, believing the abuse was deserved and/or they are not deserving of help, and/or fear that revealing the abuse will escalate the perpetrator's behavior. The way you frame questions is important to engaging the victim in disclosure. Therefore, normalizing the situation by prefacing questions is important (e.g., "Relationships between adults can sometimes become violent" or "I'm concerned that your symptoms may have been caused by someone else" or "Sometimes others are overprotective or jealous").

Further, LGBT victims experience additional barriers to gaining help when they are victims of IPV. These barriers include the following:

- Concerns about law enforcement officers' reactions to their LGBT status
- Legal definitions that exclude same-sex couples
- Concerns about "outing" themselves when seeking help, thus risking rejection and isolation from support systems (e.g.. family and friends)
- Few LGBT inclusive services
- Potential homophobia from non-LGBT staff

For all victims of IPV, the risk of suicidality is higher than the average population. People who are victims of IPV are five times more likely to die by suicide (Hart & Klein, 2013).

When conducting the assessment, timing can make a difference in whether you are able to engage the victim in treatment. Understanding the *cycle of abuse* (Focht, n.d.) is helpful in determining the best way to intervene. There are three phases to the cycle of abuse:

1. **Tension building**: The abuser experiences stress, becomes agitated and tense. Any subject matter that might evoke additional stress, such as money, housework, work/family responsibilities, results in building tension. The abuse begins to be verbally abusive, using insults or demeaning comments to criticize or control the victim. Intimidating, threatening, or even physically shoving the victim may occur during this phase.
2. **Abuse:** Occurs when the batterer becomes physically abusive, throwing objects, destroying property, harming the victim or someone important to the victim (e.g., child or pet). The abuser may hit, slap, kick, choke, smother, or sexually assault the victim. At this point the victim is unlikely to be able to stop the abuse and attempts to do so may result in an escalation in behavior.
3. **Open window:** This phase occurs between the battering and the honeymoon phase. This is the time in which victims are most amenable to seeking help and engaging in treatment.
4. **Honeymoon phase:** During this phase the perpetrator apologizes, promises to "never do it again," and may even acknowledge his or her behavior was hurtful. He or she may buy the victim gifts or become overly attentive or affectionate. Often this lulls the victim into believing the danger is over.

Risk factors that increase the likelihood abuse will occur include financial problems and unemployment, divorce or separation, addictions, the victim or the perpetrator were victims of child abuse, suicide attempts by victim or perpetrator, and any symptoms of mental illness.

The Bureau of Justice Statistics, using FBI data, estimated that 241 men (110 husbands and 131 boyfriends) and 1,095 women (603 wives and 492 girlfriends) fell victim to IPV homicides (Hart & Klein, 2013). To assess for homicidal risk, counselors should ask about the presence of a gun in the home, which would increase the likelihood of fatal consequences of an abuse episode. Additionally, ask if the abuser has threatened to kill the victim or him- or herself, both of which increase the risk of homicide. Inquire about the perpetrator's level and frequency of jealousy, violent behaviors directed at non-family members and what those behaviors were, and substance abuse issues. These issues are considered to increase the likelihood of an abuse episode ending in death. Assess the severity of injuries over time and whether they have increased in severity. Inquire whether the abuser has killed a pet and/or if he or she objectifies the victim by treating the individual like a nonperson.

If you assess that there is an IPV situation, then express that this is more common than the victim may be aware, that in fact it occurs in 1 out of 10 relationships (Black et al., 2011). Assert that the abuse is not the victim's fault, regardless of what the victim is told. Explain that IPV can result in chronic and/or long-term mental health and physical health problems for the victim, their children, and any other vulnerable persons who have been exposed to the violence. Finally, convey that IPV is cyclical and often increases in intensity and severity over time; it is a crime. As part of your informed consent, it is important that you include any limits to confidentiality regarding mandatory reporting of domestic abuse in your state. Most states have domestic abuse mandatory reporting laws, which are distinct from child abuse and elder abuse mandatory reporting (Durborow, Lizdas, O'Flaherty, & Marijavi, 2010). They generally fall into one of four categories:

1. Laws requiring reporting of injuries caused by a weapon
2. Laws requiring reporting of injuries caused by violation of criminal laws, as a result of violence, or through nonaccidental means
3. Laws specifically requiring reporting of domestic violence
4. No mandatory reporting law

It is important that you know the law in the jurisdiction you practice and follow it. Once you have informed someone of the law, you can facilitate a police report, direct the victim and any children to safe shelter, and help the victim and his or her children get counseling.

DIAGNOSIS

Although not a mental health diagnosis, women who experience IPV also demonstrate high levels of shame and guilt. They often blame themselves for the abuse and particularly for their children being exposed to abuse (Lindgren & Renck, 2008; Weaver & Clum, 1995). IPV victims identify "stress" as the biggest motivator for seeking mental health intervention (Karakurt, Smith, & Whiting, 2014). As such, mental health diagnoses are necessarily affected by these dynamics.

Posttraumatic Stress Disorder (PTSD)

Given that IPV is traumatic, by definition, many IPV victims develop PTSD. In fact, studies indicate between 40–80% of women who experience IPV demonstrate symptoms of PTSD (Black et al., 2011; Mertin & Mohr, 2001). IPV victims are three times more likely to meet PTSD diagnostic criteria than those with no IPV victimization (Coolidge & Anderson, 2002;

Fedovskiy, Higgins, & Paranjape, 2008). PTSD is more common among IPV victims who were sexually assaulted (Kilpatrick, 2004). With increased severity of abuse, victims are more likely to experience anxiety disorders and PTSD (Follette, Polunsy, Bechtle, & Naugle, 1996), and those who experience multiple types of abuse are significantly more likely to develop PTSD with comorbid suicidal depression (Bonomi et al., 2006; Bonomi et al., 2009; Buller, Devries, Howard, & Bacchus, 2014; Cerulli, Talbot, Tang, & Chaudron, 2011). Interestingly, experiencing psychological abuse is more predictive of PTSD and depression than is physical abuse victimization (Nathanson, Shorey, Tirone, & Rhatigan, 2012). The most common PTSD symptoms experienced by IPV victims are increased arousal, hypervigilance, and emotional withdrawal/numbing (Karakurt, Smith, & Whiting, 2014).

Depression

A meta-analytic study demonstrated that female victims of IPV had twice the risk of developing depressive symptoms and three times the risk of meeting diagnostic criteria for major depressive disorder (Beydoun, Beydoun, Kaufman, Lo, & Zonderman, 2012). Among those with depression, mothers who were IPV victims experienced twice as much post-partum depression as mothers who had not experienced IPV. Also, mothers are twice as likely to have current depression diagnoses (Cerilli, Talbot, Tang, & Chaudron, 2011). Female victims of severe IPV abuse by a male perpetrator exhibited four times the risk of suicide attempts (Struass & Smith, 1990). One study found that 42% of the women with depressive symptoms expressed suicidal ideation (Karakurt, Smith, & Whiting, 2014).

Addictions

According to the American Society of Addiction Medicine (ASAM), addictive disorders are also prevalent among IPV victims. Part of this is due to the fact that they are prescribed more pain medication for injuries than nonvictims (Karakurt, Smith, & Whiting, 2014). Studies indicate prevalence rates of substance abuse range from 24% to 75% (Danielson, Moffit, Caspi, & Silva, 1998; Fowler, 2007; Martin, Moracco, Chang, Council, & Dulli 2008; Watson et al., 1997). Alcohol use is most common (60%) with drug dependence slightly lower (55%). IPV victimization is associated with higher rates of both binge drinking and tobacco use (Afifi, Henriksen, Asmundson, & Sareen, 2012; Bonomi et al., 2009; Breiding, Black, & Ryan, 2008; Buller, Devries, Howard, & Bacchus, 2014). Victims of IPV are six times more likely to develop a substance use disorder (Bonomi et al., 2009). Additionally, eating disorders are significantly more prevalent among IPV victims than nonvictims (Bundock et al., 2013).

TREATMENT

Given that victims often report their first incidence of IPV occurred prior to the age of 18, it is crucial that we consider both prevention and intervention for this issue. The CDC suggests a number of *prevention activities*. First, teach safe and healthy relationship skills, including social and emotional learning programs for youth and healthy relationship programs for couples. The CDC suggests that prevention programs engage influential adults and peers as allies, including men and boys; provide bystander empowerment education; and develop family-based programs about IPV. A significant prevention measure would be the disruption of the developmental trajectory leading to IPV. This would include early childhood intervention, parenting skills training, preschool enrichment with family engagement, and treatment for at-risk children, youth, and families. Also, it is important to provide protective school, community, and organizational environments, strengthen economic supports, and support survivor services (e.g., victim-centered services, housing, first responder and civil legal protections, and treatment support) (CDC, 2017). Additional prevention or early intervention measures include raising awareness through education campaigns about dating and spousal violence in relationships. Also, crisis hotlines provide a method for early intervention for victims reaching out for help.

Shelters and Supportive Services

Victims typically seek help first from friends and family before turning to outside sources of support. When they seek outside services, most often they seek criminal justice intervention, followed by social services like medical care, crisis counseling, and mental health counseling. Support services include information on the criminal justice process, notification of criminal justice hearings/events, information on victims' rights and how to obtain information from courts, referrals to counseling services, assistance with victim's compensation applications, and sometimes immigration assistance.

Many *shelters* offer emergency housing, peer counseling, safety planning, advocacy, and community referrals for other services, like mental health counseling. Increasingly, IPV victims' programs are expanding to offer transportation assistance, medical and legal assistance, as well as housing mental health counseling services within the shelter environment. Common mental health interventions at shelters include crisis counseling (97%), individual counseling (92%), support groups (97%), parenting groups (55%), child counseling (54%), and child care (58%) (Hart & Klein, 2013). IPV programs also provide advocacy services for participants. Among IPV victim programs, 95% offered housing assistance, 82% provided support in civil courts and 81% provide criminal court advocacy (Hart & Klein, 2013). Also, 81% of IPV programs provide civil court advocacy (Heart & Klein, 2013).

Safety planning is a crucial part of DV/IPV victim interventions. A typical safety plan specifies an individualized plan of action for when a violent incident occurs, including practicing how to get out safely and determining the best route to leave, having an established location for purse and car keys so that leaving is efficient, specifying typical escalation behaviors that indicate the need to leave, having a code word or phrase that indicates to children and/or friends to call for help, a place to go to, and identifying places to avoid having an argument that may be difficult to escape from. The plan also specifies safety strategies when preparing to leave. These include leaving money and an extra set of keys with a trusted friend or family member, keeping copies of important documents or keys in a secure private location, opening a bank account to increase independence, keeping a phone or phone card that is private and used only for emergencies, and leaving extra clothes or other personal items in a safe, neutral location. The safety plan also establishes specific things the victim can do to increase safety in his or her own residence like changing locks on doors and windows, replacing wood doors with steel/metal ones, installing a security system, purchasing rope ladders to escape from second-story windows, teaching children to call emergency contacts/numbers, establishing safe people for children to stay with, and so on. The safety plan establishes steps the victim can take to get and use an order of protection, including determining where to keep the order for easy access, giving a copy to the police department in the community the victim works, visits to friends, informing employer/minister/others of the protection order, knowing how to get a copy if the batterer destroys the original, and knowing what to do if the order is violated. The safety plan establishes who the victim will tell about the abuse, how the victim will manage safety in situations where alcohol or drugs are used by the victim and/or the perpetrator, and steps to safeguard the victim's emotional and mental health. The plan specifies what the victim needs to have stored to take with them if they leave, including the following:

> Copy of protective order
>
> Identification for self and children
>
> Birth certificates for self and children
>
> Social Security cards
>
> School and vaccination records
>
> Checkbook, ATM card, money, credit cards
>
> Driver's license and registration
>
> Keys (house, car, office)
>
> Medications
>
> Welfare ID, work permits, green cards
>
> Passports, divorce papers, medical records
>
> Lease/rental agreement, house deed, mortgage payment book
>
> Insurance papers
>
> Address book
>
> Personal items (sentimental value, favorite toys/blankets of children, pictures)
>
> Phone numbers for police/sheriff (local, work, school), prosecutor's office, and battered woman's program or National Domestic Violence hotline

A copy of a safety plan can be accessed at the National Center on Domestic and Sexual Violence website at www.ncdsv.org/images/DV_Safety_Plan.pdf.

Legal Interventions

According to the National Institute of Justice, IPV victims benefit from a variety of legal interventions. First, advances in legal policy and legislation have drastically changed the way we approach IPV in the justice system over the past 40 years. Until the 1970s IPV was a misdemeanor in most states, even when the same type of behavior perpetrated against a non-spouse would have been a felony. Since 1992 the Joint Commission on Accreditation of Healthcare Organizations (JCAHO) requires all accredited facilities implement policies and procedures for identifying, treating, and/or referring victims of IPV. The Violence Against Women Act (VAWA) is a federal law passed in 1994, which provided for developing a coordinated response from the criminal justice system, social service organizations, and non-governmental organizations to domestic violence and sexual assault. It established STOP grants for educating judges and police officers, funding victim and witness counselors, and funding social service systems focused on sheltering and treating battered women. In 1996, Congress passed the Domestic Violence Offender Gun Ban, also called the Lautenberg Amendment, which bans the shipment, transfer, and ownership of guns and ammunition by anyone convicted of misdemeanor domestic violence or those under a restraining/protection order for DV.

In 2000, Congress reauthorized VAWA and expanded its scope to include dating violence and stalking as well as trafficking. The 2003 reauthorization provided expanded protection for immigrants who are victims of IPV, including making it illegal to evict a victim of DV or stalking from federal housing based on their status as a victim. The 2013 reauthorization further expanded housing protections and protections for students and immigrant survivors. In 2017 the new regulations for the Family Violence Prevention and Services Act, which provides funds for IPV services, mandated nondiscrimination related to sexual orientation and gender identity, transgender, and gender nonconforming individuals (National LGBTQ Institute on IPV, 2018).

IPV victims now have protection in every state. A *restraining order* or protective order is intended to provide additional protections for IPV victims. Some states have specific types of restraining orders for stalking and sexual assault, in addition to IPV restraining orders. Although they vary from one jurisdiction to another, they all mandate that the perpetrator is legally barred from participating in certain activities or contacting the victim or being in the vicinity of the victim. These are called "stay-away" provisions. If the perpetrator violates this order, then he or she is more likely to be arrested and jailed. Some of these orders also allow judges to order perpetrators to pay temporary support or continue paying for housing (support provisions), to vacate a home or car owned jointly (exclusive use provisions), or to pay the costs of medical or property damages stemming from the abuse (restitution provisions). Some courts also may order perpetrators to relinquish firearms. Although some studies indicate that restraining orders are effective as deterrents to future abuse, other studies indicate 40% of these orders are violated, usually with more violent episodes, and are not very effective in deterring future violent behavior (Grau, Fagan, & Wexler, 1984; Harrell & Smith, 1996; McFarlane et al., 1994; Spitzberg, 2002).

Some states require police to make arrests even when the victim does not press charges, requiring them to go to the victim's home with them to get children and belongings, and informing victims of their rights as victims of IPV. Legal remedies vary from state to state. Generally, victims can seek civil relief form civil courts when they are the girl/boyfriend, spouse or former spouse, or related by blood or marriage to an abuser; are stalked or harassed;

or have a child with the abuser. Civil remedies can provide financially for the victims of IPV. Criminal charges are intended to punish the abuser and can be filed if a victim experiences violence, regardless of whether the victim and abuser are living together or married. It is best for victims to file civil and criminal charges at the same time based on the same incident. Additionally, victims should stay in a shelter or with relatives/friends, seek medical attention for injuries, and seek counseling to help process the psychological and emotional impact of the abuse. Guidance on how to pursue legal, medical, economic, and psychological help is available through local shelters or victim treatment programs and/or the National Domestic Violence Hotline (800-799-SAFE/7233 or TDD 800-787-3224).

Mental Health Services

Crisis counseling is the initial mental health service offered to victims of IPV. This type of counseling is more directive than traditional counseling. It focuses on de-escalating and containing the immediate crisis. So, the primary aim for the mental health provider is to assist the client with physical and emotional safety. Sometimes this occurs by marshalling existing resources; however, for many clients with few supports, they go into shelters and begin working with a case manager and victim advocate to find the economic, legal, social, and psychological supports they need to leave the abusive situation.

Psychoeducation is a common component of DV/IPV victim programs. Psychoeducation seeks to improve the victim's awareness of the dynamics involved in abusive relationships, the consequences of staying in the relationship to the victim and any children, and strategies for coping with being a victim of IPV. One example of a DV/IPV psychoeducation group has 12 structured sessions where the mental health provider provides didactic information on specific predetermined topics and facilitates the group members' discussion around these topics. Sample topics are as follows:

- Domestic violence and PTSD: Effects on the victim and children
- Safety planning and establishing support systems
- Coping skills
- Anger management
- The cognitive ttriangle: The relationship between thoughts, feelings, and actions
- Trusting others
- Trusting oneself
- Guilt and responsibility
- Telling your story: The first DV experience
- Telling your story: The worst DV experience
- Your child(ren)'s story: Supporting your child(ren)
- Healthier relationships

Support groups are common in DV/IPV victim programs. These groups offer fellowship and friendship from other IPV victims. These groups meet for 1 to 2 hours daily and provide a place for shelter residents to gain support and talk about their thoughts, feelings, and concerns about their current situation. They may also discuss ways to problem solve parenting issues or logistical issues related to moving forward with their lives. Most of the time these groups are led by a shelter volunteer or employee.

Individual counseling is not offered at every IPV victim program. However, when it is offered, counselors attempt to provide trauma-informed care. Essential principles of any trauma-informed approach to DV/IPV intervention include safety and stability as foundational, respect, and positive regard shown to clients, supporting courage to leave, optimism about life, sensitivity to multicultural issues, empowerment of the victim and respect for the victim's autonomy in making decisions, awareness of gender issues, movement toward growth, and building on strengths. Individual counseling provides a place to work through individualized safety plans, parenting concerns, and mental health issues related to the abuse.

Children's counseling is also offered at most DV/IPV programs. Play therapy is used with young children to provide a safe, supportive place to process their emotions about events that they may not fully understand. Older children and adolescents are generally placed in group therapy situations where they find support and learn similar, yet age appropriate, psychoeducational material as the parent/victim learns. Children also work on safety plans of their own using language and terms that are easy for them to understand.

SETTINGS

As previously described, most victims' services occur in community agencies, frequently nonprofits, or in shelters. However, for individuals who have more financial resources, some private practitioners who have previous experience in working with DV/IPV may work with victims as well. Frequently, these agencies or private practitioners are reimbursed for services through the state's Victims Assistance programs, which provide financial compensation for mental health services for victims of crime.

Beginning in the 1990s, many jurisdictions began developing domestic violence courts, modeled on drug treatment court models. There are around 200 DV courts today, which utilize mental health treatment courts that use an interdisciplinary treatment team approach to addressing DV in the community (Labriola, Bradley, O'Sullivan, Rempel, & Moore, 2010). The treatment team is led by a judge who hears all DV cases in the jurisdiction. There are specially trained probation officers who act as caseworkers for the offenders. Professional members of community agencies that treat offenders and victims also participate in the treatment team. DV courts focus on rehabilitation and deterrence of repeated offending. Victims' services establish courthouse and pretrial safety and orders of protection for victims. The DV treatment team also provides accountability procedures for offenders, including assessments, batterer's intervention programs (BIP), and monitoring of offender's in the community. Finally, there is judicial oversight of all services so that the judge is making decisions based on information from caseworkers, officers, and treatment providers in order to increase the likelihood of success and family reunification in cases where it is appropriate. Common goals of DV courts include the following:

- Consistent application of legally appropriate procedures and sentences
- Efficient case processing

- Informed decision making
- Coordinated response between criminal justice, victims' services, and offender programs
- Victim safety and services
- Offender accountability
- Reduced recidivism through rehabilitation (changing offenders' beliefs, attitudes, and behaviors) or deterrence (increasing the perceived consequences of re-offending)

There continues to be some controversy among victims' advocates about the use of DV courts. Specifically, victims' advocates express concern about whether DV courts are too focused on rehabilitation of offenders without enough support for the safety of victims. However, a study of DV courts indicated that safety and security of victims is the primary concern of DV treatment teams (Labriola, Bradley, O'Sullivan, Rempel, & Moore, 2010).

Case Study: Maria

Maria is a 16-year-old Mexican American girl who lives with her mother and younger brother. Her parents divorced when she was 8, following several incidents of domestic violence between her parents that escalated to the point that her mother was hospitalized for injuries, and Maria was also injured, which involved her family with Child Protective Services (CPS). Because of this incident, her father was placed in prison for aggravated assault with a weapon. He was already on parole for a drug-related offense, so he was ordered to complete a 10-year minimum prison sentence. Once her father was placed in prison the CPS case was closed on Maria and her brother; however, recently her mother began living with a man who has a previous history of domestic violence. When Maria's brother broke curfew, their mom's boyfriend physically assaulted her brother, which led to a new CPS case being opened.

When Maria met with the caseworker, she disclosed that she was 6 weeks pregnant with a child by her longtime boyfriend, Malcolm. The caseworker noted that Maria had bruises on her arm that appeared to be evidence of a hand wrapped around her bicep. She also had what appeared to be a healing laceration above her left eye. When asked about the injuries, Maria reluctantly acknowledged that her boyfriend was upset that she "got herself pregnant," and they didn't have the money to get an abortion. He punched her in the stomach to try to trigger a miscarriage. When he did, she began fighting back, resulting in additional injuries. Maria states that she loves her boyfriend and does not want him to get into trouble. She knows she should have been more careful and not gotten pregnant. Following the interview, Maria is mandated to undergo counseling for domestic violence by the family court judge overseeing her family's case.

She reports that Malcolm does not want her to talk to her family or friends, much less you, about their private business. She reports that she relies on Malcolm for financial support because her mom threw her out of the house since her mom believes she's making bad choices. When you assess her, you find that she is experiencing primary insomnia, night terrors, hypervigilance, and exaggerated startle response. You also notice that when asked about the abuse, currently or in the past, she tends to "zone out" and not realize that you are waiting for a response.

Case Application Questions

1. Discuss Maria's case, applying family and sociocultural contexts of the presenting issue. What challenges do you see in treating Maria and why?
2. Describe the types of abuse that might be present for Maria and what her experience is applying the power and control wheel. How would this information inform your work with Maria?
3. If you had to give Maria a preliminary diagnosis, what would it be? Support your answer with evidence from the case. What additional diagnostic categories would you want to explore and why? What additional information would you need to gather to determine if the other diagnostic categories fit for Maria or not and why?
4. Describe how prevention activities might be used in Maria's case to prevent escalation of abusive relationships.
5. Design a comprehensive intervention plan, including identification of settings(s) in which treatment or other types of support or intervention would be conducted. Explain your reasoning for the choices you make.

SUMMARY

This chapter defines both domestic violence and interpersonal violence and discusses prevalence rates of DV/IPV among different genders, ethnicities, and sexual orientations. Information is provided about what to look for in screening for potential DV/IPV victimization, including how to approach assessments, what to look for, and what to ask in assessment situations. Included in the assessment section is information on the power and control wheel indicating potential abuse situations and the phases in the cycle of abuse. Common diagnostic issues, including PTSD, depression and suicidality, and addictive disorders are discussed as they manifest among DV/IPV victims. Finally, the chapter reviews typical prevention activities and legal, social support, and mental health interventions and settings.

CHAPTER 10 REFLECTIVE QUESTIONS

1. Describe domestic and intimate partner violence, including the different types of violence common in these relationships.
2. Describe the elements of a thorough assessment, if you were working with an adult victim of domestic/intimate partner violence.
3. How would you assess risk to a victim of domestic/intimate partner violence?
4. If you were conducting a psychoeducational workshop in your community, how would you explain the cycle of abuse to participants of different demographics (e.g., teens, persons with limited formal education, LBGTQ)?

5. Discuss the types and prevalence of different mental health issues domestic/intimate partner violence victims experience.
6. If you were designing a comprehensive program to address domestic/intimate partner violence victimization, what would it look like?
7. If you were developing a safety plan with an adult victim of domestic/intimate partner violence, what would you include in the discussion and why?

RESOURCES

Intimate partner violence and sexual abuse among LGBT people: https://williamsinstitute.law.ucla.edu/wp-content/uploads/Intimate-Partner-Violence-and-Sexual-Abuse-among-LGBT-People.pdf

National LGBTQ Institute on IPV: https://avp.org/ncavp/national-lgbtq-institute-ipv/

National Coalition Against Domestic Violence: Male victims of intimate partner violence: https://www.speakcdn.com/assets/2497/male_victims_of_intimate_partner_violence.pdf

National Resource Center on Domestic Violence: Technical assistance: Serving male-identified survivors of intimate partner violence: https://vawnet.org/sites/default/files/assets/files/2017-07/NRCDV_TAG-ServingMaleSurvivors-July2017.pdf

National Institute of Justice, "Perspectives on Civil Protective Orders in Domestic Violence Cases: The Rural and Urban Divide": https://www.ncjrs.gov/pdffiles1/nij/230410.pdf

National Center for Health Research: The cycle of domestic violence: http://www.center4research.org/cycle-domestic-violence/

National Child Traumatic Stress Network: Domestic violence: https://www.nctsn.org/what-is-child-trauma/trauma-types/domestic-violence

Behind closed doors: The impact of domestic violence on children: https://www.unicef.org/media/files/BehindClosedDoors.pdf

National Domestic Violence Hotline: https://www.thehotline.org/

Domestic Violence Personalized Safety Plan: http://www.ncdsv.org/images/DV_Safety_Plan.pdf

National Institute of Justice: Intimate partner violence: https://www.nij.gov/topics/crime/intimate-partner-violence/Pages/welcome.aspx

National Institute of Justice, "A National Portrait Domestic Violence Courts": https://www.ncjrs.gov/pdffiles1/nij/grants/229659.pdf

The trend toward specialized domestic violence courts: Improvements on an effective innovation: https://ir.lawnet.fordham.edu/cgi/viewcontent.cgi?article=3628&context=flr

Crime Victims Institute, "Assessing the Risk of Intimate Partner Violence": http://www.ncdsv.org/images/CVI_Assessing-the-Risk-of-IPV_1-2010.pdf

Domestic Violence/Intimate Partner Violence Offenders

Amanda Russell and Leigh F. Holman

Upon completion of this chapter, readers will be able to do the following:

- Conduct an IPV offender assessment
- List different types of IPV offenders and determine appropriate interventions
- Explain batterer intervention programs and their relationship to DVERT teams and DV treatment courts

TABLE 11.1 Myths and Myth Busters

Myths	Myth Busters
Victims provoke perpetrators into violence.	**Regardless of the victim's behavior(s), it is not acceptable for someone to perpetrate violence in an intimate relationship, unless the person's life is in danger.**
DV/IPV results from an impulse control or anger management problem.	**Many perpetrators actually act violently in a methodical and planned manner, rather than impulsive one.**
Anger management is a shorter, more cost conscious method to treat batterers.	**Batterer intervention programs (BIPs) are specialized treatment programs that address the interpersonal and contextual dynamics of abuse beyond anger management.**

INTRODUCTION

According to the National Violence Against Women Survey (NVAWS), just over 5 million people experience incidents of intimate partner violence (IPV) annually, resulting in 2 million injuries, a quarter of which require medical attention (Gerberding, Binder, Hammond, & Arias, 2003). However, there are a number of challenges to estimating prevalence rates because of lack of consensus in how IPV is defined, variations in data collection, sampling, survey instruments, repetitive nature of IPV, and other methodological issues (Gerberding, Binder, Hammond, & Arias, 2003; National Institute of Justice [NIJ], 2010). Additionally, many victims simply do not want to acknowledge DV/IPV.

IPV offenders do not neatly fit a simple description. They vary in age, socioeconomic level, ethnicity/race, sexual orientation, and religion (NIJ, 2010). However, rates of IPV in LGBT populations tend to be higher. The victims find it more difficult to disclose due to discrimination; therefore, only a small percentage of LGBT IPV offenders have charges for IPV (Healey, Smith, & O'Sullivan, 1998). We know, however, that both men and women may perpetrate DV/IPV, although most studies indicate that the majority (85–95%) of perpetrators are male (Bagshaw & Chung, 2000; Gerberding, Binder, Hammond, & Arias, 2003; Healey, Smith, & O'Sullivan, 1998; NIJ, 2010). Over half report that IPV is bi-directional with over 69% of African American's reporting bi-directional abuse. In addition, estimates range from 3.3 to 10 million children annually who witness IPV, and among these, resulting injuries are common (Bragg, 2003). Among those charged with IPV, less than 10% result in a conviction or guilty plea, with less than a third of those ever receive any jail time. Therefore, forensic counselors are most likely to work with batterers in the community, rather than in correctional institutions (Hamby, 2014).

Research also indicates that violent behaviors have neurological correlates related to brain structure, neurotransmitter functioning, and hormonal factors (Farrell, 2011). Aggression involves the activation of parts of the hypothalamus, triggering the emotional center of the brain in the amygdala, resulting in dysregulated fear and anxiety, which then results in defensive aggression (Farrell, 2011). Additionally, executive functioning functions, such as inhibition and judgment, located in the prefrontal cortex, do not engage during aggression among batterers (Kavoussi, Armstead, P., Coccaro, 1997). Neurochemically, low levels of serotonin and GABA result in impulsive aggression. Additionally, higher concentrations of noradrenaline, acetylcholine, and dopamine may increase aggression (Renfrew, 1997). Finally, research indicates strong support, although not conclusive, between high levels of androgynous hormones, cortisol, a stress hormone, and dehydroepiandrosterone sulfate (Renfrew, 1997).

State laws vary in how they address IPV behaviors. However, federal laws that address IPV include the Family Violence Prevention and Services Act (FVPSA) of 1984 (P.L. 98–457), the Violence Against Women Act (VAWA), Title IV of the Violent Crime Control and Law Enforcement Act (P.L. 103–322), and the Personal Responsibility and Work Opportunity Reconciliation Act of 1996 (PRWORA) Wellsonte/Murray Amendment (P.L. 104–193). FVPSA was the first attempt at legislation to effect IPV, and it provides funds to raise awareness about IPV, as well as grant funding for DV shelters and victim services. VAWA was significant in that it demonstrated acknowledgment of the seriousness of IPV through improving law enforcement and criminal justice responses to IPV. There are four parts to the act, including safe streets, safe homes for women, civil rights for women and equal justice for women in the courts, and protection for battered immigrant women and children. As a result, new criminal offenses with tougher penalties were created, including mandated restitution to victims and more protections for victims during prosecution. This legislation also increased funding for prevention and education programs, victims' services, IPV training for community profession-als, and protection from deportation for immigrant women. Finally, PRWORA replaced Aid to Families with Dependent Children (AFDC) with Temporary Assistance to Needy Families (TANF). Under new provisions, states were able to temporarily exempt identified victims of IPV from meeting time limits and other work requirements necessary for economic assistance.

ASSESSMENT

When assessing clients for IPV behaviors, it is important to understand what constitutes abuse in this context. When we talk about IPV, usually people think of *physical abuse* behav-iors ranging from pushing and slapping to strangulation or other behaviors ending in serious injury or death. *Emotional, verbal, or psychological abuse* includes any verbal or nonverbal behavior intended to tear down the self-esteem of their partner in order to manipulate or control the behavior of the victim. *Sexual abuse* ranges from restricting access to birth control to pressure or coercion to do something sexually that they do not want to do. *Digital abuse* is the use of technology in a manner that the offender intends to control (e.g., cyberstalking or surveilling) or harm (e.g., posting naked pictures on social media) the victim. *Economic abuse*, also called financial abuse, involves any use of money or other tangible resources intended to control or influence the victim. This can include a perpetrator working and "not allowing" the victim to work, thus limiting the victim's economic resources. *Spiritual abuse* involves the use of spiritual or religious beliefs to manipulate or control the victim. This can range from restricting the victim from attending religious services to a minister telling a victim (e.g., woman) to go back to an abusive partner because the Bible mandates she submit to her husband's will or that the victim should return to the relationship because there is no religious support for termination of the relationship. Finally, *stalking* is the act of tracking the victim's movements without his or her consent. Stalking may involve physically following the victim, hiring someone to follow the victim, or using technology to surveille the victim.

IPV perpetrators use a variety of common tactics to manipulate and control victims. Abusing power and control is the primary goal of any IPV offender. They coerce victims into feeling helpless, scared, and shameful through randomly changing expectations for the victim's behavior in order to avoid abuse with corresponding increasing demands on the victim. IPV offenders commonly act nice, normal, and loving in public and then change into violent or degrading behavior in private. They also frequently avoid accountability for their behavior by projecting blame onto the victim (e.g., "If you wouldn't have …. I wouldn't get so angry"). Although 5–10% of IPV offenders act impulsively, most do not, so when they claim they cannot control their anger, this is another strategy to control the victim's response to abuse. Finally, almost all abusers minimize, rationalize, and/or deny the abusive behavior.

During a *domestic violence risk assessment* the counselor gathers information from behavioral observation, formal assessments, a clinical interview, review of collateral resources (e.g., arrest report, prior psychological evaluations), and reflection on his or her own interaction with the client, in order to help him or her understand the context and extent of domestic violence behaviors and the extent of harm present.

Risk assessment involves both static and dynamic risk factors. *Static risk factors* are those based on the individual's history, background, and demographics. They do not change. We use these to determine the basic level of risk a perpetrator poses. Then we may use dynamic factors to adjust opinion of risk, moderately, based on context. *Dynamic risk factors* can change because of intervention, treatment, or even just the passage of time. They include information about the person's current attitudes, beliefs, and behaviors (e.g., expressions of empathy, insight, or motivation) that may indicate a change in level of risk. However, a skillful or personality disordered offender can more easily manipulate these factors, and therefore should not result in major adjustments to level of risk.

These offenders are usually court mandated to treatment and therefore resistant to intervention. You can expect that the offender will use similar tactics used in his or her IPV behaviors to gain control of the interview, which can range from manipulation and flattery to minimization and rationalization to coercion, threats, and use of demeaning comments. Therefore, the counselor must maintain a posture that is both assertive and professional. During the assessment phase, in particular, it is important to remember that the counselor is gathering information, not intervening therapeutically. When the focus is on information gathering, counselors take note of the way the client interacts with them and with others in the facility, the ease or difficulty with which they are able to obtain information, any strategies used to gain control or manipulate them, as well as the actual information the perpetrator shares verbally. Often counselors' interpersonal experiences and behavioral observations of the client are as valuable, if not more, than the verbally articulated information provided by the offender during the clinical interview. During this phase, counselors will not confront or attempt to change any of the clients' thinking errors or behaviors beyond calmly and professionally setting boundaries when necessary to maintain their safety.

Clinicians should view the importance of rapport building and the therapeutic alliance with equal importance as they would with any other client. Without any rapport, the counselor will have great difficulty gaining insight into the client's motives and underlying issues driving his or her abusive behavior. It is important for interviewers to remember that not every person who has been abusive to a partner is the same. People act in abusive ways for a variety of reasons and can have very different emotional reactions to their own behavior. If the clinician is able to connect with the IPV offender, he or she is much more likely to understand the roots of the abusive behavior and make appropriate choices regarding the treatments and services that will be most likely to promote change.

It is important when interviewing someone who has committed intimate partner violence to assess his or her level of accountability taking and stage of change. Motivational interviewing may be a useful tool for assisting clients in navigating these stages of change. As discussed in chapter 3, the pre-contemplation stage is characterized by a client's assertion that violent/aggressive behavior is not causing problems and therefore does not need to change. When working with IPV offenders, this stage often includes victim blaming, minimization, normalization, and justification. Clients may state that they would not have become aggressive if their partner had not been unfaithful or refused to listen to them. Therefore, it is not their behavior that needs to change, it's their partner. They also may blame the neighbor, friend, or family member who called the police, or they may blame law enforcement. Clients may believe that their behavior was not the problem; other people getting involved and overreacting was the problem. Offenders may also report that they fight with their partner just as everyone else does. They may point to their peers or family members who are also involved in abusive relationships and assume that their behavior does not need to change because fighting and abuse is a "normal" part of being in a relationship. Questions that may be helpful in assisting the client in becoming more open to new behaviors include the following:

1. What consequences have you faced because of the way you handled this situation?
2. What would happen if your partner or a future partner demonstrates this behavior again? Is it possible that you could end up facing these consequences again in the future? If so, why? If not, why not?
3. Has the way you reacted when angry or upset ever caused you problems in the past?

Clients who are in the contemplative state of change can benefit from finding motivation and hope that change is possible and that change would be worth the effort. Counselors can provide encouragement and support during this stage by asking questions that allow the client to imagine positive alternatives to abuse:

1. What are some things about the way you react in arguments that you'd like to change?
2. Describe how you'd like to react when you feel upset with your partner.
3. What stands in the way of you reacting in a different way when you feel upset or angry with your partner?
4. Tell me about a time when you were able to react differently when you were upset with your partner. What was different in that situation?
5. If you could imagine an ideal relationship, what kind of partner would you be in that relationship?

During the preparation stage, counselors can assist clients with making a plan to learn new, workable behaviors and curtail any likely roadblocks. This includes assisting the client in finding appropriate treatment services, whether that may include a domestic violence intervention program, anger management, individual counseling, psychiatric treatment, addiction treatment, or a combination of these. Assisting clients with increasing their literacy skills or education level may be necessary at this time as well as helping with employment and housing needs.

Even when a client appears to be in the action or maintenance stage of change, it is important for treatment providers to be aware of the importance of continued oversight, accountability, and monitoring for victim safety. Table 11.2 offers some do's and don'ts in working with offenders.

TABLE 11.2 Do's and Don'ts When Working With IPV Offenders

Do's	Don'ts
Do gently confront inconsistencies once you have created a rapport with the client.	Don't assume if someone lies then he or she absolutely isn't ready to change.
Do address inappropriate comments or gestures.	Don't react defensively.
Do verbalize clients' strengths.	Don't "cosign their BS" or express empathy while not excusing behavior.
Do redirect when clients ask personal questions.	Don't share information that may compromise your safety.
Do remain curious. What is driving this person's behavior?	Don't make assumptions.
Do listen closely for inconsistencies.	Don't point out inconsistencies just for the purpose of calling the client out.
Do use extraneous information (victim, collaborative data, and criminal history).	Don't get into a power struggle (there is no point).
Do be aware of safety concerns.	Don't take extraneous information as fact.
	Don't treat this person like a criminal.
	Do treat this person with respect.

Offenders are likely to continue to react in abusive ways when experiencing difficult emotions or a lack of control until they learn and habitually practice new, healthier methods of managing their emotions.

During assessments, the forensic mental health counselor must assess *level of dangerousness* by gathering information such as the following:

- The nature and extent of domestic violence
- The impact of the domestic violence on adult and child victims
- The risk to and protective factors of the alleged victim and children
- The help-seeking and survival strategies of the alleged victim
- The safety and service needs of family members
- The availability of practical community resources and services

This assessment also involves identifying *high-risk behaviors* that may end in severe attacks or even homicides. Indicators include the following:

- Possession or use of weapons
- Threats of suicide or homicide
- Demonstration of extreme jealously and/or obsession with the victim
- Prior behavior resulting in serious injury
- History of violent behavior toward previous partners and/or children
- During separations/divorce, demonstrations of physical attacks, verbal threats, and stalking behaviors
- Kidnapping or taking the victim hostage
- Sexually assaulting the victim

The more indicators, the higher the risk of severe harm and/or impending homicide. This indicates risk not only to the identified victim but also toward other people in the victim's life, those trying to help, including a professional (e.g., counselor), and/or the victim's children.

When assessing offenders with children in the home, you also need to assess for actual or potential abusive behavior toward children. Commonly, these offenders demonstrate rigid and demanding expectations outside of normal development, resulting in children being fearful around the perpetrator. The offender may often neglect his or her parental responsibilities, deferring these to the adult victim. Additionally, IPV offenders often use their children to manipulate the adult victim and/or to undermine the adult victim's relationship with the children through manipulation. Examples of severity exhibited by different types of abusive behavior are listed in Table 11.3.

Table 11.4 provides examples of questions that may be helpful to use during a *clinical interview* in order to assess the topics discussed in this section. Ideally, during the interview, information should be gathered about these topics from both the clinical interview and from other sources (e.g., collateral sources, victim interviews, behavioral observations, etc.). Having multiple sources of data increases understanding of the situation in context, the extent of the behaviors being assessed, and the potential cognitive distortions the client has regarding the aggressive behaviors. The questions from the clinical interview should be asked in a manner so as to reduce the likelihood that the client becomes defensive. The information in this table can assist with preparation in asking questions when the opportunity presents itself. If you refer to a list of questions on a paper, then the client is more likely to feel analyzed and judged, which will likely result in increasing defensiveness and limiting the quality or amount of information gathered. Begin the interview with open-ended questions (e.g., "People often have a different view of what brought them to counseling than the person who referred them, so can you give me your take on what brought you here?"; You may ask,

TABLE 11.3 Examples of Abuse Severity Levels

	Minor	Moderate	Severe
Physical abuse	Grabbing, pushing, slapping. Acts unlikely to result in injury or require professional medical attention.	Punching, kicking, or head butting. Acts likely to result in temporary injury and potential need for medical attention.	Extreme violence. Strangulation, forceful blows to the head or striking with an object. Acts likely to result in serious or even permanent injury or death.
Emotional abuse	Infrequent incidences of rejection, criticism, name-calling, and/or put-downs. Unlikely to have lasting negative consequences for the victim's self-esteem or sense of agency.	Multiple incidents of severe rejection, criticism, insults, name-calling, put-downs, and/or humiliation. Likely to have lasting impacts on the victim and undermine his or her self-esteem and sense of agency.	Frequent rejection, criticism, insults, name-calling, put-downs, and/or humiliation. Likely to have a devastating impact on the victim's self-esteem and sense of agency.

TABLE 11.4 Clinical Interview Questions

Topic	Questions
Expectations of the abused partner and the relationship	I'd like you to describe your relationship with your partner. For example, how do you communicate with one another?
	What type of things do you expect from your partner?
	How would you describe your partner?
	What do you do when you and your partner disagree?
	What do you do when you become angry?
Types of abusive behavior and tactics	Have people told you that your temper is a problem? Who? How do you make sense of that?
	How do you feel about your partner visiting his or her friends and family?
	How do you and your partner manage your household duties and income?
	Do you ever yell at your partner? Call your partner degrading names? Put your partner down?
	Have you ever physically harmed or used force on anyone in your family? In what way? When did that happen?
	Has your partner made you so mad that you pushed, kicked, or slapped him or her? Held him or her down? Grabbed him or her by the neck?
	Have you ever threatened to harm or kill yourself, your partner, your children, or a pet?
	Ave you ever threatened or used a weapon or gun against your partner? Do you have access to a weapon or gun?
	Have the police ever come to your home? Tell me about that (how many times, what happened, etc.).
	Have you ever been arrested, charged, or convicted of a domestic violence assault or any other violent crime? What happened as a result?
Risks to the children	How would you describe your children?
	What kinds of things do you expect from your children?
	How do you discipline your children?
	How do you think the children are affected when they see or hear you and your partner fighting?
	Have your children ever intervened during an argument with your partner? Tell me more about that (what happened and why).
Risk factors that may increase level of dangerousness	Did you ever see either of your parents harmed by a romantic partner? If so, what did you do and how did you feel about it?
	Were you ever harmed as a child?
	When was the last time you drank alcohol or used drugs? Tell me more about your drinking/drug use (when, how much, beliefs about why they use, what circumstances, etc.)
	Have you ever attended a substance abuse program or been arrested for a DUI?
	Have you ever been treated for depression or felt like you wanted to die?
	Have you previously been violent with your partner? With others?
	Have you had thoughts you wanted to kill yourself? Others? Have you ever tried to do that?

Topic	Questions
	Have you ever violated conditional release or community supervision requirements of a court order? Have you ever violated a no-contact order?
	Have there been any recent changes in your employment? New relationship problems at home or work?
	Have you ever been diagnosed with a mental illness? If so, what was the diagnosis? (check out depression, bipolar mania, psychosis, and addictive disorders, conduct disorder as a child, in particular)

H. Lien Bragg, "Clinical Interview Questions," *Child Protection in Families Experiencing Domestic Violence*, pp. 97-98, U.S. Department of Health and Human Services, 2003.

P. Randall Kropp, et al., "Clinical Interview Questions," *Spousal Assault Risk Assessment Guide.* Copyright © 1999 by Multi-Health Systems Inc.

"Can you tell me about your relationship with (the victim's name)?" or "Tell me about how things are done in your home, for instance how household responsibilities are divided, who's in charge, that sort of thing." These will be "warm-up" questions to begin establishing the therapeutic relationship and get a sense of the offender.

It is also beneficial to review the client's probation/parole orders from the court, as a part of the clinical interview. I generally ask the client to tell me what the court has ordered regarding his or her IPV charge. Then I compare that to what the order actually says, highlighting any discrepancies between the client's beliefs about the order and what my reading of the order states. The point here is to communicate to the client that I will check out what they are saying against another source, if available, so being straight with me is the better way to go. In addition, I want to make sure the client has no "wiggle room" to say he or she violated an order because of lack of understanding about what the court intended with the order. This sets the stage for treatment.

We also commonly use formal psychometrically validated assessment measures, in order to gather more data that may either support or contradict our behavioral observations and clinical interview data gathered. These instruments may be administered as part of a comprehensive psychological evaluation or as a standard part of the intake process for a batterer's intervention program. Table 11.5 describes some common risk assessment instruments.

Two of the most used risk assessments are the *Spousal Assault Risk Assessment* (SARA) (Kropp, Hart, & Webster, 1999) and the *Ontario Domestic Assault Risk Assessment* (ODARA) (Hilton, Harris, Rice, Lang, Cormier, & Lines, 2004). The items included in Table 11.2 include the items asked by the SARA and the ODARA. The *Conflict Tactics Scale* (Straus, 1979, 1990, 1995) is another instrument used to assess batterers and is an 80-item validated scale that explores how the batterer handles family conflict, including questions about negotiation, physical assault, sexual coercion, injury, and reasoning. *The Attitudes Towards Violence Scale* (Anderson, Benjamin, Wood, & Bonacci, 2006) is a validated instrument that asks the batterer to choose from 1 (strongly disagree) to 5 (strongly agree) for 39 statements that indicate attitudes toward violent behavior. Higher scores indicate the client has more beliefs that support using violence for solving conflict. Finally, the level of psychopathy an offender displays often correlates with level of dangerousness and pervasive nature of his or her violent behavior. Therefore, some programs also use the Hare Psychopathy Checklist, revised (PCLR) (Hart & Hare, 1997) to evaluate whether the client exhibits behaviors consistent with psychopathy.

TABLE 11.5 Common Risk Assessment Instruments

Risk assessment instrument	Description
Danger assessment (DA)	Used by law enforcement, healthcare professionals, and IPV advocates assessing risk of homicide resulting from IPV. Clients mark number of times they experienced different types of abuse in the previous year and answer yes/no to 18 questions. Scores range from 0–25.
Domestic Violence Screening Instrument (DVSI)	Completed by a third party by reviewing prior court/probation records. Used to inform pre-trial evaluations and as a management tool in correctional settings.
Ontario Domestic Assault Risk Assessment (ODARA)	Police use the instrument that is a 13-item yes/no questionnaire about the individual's substance abuse, violence, criminal behavior history, and victim vulnerabilities used to assess the likelihood that a person has committed IPV.
Spousal Assault Risk Assessment (SARA)	20 items, which gather data about dangerousness of IPV behaviors. It provides a standardized measure of physical and emotional abuse of substance use and a review of police reports, victim statements, and criminal records.
CAADA-DASH risk identification checklist	24-item tool used by law enforcement, IPV advocacy organizations, batterer intervention programs, health and mental health series, and children's courts. Designed to predict lethality of violence.
Lethality screen	11 of the 20 questions asked by the Domestic Violence Lethality Assessment Program (DVLAP), which law enforcement uses to identify high-risk victims and connect them with advocates.
Duluth police pocket card	Guides for responding officers in asking open-ended questions of victims. Intended to provide a description of the IPV to the court.

DIAGNOSIS

Diagnoses are methods for classifying behavioral symptoms or syndromes. However, there are also theoretically based typologies, which also serve to classify behavior. Diagnoses given batterers vary because each individual is different; the level of control they exhibit, the underlying mental health issues, and the potential characterological (personality) patterns also influence violent behavior. As such, there is no specific diagnosis for batterers. However, there is a *batterer typology* (Holtzworth-Munroe, & Stuart, 1994) that we can use to classify battering behavior. This typology resulted from a meta-analytic review of existing typologies and statistical analysis of the components of these typologies, including both rational/deductive approaches and empirical/inductive approaches. It resulted in three descriptive dimensions common across typologies:

1. The severity of marital physical violence and related abuse, such as frequency of the violence and psychological and sexual abuse
2. The generality of the violence (e.g., family only or extrafamilial violence) and related variables such as criminal behavior and legal involvement
3. The batterer's psychopathology or personality disorders (Holtzworth-Munroe & Stuart, 1994)

The typology that developed include three categories of IPV offenders: the family-only batterer, the dysphoric/borderline batterer, and the generally violent/antisocial batterer.

The *family-only batterer* (Farrell, 2011; Holtzworth-Munroe & Stuart, 1994) accounts for half of all IPV offenders. Violent behavior is related to misinterpretation of social cues. They generally have no history of psychopathy, criminal behavior, severe mental health issues, or addictive behaviors. For this group of batterers, violence is limited to extreme frustration. They tend to be passive or dependent in relationships and have a low to moderate risk of depression and a moderate level of anger.

The *dysphoric/borderline batterer* (Farrell, 2011; Holtzworth-Munroe & Stuart, 1994) demonstrates signs of emotional volatility and psychological issues. Addictive behaviors are common among this group. Their IPV behaviors, including both physical and sexual, tend to be moderate to severe. However, they have low to moderate levels of criminality and violent behaviors outside of their family. These offenders may exhibit borderline or schizoid personality disorders. Additionally, they often have diagnosable mood disorders and high levels of anger.

Finally, the *violent batterer* (Farrell, 2011; Holtzworth-Munroe & Stuart, 1994) accounts for a quarter of batterers. This group exhibits the most pervasive and severe patterns of violent behavior, including moderate to high levels of psychological and sexual violence within their intimate partner relationships and high levels of criminality and violence in the community. These offenders frequently score high on psychopathy, frequently have diagnoses of antisocial personality disorder, have extensive histories of criminality, and demonstrate substance abuse or addictive behavior patterns. IPV offenders in this category also demonstrate only moderate levels of anger, although they are often more violent, which is indicative of their psychopathy. They have control over their behavior and choose when to be violent in order to gain control of a situation or person, often "just for fun." They have low levels of depression and are unlikely to kill themselves. These offenders may have additional serious mental health issues, which need to be assessed.

TREATMENT

It helps to understand the developmental trajectory of abusive behaviors in order to understand, for an individual client, how to best intervene. The ecological model explains the development of IPV stemming from a variety of interrelated factors described in Table 11.6.

According to the World Health Organization (Garcia-Moreno, Guedes, & Knerr, 2012), some common beliefs and social norms that create a culture where IPV may flourish can be areas for intervention, including the following:

TABLE 11.6. Ecological Model of IPV Risk Factors

Individual factors	Young age
	Low education
	Witnessed IPV as a child
	Believes IPV is acceptable
	Past IPV behavior
	Substance abuse
	Personality disorders
Relationship factors	Conflictual relationships resulting in dissatisfaction
	Economic stressors
	Belief that men should be dominant over women
	Men having multiple partners
	Woman having higher education or wealth than the man
Community and societal factors	Poverty
	Low socioeconomic status of women
	Few legal or social consequences for IPV
	Women not having equal rights
	Social norms that accept or encourage violence as a way to resolve conflict

(Garcia-Moreno, Guedes, & Knerr, 2012)

- Physical violence is an acceptable way to resolve relational conflict.
- There are times a woman deserves to be beaten.
- A man is superior to women and has the right to assert power over women.
- Men have the right/responsibility to correct women, verbally or physically.
- Women should focus on keeping their families together, even if it means tolerating violence.
- Rape is evidence of masculinity, and sexual intercourse is a man's right in marriage.
- Girls are responsible for controlling whether men are sexually aroused or not.

As a result, prevention and early intervention should focus on changing these beliefs and norms through changing legal and social sanctions against IPV, strengthening women's rights and economic empowerment, building awareness of the problem and consequences of IPV, and promoting progressive attitudes toward gender equality and appropriate ways to deal with conflict.

In order to work with IPV offender-parents, treatment providers use psychoeducation to help abusers understand the damaging impact of IPV on both partners and children. Interventions for parenting offenders may include intensive, directive parenting skills training, supervised visitation and safe exchange locations, encouraging abusers to support their children's access to treatment resources, and recruiting nonviolent men to mentor IPV offenders' parenting. Parenting training involves discussions of the offender's parental role in the family; communication skills, assertiveness, and expressing feelings in a healthy responsible manner; understanding differences between discipline and punishment; nonviolent methods for addressing children's behavior problems; information about normal child development; and common behavioral and emotional manifestations when a child has been exposed to domestic violence.

Criminal justice responses have developed since laws against IPV began strengthening in the 1980s. Some key actions within the criminal justice system that support treatment include the following:

- Expediting IPV cases
- Using specialized units and centralized dockets for batterer cases (e.g., domestic violence court)
- Gathering broad-based offender information in an efficient manner
- Taking advantage of culturally competent specialized interventions (e.g., veterans, high risk, female, mentally ill, etc.)
- Coordinating batterer intervention with addiction treatment; being alert to risks to children exposed to IPV
- Creation of a continuum of supports and protection for victims; encouraging interagency cooperation

A court-based intervention advocated by treatment providers includes use of temporary or permanent protective court orders. A *restraining or protective order* requires the perpetrator to stay a certain distance from the victim's home, work, or places the victim commonly goes, as well as places limitations on electronic communication or surveillance of the victim. An emergency protective order goes into effect immediately and can last from 31–91 days. Having a protective order ensures immediate response from law enforcement if a victim reports the offender is violating the order. Violations tend to be misdemeanors, which may result in fees up to $5,000 and/or jail time. A temporary order will not show up on a background check, although a permanent order will appear on your criminal record, even though it is a civil order.

Most (80%) offenders are court ordered to attend a standardized *batterer's intervention program* (BIP) (Healey, Smith, & O'Sullivan, 1998). There are *family systems models*, which view IPV as stemming from problematic family interactions where each family member contributes to the behavior of others. These models tend to work with both partners and focus on more effective communication and conflict resolution strategies. These models directly oppose the justice system's emphasis on offender accountability. In fact, 81% of state standards for

BIPs prohibit use of couples or family counseling in IPV orders (Austin & Dankwort, 1999). Most state-approved BIP programs rely on all-male group formats, ranging from 12 to 52 weeks (Clus & Bodea, 2011). Another common model is *cognitive behavioral treatment* (CBT) interventions that focus on identifying and changing thinking errors and development of anger management skills (Gondolf, 1997a; Harrell, 1991). Anger management programs teach offenders to recognize signs of anger and anger escalation, to resolve anger with relaxation techniques or use of nonviolent expression of conflict. *Group practice models*, like Emerge (40 weeks), Men Stopping Violence (24 weeks), and Abusive Men Exploring New Directions (AMEND) (40 weeks), are based on the premise that battering results from multiple reasons (Jackson, 2005). As a result, they combine methods like psychoeducation, CBT techniques, and assessment of individual needs. Finally, there are newer *psychological models* like attachment trauma-based or criminal justice–based typology models gaining popularity, but which have not really been studied sufficiently (Gondolf, 1997b).

Emerge developed in 1977 to improve prevention and intervention among those who abuse others. It involves two stages. The first stage is eight group sessions, which provides a psychoeducational foundation for group members and allows two group facilitators to evaluate the member for appropriateness for the program. Stage two is 32 group sessions, which are also psychoeducational, in part, but are also more process oriented, utilizing the counselor's clinical training to facilitate group processing therapeutic issues as interpersonal dynamics manifest in the group.

The *Duluth model* (Jackson, 2005) is the most used and in many states mandated. It was the first multidisciplinary program approach to deal with IPV. This model requires 26 weeks of intervention, based on the feminist theory that patriarchal society encourages men to control their partners and result in IPV (Jackson, 2005). Treatment focuses on psychoeducation and gender role resocialization and challenging batterer beliefs about men's rightful dominance over women. The model asserts that the primary responsibility for control of abusive behavior belongs to the community and the abuser, not the victim (Pence, n.d.). It has four principles that drive interagency interventions:

1. Basic infrastructure must support multiple agencies and resources working in a coordinated and cooperative manner.
2. The overall focus is on victim safety, and all activities must support that.
3. Each agency agrees to identify, analyze, and find solutions to any ways their practices may compromise the collective intervention goals.
4. All partners hold IPV offenders accountable for their violent behavior.

In short, the Duluth model requires a coordinated community response to the problem of IPV. In 1984, the Domestic Abuse Intervention Project (DAIP) developed the curricula that became the psychoeducational piece of the Duluth model. Part of the curriculum development resulted in the *power and control wheel* (Figure 11.1), which represents the lived experiences of women who were abused in an IPV relationship. By naming power differences in relationships, treatment providers can more easily provide accurate advocacy and support for victims, as well as accountability and opportunities for change among offenders. A video and explanation of the wheel is available at www.theduluthmodel.org/wheels/.

Regardless of the model used, there is limited evidence that any of these are effective over time (Adams, 2003; Jackson, 2005: Healey, Smith, & O'Sullivan, 1998). However, research indicates that batterers who attend BIP of any kind are less likely to recidivate than those who do not attend any treatment (Tsai, 2000). Given there is little evidence supporting one approach, the current trend is more specialized interventions tailored to the specific type of batterer that takes into account the batterer's psychological profile, risk assessment data, and other contextual information.

SETTINGS

IPV offenders generally receive treatment in a specialized BIP program that is part of a nonprofit IPV agency. However, increasingly criminal justice–trained, rather than mental health–trained, "counselors" employed by privatized correctional corporations provide treatment that was traditionally facilitated by a mental health professional. Batterers may also present in substance abuse or mental health agencies due to comorbid diagnoses. Couple's or family counseling is likely to place victims at increased risk and therefore is not recommended. We also do not recommend standard anger management classes because they often do not address the pervasive patterns of behavior involved in IPV relationships, and they generally are not as effective in holding IPV offenders accountable. Even the term "anger management" minimizes the extent and severity of behaviors exhibited in IPV because it indicates that abusive behavior is solely an "anger problem," which is an oversimplification of the complex interpersonal dynamics involved between two people engaged in a violent relationship.

Domestic violence treatment courts (DV Courts) are common among larger jurisdictions, with over 300 established around the country. The first was established as the Brooklyn Felony Domestic Court in 1996, which required IPV offenders to have formal reviews in the court regarding their order of protection once paroled. The more common format is integrated domestic violence courts. These treatment courts involve a single judge hearing all IPV cases in order to improve efficiency and consistency in prosecuting these cases (Tsai, 2000). DV courts use a variety of tactics to improve the handling of IPV cases, including

- establishing intake units for protection order cases;
- case coordination and standardized service referral procedures;
- tracking procedures for offender, victim, and children;
- court calendars for protection orders and criminal cases to address special circumstances involved in these cases; and
- establishment of integrated systems to gather and analyze data from all stakeholders, which informs case coordination and compliance monitoring (Keiltz, 2004).

For an analysis of the positive and negative issues related to DV courts, see Table 11.7.

TABLE 11.7 DV Courts Benefits and Concerns

Benefits	Concerns
Enhanced coordination of cases and consistent orders in different cases involving the same parties	The assignment of judges who are not interested in gaining the expertise necessary to be effective with IPV cases.
More comprehensive relief for victims at an earlier stage of the judicial process	The fast-paced decision making may result in less effectiveness, due to the emotionality and complexity associated with these cases.
Advocacy services that encourage victims to establish abuse-free lives	These courts may ignore the special needs of victims in favor of assembly-line justice for offenders.
Victims provided with immediate access to advocates	Defense counsel object to the name of the court as prejudicial labeling that presupposes guilt of all court participants.
Victims are informed about progress of the case from advocates	Judges may be too closely aligned with the victim's perspective and lose impartiality.
Greater understanding by judges of how domestic violence affects victims and their children	Victims' advocates do not like the term problem-solving court or treatment court for IPV cases because there are substantial differences between IPV and other types of treatment courts (e.g., mental health treatment courts).
More consistent procedures, treatment of litigants, rulings, and orders	
Greater availability of mechanisms to hold batterers accountable for the abuse	
Improved batterer compliance with orders	They primarily offer services to help the victim become independent of the batterer, rather than focusing on effective rehabilitation of the batterer's IPV behaviors.
Greater confidence on the part of the community that the justice system is responding effectively to domestic violence	
Greater system accountability	High rates of burnout among judges and advocates who focus on IPV cases.

(Keiltz, 2004; Mazur & Aldrich, 2003)

Another innovative approach is *domestic violence enhanced response teams* (*DVERT*). DVERT is a multidisciplinary team consisting of police, prosecutors, social services, and animal abuse programs, formed to address serious IPV cases. Judges refer cases identified as serious and high risk to the DVERT team, who focus on containing high-risk violent offenders through community policing efforts. The DVERT team directs all aspects of intervention, including investigation, intervention, and advocacy services. You can find more information about DVERT at www.dvert.org.

Case Study: Leroy Part II

(Part I provides history for this client, which you can find at the end of chapter 6).

Leroy is a 62-year-old African American man who is currently serving 15 years for attempted murder of his live-in girlfriend, Jenny, a White 32 year-old woman he calls his "snow bunny." He acknowledges that he beat Jenny to the point that she had to be hospitalized and was in a comma for 3 weeks. He justified his beating Jenny because he said "that White bitch thought she could get over on me with another guy, but she's my property. I pay for her, and she's mine."

This is Leroy's fifth arrest as an adult, having also been very involved in the juvenile justice system beginning at 13 years old. Leroy identifies as a member of the "Gangsta Disciples" and refers to himself with pride as an "OG" (original gangster). He uses this status to offer advice and guidance to younger inmates. Leroy appears to be a relatively healthy man, standing over 6' tall with a muscular build. However, his records indicate chronic gastrointestinal issues, including a bleeding ulcer and back pain attributed to gunshot wounds suffered as he ran from a rival gang member when he was 23 years old. He attends church services regularly and leads a Bible study on the unit. Having grown up singing in the choir, he enjoys singing and writing songs and has even written songs for a group of correctional officers who are in a band together.

Currently, Leroy is struggling with his mother's ailing health. She has not been able to travel to visit him in the state penitentiary for several years, and he recently found out that she has terminal metastasizing breast cancer. He does not believe he will be able to talk to her or attend her funeral when she passes away. He also reports struggling with his own mortality and his identity, worth, and the meaning of his life in his current circumstances and life trajectory. Additionally, he frequently expresses a desire, almost an obsession with, helping younger inmates learn from his life experience. He is up for compassionate release, due in part to his mother's ailing health and due in part to his own health troubles combined with his "good behavior" as a prisoner. He states he intends to go home to live with his girlfriend again because she's forgiven him and understands what she did to disrespect him that resulted in the beating.

Case Application Questions

1. Describe the likely neurobiological impacts of Leroy's life experiences on his current behavior.
2. Discuss how you would evaluate Leroy's DV/IPV behaviors. Specifically, identify assessment of types of abuse you would want to evaluate, static and dynamic risk factors he possesses, and your assessment of risk for violence. Provide examples of collateral data you would want to review, questions you would ask in an interview to gather the information needed for your assessment, and the formal assessment measures you would consider using and why.
3. Apply the batterer typology from this chapter to Leroy's case. Discuss your reasons for placing him in the category you choose.
4. Analyze Leroy's case and discuss the potential interventions you would recommend using with him and why. What about once he is released on parole? What settings or agencies might be involved in working with Leroy?

SUMMARY

This chapter provided information about the prevalence and characteristics of IPV offenders in the United States, as well as an understanding of the federal laws addressing IPV. The reader learned about the unique aspects of assessing IPV offenders, including types of questions to ask in a clinical interview, the therapeutic approach best used in the assessment, and how to identify additional, more objective, data sources for assessments. A typology of different types of offenders is discussed, as is the common comorbid diagnoses forensic mental health counselors may treat when working with this population. The reader learned about prevention and interventions, including different types of batterer intervention programs commonly mandated. Finally, we discussed different treatment settings, including substance abuse and mental health agencies, correctional corporations, DVERT teams, and DV treatment courts.

CHAPTER 11 REFLECTIVE QUESTIONS

1. If you were presenting a community information session on domestic violence, how would you describe batterers and battering behaviors?
2. Compare the different offending behaviors of batterers and the most appropriate interventions for each.
3. Discuss the role of rapport building in counseling batterers and describe how you would facilitate the clients becoming more open to the counseling process. Give specific examples.
4. Describe how you would work with batterers during different stages of change to engage them in the process and move them toward change behaviors.
5. If you were working as a counselor associated with a domestic violence court program, how would you assess level of dangerousness of a batterer for the court? Be specific about the types of information you would gather, as well as how this information would inform your understanding of the batterer's risk level.
6. Compare the different types of batterers.
7. Compare the different types of batterer intervention programs you might work in as a forensic mental health counselor. Specifically, discuss your assessment of the strengths and challenges of each.
8. Discuss the strengths and challenges of domestic violence courts and DVERT teams.

RESOURCES

National Center on Domestic and Sexual Violence. Battering Intervention Related Publications. http://www.ncdsv.org/publications_battintervention.html

National Institute of Justice, "A National Portrait Domestic Violence Courts": https://www.ncjrs.gov/pdffiles1/nij/grants/229659.pdf

"The Trend Toward Specialized Domestic Violence Courts: Improvements on an Effective Innovation": https://ir.lawnet.fordham.edu/cgi/viewcontent.cgi?article=3628&context=flr

Crime Victims Institute, "Assessing the Risk of Intimate Partner Violence": http://www.ncdsv.org/images/CVI_Assessing-the-Risk-of-IPV_1-2010.pdf

"Batterers: A Review of Violence and Risk Assessment Tools": https://pdfs.semanticscholar.org/4092/f92b38c5efd5dd4c89f2a909cd8024508a31.pdf

Battered Women's Justice Project: Risk assessment in batterer intervention: https://www.bwjp.org/resource-center/resource-results/batterer-intervention-risk-assessment.html

The Duluth model: https://www.theduluthmodel.org/

Child Welfare Information Gateway: Batterer intervention programs: https://www.childwelfare.gov/topics/systemwide/domviolence/treatment/intervention/

Integrating ACEs science into batterer intervention programs: https://www.acesconnection.com/blog/if-you-integrate-aces-science-into-batterer-intervention-programs-recidivism-plummets-and-men-and-women-heal

National Institute of Justice, "Batterer Intervention Program Approaches and Criminal Justice Strategies": https://www.ncjrs.gov/pdffiles/168638.pdf

IMAGE CREDITS

Counseling Sexual Assault Survivors

- Assess clients for child and adult sexual assault experiences in a trauma-sensitive way
- Describe the inter-relationship between different affective and behavioral manifestations of sexual trauma as they affect diagnosis and treatment
- Explain the BASK model and the structural model of dissociation
- Apply the process of trauma-informed counseling and related interventions for sexual assault survivors

TABLE 12.1 Myths and Myth Busters

Myths	Myth Busters
Victims provoke sexual assault by not taking safeguards to keep themselves safe.	Perpetrators of sexual violence may identify victims who are easy to discredit based on sociocultural myths, but victims are never to blame for a sexual assault.
If someone is victimized, he or she will report it to authorities, and if he or she does not report, then it probably did not happen.	Many sexual assaults are not reported, and when they are there may be a significant time delay in the report due to fear they will not be believed, fear of being blamed/shamed, fear the sex offender will harm them, distrust of law enforcement, etc.
If someone is under the influence of substances at the time of the sexual encounter, it cannot be a sexual assault.	Being under the influence of substances diminishes a person's ability to consent to any sexual encounter, and therefore, sexual assaults commonly happen when the victim is drunk or on drugs.

INTRODUCTION

Forensic mental health counselors work with sexual assault victims at child advocacy centers, rape crisis centers, psychiatric hospitals, residential treatment facilities, community agencies, private practices, and correctional facilities. The definition of *sexual assault* is

> any sexual act, attempt to obtain a sexual act, unwanted sexual comments or advances, or acts to traffic, or otherwise directed, against a person's sexuality using coercion, by any person regardless of their relationship to the victim, in any setting, including but not limited to home and work. (Jewkes, Garcia-Moren, & Sen, 2003)

Although prevalent, the extent of the problem is limited due to barriers to reporting. Additionally, having been the victim of a prior sexual assault increases the chances of subsequent victimization (Jewkes, Garcia-Moren, & Sen, 2003; Murray & Lopez, 1996). *Sexually violent behavior* includes

- unwanted sexual advances or harassment;
- sexual abuse of a child or mentally or physically disabled person;
- forced marriage or cohabitation including child marriage;
- denial of the right to contraception or measures to protect from sexually transmitted diseases;
- forced abortion;
- forced prostitution and trafficking for the purpose of sexual exploitation; and/or
- rape by a stranger, spouse, or intimate partner; systematic rape during armed conflicts (Krug, Dahlberg, Mercy, Zwi, & Lozano, 2003).

The text discussed child sexual abuse in section II, so we will focus on non-child sexual violence.

We consider most sexual assaults counselors treat in the United States *domestic sexual violence* perpetrated by intimate partners or other household members, or *criminal sexual assault* of a child or an adult, perpetrated by someone who does not live with or is in close relationship to the victim. Counselors in the United States are less likely to treat *conflict-related sexual violence*, perpetrated by governments or militias as a weapon of war, although not unheard of. Sexual assault victims occur among all age ranges, ethnicities, socioeconomic status, and religious traditions, and male, female, transgender, and gender nonconforming individuals all experience sexual assault. **Table 12.2** provides information on some major sexual assault laws and court decisions (Rape, Abuse, and Incest National Network [RAINN], n.d.).

According to the Rape, Abuse, and Incest National Network (RAINN), there are 60,000 children and 321,500 adolescents and adults (12 and older) sexually assaulted annually (Truman & Langston, 2015). Over 80,000 experience sexual assault while incarcerated and almost 19,000 military personnel experience sexual assault. Although these are large numbers, the rate is actually 63% lower than it was in 1993. One out of six women and 1 in 33 men, (around 3 million) reports being the victim of attempted or completed rape. Although women report

TABLE 12.2 Notable Sexual Assault Laws and Court Decisions

Debbie Smith Act	Provides resources to process DNA evidence and adds the samples to the DNA database
Clery Act	Requires greater transparency and timely warnings from colleges/universities about crimes committed on campus, including sexual violence
Campus SaVE Act	Amended from the Clery Act to increase transparency requirements for colleges, guarantee rights for survivors, establish disciplinary proceedings, and require education programs
SAFER Act	Supports efforts to audit, test, and reduce the backlog of DNA evidence in sexual assault cases
Title IX	Prohibits discrimination on the basis of sex by educational institutions that receive federal funding
Victims of Crime Act	Provides monetary support to crime victims to pay for medical bills, counseling, and lost wages related to their victimization

(RAINN, n.d.)

most rapes, there are potential barriers to boys and men reporting rape that likely impact the overall estimate of males experiencing sexual assault. Twenty one percent of transgender, genderqueer, or nonconforming (TGQN) college students experience sexual assault, whereas, 18% of non-TGQN females and 4% of non-TGQN males have sexual assault experiences.

Indigenous populations are two times more likely to experience rape/sexual assault than all other races, putting them at highest risk of sexual violence (Perry, 2004). Although most sexual assaults occur at or near a person's home (55%), another 12% occur at or near a relative's home. However, 41% of indigenous people are likely to experience victimization by a stranger (Perry, 2004). Correctional staff perpetrate most sexual assaults against inmates (Beck, Berzofsky, Caspar, & Krebs, 2013). Although all sexual contact between correctional staff and inmates is illegal, due to the power differential, over half is nonconsensual as well (Beck, Berzofsky, Caspar, & Krebs, 2013). According to the Department of Defense (DOD) (2014) among the military personnel who experienced unwanted sexual contact, most were female.

Sexual violence on college campuses is more likely in the fall months and during the first year of college (Kimble, Neacsiu, Flack, & Horner, 2010). Women 18–24 who are not in college are four times more likely to experience sexual violence than older women (Kimble, Neacsiu, Flack, & Horner, 2010). Women attending college are slightly less (three times as likely) to be at risk. Almost a quarter (23.1%) of women and 5.4% of males in undergraduate programs and almost 9% of women and 2% in graduate and professional programs fall victim to sexual assault precipitated by physical violence, force, or incapacitation (Sinozich & Langston, 2014). College men 18–24 are 78% more likely to be sexually victimized than nonstudents. Also, 21% of TGQN college students experience sexual assault, only slightly more than non-TGQN females (18%) (Sinozich & Langston, 2014). Although these statistics are harrowing, only 20% of college women and 32% of nonstudent females 18–24 report their assaults to the police (Sinozich & Langston, 2014).

ASSESSMENT

When counseling CSA/SA survivors it is important to approach assessment as a collaboration between you and the client. This approach results in minimizing power differentials while maintaining professional boundaries. This balance is important with clients who experienced violations of intimacy in which they felt disempowered. During the assessment, it is important for counselors to explore not only challenges the client experienced, but also the resources and resiliencies embodied in the client and his or her experience, as counselors may draw on these resources to support the client's recovery.

Prior to asking about any sexual assault, it is crucial to establish physical and psychological safety through rapport building. If a client does not feel safe, then he or she is less likely to disclose. Alternatively, if he or she discloses without feeling safe, then the person may experience re-traumatization because of the disclosure. An important part of providing a psychologically safe environment is remembering that your role as a counselor is to attend to the victim's needs, even during assessment. Your role is not to investigate where a crime happened, who committed the crime, and/or whether they need reporting to law enforcement or protective services. Although information gathered may result in a report to the authorities, this is not your primary goal. When a counselor's curiosity or desire for justice overtakes the primary role of attending to client welfare, then the client is likely to experience the clinical interview as an interrogation, thereby creating a psychologically *un*safe environment. Additionally, you should approach questions about sexual abuse/assault in a professional, matter-of-fact tone that is also empathic. If you appear nervous asking these questions, then the client may perceive your discomfort as indicative that you cannot handle hearing about his or her sexual abuse/assault. As a result, he or she may protect you by not disclosing.

There are several types of sexual assault, which you should summarily assess during an intake interview, whether the individual presents with this as the primary complaint. The first is childhood sexual abuse, which many adults experienced but have not previously disclosed or received treatment. *Childhood sexual abuse* (CSA) includes any sexual contact as a child or adolescent with someone 4 or more years older or whom had more power than they did, at the time of the sexual contact. Many adult survivors of CSA present with other mental health concerns (e.g., anxiety, depression, addictive disorders, etc.) that may relate directly or indirectly to their childhood victimization.

They may minimize or deny experiences of CSA as a survival mechanism, often out of shame or fear (e.g., fear of retribution, fear you will think they abuse their children, fear of the criminal justice system arresting a family member/perpetrator). Other CSA survivors do not believe their experience meets a level of misconduct considered abusive. By asking about CSA as a standard part of any interview, it communicates to the client that CSA is a common experience that people talk about in counseling. Often, just doing this provides enough psychological safety for the client to disclose this experience. You should be direct in asking about sexual abuse. Some examples of questions include the following:

- Did anyone ever touch you sexually as a child?

- Can you tell me about any experiences you had as a child where you experienced sexual, physical, or emotional abuse?
- Has anyone in your family ever been involved with Child Protective Services?
- Did you ever live away from your parents? Were you in foster care? Were any of your siblings ever in foster care?
- When you were a kid, did you ever feel like you were in danger?

If a client is not presenting for CSA, but acknowledges sexual victimization as a child, then follow up by asking if he or she believes the sexual victimization may relate to the mental health symptoms that bring him or her to counseling. It is important to understand their perception of CSA in relationship to the presenting issues because it informs how you proceed in treatment regarding working on residual CSA trauma. Using the Adverse Childhood Experiences (ACE) questionnaire discussed in the assessment chapter of this text is one way to explore CSA in a standardized manner. **Table 12.3** provides some examples of formal assessments, which you may use for further assessment of CSA and its' after effects (e.g., PTSD, dissociation).

After exploring CSA, you should explore any client experiences of unwanted sexual behavior from another person as an adult. *Sexual assault* (SA) may include sexual harassment,

TABLE 12.3 Formal Assessment Measures of Sexual Trauma

Instrument	Description
Childhood Trauma Questionnaire (Bernstein, Fink, Handelsman, & Foote, 1994)	Twenty-eight-item self-report instrument screening for physical, sexual, and emotional abuse, emotional neglect, and family dysfunction, which takes about 10–15 minutes to complete.
Child Maltreatment Interview Schedule (CMIS) (Briere, 1992).	Forty-six-item measure of behaviorally described manifestations of emotional, physical, and sexual abuse occurring prior to age 17, including five domains (level of parental physical availability, psychological availability, parental history of substance or mental health disorder, perception of physical/sexual abuse status, and psychological/physical/emotional/sexual/ritualistic abuse). Questions age of onset, relationship to abuser, and severity of abuse.
Child Trauma Interview (CTI) Fink, Bernstein, Handelsman, Foote, & Lovejoy, 1995).	Forty-nine screening items and multiple follow-up probes of six categories (childhood separation and loss, physical neglect, emotional abuse/assault, physical abuse/assault, exposure to violence, and sexual abuse/assault), which takes between 30–90 minutes to complete, depending on extent of child trauma experiences. Collects detailed information including frequency, duration, and severity, persons involved, nature of events, age at the time of events, threats during events, client's previous disclosures, and nature of injuries sustained.
National Women's Study Event History (NIWSEH) (Resnick, Falsetti, Kilpatrick, & Freedy, 1996)	Used to examine detailed information about traumatic experiences (e.g., rape, attempted sexual assault, molestation, physical assault, accidents, disasters, exposure to death or serious injury, and death of a friend/family member) including first, most recent, and worst rape; single molestation; attempted sexual assault). Questionnaire takes 10–20 minutes to complete with follow-up interview taking 1–3 hours.

Instrument	Description
Trauma Symptom Inventory (TSI) (Briere, 1996)	One-hundred-item assessment of symptoms following traumatic events utilizing 10 scales including anxious arousal, depression, anger/irritability, intrusive experiences, defensive avoidance, dissociation, sexual concerns, dysfunctional sexual behavior, impaired self-reference, and tension-reduction behavior). Twelve critical items including suicidal ideation/behavior, psychosis, and self-mutilation also evaluated. TSI has three validity scales. Takes about 20 minutes to complete.
Traumatic Events Survey (TES) (Elliot, 1992)	Evaluates 30 different child and adult trauma experiences including sexual trauma. Details include characteristics of sexual abuse (age at first and last event, relationship to the abuser, and past and current levels of distress associated with the abuse).
Trauma Symptom Checklist-40 (TSC-40) (Elliott & Briere, 1992)	Forty-item self-report tool evaluating child and adult trauma experiences and related symptomology like anxiety, dissociation, and sexual concerns.
Trauma and Attachment Belief Scale (TABS) (Pearlman, 2003)	Measures disrupted cognitive schemas and need states associated with complex trauma using five scales: safety, trust, esteem, intimacy, and control. It helps counselors understand assumptions the client has regarding his or her relationship to others, including the counselor.
Screen for Posttraumatic Stress Symptoms (SPTSS) (Carlson, 1997)	Seventeen-item self-report screening tool for PTSD symptoms, particularly useful for clients with histories of multiple trauma experiences.
PTSD Checklist-5 (PCL-5) (Weathers et al., 2013)	Twenty-item self-report measure assessing DSM-5 symptoms of PTSD used for PTSD screening, provisional diagnosis of PTSD, and monitoring symptom change during and after treatment intervention.
Clinician-Administered PTSD Scale (CAPS) (Blake et al., 1995)	Thirty-item structured interview measuring symptoms of acute stress and posttraumatic stress related to one to three trauma events. Thirty to 60 minutes to administer.
Dissociative Experiences Scale (Bernstein & Putnam, 1986)	Brief 28-item measure of the frequency of dissociated experiences (e.g., dissociative amnesia, gaps in awareness, de-realization, depersonalization, absorption, and imaginative involvement).
Symptom Checklist 90-Revised (SCL-90-R) (Derogatis, 1983)	Ninety-item self-report that takes about 15 minutes to administer, measuring nine primary dimensions of mental health including somatization, obsession compulsion, interpersonal sensitivity, depression, anxiety, hostility, phobic anxiety, paranoid ideation, and psychoticism. Provides a severity index and intensity index. Can be used as part of a comprehensive initial assessment or to evaluate treatment progress.

exhibitionism, voyeurism, or frotteurism, acquaintance rape, domestic sexual assault, or stranger rape. Some clinical interview questions used to explore SA examples are the following:

- Have you ever had sexual contact with someone whom you did not want to?
- Have you ever been forced into a sexual experience?
- Unfortunately, it's not uncommon for teens or young adults to have sexual experiences. Has that ever happened to you?

Many people who experience one sexual assault may experience multiple sexual assaults; therefore, it is crucial to ask if the client experienced additional episodes of sexual victimization. Often, I preface this by saying, "It's not uncommon for someone to experience multiple sexual assaults over their lifetime, so I'm wondering if you've had other experiences where someone violated your sexual boundaries." By saying this, I prepare the client that if he or she experienced multiple victimizations it is safe to disclose these. Often when people experience multiple victimizations they blame themselves and are less likely to disclose subsequent victimizations. Additionally, you can use many of the formal assessments in **Table 12.3** to assess adult trauma experiences, general symptomology associated with experiences of adult SA, and some assessments for dissociative or traumatic stress symptomology.

Follow up any disclosure of sexual abuse/assault by asking what it is like for them to tell you about this/these experience(s). This provides some information about the client's level of comfort in talking about the CSA/SA. Additionally, the client's response may signal areas of psychological safety, trust, or mental health symptoms that need immediate attention in order to sustain the client through the remaining interview. When clients first disclose sexual abuse/assault, they often feel like a "raw nerve" exposed to the elements. They need you to attend to this feeling of vulnerability in the moment before proceeding to other parts of the interview. If you do not do this, then some clients' autonomic nervous system (ANS) responses will result in them *dissociating* (flight), becoming *defensive* (fight), or being *non-responsive* (freeze) to the remaining clinical interview. Once you establish the client's level of safety following disclosure, explore details of CSA/SA including the following:

- Age at first event and last event
- Duration, frequency, and severity of the CSA/SA event(s)
- Relationship to the abuser(s)
- Other people involved in the CSA/SA
- Most recent CSA/SA event and worst CSA/SA event
- Level of distress experienced at the time of the CSA/SA *and* current level of distress
- Threats experienced during or after the event(s)
- Previous disclosure of CSA/SA and response

Inquire what happened in response to the abuse/assault (e.g., Did the client immediately disclose to anyone? Was there a consequence to the perpetrator? If the victim knows the perpetrator, how did he or she relate to the victim following the abuse/assault?). Also, ask how the client coped. The following list includes some coping questions you may ask to explore the client's experience:

- *Potential dissociative experiences:*
  - What went through your mind during the abuse/assault?
  - Where you aware of any physical sensations during the abuse/assault?
  - What emotions did you experience leading up to the abuse/assault? During the event(s)? Afterward?
- *Cognitive attribution:*
  - How did you make sense of the abuse/assault?
  - What does experiencing sexual abuse/assault mean in terms of your identity? How does it affect the way you "see" yourself?

■ *Coping:*
  ● What did you do immediately following the event(s)?
  ● What feelings do you most associate with the experience(s)?
  ● How do you experience memories of the abuse? (e.g., intrusive memories, flash-backs, nightmares).

Specifically inquire about any physical, emotional, or interpersonal/relational conse-quences he or she experienced. You may also take this as an opportunity to provide some basic psychoeducation about the common effects of sexual assault, including using sub-stances to manage trauma symptoms (e.g., flashbacks, intrusive memories, hypervigilance, and/or nightmares). Additionally, it is common to experience increased anxiety, distrust in other people, fear, and different levels of sadness or depression, as a result. By providing this information, you open the door for the client to talk about additional mental health symptoms, which may be the target of treatment. Finally, due to the nature of trauma, it is crucial that you assess the client's thoughts of self-harm, suicidality, and/or harm to others (e.g., abuser).

Sexual assault can result in physical injuries, gynecological complications, and death (Fernandez, 2011). However, SA victims also present for counseling with a variety of mental health issues including

> rape trauma syndrome; … . post-traumatic stress disorder; … depression; social phobias (especially in marital or date rape victims); anxiety; increased substance use or abuse; suicidal behaviour; … . chronic headaches; fatigue; sleep disturbances (i.e.[,] nightmares, flashbacks); rec[u]rrent nausea; eating disorders; menstrual pain; [and] sexual difficulties. (Fernandez, 2011).

Table 12.4 illustrates some common responses to CSA/SA, organized according to re-experiencing symptoms and avoidance symptoms. Counselors should explore or note behavioral observations of each of these during the assessment process in order to aid with diagnosis.

Remember that sexual assault victims (70%) experience moderate to severe distress, more than victims of any other violent crime do (Langston & Truman, 2014). Therefore, fol-lowing assessment of CSA/SA, it is crucial that the counselor check in with the client about level of distress currently experienced and help the client reduce distress to safe levels prior to allowing the client to leave the office. Otherwise, the person is likely to experience the assessment as invasive and you as a therapist as an unsafe person or someone unable to help him or her manage his or her serious trauma-related psychological distress.

TABLE 12.4 Common Peri-Traumatic Responses to Sexual Trauma

Domain	Re-experiencing symptoms	Avoidance symptoms
Cognitive	Intrusive thoughts and images Self-blame/attribution	Amnesia De-realization/depersonalization Dissociation
Affective	Irritability or anger Anxiety or nervousness Depression Shame Hopelessness Loneliness Fear	Emotional numbing Isolation of affect
Behavioral	Psychomotor agitation Psychomotor retardation Hypervigilance Aggression Exaggerated startle response High tolerance for inappropriate behavior Attempts to master the abuse (e.g., getting into risky sexual situations)	Sleeping more than normal Appear to be "zoning out" Engaging in addictive behaviors (e.g., substance use/abuse, disordered gambling, eating disorders) and intended to numb or escape from distressing thoughts/feelings associated with the trauma Self-mutilation
Physiological	Hyperarousal of ANS symptoms resulting in overreaction to environmental/cognitive/sensory/affective triggers associated with the trauma	Sensory numbing Reacting abnormally to otherwise violent or risky situations
Multiple domains	Flashbacks Age regression Nightmares/night terrors	Dissociation from reality Psychosis

DIAGNOSIS

Survivors of CSA/SA present with a variety of mental health concerns. In fact, functional impairments at school or work (38%) are common among SA victims. Additionally, 37% report more frequent interpersonal conflict following the assault (Crime Victims Research and Treatment Center [CVRTC], 1992). In a meta-analytic study, Chen and colleagues (2010) identified strong support for diagnoses of anxiety, depression, suicidality, eating disorders, PTSD, sleep, and somatoform disorders among people who experience CSA/SA. *Anxiety disorders* employ the same neurobiological mechanisms as traumatic stress disorders, so it is no surprise that these are common among CSA/SA survivors. *Generalized anxiety disorder* involves an "increase in non-specific anxiety symptoms after a traumatic event" (Briere & Scott, 2006). Additionally, many trauma survivors experience *panic attacks* or *specific phobias* of certain environmental stimuli associated with the trauma. Manifestations of *depression* among trauma survivors include feelings of extreme sadness related to irrevocable loss, hopelessness about future safety, a sense of worthlessness and excessive shame and guilt, suicidality, lost interest in pleasurable activities, problems concentrating, sleep difficulties, eating difficulties, and extreme fatigue (Briere & Scott, 2006). Additionally, *psychotic depressions* are four times more common among trauma survivors with PTSD (Briere & Scott, 2006). Among depressed CSA/SA survivors, 30% contemplate suicide (CVRTC, 1992).

Most (94%) SA survivors experience some symptoms of *acute stress disorder* (ASD) and about one-third (30%) have *PTSD* 9 months after rape (Davidson & Foa, 1993). The symptoms of ASD or PTSD are categorized as *re-experiencing* the traumatic event; *avoidance* of the trauma-related environmental, sensory, or affective stimuli associated with the trauma and numbing; and persistent *hyperarousal* of the ANS system, resulting in desire to fight, flee, or freeze when triggered, whether the current trigger actually presents a risk or not. **Table 12.4** reflects each of these trauma symptom categories.

The more trauma experiences, the more complex symptoms may be. In fact, Herman (1992, 1997), in her seminal work *Trauma and Recovery* called for a new diagnosis of *complex PTSD*. Complex trauma results from prolonged periods of trauma. Symptoms include alterations in affect regulation, consciousness (e.g., dissociation), self-perception (e.g., helplessness, shame/guilt/self-blame, stigma), perception of the perpetrator, interpersonal relationships (e.g., isolation, disruption, persistent distrust), and systems of meaning (e.g., hopelessness, loss of faith). Complex PTSD "arise[s] from severe, prolonged, and repeated [relational] trauma (Briere & Scott, 2006, p. 31). In their descriptions of complex PTSD, several prominent trauma experts (Briere & Scott, 2006; Herman, 1992, 1997; van der Kolk, 1987) describe the need for these survivors to engage in external regulation of dysregulated emotion, also called *tension-reduction behaviors* (Briere & Scott, 2006). These tension-reduction behaviors include addictive behaviors and interpersonal strategies that may develop into personality disorders.

CSA/SA victims exhibit increased risks for developing addictive disorders (SAMHSA, 2014). Substance use/abuse is the most common behavior engaged in that helps survivor's initially numb symptoms of anxiety and traumatic stress disorders. In fact, SA survivors develop high rates of *substance use disorders* (SUDS). They are 3.4 times more likely to use marijuana, six times more likely to use cocaine, and 10 times more likely to use other major drugs (CVRTC, 1992). However, some CSA/SA survivors utilize other addictive behavioral processes, which trigger the same pleasure/reward centers of the brain as SUDs, to numb or escape the emotional and physiological dysregulation resulting from traumatic stress disorders, anxiety, and depression. These include *gambling disorder*, *sexual addiction*, and *eating disorders* (APA, 2013; Carnes, 1989; Rosenberg & Feder, 2014; Sun, Ashley, & Dickson, 2012). It is important to note that when CSA/SA survivors stop engaging in addictive behaviors during treatment, their trauma symptoms, which triggered the addiction, are likely to be more intense and increase potential for relapse (SAMHSA, 2014). Therefore, the preferred treatment method for addicted trauma survivors is treatment for trauma and addiction concurrently. Interestingly, in Bessel van der Kolk's (1987) seminal work *Psychological Trauma*, he identified a common *addictive response to traumatic re-exposure* experienced by some CSA/SA victims. This includes seeking out situations or engaging in behavior in which the survivor is likely to experience additional trauma. Some consider this an effort to "master" the trauma already experienced.

Another common set of diagnoses associated with avoidance of trauma symptoms are *dissociative disorders* (Briere & Scott, 2006; Herman, 1992, 1997; van der Kolk, 1987). When someone experiences trauma, he or she may have difficulty integrating all of the thoughts, feelings, behaviors, and meaning of a traumatic event into his or her experience and/or sense of self. According to the *BASK Model of Dissociation* (Braun, 1988), a trauma survivor may dissociate one or more of the following functions associated with a traumatic event or series of events:

- **Behavior:** The actions that occurred during the trauma
- **Affect:** The emotions associated with the trauma
- **Sensation:** The physical sensations or body memories of the trauma, which may include sights, smells, sounds, sense of pressure on the body, sense of physical orientation in space, or other physical sensations including sexual arousal or pain
- **Knowledge:** The meaning of the trauma

According to Braun (1988), dissociation can occur in one or more of these functions along a continuum from complete awareness, through suppression (putting it out of one's mind), denial (choosing not to acknowledge the reality of the event until the ability to cope is developed), repression (a psychological response to intrapsychic conflict), to complete dissociation or lack of awareness. A traumatized person experiences an environmental trigger reminding them of the trauma in situations such as the following:

- The presence of the perpetrator or someone who reminds the victim of the perpetrator;
- Similar sights/sounds/smells, physical pressure or sensation, including sexual arousal, to the trauma event
- Witnessing another assault
- Being in the presence of someone the same age the victim was at the time of the assault
- Being in the same or similar location (e.g., college dorm room) as the assault
- The victim may re-experience the dissociated trauma through intrusive memories, flashbacks, or nightmares. The victim may also demonstrate behavior that does not make sense without the awareness of the traumatic event like exaggerated startle response or hypervigilance

Another valuable model conceptualizing dissipative trauma experiences is the *structural model of dissociation* (van der Hart, Nijenhuis, & Steele, 2006), which involves primary, secondary, and tertiary dissociative experiences. *Primary dissociation* is when traumatic memories are encoded as fragmented sensory (e.g., sights, smells, sounds, physical sensations) components of the event (van der Kolk, McFarlane, & Weisaeth, 1996). Therefore, there is not a consistent narrative of events or experiences. Many people have experiences of primary dissociation related to what we call *little 't' traumas*, like a car accident or death of a loved one. The combination of this reality and the fact that people tend to fill in missing narrative details when questioned about a trauma is why it can be problematic for a counselor to question a CSA/SA survivor about the details of his or her experience. To minimize this occurrence, let the client know soon after disclosure how traumatic memory works. So I might say, "Traumatic memories often result in missing elements of what happened (almost like flashes of pictures or sounds or sensations without a clear connection to one another), so if there is anything that I ask about that you do not remember, it makes perfect sense because that is how traumatic memory works." Additionally, when clients seem "stuck in their head," as if trying to find words for what they remember, I often say to them, "Just spit out whatever is going through your mind, it doesn't have to make sense." This gives the client permission to have disjointed memories, which are often very common in trauma experiences.

Secondary dissociation, also called peri-traumatic dissociation, involves "alterations in the experience of time, place, and person, which conferred a sense of unreality on the event as it was occurring" (van der Kolk, McFarlane, & Weisaeth, 1996, p. 307). Secondary dissociation can result in *depersonalization*, which is when a person experiences an event as if it is happening to someone else outside the client's body. Often survivors describe these memories as if they are watching it on TV or in a movie. Another symptom of peri-traumatic dissociation is *de-realization*, which is the experience that what is happening is not real. As a result, some survivors have a mental image of what happened when they experienced sexual abuse, but they do not trust their memory. This is common when the perpetrator was someone they knew or trusted and they cannot resolve the cognitive dissonance between their trust or love for the person and the abusive behavior perpetrated.

Although secondary dissociation can happen to anyone experiencing a significant *big 'T' trauma*, like CSA/SA, it is particularly common among people who develop identity disturbance associated with prolonged or complex trauma, like *borderline personality disorder*. As a result, victims of complex trauma may develop maladaptive interpersonal relationships characterized by

- difficulty with negotiating interpersonal boundaries;
- demonstrated emotional lability when their identity is threatened by perceived rejection or abandonment by a significant attachment figure; and
- self-destructive impulsive behaviors like self-mutilation, eating disorders, suicidal gestures, or addictions in which they attempt to use the behavior to re-engage a significant person into the relationship when they perceive the attachment figure is rejecting them.

Finally, *tertiary dissociation* occurs when a client experiences complex trauma and dissociates different experiences as if they happened to different personalities. It results in a total split in consciousness into different personalities within the same individual. We generally diagnose this level of dissociation as *dissociative identity disorder* (DID). People with DID have at least two distinct personality states, sometimes two different developmental ages, that the person may switch between when he or she undergoes stress, particularly if the stress is triggered by an environmental trigger of the trauma. People with DID lose track of time when they dissociate into an *alter* (not their primary) personality. The alter personality may actually have a different age, gender, and/or name in addition to other personality characteristics.

TREATMENT

This section relates to the earlier discussion in the text about neurosequential development where the brain develops sensory emotional experiences, or affective experiences, before developing executive cognitive functions. Posttraumatic affective manifestations are complex and often trigger additional behavioral and relational/interpersonal symptoms, which ultimately lead to diagnosable disorders described previously.

Psychological or Affective Reactions Common in Treatment

According to Herman (1992, 1997) the core experience of psychological trauma is *disempowerment* (a decreased sense of personal power/control over one's environment) and relational *disconnection* (feeling different or alienated from others). When someone experiences a relational aggression like CSA/SA, it makes sense that the survivor may feel as though he or she *cannot trust* other people. This can be particularly significant for those victimized by someone they knew and trusted, like a close friend or family member or trusted community member (e.g., police or priest). As a result, the victim may choose to isolate him- or herself because of fear that he or she might experience victimization again. Often the victim may believe he or she cannot trust his or her own instincts about people. This may also lead to significant feelings of *grief* related to lost relationships or a lost sense of self (who the victim thought he or she was before the CSA/SA compared to after). The victim may experience lost hope for the future, as well as loss of enjoyment in "normal" experiences like intimate relationships, having children, or other events that may remind them of the offender or the abuse.

Relational disconnection can also be rooted in feelings of *shame* or blaming oneself for the trauma event(s). This is even more common when the victim experiences repeated traumas. Shame results in difficulty for clients who want to talk about their sexual trauma because they fear you will not believe them or will criticize them or reject them. Another reason for disconnection is *anger* or even rage resulting from the victimization. Sometimes it is difficult for CSA/SA survivors to go through the day without feeling driven by out-of-control anger, sometimes even resulting in verbal or physical aggression toward others. For women socialized to be "nice," this is particularly disconcerting. It is also confusing for people the survivor is in relationship with, especially when the anger is out of proportion to the current situation. When a victim does not express his or her anger, particularly when combined with grief and shame, he or she may develop profound *sadness* or even depression, as a result. Sadness may result in feelings of hopelessness or the experience of a spiritual or existential crisis related to the victim's difficulty integrating the trauma experience(s) into the meaning he or she finds in the world or into the victim's story of his or her life.

Fear can also be intense. Although a normal reaction to victimization, posttraumatic fear may result in generalized fear. For instance, if abused by a male teacher, the victim may begin to fear all men or all teachers. Fear and anger together can result in the experience of *powerlessness* or loss of control over one's sense of agency. The fear and powerlessness can lead to intrusive sensory memories (sights, sounds, smells, physical sensations, etc.), flashbacks, nightmares, and other experiences related to dissociative or posttraumatic stress disorders previously explained. The fear and loss of agency combined with shame or disconnection can also result in development of *sexual intimacy problems*, *somatization* of psychological experiences into physical symptoms, and/or *relational disturbances* and even personality disorders.

Trauma-Informed Care

A trauma-informed approach requires treatment providers realize the widespread impact of trauma and understand potential treatments and paths to recovery. Trauma-informed providers recognize the signs and symptoms of trauma and work to help the client heal while also actively working *not* to re-traumatize the client during the recovery process. SAMHSA articulates six key principles of trauma-informed therapy. These include the following:

1. Safety
2. Trustworthiness and transparency
3. Peer support
4. Collaboration and mutuality
5. Empowerment, voice, and choice
6. Cultural, historical, and gender issues

According to SAMHSA, trauma-informed care recognizes the survivor's need for respect, information, connection, and hopefulness regarding recovery. The following description of the trauma therapy process, drawing on the work of Briere and Scott (2006); Herman (1995, 1997); Ogden, Minton, and Pain (2006); Perry (2006); Shapiro (2010); van der Kolk (1987); and van der Kolk, McFarlane, and Weisaeth (1996), is helpful. These original works are highly recommended reading if you choose to work with trauma survivors.

Phase I: Safety and Stabilization

In the beginning of the therapeutic relationship, counselors attend closely to establishing a safe trusting relationship with the client through collaboration and minimization of power differentials, while still maintaining professional boundaries. *Boundaries* provide safety for clients. They are like guardrails on a highway that keep a vehicle (e.g., the client) from going off into a ditch (e.g., losing control or becoming overwhelmed). Counselors establish boundaries related to when and where meetings will occur, methods and parameters of communication, and consequences when clients violate boundaries (e.g., missed sessions). In order to communicate safety to clients, it is important for counselors to maintain boundaries and only deviate if there is a well-thought-out therapeutic rationale for doing so.

Professional boundaries include setting limits on the level of personal information you share with a client. Think about how much information you would share with a small child if you were parenting the child. Emotionally, the client is like a child. There is some information that may be helpful to the process, but much personal information is not appropriate to share with a client. Often when trauma survivors ask personal questions (e.g., Are you married?

Do you have kids? Has this ever happened to you?), they are trying to figure out whether you are safe to talk to and whether you can understand their perspective. When the client asks personal questions, it may be more therapeutic to explore what the question is about rather than answering it directly. For instance, you may say something like "It sounds that's important to you, before answering; I'm curious what it is about that information that is important to you." Often this is when a client will say: "Well if you have kids it might be hard for you to hear about what happened to me," or "If you are married, you couldn't possibly understand what it's like to be single and get into a situation where you are raped," or "If you haven't gone through this, how can you possibly understand how I feel?" These are all opportunities to explore the client's fears about trusting someone.

Reflecting this concern/fear of trust and normalizing it within the context of the trauma is often helpful. "I can imagine it's hard to know whether it's safe to trust someone when you are feeling really vulnerable. It's very common for CSA/SA survivors to have difficulty trusting other people after they've been victimized." The key is to turn the session back toward processing what is motivating the question and addressing the underlying issues. If you are a survivor, this experience can be helpful as a counselor, but remember that your experience is not like any other person's, so it may be more helpful to use the experience in this manner: "I know a lot of survivors feel/think/experience . . ." You are going to insert your feelings, thoughts, experiences, but the client does not know they are yours. By doing this, you can provide validation and communicate understanding, but you also are providing the client with space to reject these feelings/thoughts/experiences as inconsistent with his or her own.

Many new counselors have anxiety about this process. The counselor, not having been through this process before, may be concerned that he or she will be unable to handle the client's intense emotions, the sometimes horrifying stories shared, or the feelings of helplessness and worthlessness victims often experience when they begin to emerge themselves in trauma work. It is crucial that new counselors, in particular, maintain competent supervisory relationships through this process. Otherwise, the counselor risks vicarious trauma, which can result in colluding with the client's defenses or undermining the client's progress. The supervisor provides guardrails for the inexperienced counselor, in a parallel process to the counselor's guardrails for the trauma client. I refer to this process as *holding the hope* for the client. Often clients do not believe they are capable of processing through their trauma and coming out the other side as a whole, functioning person because they feel fragmented and disempowered currently. Therefore, they need counselors to "hold the hope." In order to do that, the counselor must provide a safe, nonjudgmental, supportive environment that attends to pacing concerns so that the client feels safe from becoming overwhelmed with traumatic stress symptoms like intrusive memories or intense emotions.

The counselor acts as an *interpersonal regulator* of the client's dysregulated emotions. The counselor may utilize interpersonal or relational interventions to help regulate the client's emotional state. *Theraplay* interventions are another method for engaging the client through interpersonal regulation of emotion while building trust and attachment in the relationship, with the goal of moving the client toward intra-personal (self) regulation of emotion. Early in the relationship, counselors help clients deduce distress and begin learning to regulate dysregulated affective states (Briere & Scott, 2006). Any new or deeper disclosure can lead the client to become destabilized and increase distress. The counselor does the following:

- Reflects the client's experience
- Validates through reflections and affirmations
- Dispels misconceptions about CSA/SA through psychoeducation and cognitive restructuring
- Normalizes the client's response to trauma
- Provides space and support for the client to express a full range of emotions
- Works to be culturally sensitive
- Offers options, rather than advice
- Provides advocacy, psychoeducation, and referrals as needed
- Helps the client develop constructive ways for coping (e.g., physical activity, sleep, hygiene, engaging support groups, use progressive muscle relaxation or mindfulness meditation to manage anxiety, developing visualizations for containment, learning grounding exercises, etc.)

Ogden and colleagues (2006) discuss phase one of trauma treatment in relationship to *development of somatic resources for stabilization*. Some techniques discussed include the following:

- *Oscillation techniques* "directing the client to repeatedly and mindfully orient back and forth between calm or 'resourced' body areas, experiences, or sensations and areas or experiences that are painful or uncomfortable" (Ogden, Minton, & Pain, 2006, p. 217).
- *Facilitating awareness and management between physical sensations, dysregulated arousal, and emotions* by helping them learn to acknowledge, tolerate, and give voice to unregulated sensations and modulate arousal and control over reflexive responses (e.g., acting out, numbing, etc.).
- *Differentiating between body sensations, emotions/feelings, and cognitions.* For instance, a counselor may address undifferentiated affect, which has become fused with cognition and meaning by asking the client to attribute a thought/cognition to the affect experienced or ask the client to "make sense" of the physical sensations he or she is currently having.
- *Containment exercises.* These interventions assist the client to "contain" sometimes overwhelming emotions (e.g., anger, grief), so that they do not feel they are losing control. By providing containment, the counselor creates a sense of safety for the client, which allows the client enough confidence to continue opening up in counseling. Visualizations can be used (e.g., plugging a dam of overwhelming emotions or packing up distressing memories into a suitcase that will be left in a safe place in the therapist's office, or taking down (building up) a brick wall one brick at a time). Each of these can facilitate opening memories, emotions, and processing during sessions and contain them when the client leaves sessions so that he or she can function in the world without being overly vulnerable. In addition, sand trays, art, music lyrics

or CDs, and genograms can be used to act as "containers" for the emotional material they help the client process during sessions. Sometimes, it is helpful to have clients make a container in session using a variety of materials to decorate it on the outside with how people view them and then decorate the inside with things people do not see/know about them. They may also bring or make trinkets or art or take photos of sand tray or art created in sessions, which represent their trauma memories, and place these inside the container to leave with the counselor when they leave session.

- *Autoregulation skills.* Trauma counselors help clients begin to experience what it is like to regulate emotional arousal within sessions using autoregulation skills that they can integrate into their daily lives to help self-regulate outside of therapy. These include directed practice in session when the client becomes dysregulated during processing traumatic material and then verbally processing the experience in order to raise the client's awareness of control he or she has in those moments to use the same skill(s) to autoregulate. These include the following:
  - *Grounding exercises*: Feeling the seat beneath you, putting your feet firmly on the ground and your arms on the armrests of a chair, moving your feet back and forth to feel the support of the ground under you or shifting weight in a seat to feel the support of the chair beneath you, etc.
  - *Controlled breathing exercises*: Asking the client to take long controlled deep breaths in, allowing peace and relaxation to enter the body, and then exhale all the negative emotion and energy built up in their body, guiding them several times through this exercise.
  - *Progressive muscle relaxation* (PMR): Guiding clients through a progressive muscle relaxation exercise to raise awareness of where they hold stress in their body and how they have the power to release this stress and reach a state of relaxation and peace without negative or self-destructive behaviors (e.g., self-mutilation, addictive behaviors, etc.)
  - *Sensorimotor sequencing*: Facilitating clients' processes of becoming aware of involuntary physiological responses to environmental traumatic triggers, slowing the process by engaging in a cognitive processing of their observations of physiological processes, separating out thoughts and feelings associated with or meanings attributed to the physiological responses, and beginning to voluntarily/consciously take control of these processes. For instance, if someone becomes anxious and trembles, then we would first draw awareness without trying to change anything, describe the sensations experienced, placing aside thoughts/feelings/meanings associated with the trembling and then utilizing deep breathing to slow the physiological response, thus gaining control and reducing anxiety in the process.

The final, although not insignificant, support in counselor work with clients is identifying *safe supports and resources* the client can access during times of dysregulation outside of therapy. This may include identifying safe friends and/or family members who can provide support.

It may include involvement in a trauma-specific counseling group or a peer support group for survivors of incest, CSA, or SA/rape. If the client still comes into contact with "unsafe" people (e.g., the offender, other unsupportive people), then the counselor must work with the client on ways to deal with these situations and access support resources or make safety plans in order to minimize the chances of re-traumatizing experiences.

Counselors also use their relationship with the client to help the client maintain a pace in therapy that honors his or her experience while also moving him or her forward. *Pacing* is a regulatory method used when clients begin to move too fast and become overwhelmed with emotion, resulting in dysregulation, possible externalization through engaging in addictive behaviors or aggression, or possible internalization through self-harm or dissociation. When the client becomes "stuck" and retraumatized, the counselor increases the pace in order to help the client move forward and process through the trauma. When we review the *neurosequential model of therapeutics* (Perry, 2006) discussed earlier in the text, phase one focuses on the calming the limbic system responses to trauma.

Phase 2: Processing Traumatic Experiences

Movement from phase 1 to phase 2 of treatment is not a clear step-by-step process as much as it is an enmeshment where safety and stability engenders therapeutic risk taking, which involves accessing memories, willingness to tolerate emotion, and then processing what is coming up in the moment. However, as we move into the next phase, we focus on building the connections between limbic system responses and cognitive executive functions illustrated in Perry's (2005) NMT model. Once the client has established a safe therapeutic relationship with the counselor, the counselor is able to track and help modulate the client's dysregulated emotion and behavior, and the client has practiced and is beginning to use, outside counseling, those self-regulation skills and supports, then the counselor can facilitate movement into processing the client's traumatic memories.

During this phase, counselors help clients acknowledge and process through the cognitive, affective, and sensory memories related to traumatic events. However, these memories may not be linear or have clear narratives easily communicated through words. These interventions include sand tray, psychodrama, music therapy, art therapy, and so on. Creative, experiential, neurosequential interventions help clients access and begin processing memories. These include use of psychodrama, art, music, sand tray, and animal-assisted therapy, among other interventions, which access sensory material and provide a medium for expressing and processing through emotional material. Counselors use these methods to facilitate the client's emotional abreaction and corrective emotional experiences while remaining a nonjudgmental supportive presence bearing witness and giving voice to the client's pain.

Pacing continues to be important during this stage. Counselors must carefully attend to pacing because clients can become "stuck" on one memory or series of memories, thus becoming re-traumatized. If this occurs, then counselors may use directive interventions to help the client move through these memories. Directive interventions may include directed role playing, empty chair, or the counselor asking the client if he or she can make a change to the client's sand tray/art, which is a targeted intervention to move the client forward. When any experiential intervention occurs, it is important for the counselor to facilitate the client's verbal processing of his or her experience.

Counselors continue to utilize the client's somatic resources from the previous phase of treatment. Additionally, counselors work more with cognitive interventions directed at challenging and changing trauma-related assumptions that support self-blame or other destructive thought processes. Through cognitive work, clients improve insight into what the trauma means in terms of their identity, their spirituality, and their resiliency. Over time, the process helps the client develop a coherent trauma narrative.

Phase 3: Integration and Meaning Making

Although integration begins in phase three, in reality, as client's process trauma in phase two, they begin integrating these experiences into a unified story of self and begin a meaning-making process. During phase three, the counselor facilitates the client's process of meaning making. Part of this process includes restructuring communication between limbic system physiological and emotional responses and cognitions that help the client "make sense of" or develop a story about the experiences. The CSA/SA experiences integrate into the client's sense of self or identity without overwhelming his or her identity. In other words, the trauma is part of who the person is; part of one's personal experience, not the sum total of one's identity.

During this phase, clients may process grief and loss issues related to the CSA/SA experiences or related to those relationships or roles impacted by the trauma. Sometimes clients decide to forgive those who abused them or who supported the abuser(s) because it is freeing for the trauma survivor to forgive and move forward with life. Periodically, after treatment, trauma survivors may reach different developmental periods (e.g., first intimate partner relationship following therapy), and the client may experience a *transcrisis* situation because the trauma experience/memory is triggered. These are predictable, and counselors should share this information with clients, letting them know that it is normal, and that it is a good indication that they may need to re-enter counseling for a short period to resolve the transcrisis situation.

Case Study: Kirsten

Kirsten is a 19-year-old Caucasian female college sophomore at a prestigious college majoring in chemistry. She is an honor student who plans to become a pharmacist or an anesthesiologist, although she has not decided for certain which way to go with her future studies. Kirsten is also a cheerleader for her college, as well as an officer in her sorority. She presented at the emergency room for treatment for an unknown infection with a high white count and associated physical symptoms. During her initial interview with a male resident, she had an extreme reaction to being asked if she could be pregnant or have any STDs. She demonstrated hostility and anger and resistance to being physically examined. He ordered the nurse to treat her with a mild sedative intravenously. Kirsten began crying uncontrollably when the nurse explained what she was doing, and at that time, Kirsten disclosed she had been raped by one of the football players at school, whom she'd been flirting with for a few weeks, while at an "away game" two nights ago.

Following the disclosure, the resident called for a psychological consult, and you were called in from the Rape Crisis Center to assess Kirsten and provide crisis intervention. Kirsten demonstrates exaggerated startle response, tearfulness, emotional liability inconsistent with her previous medical or mental health history, and appears to be reacting to the male resident as if she is reliving the assault. She expresses to you that she had not considered that she could be pregnant or that she could have contracted a STD because of the rape. She keeps repeating that she "should have known better" than to go to his room and drink with him by herself and that she feels "stupid for making that mistake." She says she cannot tell her parents about what happened because they will come take her out of school, and that will ruin her chances for a special research scholarship she is in the running for at school. She also states that she doesn't want to tell any of the other students or the school officials what happened because she's sure they will blame her for placing herself in a situation where this could happen and likely ruin her chances at the scholarship she's pursuing because the rape would "look bad for the university."

Case Application Questions

1. What are the potential laws that may impact Kirsten's case?
2. Describe how you would assess Kirsten. Specifically describe how you would approach her and why you would choose the approach you do. Also, identify questions you would ask her to further assess her situation and identify formal measures you might use to assess Kirsten. Support your responses with logical reasoning.
3. What peri-traumatic responses might you expect from Kirsten? What diagnostic categories would you explore, if you needed to give a diagnosis for her insurance company to pay for services?
4. Consider that during the assessment you find out that Kirsten has been having intrusive memories to being raped by her brother when she was 8 years old and he was 13. Apply the BASK model to describe potential dissociative reactions Kirsten might have had that allowed her to "survive" this earlier attack. Discuss why these memories might be surfacing now, following the rape, using your understanding of traumatic neurobiology. Discuss how your understanding of dissociation might inform your treatment plan.
5. Imagine you are working with Kirsten as an outpatient counselor at the Rape Crisis Center. Describe the therapeutic process you would follow to guide Kirsten through treatment. Also discuss the potential reactions she might have during treatment and how you can address these during treatment.

SUMMARY

This chapter on sexual assault focuses on adult survivors of child sexual abuse and adult sexual assault. Incidence, prevalence, and types of sexual assault behaviors are discussed.

Additionally, the chapter identifies significant laws and court decisions governing sexual assault cases. The chapter discusses affective, cognitive, behavioral, and psychological reactions, including two models of dissociation, applicable to counseling sexual assault survivors. Both informal and formal trauma-sensitive approaches to assessment of CSA and SA, common diagnostic issues stemming from CSA/SA experiences, and phases and interventions used in trauma-informed care are described in depth.

CHAPTER 12 REFLECTIVE QUESTIONS

1. If you were presenting a workshop on sexual assault to a community group, how would you describe the different types of sexual violence? How would you describe the characteristics of individuals who are at increased risk for sexual victimization?
2. Describe how you would assess the potential of past sexual abuse/assault with an adult client during an intake session.
3. If you were providing psychoeducational information to a group of sexual assault survivors or their spouses, how would you describe the effect of a sexual assault on the victim's ANS system?
4. During an intake assessment with an adult sexual abuse/assault client, how would you assess the client's coping following the abuse/assault? Provide specific examples.
5. Compare common peri-traumatic responses to sexual trauma.
6. Describe the common diagnostic issues that sexual abuse/assault survivors deal with.
7. Compare the BASK model of dissociation with the structural model of dissociation. How would you use this information to assess dissociation with a sexual abuse/assault survivor?
8. Discuss the common psychological or affective reactions to sexual abuse/assault and discuss how trauma-informed care addresses these concerns.
9. If you were planning treatment with an adult who suffered child sexual abuse and then was sexually assaulted again in college, what would the treatment process look like? Describe how each phase of treatment builds on the previous phase.
10. Describe techniques you might use to help a client develop somatic resources for stabilization.

RESOURCES

Darkness to Light: Mandatory reporting: https://www.d2l.org/get-help/reporting/mandatory-reporting/

"Safety Planning with Adult Sexual Assault Survivors; A Guide for Advocates and Attorneys": https://www.victimrights.org/sites/default/files/Safety%20Planning%20with%20Adult%20Sexual%20Assault%20Survivors_A%20Guide%20for%20Advocates%20and%20Attorneys.pdf.

"Adult Sexual Assault Law Enforcement Guidelines (2017) for the Commonwealth of Massachusetts": https://www.mass.gov/files/documents/2018/07/24/2017-sexual-assault-law-enforcement-guidelines.pdf

National Sexual Violence Resource Center: https://www.nsvrc.org/

National Child Traumatic Stress Network: Trauma-informed care: https://www.nctsn.org/trauma-informed-care

National Center on Domestic and Sexual Violence: http://www.ncdsv.org/

Rape, Abuse and Incest National Network (RAINN): https://www.rainn.org/

U. S. Department of Justice Violence Against Women Office: https://www.justice.gov/ovw

National Alliance to End Sexual Violence: https://www.endsexualviolence.org/

EMDR Institute, Inc.: http://www.emdr.com/

International Somatic Movement Education and Therapy Association: https://ismeta.org/about-ismeta

Intensive trauma treatment course with Dr. Bessel A. van der Kolk: https://catalog.pesi.com/sales/bh_001087_trauma_organic-16108

Child Trauma Academy: http://childtrauma.org/

CHAPTER 13

Counseling Sex Offenders

Leigh F. Holman and Rebekah Lemmons

Upon completion of this chapter, readers will be able to do the following:

- Discuss the aspects of a comprehensive psychosexual assessment of sex offenders
- Explain the differences between different types of psychobiological tests utilized in the assessment and their uses in treatment
- Compare different methods of classifying sex offenders
- Describe the common elements of sex offender treatment program interventions

TABLE 13.1 Myths and Myth Busters

Myths	Myth Busters
Sex offenders are strangers who lurk in bad areas.	Sex offenders are commonly known to the victim(s) and often have a personal relationship with the victim(s).
Sex offenders can be identified through background checks.	Many sex offenders are not caught or convicted of a sex crime, so they may not have a criminal history that would raise concerns during a background check.
Most sex offenders reoffend.	According to the Council on Sex Offender Management, reconviction data suggests most sex offenders are never convicted a second time, and for those who are, it is more likely related to the severity and type of sexual offense than that the person sexually offended previously.
Sex offenders are male.	Increasingly, more females arrested and convicted on sexual offending behavior.
Juveniles do not commit sexual offenses.	Many sex offenders begin offending during their youth, many in response to their own victimization.

INTRODUCTION

Considered "hidden crimes," many victims do not report sexual offense victimization. Keeping this in mind, there are about 100,000 arrests for sex offenders (SO) in the United States annually; about one-third are for forcible rape (Center for Sex Offender Management [CSOM], n.d.). Currently, there are approximately 150,000 sex offenders housed in state and federal correctional facilities. Between 1980 and 1994, the number of incarcerated sex offenders rose by 300%. However, this corresponded with the increased publicity about sexual abuse and sexual assault, due to public figures like Oprah Winfrey talking about their own abuse. Many people expressed concern at the time that sexual offending behaviors were becoming an epidemic. The reality is that these offenders had always been in the community but due to a variety of sociocultural norms and corresponding public policies, they avoided report or arrest for sexual offenses. **Table 13.2** provides a list of sociocultural, policy, and legal trends from 1930 to present.

According to the Center for Sex Offender Management (CSOM) (n.d.), adults account for most (80%) arrests, as do males (95%); however, we know that there are many juvenile sex offenders, as well as female offenders. One complication when we review data about sex offender prevalence and incidence is that many juveniles and female offenders do not have arrests, or they either plead down to a non-sex offense charge or are placed on deferred adjudication, rather than being prosecuted. According to CSOM, victims 5 years old or younger are equally as likely to be victimized by a family member (49%) or acquaintance (48%), with

TABLE 13.2 Trends in Sex Offender Norms, Laws, and Policies

Time period	Trends, norms, laws, and policies
1180–1930	Stereotypes about sex offenders promoted through sociological and psychological research.
	Large families living in small quarters, migrant farm work, and other socioeconomic trends resulted in intra-familial sex practices for some groups.
1930–1955	Waves of predator panic. Increased focus on psychiatric influence on policy.
	Sex crimes focused on interracial sex (e.g., the Scottsboro Boys rape trial 1931).
	1932: Lindbergh baby kidnapped.
	1935: Albert Fish: Pedophile and child murderer viewed as the stereotypical stranger-monster. Hoover becomes FBI director and begins a campaign to raise awareness and prosecution of sex offense crimes.
	1937: Michigan and 1938 Illinois pass the first sexual psychopath laws.
	1940: NYC mayor established a committee for the study of sex offenses, which debunked many myths about this population.
	1944: Chemical castration of sex offenders first tried.
	1947: California passed the first sex offender registration law to track known sex offenders, which corresponded with the Black Dahlia case.
	1948: Kinsey's *Sexual Behavior in the Human Male* is published as is *the Outer Edges* (fictional account of a child sex-murderer).
	Many sex offenders diagnosed with manic depression.

(Continued)

Time period	Trends, norms, laws, and policies
1950–1970	Experimentation with sex offender policies, dialogue outside the dominant "monster-type" view. Corresponding social distrust in law enforcement and psychiatry in the country. Concerns about restrictive views of sexuality (e.g., pre-marital sex, non-monogamous sex) led to more lax views of sexual deviancy.
	1950: California passed the Sexual Deviation Research Act.
	1952: First DSM included homosexuality, fetishism, pedophilia, transvestism, exhibitionism, voyeurism, sadism, masochism, and other unspecified sexual deviations.
	1953: Kinsey's *Sexual Behavior in the Human Female* was published.
	1955: The term "child molestation" first appeared in *Reader's Digest* to differentiate sexual interest in adolescents. The novel *Lolita* was published.
	1957: Kurt Freund developed the penile plethysmograph (PPG) to aid the Czechoslovakian army screen for homosexuals.
	1958: *The Mark*, a fictional novel about a man living under sex offender laws, was published.
	1960: *To Kill a Mockingbird* published.
	1962: Illinois becomes the first state to decriminalize sodomy.
	1963: Dr. C. Henry Kempe's *The Battered Child Syndrome* is published.
	1965: Gladys Schultz wrote *How Many More Victims?* stating that rape of women and children was common and resulted in long-term psychological damage.
	1969: Stonewall riots brought national attention to the gay rights movement.
1970–1979	1970: The Lockhart commission (U.S. Commission on Obscenity and Pornography) does not find a link between obscene materials and criminality.
	1973: APA membership votes to exclude homosexuality from the DSM.
	1974: Child Abuse Prevention and Treatment Act (CAPTA) creates mandatory abuse reporting requirements; Diana Russell's *The Politics of Rape: The Victim's Perspective* was published; and rape awareness campaigns begun by feminist groups.
	1977: Child sexual abuse established as a term; Child pornography production, distribution, and possession made illegal by the Kildee-Murphy Bill; The journal *Child Abuse and Neglect* began publishing; sexual harassment ruled illegal by courts.
	1978: National Man-Boy Love Association (NAMBLA) formed in Boston.
	1979: First national conference devoted to child abuse
1980–1990	1979–1981 stories of child murders prominent in media; Adam Walsh, Etan Patz cases raised concerns about child abduction, sexual torture, and murder; John Wayne Gacy, Randy Kraft led people to incorrectly link homosexuality to pedophiles and child killers.
	1980: *Michelle Remembers* cowritten by a Canadian psychiatrist and his patient highlighting concerns about Satanic ritual abuse and memories of sexual abuse recovered using hypnosis.
	1982: *New York v. Ferber*: The Supreme Court (SC) asserted that the government has compelling interest in child protection upholding a law stating it was illegal to "promote any performance which includes sexual conduct by a child less than 16."
	1982: Bakersfield, California became the site of the first major claim of Satanic ritual abuse.
	1984: The National Center for Missing and Exploited Children (NCMEC) was formed; *Silent Shame* was broadcast on NBC, a documentary on child sexual abuse.
	1985: The *Meese Report* on pornography was released.
	1986: Oprah Winfrey disclosed her personal history of child sexual abuse on national TV.
	1988: U.S. Parole Commission, state, and local jurisdictions began experimenting with electronic monitoring.

Time period	Trends, norms, laws, and policies
1990–2000	1990: Washington state creates the first sexual predator law, establishing a registry, community notification, indefinite sentencing, civil commitment, and tiered risk in response to two high-profile cases, thus starting the "memorial law" trend in sex offender laws.
	1991: *Predator* book popularized the term "sexual predator."
	1992: World Health Organization (WHO) removed homosexuality from ICD.
	1992: Fran Henry started one of the first child sexual abuse prevention groups, Stop it Now!
	1993: Polly Klaas murder coined as *murder of America's child*.
	1994: Jacob Wetterling Act (Jacob's Law) established the first national sex offender registry law. Requires states to track sex offenders by validating place of residence annually for 10 years from time of release into the community. Those convicted of violent sex offenders must validate quarterly for the rest of their lives.
	1994: Indiana's Zachary's Law places sex offender registry online.
	1994: California passes One Strike for some categories of rapists.
	July 1994: Megan Kanka murdered in New Jersey, leading to the national sex offender registry called Megan's Law.
	1995: Amendments to the Communications Decency Act (CDA) address fears about online predators.
	1995: Florida passes the first residence restriction laws against sex offenders.
	1995: Louisiana becomes the first state to reinstitute the death penalty for child rape.
	1996: Megan's Law passed, a federal law forcing states to maintain publicly accessible registries and community notification.
	1996: California passes the first chemical castration law.
	1996: Pam Lyncher Sexual Offender Tracking and Identification Act required registered sex offenders moving to a new residence after release from prison or placement on parole/probation to inform state authorities within 10 days of moving.
	1996: Communications Decency Act (CDA) of 1996: First attempt to regulate pornographic material on the Internet in response to fears about online predators.
	1997: Supreme Court upholds civil commitment of sex offenders in *Kansas v. Hendricks*.
	1998: Delaware passes the first sex offender ID card law, marking state-issued ID cards with a "Y."
	1999: Static-99 is developed by Karl Hanson, becoming the leading risk assessment tool used to evaluate sex offenders.
2000–current	2000: Campus Sex Crimes Prevention Act signed, amending FERPA to assure that educational institutions may give out information regarding sex offenders, which they receive through state sex offender registration and community notification programs.
	2000: Legal Defense Fund is established to fight Oregon's public registry.
	2001: *Seling v. Young*: civil commitment is judged not to be a second punishment.
	2002: Three high-profile cases of abducted White girls dominated media (Elizabeth Smart, Danielle Van Dam, and Samantha Runnion).
	2003: U.S. Supreme Court (SC) upheld Megan's Law in Connecticut.
	2003: PROTECT act creates the national Amber alert program.
	2005: Florida passes the Jessica Lunsford Act (Jessica's Law) including strict mandatory minimum sentencing laws for sex offenders, mandatory minimum 25 year and max life sentence for first-time child sex offenders. Shortens the address registry period to 3 days, and requires any person convicted of a sexual offense against a child under 13 be electronically monitored for life.
	2006: California Sex Offender Punishment, Control and Containment Act passed.

(Continued)

Time period	Trends, norms, laws, and policies
	2006: Adam Walsh Act (Adam's Law) implemented nationally, which organizes sex offenders into three tiers with differentiated registry requirements based on level of risk. Set criteria for states for posting offender data on Internet.
	2007: Ohio becomes first state to become "substantially compliant" with federal Adam Walsh Act.
	2008: U.S. SC rules the death penalty cannot be applied to rape cases where there is no murder (*Kennedy v. Louisiana*).
	2008: First state specific sex offender reform groups forms (Texas Voices).
	2009: Iowa becomes the first state to repeal residency restriction laws for most sex offender registrants; Reform Sex Offender Laws has first conference.
	2010: U.S. SC upholds indefinite commitment of the Adam Walsh Act in *U.S. v. Comstock*.
	2011: Erin's Law first passed in Illinois requiring public schools in the United States to implement prevention-oriented child sex abuse programming to students, faculty, and parents about how to avoid sexual abuse and how to recognize warning signs. (Most states now have this requirement.)

very few sexually abused by strangers (3%). Elementary-age children (6–11) similarly are victimized by family members 42% of the time and someone known to the victim 53% of the time, with only 5% victimized by strangers. However, from ages 12–17 there is a sharp jump in the number who experience victimization by an acquaintance (66%), compared to 24% victimized by family and 10% by strangers. For 18–24-year-olds, the acquaintance sexual assault stays virtually the same (67%), while the family (10%) and stranger assault frequencies flip (24%). Finally, for those victims 25 or older, 57% experience sexual assaults from someone they know outside their family, 13% within the family, and 30% strangers.

Working as a *sex offender treatment provider* (SOTP) requires specialized knowledge and clinical training. Some states have certifications or licenses, which specify training and continuing education requirements. The national professional organization that represents professional SOTPs is the Association for Treatment of Sexual Abusers (ATSA), and they have their own standards (adult and adolescent practice guidelines), policy statements, code of ethics, educational opportunities, and conference, which you can explore on their website atsa.com.

ASSESSMENT

Assessments for sexually inappropriate or illegal behavior generally only occur post-adjudication and only on adolescent (over 10 years old) or adult offenders. Therefore, this section will focus on these populations.

Psychosexual Evaluations

Sex offenders undergo what we call a *psychosexual evaluation*, which is an evaluation conducted by one or more trained professionals to assess the level of risk for continued offending and the client's treatment needs. They include the following:

- *Document review*: Review of referral documents, offense reports from law enforcement, potentially collateral interviews or review of past criminal history, child protective services history, and/or psychological evaluations, depending on the client's situation and program resources

- *Clinical interview*: Standard psychosocial history and mental status exam
- *Psychological assessment*: Usually referred out to a psychologist, including test of general cognitive functioning (IQ test), assessment of adaptive functioning (e.g., scales of independent behavior-revised, Vineland), and psychological characteristics (psychometrically validated personality test, e.g., MMPI)
- *Psychosexual assessment*: This is a sex offender–specific evaluation of sexual history, attitudes and beliefs about sex, deviant sexual interest (Abel Assessment for Sexual Interest) and/or arousal (penile plethysmograph [PPG]). A treatment provider trained at the program will likely conduct this part of the assessment. The final part of the psychosexual assessment evaluates the client's truthfulness against his or her report of the instant offense and sexual history using a clinical polygraph, conducted by a trained credentialed polygrapher in consultation with the treatment provider.

Sexual history includes questions about sexual fantasies, urges, and behavior; early sexual experiences; number and duration of sexual relationships; gender identity and sexual orientation; frequency of sexual activity, including masturbation and intercourse; sexual functioning; and unusual sexual interests or behavior, which are not necessarily deviant or illegal (e.g., cross-dressing). Counselors analyze all assessment data to identify abnormal patterns in sexual development, attitudes, and beliefs, including identification of cognitive distortions indicative of sexual offending and/or criminal thinking, which may contribute to offending patterns. We evaluate all the data gathered from interviews and tests against collateral data sources (e.g., criminal history, law enforcement or protective services documentation, prior psychological evaluations, interviews with family or victim, etc.).

Psychophysiological Testing

Deviant sexual interest or arousal is a classic sign of SO behavior. *Deviant sexual interest* is any interest in sexual activity with a human or animal (e.g., bestiality) who cannot or does not consent, or using coercion, force, incapacitation, or power differential (e.g., social/occupational position or age) to gain sexual compliance from a victim. Deviant sexual interest indicates the likelihood of *deviant sexual arousal*, meaning that sexual arousal results from these same thoughts or behaviors.

The *Abel Assessment for Sexual Interest* (AASI) evaluates sexual interest using a psychometrically validated test of visual reaction time. The client looks at and rates pictures on a computer of models of different ages, who are clothed (some in bathing suites), in various poses, and with various facial expressions. Photos indicate some pictures of people who are happy, some unhappy or even in distress, some in normal situations, and others bound with rope or otherwise restrained. The models (or their legal guardians) understood the purpose and use of the pictures when they agreed to participate. The test evaluates the length of time the client looks at each picture as an indication of interest. Additionally, information about the consistency or inconsistency between client ratings of the pictures and the visual reaction time are noted.

The *penile plethysmograph* (PPG) evaluates sexual arousal. It is currently considered the only objective means for assessing pedophilic interest because it directly measures the level of arousal in a penis. There are two types of PPGs. One measures volume and the other circumference. *Volume PPGs* measure "the displacement of air in a cylinder enclosing the penis—typically, a glass or rigid cylinder placed over the penis with an inflatable cuff that encloses the base of the penis" (Coric et al., 2005, p. 27). The *circumferential PPG* measures direct changes in penis diameter, in response to sexual stimuli by placement of a calibrated mercury strain gauge at the base of the penis. It connects to an instrument that monitors small alterations in voltage through the strain gauge. Whichever type is used, the client places the penis in a private environment of a controlled clinical assessment setting. The evaluator is in an adjacent room. The evaluator directs stimuli (visual or auditory depictions of sexual material, some are 911 calls during sexual assaults, others include child pornography, and a host of other materials). The evaluator also records changes in PPG readings. There is controversy around use of the PPG because it uses material gathered during criminal investigations, and the victims may be unaware they are used for this purpose. Additionally, it involves pictures of nude individuals and some illegal depictions of child pornography. As a result, the PPG generally is only used with adult SOs.

Psychosexual assessments commonly utilize clinical polygraphs to assess truthfulness of the client's reports in clinical interviews. There are two types of *clinical polygraphs* utilized in the assessment phase, instant offense and sexual history. Hindman and Peters (2001) reviewed studies of clinical polygraphs with sex offenders and found "it was common for sex offenders to lie about the numbers of their victims, falsely claim a history of being sexually abused themselves, and minimize or deny their juvenile sex offenses" (p. 15).

- *Instant offense polygraph*: This may also be called a specific issue polygraph. It consists usually of three to five target questions that test facts related to the most recent offense the client is charged with. It can help indicate discrepancies between the victim's and offender's descriptions of the offense when combined with a review of the victim statement and/or witness statements. This information can be useful when engaging the client in treatment, as well.
- *Sexual history polygraph*: Evaluates whether the client has fully disclosed an accurate sexual history during the clinical interview and psychological assessment portions of the psychosexual evaluation.

The remaining types, used during and/or after treatment, when a client is on community supervision, we discuss in the treatment section.

Risk Assessment

Risk assessment is the process of identifying the probability of future criminal behavior and sexual reoffending. It takes place in both criminal justice and clinical settings. Assessment of risk is an ongoing process throughout treatment, which provides information about the appropriate placement of the offender, the goals of treatment and management, community notification, and potential referral for civil commitment. Counselors originally provided SO risk assessment based on *clinical judgment*. Whether using structured psychometrically validated instruments or unstructured, these assessments were non-standardized nor replicable. The second generation of SO risk assessment focused on actuarial assessments, which provided standardized and replicable risk assessment. Unstructured clinical judgment risk assessment has low predictive validity and structure is low to moderate at best (Tully, Chou, & Browne, 2013).

Actuarial assessments utilize clearly stated definitions and coding rules, utilization of historical artifacts, and assessment of risk factors empirically related to re-offense. These were moderately reliability in predicting re-offense. The Static-99 was the first and most used actuarial assessment of SO risk. However, these assessments relied on static variables, meaning they could not change based on treatment intervention. This is problematic if we believe treatment can reduce risk of re-offense. Actuarial assessments vary in predictive validity from low-moderate (SVR-20) to moderate (Static 99, Static 99R, SORAG, STABLE, and ACUTE) (Tully, Chou, & Browne, 2013).

Therefore, the third generation relies on a *dynamic assessment* of risk. These assessments attempt to combine the best of the previous approaches. They have characteristics of actuarial assessments in that they have clearly stated definitions and coding rules that utilize risk factors empirically related to re-offense and are standardized and replicable. However, they also consider not only static variables but dynamic ones as well, which contextualize risk based on sociocultural, environmental, and individual characteristics. Dynamic assessments address illegal SO behaviors and other challenging sexual behaviors that are not illegal, such as compulsive use of pornography (legal), exposure to others in a group home setting, unwanted touching of others' genitals over clothing, sexually explicit phone calls, and/or spying on someone in the shower, when dressing, and so on.

Although risk assessment continues to improve, there are limits to this process. No risk assessment can provide a complete guarantee of community safety. Most sexual offenses are never reported, and therefore undetected by actuarial calculations. Actuarial risk also relies on studies utilizing varying methodologies with different levels of rigor. Because of the heterogeneity of sex offenders, as a population, risk assessment based on any statistical probability (which increases accuracy) is indicative of generalities across the group, not a specific reflection of an individual's risk. This is another reason sole reliance on actuarial risk assessment is problematic.

DIAGNOSIS/CLASSIFICATION

We classify sexual behaviors developmentally as well as diagnostically. Sexually inappropriate behavior exhibited by children are those behaviors that are developmentally inappropriate for their age. Some children (0–9 years) who experience sexual abuse become *sexually reactive* and demonstrate sexualized behaviors because of their direct victimization or viewing highly sexualized content (e.g., observing sexual intercourse; pornography exposure). They are not developmentally capable of understanding their behavior could be abusive to another person. These behaviors can include self-stimulation, sometimes to the point of bleeding or pain. However, some sexually reactive children can become aggressive and attempt to coerce other children into simulated or real sexual acts, including oral, anal, and/or vaginal penetration. Studies indicate a link between sexually reactive behavior and exposure to family sexuality, nudity, and sexual behavior in the media, domestic violence, as well as physical abuse and neglect (Burton, Rasmussen, Bradshaw, Christopherson, & Huke, 1998; Chaffin et al., 2006; Grady & Reynolds, 2001).

Children 10–12 years old may develop what we call *problem sexual behavior* (PSB), which is sexually manipulative or aggressive behavior resulting in victimization of another child. Un-adjudicated youth in this category are considered to exhibit PSB. However, depending on the jurisdiction, law enforcement may pursue criminal charges. Generally, this group is referred to as *juvenile sex offenders* (JSOs). Some may receive reduced charges under a plea agreement that requires therapeutic intervention, and courts place others on deferred adjudication where they have a chance to eliminate or reduce charges, if they successfully complete an authorized JSO treatment program.

According to ATSA, *Internet-facilitated sexual offending* (IFSO) is another form of sexual offending increasingly presenting for treatment. IFSO includes a range of behaviors, including the following:

- Viewing, trading, or producing child pornography to be traded or posted online
- Making contact with a child, adolescent, or other vulnerable person for sexual chats (electronic correspondence) or exploitation such as convincing a child to view or produce pornographic images (e.g., having the child take and e-mail a nude picture of him- or herself)
- Arranging face-to-face meetings to commit sexual offenses (sometimes referred to as "luring" or "traveler" offending) (Association for Treatment of Sexual Abusers [ATSA], 2010)

Clinical referrals for IFSO are a growing problem common in specialized treatment as well as general counseling settings. Several studies indicate these offenders are at less risk for future contact offenses than other types of sex offenders, which is partially attributed to lower levels of generalized antisocial characteristics (Elliott, Beech, Mandeville-Norden, & Hayes, 2009; Seto & Ekke, 2005). However, this is not true of Internet child pornography traffickers who have high levels of pedophilic sexual arousal patterns on the PPG (Seto, Cantor, & Blanchard, 2006; Seto & Eke, 2005).

Most convicted sex offenders receive one or more paraphilia diagnoses (Abel, Becker, Cunningham-Rathner, Mittleman, & Rouleau, 1988). *Paraphilias* are "a class of mental disorders defined by an atypical sexual interest and/or behavior that causes mental distress to a person and/or makes the person a serious threat to the psychological and physical well-being of other individuals" (ATSA, 2015, p. 2). Sex offenders receiving treatment, although they may have histories of exhibitionism, voyeurism, or frotteurism, or another paraphilia, generally have diagnoses of pedophilia or sadism (rapists). In addition, many sex offenders

(93%) experience comorbid mental health issues like mood disorders, anxiety disorders, and psychosis (Raymond, Coleman, Ohlerking, Christenson, & Miner, 1999). Some have learning disabilities or low cognitive functioning, which can affect treatment intervention choices. Finally, personality disorders are common among sex offender populations (Sigler, 2017), particularly antisocial personality disorder and narcissistic personality disorder, although more so for rapists (46%–50%) than pedophiles (20%–40%) (Curtin & Niveau, 1998; Raymond, Coleman, Ohlerking, Christenson, & Miner, 1999). Gudjonsson, Sigurdsson, and Einarsson's (2003) study also identified higher rates of certain personality traits among sex offenders, including higher rates of introversion and social desirability.

There are several typologies of sex offenders conceptualizing this group of perpetrators. Some classify as pedophiles (attracted to pre-pubescent children) and rapists (sexual arousal by forcing someone, child or adult, into unwanted or painful sexual activity). Some further classify child sex offenders as regressed (attracted to both adults and children) or fixated (attracted only to children (Elliott, Beech, Mandeville-Norden, & Hayes, 2009; Laws & O'Donohue, 1990; Marshall, Laws, & Barbaree, 1990). The Federal Bureau of Investigation (FBI) classifies child sexual offenders using a typology that categorizes situational or preferential offenders (Holmes & Holmes, 2009). *Situational offenders* may be the following:

- **Regressed:** Poor coping skills, target accessible victims, substitute children for adult relationships
- **Morally indiscriminate:** Do not prefer children, but tend to use children or any accessible victim for their own gain, sexual or not
- **Sexually indiscriminate:** Primarily interested in sexual experimentation; abuse children out of boredom
- **Inadequate:** Social misfits, insecure, low self-esteem, "relationships" with children perceived as their sole sexual outlet

The FBI further classifies *preferential offenders* as the following:

- **Seductive:** Groom children through love, affection, gifts, and enticements in order to develop a "relationship" with the child and seduce the child into engaging in sexual acts
- **Fixated:** Have poor psychosexual development; desire affection from children; compulsively and solely attracted to children
- **Sadistic:** Aggressive, sexually excited by violence; target strangers for victimization; extremely dangerous.

Nicholas Groth (Groth & Birnbaum, 1979) describes three types of rapists, based on the rapist's goal. The first is the *anger rapist*, who consciously intends to humiliate and physically and psychologically harm the victim. They express contempt for the victim through physical violence and profanity during the rape. Sex is a weapon, and the level of force used during the attack is beyond what would be necessary to carry out the act. *Power rapists* compensate for feelings of inadequacy by raping in order to assert competency, control, authority, or capability. They usually fantasize about rape and other sexual conquests where the victim may initially resist, but actually "wants" the rape to occur. Power rapists primarily rely on verbal threats or intimidation with a weapon or social position. They usually only use the amount of force necessary to gain compliance, and they may actually ask the victim for a date following the rape. Due to the inadequacy the rapist experiences, the perpetrator may feel compelled to continue the behavior with subsequent victims in a serial fashion. *Sadistic rapists* are calculated, often wearing a disguise or blindfolding victims. They often target victims who are easily dismissed like prostitutes or "promiscuous" people. There is usually prolonged ritualistic torture and restraint involved. Inflicting pain, watching the victim in distress and in suffering pair with sexual excitement for the sadistic rapist. These rapists are very dangerous, may use a weapon as an implement of the rape itself, and may severely injure or kill the victim. Finally, for *gratification rapists*, the only motivation is to obtain sex to alleviate loneliness. Generally, this person has difficulty finding socially acceptable outlets for sexual desires and has poor social skills with desired partners.

TREATMENT

Working as a SOTP means that along with being the counselor for offenders, you will work closely with probation and parole officers trained to supervise and manage SOs in the community. There is a new trend toward victim-centered community management approaches in the justice system. The Council for Sex Offender Management (CSOM) published guidelines for sex offender programs using the victim-centered approach. They define the *victim-centered approach* as "a philosophy, principle, and practice that recognizes sexual assault victims as primary clients of the justice system, and whose safety, rights, and interests are a paramount consideration when designing and implementing perpetrator management strategies" (Brumby, Baker, & Gilligan., 2018, p. 4). This approach prioritizes victim safety and well-being, and they define primary victims as the direct victims of sexual offending behavior and secondary victims as any other person affected by the offending behavior, which can include spouses, parents, or children of the offender or victim.

CSOM advocates trauma-informed care that facilitates healing and prevention of harm to others. Treatment is just one of the principles of *victim-centered management approaches*. The fundamental principles of this approach include victim centeredness, specialized training of probation/parole officers and treatment providers, use of evidence-based practices, and raising public awareness through education, engagement, monitoring, evaluation, and collaboration. These principles are manifested from investigation, prosecution, and sentencing to assessment, to community supervision, whether probation or upon reentry through parole, treatment both in correctional facilities and in the community, registry compliance, and community notification. CSOM advocates for specialized training on risk factors, assessment tools, and treatment interventions specific to sex offending behavior. *SO specific treatment*, according to ATSA, is any treatment focused on the following:

1. Preventing reoccurring sexually abusive/aggressive behavior by helping men at risk of sexually offending to do the following:
    a. Effectively manage the factors that contribute to sexually abusive behaviors
    b. Develop strengths and competencies to address needs

    c.   Identify and change thoughts, feelings, and actions that may contribute to sexual offending

    d.   Establish and maintain stable, meaningful, and prosocial lives (ATSA, 2016)

Specialized SO treatment interventions address the SO's *motivation* for sexually offending, including deviant sexual interest/arousal patterns, social and emotional skills deficits, power and control, and anger. Intervention also must address issues affecting the client's *willingness to engage* in treatment, including identifying and challenging cognitive distortions that support offending behaviors, addictive issues that lower inhibitions to offending, management of current and ongoing stressors, and any long-standing characterological issues like personality disorders and psychopathy. Finally, treatment must address the need for building *external and internal barriers* to prevent offending.

Cognitive Interventions

The most common cognitive intervention in SO treatment is psychoeducation. Psychoeducational intervention components usually occur in a group setting. Each session the counselor presents one of several predetermined topics as part of a curriculum. Often there is an activity associated with the topic, and the counselor facilitates a discussion about the topic as it relates to those attending group. *Psychoeducational* topics in SO treatment programs include things like the following:

- **Sex education**: Interpersonal relationships, understanding intimacy, appropriate and inappropriate sexual behavior, gender, anatomy and physiology, self-image, relationship awareness, abuse awareness, STD awareness, deviant sexual fantasies and arousal, and healthy sexual fantasies and arousal.
- **Identifying and challenging cognitive distortions** (e.g., denial, minimization, rationalization). There are seven types of denial identified, which SOs use related to their sexual offending behavior, including the following:
  - *Denial of facts:* Claims the victim is lying or has a faulty memory
  - *Denial of awareness:* Claims no memory of the events because of a substance-induced blackout
  - *Denial of impact:* Minimizes harm the victim experienced(s)
  - *Denial of responsibility:* Blames the victim or a medical condition in an effort to minimize or avoid responsibility for the sexual offending behavior
  - *Denial of Grooming:* Claims there was not a plan for the offense to occur, or that the decisions leading up to the offense were not important. *Grooming* is the process of manipulation used to gain trust and lower defenses of the victim
  - *Denial of sexual intent:* The perpetrator acts as if the behavior was not intended to be sexual at all. S/he may claim that s/he is attempting to educate the victim about the body and this was misunderstood as sexual. Alternatively, a male offender may claim that his penis "accidently" bumped into a victim's body and was misinterpreted as a sexual assault.

- *Denial of denial*: Acts disgusted by what has happened in the hope that others will not believe it possible that he or she is capable of committing such a crime.
- **Taking accountability for offending:** Completing an offending autobiography and presenting it to the group
- **Trauma:** What is considered trauma; understanding the physical, psychological, and functional effects of trauma; identifying own trauma; identifying how one's sexually offensive behavior impacted the victim's development of trauma; trauma-management.
- **Emotional regulation** (e.g., anger, anxiety, depression): Identifying emotions in the moment, gauging intensity of emotion, and learning mechanisms to reduce heightened negative emotional states without offending. Healthy expression of emotion.
- **Coping skills training:** Communication skills, conflict management skills, stress management skills, deep breathing and progressive muscle relaxation, etc.
- **Empathy enhancement:** Writing letters to the victim taking responsibility for actions to present in group, victim empathy, impact role plays in group, potentially restorative justice activities (particularly for juvenile offenders or incest offenders likely to return to the family or community).
- **Identifying precursors to offending behaviors**: Any seemingly unimportant decision (SUDs), maladaptive coping response (MCRs), risk factors, lapses, and the abstinence violation effect (AVE), including the following
  - *Perpetrating precursors*: Chronic thoughts, feelings, and behaviors for the SO, which help him or her pretend everything is normal, but actually is the beginning of the person's offense cycle
  - *Precipitating precursors*: Thoughts, feelings, and events developed during childhood, which influence current thoughts, feelings, and behaviors (e.g., experiencing child abuse)
  - *Predisposing precursors*: Thoughts, feelings, and events acting as triggers for their offense cycle to progress through negative affective states, seemingly unimportant decisions, engaging in grooming behaviors before acting out. These are high-risk facts (HRFs)
- **Offense cycle:** Learning the elements of an offense cycle, identifying individual triggers or risk factors for offending (high-risk situations) and cognitive distortions used to facilitate grooming and offending behaviors (seemingly unimportant decisions), and identifying and putting into place barriers (internal and external) to offending behaviors (registering, community notification, electronic monitoring, trained chaperones, probation/parole officers, clinical polygraphs, coping skills implementation, emotional regulation skills implementation).

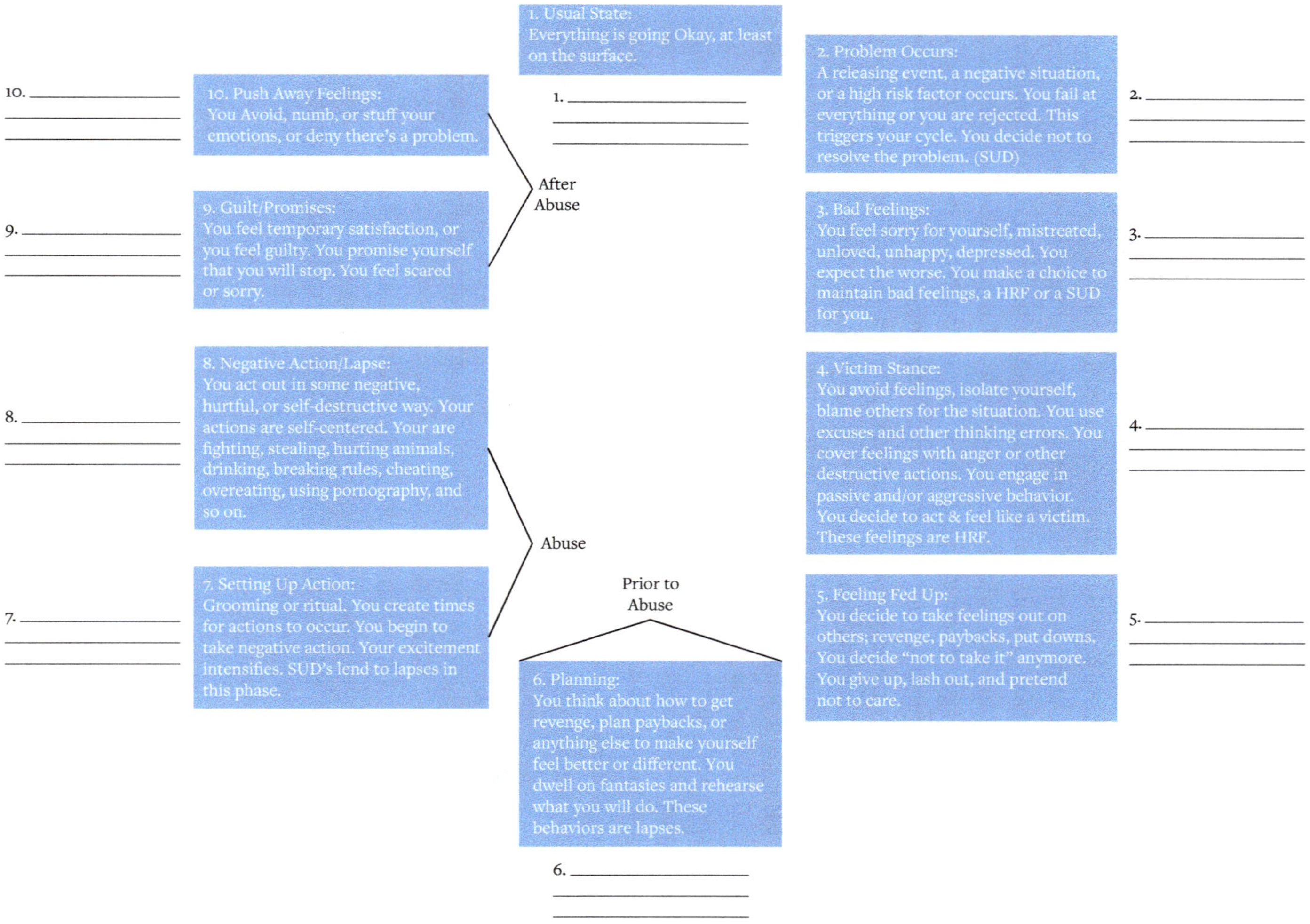

FIGURE 13.1 Offense cycle illustration

10.

10. Push Away Feelings:
You Avoid, numb, or stuff your emotions, or deny there's a problem.

9.

9. Guilt/Promises:
You feel temporary satisfaction, or you feel guilty. You promise yourself that you will stop. You feel scared or sorry.

8.

8. Negative Action/Lapse:
You act out in some negative, hurtful, or self-destructive way. Your actions are self-centered. Your are fighting, stealing, hurting animals, drinking, breaking rules, cheating, overeating, using pornography, and so on.

7.

7. Setting Up Action:
Grooming or ritual. You create times for actions to occur. You begin to take negative action. Your excitement intensifies. SUD's lend to lapses in this phase.

6. Planning:
You think about how to get revenge, plan paybacks, or anything else to make yourself feel better or different. You dwell on fantasies and rehearse what you will do. These behaviors are lapses.

6.

1. Usual State:
Everything is going Okay, at least on the surface.

1.

2. Problem Occurs:
A releasing event, a negative situation, or a high risk factor occurs. You fail at everything or you are rejected. This triggers your cycle. You decide not to resolve the problem. (SUD)

2.

3. Bad Feelings:
You feel sorry for yourself, mistreated, unloved, unhappy, depressed. You expect the worse. You make a choice to maintain bad feelings, a HRF or a SUD for you.

3.

4. Victim Stance:
You avoid feelings, isolate yourself, blame others for the situation. You use excuses and other thinking errors. You cover feelings with anger or other destructive actions. You engage in passive and/or aggressive behavior. You decide to act & feel like a victim. These feelings are HRF.

4.

5. Feeling Fed Up:
You decide to take feelings out on others; revenge, paybacks, put downs. You decide "not to take it" anymore. You give up, lash out, and pretend not to care.

5.

Abuse

After Abuse

Prior to Abuse

Cognitive restructuring also occurs as part of the processing in individual and group counseling formats throughout treatment. For those programs with a therapeutic milieu, counselors usually address psychoeducational material as well, in order to reinforce this knowledge and the associated skills. Many sex offender programs use a standard curriculum like Pathways (juveniles) or "Who Am I and Why Am I in Treatment," "Why Did I Do It Again?," and "How Can I Stop?"; and "Enhancing Empathy" by Robert Longo, Laren Bays, and Steven Sawyer.

Behavioral Interventions

Behavioral interventions involve a variety of activities intended to minimize or change the sex offender's deviant sexual arousal. They use standard behavioral conditioning principles in practice. According to research, the most effective interventions for reducing deviant sexual arousal are behavioral interventions (Dougher, 1996; Moster, Wunk, & Jeglic, 2008).

Masturbatory satiation involves the offender verbalizing healthy sexual fantasies and masturbating to the fantasy to the point of climax/ejaculation. After reaching orgasm, he or she continues masturbating while verbalizing a sexually deviant fantasy (e.g., nonconsenting adult or a child victim) for 50 minutes to 2 hours. If, during the deviant fantasy, the offender becomes aroused, then he or she is supposed to switch to verbalizing a healthy sexual fantasy. Sometimes offenders do this in a PPG lab while monitored through auditory observation and are asked to audiotape these deviant fantasies and keep a log of when they did the exercise, how long, and the effects. The person may bring the audiotape and log into individual counseling and play it, while at the same time the counselor may challenge and confront cognitive distortions contained in these ideas and fantasies. According to Abel and colleagues (1985), this technique successfully reduced deviant arousal after 12 sessions. However, due to the use of masturbation to deviant stimuli, use with juvenile offenders is limited.

Verbal satiation provides a non-masturbatory variation of the technique in which the client verbalizes deviant sexual fantasies at length until it becomes boring and unappetizing. There are two forms currently used. The first is verbal satiation with "repetition of deviant sexual thoughts until a state of psychological boredom is reached" (Hunter & Goodwin, 1992, p. 73). Research indicates that verbal satiation may be effective in reducing deviant sexual arousal among older juvenile offenders; however, the course of treatment must be a minimum of 6 to 9 months, perhaps longer, for moderate to severe levels of pre-treatment deviance (Hunter & Goodwin, 1992). Laboratory satiation uses visual stimuli to enhance concentration and conjuring of deviant sexual imagery while the juvenile offender repeats a deviant sexual phrase. Laboratory satiation allows psychophysiological arousal monitoring, with the counselor subsequently adjusting session length as needed to ensure psychological boredom occurs (Hunter & Goodwin, 1992).

Covert sensitization involves pairing deviant sexual thoughts and fantasies with extremely unpleasant consequences (e.g., thoughts of the arrest, staying in a holding cell overnight, arraignment, having the arrest or arraignment filmed and broadcast on the news, losing one's family due to the offending behavior, etc.). Again, the offender may either verbally go through this in session or bring a taped and written version to the individual session to go through with the counselor, who gives feedback about how to strengthen the unpleasant consequences.

Finally, *aversive conditioning* is a mainstay of adult sex offender treatment, which uses classical reconditioning of deviant stimuli. Aversive conditioning is necessary when the offender has longstanding ingrained or fixated sexual arousal solely to deviant stimuli. During aversive conditioning, the client goes through masturbatory satiation in a PPG lab. When the level of arousal is determined to be at a crucial point (which changes in successive approximations throughout the therapy), the offender is directed to "hit it," at which time he or she opens a container of ammonium and inhales until becoming physically ill. As a result, it is crucial that the offender has immediate access to something in which he or she can vomit. The point of the intervention is to pair the deviant arousal with an extremely noxious event in order to extinguish the reinforcing qualities of the deviant fantasy.

Another common behavioral intervention used on virtually every SO treatment program is the use of a *level system*. Based on social learning models of behaviorism, level systems involve clearly defined and consistently communicated behavioral expectations and positive associations with demonstrating desired behaviors and negative consequences or lack of movement up the level system for choosing not to engage in desired behaviors. Level systems work to engage the client in a simulated experience where increased demonstration of trustworthiness, responsibility, and accountability for behavior results in increases in freedom and privileges. Participants can move up the level system, gaining more freedom and privileges, as he or she demonstrates desired behaviors. However, the person may move down the level system, losing freedom and privileges as less desirable behaviors are demonstrated. The purpose is to develop a sense of personal agency and accountability for one's actions.

Interpersonal Interventions

Interpersonal interventions involve use of *interpersonal processes* within therapeutic relationships with therapists and frontline staff (or trained correctional officers), group relationships, community relationships in a therapeutic milieu (including prison program units), and family relationships. The use of interpersonal process interventions varies widely based on the theoretical perspective of the therapist(s) and program and specialized training of counselors and frontline personnel (including residential and prison DOC officers) in use of interpersonal process as a therapeutic medium.

Psychoeducational program components integrate *interpersonal skills modules* into the overall curricula. Table 13.3 provides examples of interpersonal skills modules from a civilly committed sex offender program in Illinois.

Some programs, particularly residential or prison based, utilize *recreational therapy* to advance interpersonal skills application and processing. Trained recreational therapists, perhaps in combination with the primary clinical counselor, design activities likely to evoke challenging or common interpersonal interactions. "The recreational therapist may review the game or activity with the offender[s] in order to integrate the game with the target skills, explaining what prosocial and self-managing behavior is desirable in the activity" (Liberty Healthcare Corporation, 1998, p. 14). Through participating in these activities, the offenders need to apply the interpersonal skills learned in the psychoeducational program component. The clinical counselor can stop the activity in the moment and facilitate a group or individual process around the thoughts, feelings, and behaviors triggered by the activity. Recreational therapists and frontline staff scan for target behaviors and reinforce positive targeted behaviors during the activity and during post-activity processing.

For those select individuals who may go through a family reunification process when they have a victim in the family (e.g., incest offenders), a process of clarification builds on all the elements of treatment. Ultimately, it is an interpersonal intervention. *Clarification* is a procedure requiring the SO to write a letter to the victim, taking responsibility for the grooming and sexual abuse in a language the victim can understand. This is allowed only

TABLE 13.3 Interpersonal Skills Modules

Interpersonal coping skills	Self-control coping skills
Conversation skills	Managing suicidal and negative thoughts
Assertiveness	Problem solving
Giving criticism	Increasing pleasant activities
Receiving criticism	Relaxation training
Drink and drug refusal skills	Anger management
Enhancing social supports	Coping with crises and persistent problems
Conflict resolution	Relapse prevention
	Avoiding high-risk situations

(Liberty Healthcare Corporation, 1998)

after both offender and victim therapists agree each have adequately demonstrated requisite progress in treatment for the interaction not to result in re-victimization. It is a supervised process that is a prerequisite for reunification to occur. The offender must do the following:

- Verbalize full responsibility for his or her sexual misbehavior and for the psychological and physical trauma it caused the victim.
- State why the perpetrator chose the victim and how the perpetrator misused those qualities to abuse the victim.
- Acknowledge "grooming" behavior.
- Support the victim's decision to report the abuse and take responsibility for making the victim endure the legal process.
- Acknowledge deviancy as a lifelong process and describe what the s/he is doing to manage it.
- Make no request for forgiveness or any other requests of the victim.

Psychopharmacological Interventions

Psychopharmacological interventions involve treatment of comorbid mental health issues like anxiety, depression, bipolar disorder, and so on. Although these medications may affect the offender's engagement in therapy and his or her emotion regulation abilities, they are effectively similar to any other mental health client. In this section, we focus on psycho-pharmacological interventions specifically used to manage sexually abusive behaviors, both hormonal and nonhormonal. *Hormonal agents* focus on reducing testosterone and sex drive in people with a paraphilia or who have engaged in sexually abusive behavior. Common anti-androgen hormonal agents include Depo-Provera, Leuprolide acetate (Lupron), cyproterone acetate, and gonadotropin-releasing hormone analog. These agents break down and eliminate circulating testosterone, which inhibits the production of luteinizing hormone in the pituitary gland, thus decreasing overall testosterone production. The research on effectiveness of these interventions is conflicting (ATSA, 2012).

These interventions involve altering medicines, so the medical ethical considerations in use must be foremost in the physician's mind when determining appropriateness of this intervention for a particular client. Some *ethical concerns* include the following:

- Many antiandrogen medications restrict freedom through chemical castration.
- The benefits and potential risks have not been evaluated by the FDA as a treatment for sexual offending behaviors, therefore prescribing these medications is "off-label."
- There are unpleasant side effects that may result in medication refusal.
- They may negatively interact with illegal steroids taken by the offender.
- There are federal laws prohibiting limitation of sexual behaviors and freedom of people with intellectual and developmental disabilities. (Refer to the first section of this text for the history on this.)
- The cost is high for many of these medications, and they may not be covered by insurance.
- Many professionals refuse to prescribe off label for this use.
- Reduction in sex drive may negatively impact the offender's ability to form healthy sexual relationships.
- Effectiveness is inconsistent.

Although counselors will not prescribe or manage medication, often counselors end up answering most of the client's questions about the medication, so it is important to develop a basic level of knowledge and psychoeducational resources to facilitate this part of your practice.

Nonhormonal agents used to manage sexually abusive or paraphilic behavior relate to managing comorbidity. Sex offender studies indicate people with hypersexuality (e.g., sex addiction) and paraphilic behaviors frequently experience comorbid mental health issues, including the following:

- Mood disorders: dysthymic disorder, major depressive disorder, bipolar spectrum disorders (Kafka & Hennen, 2002; Kafka & Prentkey, 1994)
- Anxiety disorders—especially social anxiety disorder and childhood-onset PTSD
- Psychoactive substance use disorders (Kafka & Hennen, 2002; Kafka & Prentkey, 1994)

- Neurodevelopmental disorders: attention-deficit hyperactivity disorder (ADHD), autism spectrum disorders, and other developmental disabilities (Kafka & Hennen, 2002; Kafka & Prentkey, 1994, 1998)

The evidence supporting use of psychotropic medications for treatment of comorbid mental health issues, like those listed, is well established. So, ethical concerns about use are limited. If these disorders result in dis-inhibitory functions, then not having medication may increase the likelihood the client will offend. However, there is little evidence suggesting these medications decrease sexual aggression or arousal, although there is preliminary evidence this may be so (Kraus et al., 2007).

Finally, neither hormonal nor nonhormonal pharmacological interventions address the underlying etiological factors or psychological or environmental risk factors for reoffending that other methods of intervention address. So, at most, we would use these interventions as an adjunct or support to traditional methods of therapy. Although counselors do not prescribe medications, it is important to note that using any medication "off label" (in a manner not approved by the FDA) raises ethical and legal issues for prescribing medical doctors.

Monitoring Interventions

Due to the risk of harm to others, most community-based SO treatment programs have requirements for periodic monitoring of behaviors that indicate the client is/is not following his or her treatment protocol. This may occur through subsequent unscheduled polygraph tests, random urine screening, and/or periodic sexual interest/arousal assessments to further evaluate potential changes that affect assessment of risk. *Maintenance polygraph* tests evaluate the client's level of compliance with both treatment expectations and community supervision requirements. *Monitoring polygraph* tests examine whether the client has committed additional offenses, whether sexual or nonsexual. According to Elliott and Vollm's (2018) study, use of post-conviction polygraphs in treatment and management of sex offenders is useful in increasing relevant disclosures of sexual offending behavior, and the re-offense rates are positively impacted through use of clinical polygraphs during treatment for violent sexual offenders. In addition to periodic polygraph tests, *random urine screening* provides information regarding whether the client is engaging in use/abuse of legal or illegal substances, which may increase re-offense risk. Finally, *periodic PPG and AASI evaluation* can provide periodic feedback about changes in sexual interest or arousal following intervention.

Support

For any recovery process, establishing and maintaining healthy support systems is important for successful outcomes. Supportive environments encourage engagement in therapy, provide guardrails for life in the community, and help the client manage stressful or crisis-oriented events successfully without lapsing into old behaviors or thinking patterns. Most programs engage in *crisis intervention* services to deescalate potential suicidal or homicidal thoughts or intent, as needed.

Family counseling and training includes education on how to best support the offender's treatment, maintain boundaries, and healthy relationships, identify and work through past trauma, avoid enabling behaviors, and provide appropriate social and emotional support to the offender during and after treatment. In some cases, although rare, we may employ family reunification and restorative justice techniques. For juvenile sex offenders, most of whom have victims within their families, family education and counseling is crucial. According to materials from New Hope Waypoint Program in Charleston, South Carolina (2001), family therapy should do the following:

- Provide education to family members about attachment styles and problems as contributors to maladaptive compensations for individuals
- Address the complex issues regarding patterns of abuse, attachment and trust, boundaries, and interpersonal relationships
- Clarify how current stressors for the individual or family members are experienced as the return of past traumas, and how small disruptions in present relationships may be seen as repetitions of prior abandonment
- Help family members provide a sense of safety, validation, challenges to distorted perceptions, facilitation of expression, accountability, and supervision
- Address the complex issues of attachment and bonding as to how the differing styles of attachment within the family influence relationships (Grady & Reynolds, 2001)

Chaperones are another potential support for community-based sex offenders. Chaperones may include family members or other reliable people in the community. They must go through a structured training process; and not all chaperones are approved. According to Smith (n.d.), chaperones are the following:

- A measure of safety for the offender and a boundary from contact with children, especially during times an offender is learning relapse-prevention techniques
- An extra set of eyes for the therapist; the chaperones will alert therapist of changes or concerns regarding the offender's thinking, feeling, or behaving states
- An aid in establishing a lifetime of safety; the chaperones will be there even when therapy and probation ends
- An aid to the offender when they assist the offender in recognizing intensifying build-up

Training involves approximately 8 hours of didactic training in a group format, including learning the following:

- What is expected of a chaperone
- What is a child safety zone
- What is a thinking error
- Myths regarding sexual offenders
- Characteristics of sexual offenders
- Warning signs for victims
- The cycle of abuse
- Definitions of paraphilias, warning signs, power and control, and grooming behaviors

- What are high-risk situations
- Identification of high-risk environments
- Appropriate steps to deter victimization
- Who makes a "good victim"
- No-contact rules for offenders
- Prevention and safety
- Safety planning

Prior to attending training, potential chaperones should review the police report(s) about the sexual offense(s) the offender committed and discuss these with the offender. Additionally, all potential chaperones must pass their own background checks to be eligible for this volunteer position. It is recommended that offenders have multiple chaperones and each will go through training, although attending training is not a guarantee each will become an approved chaperone.

The final support component for many offenders is the *community supervision* and management they receive. There are three types of community supervision:

- **Pretrial supervision:** Supervision of an accused person on bond after being taken into custody and currently on conditional release pending trial
- **Parole supervision:** Monitoring parolee's compliance with conditions of parole and re-entry to society
- **Probation supervision:** Monitoring probationers' compliance with court-ordered conditions of community release and providing services to offenders to support legal behavior

The PO will ensure offenders comply with sex offender registration and community notification standards through periodic planned and unplanned meetings. If an offender must have random physiological screenings (e.g., urine screen), the PO reviews these. Competent SO treatment providers work collaboratively with POs to ensure the client's compliance in treatment and thereby attempt to minimize the likelihood of potential future offending. The overall goals for community supervision are protecting the community, providing opportunities for offenders to become law-abiding members of society, and providing accurate and relevant information to courts to improve decision making about the offender's risks, needs, and responsivity to intervention.

Special Interventions: Civil Commitment

Between 1–5% (around 5,000) of sex offenders previously incarcerated are civilly committed. *Civil commitment* requires the individual to commit a "qualifying offense" and a qualifying mental condition, and the mental disorder "creates a high probability that the person will commit new sexual offenses in the future due to a serious difficulty controlling his or her behavior" (ATSA, 2015). Generally, civilly committed sex offenders have paraphilia diagnoses. Additionally, this class of offenders poses a *significant* (high) risk to reoffend; how significant risk is determined depends on the jurisdiction. Civilly committed SOs are court mandated to treatment. Most of these programs are housed within a correctional or forensic facility, but in Texas it is community based. The first program of this kind began several decades ago in Washington State. Often run by private healthcare companies that specialize in sex offender civil commitment, mental health professionals providing services in these setting would work within the community or correctional/forensic facility but would be employed by the healthcare company.

Case Study: Jo Bob Part II

Jo Bob is a 34-year-old Caucasian male currently civilly committed in a sexually violent predator program. Jo Bob was first arrested on aggravated sexual assault when he was 13 years old for multiple offenses against his younger siblings, which they disclosed while in counseling following removal from their home. Jo Bob attended a residential juvenile sex offender treatment program for 2 years and was released just before his 16th birthday. At 17, he was accused of rape by a female classmate, but he was not charged with that crime. His girlfriend became pregnant when Jo Bob was 22. After they married, they had two more children. His children include a 6-year-old girl, a 12-year-old girl, and a 16-year-old boy. Jo Bob is a trained mechanic who has maintained steady employment throughout his adulthood.

Both juvenile crimes were sealed, so that they could not be accessed through a routine background check. Therefore, it was not discovered that he had demonstrated these previous behaviors when he applied to become a Boy Scout troop leader for his son when his son was 6 years old. Following 3 years as a Boy Scout troop leader, three boys disclosed to their parents that Jo Bob had shown them pornography and "touched them inappropriately" on a camping trip. During the investigation, it was revealed that his son and daughters all reported they had been forced to perform fellatio on Jo Bob multiple times over many years. This resulted in his arrest and incarceration at age 31 for 5 years, following a plea deal that allowed the victims a reprieve from testifying. After 2.5 years, Jo Bob was released from prison on "good behavior." However, within a few months he violated his parole when he did not register as a sex offender and was arrested outside of an elementary school with child pornography magazines in his car. Under the state's sexually violent predator law, the district attorney pursued civil commitment in the state's Sex Offender Civil Commitment Treatment program.

Case Application Questions

1. What are the potential laws governing Jo Bob's behavior?
2. Imagine you are a sex offender treatment provider. Describe how you would pursue a thorough assessment of Jo Bob. Specifically identify collateral sources of information you would want to review, what questions you might ask in a clinical interview and why, what formal assessment measures you would utilize and why, and how you would evaluate risk of dangerousness.
3. Utilizing the continuum of sexually inappropriate or sexually abusive behavior, discuss how you would have diagnosed his behavior when he was a juvenile and how you would have diagnosed him as an adult. Discuss your conceptualization of how

his diagnosis might have developed over time, applying theoretical models of sexual offending behavior.

4. Imagine you are Jo Bob's sex offender treatment provider. Describe the treatment approach you would use and why. Specifically discuss cognitive, behavioral, interpersonal, psychopharmacological, and monitoring interventions you would consider using as part of the treatment plan.

5. If you were working with Jo Bob following his initial arrests, before his latest arrest, what types of support would you recommend? Describe how community and/or family supports would be developed and utilized during community release.

SUMMARY

This chapter discusses treatment of juvenile and adult sex offenders. You learned about different types of assessments involved in evaluating sex offenders' clinical needs and level of risk for reoffending. This includes elements of psychosexual assessments, psychophysiological tests (e.g., AASI, PPG, and clinical polygraphs), and criminal justice–focused risk assessments. Then you learned about different ways clinicians and the criminal justice system classify offending behaviors. Additionally, you learned about common comorbid mental health disorders that often complicate treatment. Then, we discussed methods of intervention, including cognitive, behavioral, interpersonal, pharmacologic (hormonal and psychotropic), monitoring, and support. Elements of relapse prevention (RP), integrated throughout the intervention section, are identified as the primary goal for SO treatment.

CHAPTER 13 REFLECTIVE QUESTIONS

1. Describe the elements needed to conduct a thorough psychosexual assessment of a sex offender entering treatment.

2. Compare the different types of psychophysiological testing you might choose to do as part of a comprehensive psychosexual assessment. Discuss the why you would or would not choose to use each of the tests, depending on the type of information you want to gather and the client characteristics of the individual you are assessing.

3. Compare the different types of risk assessments discussed in the chapter.

4. Describe the developmental classification of sexually abusive behaviors and the descriptive or diagnostic categories used to classify different types of sexually abusive behavior.

5. Describe the FBI classification of sexual offending behaviors.

6. Compare the characteristics of different rapist types.

7. Describe the specialized treatment approaches used in sex offender treatment under both the CSOM and the ATSA approaches.

8. If you were designing a comprehensive intervention program for sex offenders being treated in the community, what treatment elements would you include and why?

RESOURCES

Safer Society Foundation: http://www.safersociety.org/foundation/about-us/

Association for the Treatment of Sexual Abusers: http://www.atsa.com/

Center for Sex Offender Management: http://www.csom.org/

The sex-offender test: https://www.theatlantic.com/politics/archive/2015/07/the-sex-offender-test/397850/

Ridgeway, J. (2013, September 23). How "civil commitment" enables indefinite detention of sex offenders. *The Guardian*. Retrieved from https://www.theguardian.com/commentisfree/2013/sep/26/civil-commitment-sex-offenders

Yung, C. R. (2013). Civil commitment of sex offenders. *American Medical Association Journal of Ethics, 15*(10), 873–877. Retrieved from https://journalofethics.ama-assn.org/sites/journalofethics.ama-assn.org/files/2018-05/pfor2-1310.pdf

References

Abel, G. G., Becker, J. V., Cunningham-Rathner, J., Mittleman, M., & Rouleau, J. L. (1988). Multiple paraphilic diagnoses among sex offenders. *Bulletin of American Academy of Psychiatry Law, 16*(2), 153–168. Retrieved from https://fairplayforwomen.com/wp-content/uploads/2017/11/153.full_.pdf

Abel, G. G., & Mittleman, M. S., & Becker, J. V. (1985). Sex offenders: Results of assessment and recommendations for treatment. In M. H. Ben-Aron, S. J., Hucker, & C. D. Webster (Eds.), *Clinical criminology: The assessment and treatment of criminal behavior* (pp. 191–205). Toronto, Ontario, Canada: M & M Graphics.

Acker, G. M. (1999). The impact of clients' mental illness on social workers' job satisfaction and burnout. *Health & Social Work, 24*(2) 112–119.

Adam Walsh Child Protection and Safety Act of 2006 (42 USC 16971).

Adams, D. (2003). Certified batterer intervention programs: History, philosophies, techniques, collaborations, innovations, and challenges. *Clinics in Family Practice, 5*(1), 1–23 Retrieved March 8, 2019 from: https://www.futureswithoutviolence.org/userfiles/file/Children_and_Families/Certified%20Batterer%20Intervention%20Programs.pdf.

Adams, S. A., & Riggs, S. A. (2008). An exploratory study of vicarious trauma among therapist trainees. *Training and Education in Professional Psychology, 2*(1), 26–34.

Aday, R. H., & Krabill, J. J. (2011). *Women aging in prison: A neglected population in the correctional system*. Boulder, CO: Lynne Rienner.

Afifi, T. O., Henriksen, C. A., Asmundson, G. J., & Sareen, J. (2012). Victimization and perpetration of intimate partner violence and substance use disorders in a nationally representative sample. *Journal of Nervous and Mental Disorders, 200*(8), 684–591.

Akyuz, G., Kugu, N., Sar, V., & Dogan, O. (2009). Trauma and dissociation among prisoners. *Nordic Journal of Psychiatry, 61*(3), 167–172.

Alaggia, R. (2005). Disclosing the trauma of child sexual abuse: A gender analysis. *Journal of Loss and Trauma, 10*(5), 453–470.

Alaggia, R., & Mishna, F. (2014). Self psychology and male child sexual abuse: Healing relational betrayal. *Clinical Social Work, 36*(3), 265–275. doi:10.1007/s10615-013-0453-2

Alarcon, G., Eschleman, K. J., & Bowling, N. A. (2009). Relationships between personality variables and burnout: A meta-analysis. doi: 10.1080/02678370903282600.

Alcoholics Anonymous. (2001). *Alcoholics Anonymous* (4th ed.). New York, NY: Author.

Allen, F. A. (1962). The rule of the American Law Institute's model penal code. *Marquette Law Review 45*(4), 494–505. Retrieved from http://scholarship.law.marquette.edu/cgi/viewcontent.cgi?article=2757&context=mulr

Altinatas, M., & Bilici, M. (2018). Evaluation of childhood trauma with respect to criminal behavior, dissociative experiences, adverse family experiences and psychiatric backgrounds among prison inmates. Comprehensive Psychiatry, 82, 100–107. doi:10.1016/j.comppsych.2017.12.006

American Bar Association. (ABA). (n.d.). *The history of juvenile justice: Part I*. Retrieved from https://www.americanbar.org/content/dam/aba/migrated/publiced/features/DYJpart1.authcheckdam.pdf

American Counseling Association. (2014). *ACA code of ethics*. Alexandria, VA: Author. Retrieved from https://www.counseling.org/Resources/aca-code-of-ethics.pdf

American Federation of State, County, and Municipal Employees. (2011). *Double jeopardy: Caseworkers at risk helping at-risk kids*. Washington, DC: Author. Retrieved from https://www.afscme.org/news/publications/workplace-health-and-safety/double-jeopardy-caseworkers-at-risk-helping-at-risk-kids

American Law Institute 1962 § 4.01 (1).

American Psychiatric Association (APA). (2013). Cautionary statement for forensic use of DSM-5. In *Diagnostic and statistical manual of mental disorders* (5th ed.) (p. 25). Washington, DC: Author.

American Society of Addiction Medicine's Practice Improvement and Performance Measurement Action Group & Standards and Outcomes of Care Expert Panel. (n.d.). The ASAM standards of care for the addiction specialist physician. Oak Brook, IL: American Osteopathic Academy of Addiction Medicine. Retrieved from https://www.asam.org/docs/default-source/publications/standards-of-care-final-design-document.pdf

Americans With Disabilities Act of 1990 (ADA; 1990). Pub. L. No. 101–335. 104 Sat. 328.

Anderson, C. A., Benjamin, A. J., Wood, P. K., & Bonacci, A. M. (2006). Development and testing of the Velicer Attitudes Towards Violence Scale: Evidence for a four-factor model. *Aggressive Behavior, 32*(2), 122–136.

Andrews, D. A., & Bonta, J. (Eds.). (2010). *The psychology of criminal conduct* (5th ed.). New Providence, NJ: Anderson.

Andrews, D. A., & Dowden, C. (2006). Risk principle of case classification in correctional treatment: A meta-analytic investigation. *International Journal of Offender Therapy and Comparative Criminology, 50*(1), 88–100.

Andrews, D. A., Zinger, I., Hoge, R. D., Bonta, J., Gendreau, P., & Cullen, F. T. (1990). Does correctional treatment work? A clinically-relevant and psychologically-informed meta-analysis. *Criminoogy, 28*(3), 369–404.

Ardino, V. (2012). Offending behavior: The role of trauma and PTSD. *European Journal of Psychotraumatology, 3*(10), doi 10.3402/ejpt.v3i0.18968

Ardito, R. B., & Rabellino, D. (2011). Therapeutic alliance and outcome of psychotherapy: Historical excursus, measurements, and prospectus for research. *Frontiers in Psychology, 270*(2), 1–26. doi:10.3389/fpsyg.2011.00270

Arnetz, B. B., Lucas, T., & Arnetz, J. E. (2011). Organizational climate, occupational stress, and employee mental health: Mediating effects of organizational efficiency. *Journal of Occupational and Organizational Medicine, 53*(1), 34–42.

Asmundson, G. J. G., Stapleton, J. A., & Taylor, S. (2004). Are avoidance and numbing distinct PTSD symptom clusters? *Journal of Traumatic Stress, 17*(6), 467–475.

Association for Treatment of Sexual Abusers (ATSA). (2010). *Internet-facilitated sexual offending*. Retrieved from http://www.atsa.com/internet-facilitated-sexual-offending#iii

Association for Treatment of Sexual Abusers (ATSA). (2012). *ATSA policy: Pharmacological interventions with adult male sexual offenders*. Retrieved from http://www.atsa.com/pdfs/PharmacologicalInterventionsAdultMaleSexualOffenders.pdf

Association for Treatment of Sexual Abusers (ATSA). (2015). Civil commitment of sexual offenders: Introduction and overview. Beaverton, OR: Author. Retrieved from http://www.atsa.com/sites/default/files/%5BCivil%20Commitment%5D%20Overview.pdf

Association for Treatment of Sexual Abusers (ATSA). (2016). *Sex offender treatment for adult males*. Beaverton, OR: Author. Retrieved from http://www.atsa.com/pdfs/Policy/Sex_Off_Tx_for_Adult_Males_ATSA_2016.pdf

Auehahn, K., & Leonard, E. D. (2000). Docile bodies? Chemical restraints and the female inmate. *Journal of Criminal Law and Criminology, 90*(2), 599–634.

Austin, J. B., & Dankwort, J. (1999). The impact of a batters' program on battered women. *Violence Against Women, 5*(1), 25–42. Retrieved from https://journals.sagepub.com/doi/pdf/10.1177/10778019922181130.

Bagshaw, D., & Chung, D. (2000). Gender politics in research: Male and female violence in intimate relationships. *Women Against Violence: An Australian Feminist Journal, 8*, 4–23.

Baker, N. (2017). *6 common family roles in an addicted household.* Retrieved from https://www.rehabs.com/6-common-family-roles-in-an-addicted-household/

Bakker, A. B., Albrecht, S. L., & Leiter, M. P. (2011). Key questions regarding work engagement. *European Journal of Work and Organizational Psychology, 20*(1), 4–28.

Bakker, A. B., & Demerouti, E. (2008). Towards a model of work engagement. *Career Development International, 13*(3), 209–223.

Bakker, A. B., & Demerouti, E. (2014). Job-demands-resources theory. In P. Y. Chen & C. L. Cooper (Eds), *Work and wellbeing: Wellbeing: A complete reference guide* (pp. 37–64). Hoboken, NJ: Wiley.

Bakker, A. B., Demerouiti, E., Taris, T. W., Schaufeli, W. B., & Scheurs, P. J. G. (2003). A multigroup analysis of the job-demands-resources model in four home care organizations. *International Journal of Stress Management, 10*(1), 16–38.

Bandura, A. (1977). *Social learning theory.*

Barbell, K., & Freundlich, M. (2001). *Foster Care Today.* Washington, D.C.: Casey Family Programs National Center for Resource Family Support.

Barrett, E. L., Indig, D., Sunjic, S., Sannibale, C. Sindicich, N., Rosenfeld, J., ... & Mills, K. (2015). Treating comorbid substance use and traumatic stress among male prisoners: A pilot study of the acceptability, feasibility, and preliminary efficacy of Seeking Safety. *International Journal of Forensic Mental Health, 14*(1), 45–55. doi:10.1080/14999013.2015.1014527

Bartol, C., & Bartol, A. (2009). *Juvenile delinquency and antisocial behavior: A developmental perspective* (3rd ed.). Upper Saddle River, NJ: Pearson.

Bauer, S. (2016, July/August). My four months as a private prison guard. *Mother Jones.* Retrieved from https://www.motherjones.com/politics/2016/06/cca-private-prisons-corrections-corporation-inmates-investigation-bauer/

Bearse, J. L., McMinn, M. R., Seegobin, W., & Free, K. (2013). Barriers to psychologists seeking mental health care. *Professional Psychology: Research and Practice, 44*(3), 150–157. doi:10.1037/a0031182

Beck, A. J., Berzofsky, M., Caspar, R., & Krebs, C. (2013). *Sexual victimization in prisons and jails reported by inmates, 2011–12.* Washington, DC: Bureau of Justice Statistics, Office of Justice Programs. U.S. Department of Justice.

Bedard, R., Metzger, L., & Williams, B. (2017). Ageing prisoners: An introduction to geriatric health-care challenges in correctional facilities. *Detention: Addressing the Human Cost, 98*(903), 917–939. doi:10.1017/S1816383117000364

Belcher, J. R., (1988). Are jails replacing the mental health system for the homeless mentally ill? *Community Mental Health Journal, 24*(3), 185–195.

Berg, M. T., & Loeber, R. (2011). Examining the neighborhood context of the violent offending victimization relationship: A prospective investigation. *Journal of Quantitative Criminology, 27*(4), 427–451. doi:10.1007/s10940-011-9129-7

Berg, M. T., Stewart, E. A., Schreck, C. J., & Simmons, R. L. (2012). The victim-offender overlap in context: Examining the role of neighborhood street culture. *Criminology, 50*(2), 359–390.

Berman, J. (2005). *Women offender transition and reentry: Gender responsive approaches to transitioning women offenders from prison to the community.* Washington, D.C.: National Institute of Corrections. Retrieved from: https://s3.amazonaws.com/static.nicic.gov/Library/021815.pdf.

Bernstein, D. P., Fink, L., Handelsman, L., & Foote, J. (1994). Initial reliability and validity of a new retrospective measure of child abuse and neglect. *American Journal of Psychiatry, 151*(8), 1132–1136.

Bernstein, E. M., & Putnam, F. W. (1986). Development, reliability, and validity of a dissociation scale. *Journal of Nervous and Mental Diseases, 174*(12), 727–734.

Beydoun, H. A., Beydoun, M. A., Kaufman, J. S., Lo, B., & Zonderman, A. B. (2012). Intimate partner violence against adult women and its association with major depressive disorder, depressive symptoms and postpartum depression: A systematic review and meta-analysis. *Social Science & Medicine, 75*(6), 959–975.

Bigby v. Dretke. (2005). 402 F. 3d 551.

Black, M. C. (2011). Intimate partner violence and adverse health consequences: Implications for clinicians. *American Journal of Lifestyle Medicine, 5*(5), 428–439.

Black, M. C., Basile, K. C., Breiding, M. J., Smith, S. G., Walters, M. L., Merrick, N.T., Chen, J., & Stevens, M. R. (2011). *The National Intimate Partner and Sexual Violence Survey* (NISS): 2010 summary report. Atlanta, GA: National Center for Injury Prevention and Control, Centers for Disease Control and Prevention. Retrieved from: https://www.cdc.gov/violenceprevention/pdf/nisvs_report2010-a.pdf

Blake, D. D., Weathers, F. W., Nagy, L. M., Kaloupeck, D. G., Gusman, F. D., Charney, D. S., & Keane, T. M. (1995). The development of a clinician-administered PTSD scale. *Journal of Traumatic Studies, 8*, 75–90. doi:10.1002/jts.2490080106

Bly, N. (2015). *Ten days in a mad house.* New York, NY: Nellie Bly.

Bonomi, A. E., Anderson, M. L., Reid, R. J., Rivara, F. P., Carrel, D., & Thompson R. S. (2009). Medical and psychological diagnoses in women with a history of intimate partner violence. *Archives of Internal Medicine, 169*(18), 1692–1697.

Bonomi, A. E., Thompson, R. S., Anderson, M., Reid, R. J., Carrell, D. Dimer, J. A., & Rivara, F. P. (2006). Intimate partner violence and women's physical, mental, and social functioning. *American Journal of Preventative Medicine, 30*(6), 458–466.

Booth, P. B., & Jernberg, A. M. (2010). *Theraplay: Helping parents and children build better relationships through attachment-based play.* (3rd ed.). San Francisco, CA: Jossey-Bass.

Borja, S. E., & Callahan, J. L. (2009). The trauma outcome process assessment model: A structural equation model examination of adjustment. *Journal of Child Sexual Abuse, 18*(5), 523–552.

Bostwick, J. M., Pabbati, C., & Geske, A., J. M. (2016). Suicide attempt as a risk factor for completed suicide: Even more lethal than we knew. *American Journal of Psychiatry, 173*(11), 1094–1100.

Braga, L. L., Mello, M. F., & Fiks, J. P. (2012). Transgenerational transmission of trauma and resilience: A qualitative study with Brazilian offspring of Holocaust survivors. *BMC Psychiatry, 12*(134), 1–11.

Bragg, H. L. (2003). *Child protection in families experiencing domestic violence.* Washington, DC: U.S. Department of Health and Human Services Administration for Children and Families, Children's Bureau, Office on Child Abuse and Neglect. Retrieved from https://www.childwelfare.gov/pubpdfs/domesticviolence.pdf

Braggs v. Dunn. (2017). 257 F. Supp.3d 1171. Retrieved from https://www.leagle.com/decision/infdco20170705e28.

Braun, B. G. (1988). The BASK model of dissociation. *Dissociation, 1*(1), 4–23. Retrieved from https://core.ac.uk/download/pdf/36679914.pdf

Breed v. Jones. 421 U. S. 519, 95 S.Ct. 1979, 1975.

Breiding, M. J., Black, M. C., & Ryan, G. W. (2008). Chronic disease and health risk behaviors associated with intimate partner violence: 18 U.S. states/territories, 2005. *Annals of Epidemiology, 18*(7), 538–544.

Briere, J. (1992). Medical symptoms, health risk, and child sexual abuse. *Mayo clinic Proceedings, 67*(6), 603–604.

Briere, J. (1996). *Trauma symptom inventory*. Odessa, FL: Psychological Assessment Resources.

Briere, J. N., & Scott, C. (2015). *Principles of trauma therapy: A guide to symptoms, evaluation, and treatment* (2nd ed.). Thousand Oaks, CA: SAGE.

Briere, J., & Runtz, M. (1987). Post sexual abuse trauma: Data and implications for clinical practice. *Journal of Interpersonal Violence, 2*(4), 367–379.

Briere, J., & Scott, C. (2006). *Principles of trauma therapy: A guide to symptoms, evaluation, and treatment*. Thousand Oaks, CA: SAGE.

Bronson, J., & Berzofsky, M. (2017). Indicators of mental health problems reported by prisoners and jail inmates, 2011–12. *Bureau of Justice Statistics Report*. Retrieved from https://www.bjs.gov/content/pub/pdf/imhprpji1112.pdf

Brown, A. (2011). Federal Children's Bureau: A brief history. *Social Welfare History Project*. Retrieved from https://socialwelfare.library.vcu.edu/programs/child-welfarechild-labor/childrens-bureau-a-brief-history-resources/

Brumby, K., Baker, K., Gilligan, L. (2018). *Advancing a Victim-Centered Approach to Supervising Sex Offenders: A Toolkit for Practitioners*. Washington D.C.: Center for Sex Offender Management. Office of Justice Programs. U. S. Department of Justice. Retrieved from https://csom.org/pubs/Probation_toolkit_web.pdf.

Buchanan, A., Binder, R., Norko, M., & Swartz, M. (2012). Resource document on psychiatric violence risk assessment. *American Journal of Psychiatry, 169*(3), 1–10.

Buller, A. M., Devries, K. M., Howard, L. M., & Bacchus, L. J. (2014). Associations between intimate partner violence and health among men who have sex with men: A systemic review and meta-analysis. *PLoS Medicine, 11*(3), e1001609.

Bumby, K., Baker, K., & Gilligan, L., 2018). *Advancing a victim-centered approach to supervising sex offenders: A toolkit for practitioners*. Washington, DC: Department of Justice. Council on Sex Offender Management.

Bundock, L., Howard, L. M., Trevillion, K., Malcolm, E., Feder, G., & Oram, S. (2013). Prevalence and risk of experiences of intimate partner violence among people with eating disorders: A systematic review. *Journal of Psychiatric Research, 47*(9), 1134–1142.

Bureau of Justice Statistics. (2017). *Prison Rape Elimination Act of 2003 Data Collection Activities, 2017*. Retrieved from https://www.bjs.gov/content/pub/pdf/pdca17.pdf

Burnette, M. L., Ilgen, M., Frayne, S. M., Lucas, E., Mayo, J., & Weitlauf, J. C. (2008). Violence perpetration and childhood abuse among men and women in substance abuse treatment. *Journal of Substance Abuse Treatment, 35*(2), 217–222.

Burton, J. E., Rasmussen, L. A., Bradshaw, J., Christopherson, B. J., & Huke, S. C. (1998). *Treating children with sexually abusive behavior problems: Guidelines for child and parent intervention*. Binghamton, NY: Haworth Maltreatment and Trauma Press.

Callahan, J. L., Borja, S. E., Herbert, G. L., Maxwell, K., & Ruggero, C. J. (2013). Test of the trauma outcome process assessment model: One model of individual and environmental factors to explain adjustment. *Traumatology, 19*(4), 368–279.

Campbell, J. C. (2007). *Danger assessment, revised*. Washington, DC: Johns Hopkins University, School of Nursing. Retrieved from https://www.dangerassessment.org/uploads/SameSexDangerAssessment.rev2007.pdf

Carlson, E. B. (1997). *Trauma assessments: A clinician's guide*. New York, NY: Guilford.

Carmichael, S., & Hamilton, C. V. (1967). *Black power: Politics of liberation*. New York, NY: Vintage.

Carnes, P. (1989). *Contrary to love: Helping the sexual addict*. Minneapolis, MN: Comp Care Publishers.

Carson, A. (2018). Prisoners in 2016. *U.S. Department of Justice, Office of Justice Programs, and Bureau of Justice Statistics.* Retrieved from https://www.bjs.gov/content/pub/pdf/p16.pdf

Carson, E. A. (2016). Prisoners in 2014. Washington, DC: Bureau of Justice Statistics, U.S. Department of Justice.

Caruth, C. (Ed.). (2014). *Lost in transmission: Studies of trauma across generations.* London, UK: Karnac.

Casey, P. M., Warren, R. K., & Elek, J. K. (2011). *Using offender risk and needs assessment information at sentencing: Guidance for courts form a national working group.* Williamsburg, VA: National Center for State Courts.

Celebrate Recovery (n.d). *Celebrate Recovery's eight recovery principles.* Retrieved from https://www.celebraterecovery.com/resources/cr-tools/8principles

Center for Addiction and Mental Health (CAMH). (2009). *Screening for concurrent substance use and mental health problems in youth.* Retrieved from https://www.porticonetwork.ca/documents/489955/494758/Screening+for+Concurrent+Substance+Use+and+Mental+Health+Problems+in+Youth+PDF/aa31224c-ff0e-41ff-aeb8-900075fd855c

Center for Genetics Education (2012). *Fact sheet 58: Mental illness and inherited predisposition—schizophrenia and bipolar disorder.* Retrieved from http://www.genetics.edu.au/genetics/Genetic-conditions-support-groups/FS58KBS.pdf

Center for Justice & Reconciliation. (2018). *Reforming justice for 20 years: What is restorative justice?* Retrieved from http://restorativejustice.org/#sthash.9nqNf47J.dpbs

Center for Sex Offender Management (COSM) (n.d.). Retrieved from http://www.csom.org/

Center for Substance Abuse Treatment (2000). Substance abuse treatment for persons with child abuse and neglect issues. *Treatment Improvement protocol Series, 36.* Rockville, MD: U.S. Department of Health and Human Services.

Center for Substance Abuse Treatment. (2003). *The child welfare-substance abuse connection: A compendium of training curricula and resources.* Rockville, MD: U.S. Department of Health and Human Services.

Center for Substance Abuse Treatment. (2009). Incorporating alcohol pharmacotherapies into medical practice. *Treatment Improvement Protocol (TIP) Series, 49.* Rockville, MD: U.S. Department of Health and Human Services.

Center on the Developing Child. (2005). *Excessive stress disrupts the architecture of the developing brain.* Retrieved from https://developingchild.harvard.edu/wp-content/uploads/2005/05/Stress_Disrupts_Architecture_Developing_Brain-1.pdf

Centers for Disease Control and Prevention. (2003). Costs of intimate partner violence against women in the United States. Atlanta, GA: CDC, National Center for Injury Prevention and Control. Retrieved from https://www.cdc.gov/violenceprevention/pdf/IPVBook-a.pdf

Centers for Disease Control (2009). *Parent training programs: Insight for practitioners.* Division of Violence Prevention. Atlanta, GA: CDC, National Center for Injury Prevention and Control. Retrieved https://www.cdc.gov/violenceprevention/pdf/parent_training_brief-a.pdf

Centers for Disease Control. (2014a). *Understanding child maltreatment: Fact sheet.* Retrieved https://www.cdc.gov/violenceprevention/pdf/understanding-cm-factsheet.pdf

Centers for Disease Control. (2014b). *Essentials for childhood: Steps to create safe, stable, nurturing relationships and environments.* Retrieved from https://www.cdc.gov/violenceprevention/pdf/essentials_for_childhood_framework.pdf

Centers for Disease Control (CDC) (2015). *The Adverse Childhood Experiences (ACE) study.* Atlanta, GA: Author. Retrieved from https://web.archive.org/web/20151227092712/http://www.cdc.gov/violenceprevention/acestudy/index.html

Centers for Disease Control and Prevention. (2017). *Preventing intimate partner violence.* Retrieved from https://www.cdc.gov/violenceprevention/pdf/ipv-factsheet.pdf

Cerulli, C., Talbot, N. L., Tang, W., & Chaudron, L. H. (2011). Co-occurring intimate partner violence and mental health diagnoses in perinatal women. *Journal of Women's Health, 20*(12), 1797–1803.

Chaffin, M. Berliner, L., Block, R., Johnson, T. C., Friedrich, W. N., Louis, D. G., et al. (2006). *Report of the Task Force on Children with Sexual Behavior Problems.* Beaverton, OR: Association for the Treatment of Sexual Abusers.

Chavez-Garcia, M. (2012). *States of Delinquency: Race and Science in the making of California's Juvenile Justice System.* Los Angeles: University of California Press.

Chen, L. P., Hassan, M. M., Paras, M. L., Colbenson, K. M., Kattler, A. M., Goranson, E. M., … & Zirakzadeh, A. (2010). Sexual abuse and lifetime diagnosis of psychiatric disorders: Systematic review and meta-analysis. *Mayo Clinical Procedure, 85*(7), 618–629. Retrieved from https://www.ncbi.nlm.nih.gov/pmc/articles/PMC2894717/pdf/mayoclinproc_85_7_003.pdf

Chen, L. P., Murad, H. M., Para, M. L., Cobenson, K. M., Sattler, A. L., Goranson, E. N., & et al. (2010). Sexual abuse and lifetime diagnoses of psychiatric disorder: Systemic review and metaanalysis. *Mayo Clinic Proceedings, 85*(7), 618–629.

Chermack, S. T., Murray, R. L., Walton, M. A., Booth, B. A., Wryobeck, J., & Blow, F. C. (2008). Partner aggression among men and women in substance use disorder treatment: Correlates of psychological and physical aggression and injury. *Drug Alcohol Dependence, 98*(0), 35–44.

Cherniss, C., Egnatios, E., & Wacker, S. (1976). Job stress and career development in new public professionals. *Professional Psychology, 7*(4), 428–436.

Child Abuse Prevention and Treatment Reauthorization Act of 2010. Pub. L. No. 111–320.

Child Welfare Information Gateway. (n.d.a.). *Administration for children and families.* Retrieved from https://www.childwelfare.gov/

Child Welfare Information Gateway. (n.d.b.). *State child abuse and neglect reporting numbers.* Retrieved from https://www.childwelfare.gov/organizations/?CWIGFunctionsaction=rols:main.dspList&rolType=Custom&RS_ID=%205

Child Welfare Information Gateway. (2016). *Racial disproportionality and disparity in child welfare.* Washington, DC: U.S. Department of Health and Human Services, Children's Bureau. Retrieved from https://www.childwelfare.gov/pubPDFs/racial_disproportionality.pdf

Children's Bureau. (n.d.). *Making and screening reports of child abuse and neglect.* Retrieved https://www.childwelfare.gov/pubPDFs/repproc.pdf

Choi, G. (2011). Organizational impacts on the secondary traumatic stress of social workers assisting family violence or sexual assault survivors. *Administration in Social Work, 35*(3), 225–242.

Cieslak, R., Korczynska, J., Strelau, J., & Kaczmarek, M. (2008). Burnout predictors among prison officers: The moderating effect of temperamental endurance. *Personality and Individual Differences, 45*(7), 666–672.

Clus, P., & Bodea, A. (2011). *The effectiveness of batterer intervention programs: A literature review and recommendations for next steps.* Pittsburgh, PA: University of Pittsburgh.

Coalition for Juvenile Justice (n.d.). *Juvenile Justice and Delinquency Prevention Act.* Retrieved from http://www.juvjustice.org/federal-policy/juvenile-justice-and-delinquency-prevention-act

Cocozza, J., & Skowyra, K. (2000). Youth with mental health disorders: Issues and emerging responses. *Office of Juvenile Justice and Delinquency Prevention Journal, 7*(1), 3–13.

Cohen, L. E., & Felson, M. (1979). Social change and crime rate trends: A routine activity approach. *American Sociological Review, 44*, 588–608. Doi. 10.2307/2094589.

Colorado Department of Human Services. (2012). *Domestic violence practice guide for child protection services*. Retrieved August 7, 2018 from http://longmontdomesticviolence.org/wp/wp-content/uploads/2013/03/DV-CPS-Practice-Guide-Draft-12.17.12.pdf.

Comanor, W. S., & Phillips, L. (2002). The impact of income and family structure on delinquency. *Journal of Applied Economics, 5*(2), 209–232.

Community Mental Health Centers Construction Act of 1963 (Pub. L. 88–164).

Compalbert, N., Pennequin, V., Ferrand, C., Vandevyvere, M. A., & Geffray, B. (2016). Mental disorders and cognitive impairment in aging offenders. *Journal of Forensic Psychiatry & Psychology, 37*(6), 853–866. doi:10.1080/14789949.2016.1244277

Connery, H. S. (2015). Medication-assisted treatment of opioid use disorder: Review of the evidence and future directions. *Harvard Review of Psychiatry, 23*(2), 63–75. doi:10.1097/HRP.0000000000000075

Cook, D. J., & Michie, C. (2010). Limitations of diagnostic precision and predictive utility in the individual case: A challenge for forensic practice. *Law and Human Behavior, 34*(4), 259–274.

Cooke, B. J., & Farrington, D. P. (2016). The effectiveness of dog-training programs in prison: A systematic review and meta-analysis of the literature. *Prison Journal, 96*(6), 854–876. doi:10.1177/0032885516671919

Coolidge, F. L., & Anderson, L. W. (2002). Personality profiles of women in multiple abusive relationships. *Journal of Family Violence, 17*(2), 117–131.

Cooper, A., & Smith, E. L. (2011). *Homicide trends in the United States, 1980–2008*. Washington, DC: Bureau of Justice Statistics.

Coric, V., Feurstein, S., Fortunati, F., Southwick, S., Temporini, H., & Morgan, C. A. (2005). Assessing sex offenders. *Psychiatry, 2*(11), 26–29.

Cothern, L. (2000). *Juveniles and the death penalty*. Washington, DC: Coordinating Council on Juvenile Justice and Delinquency Prevention.

Coulton, C., Crampton, D., Cho, Y., & Park, J. (2016). Multiple system involved youth: A descriptive analysis of pathways traversed between juvenile justices and child welfare for youth in Cuyahoga County. *Center on Urban Poverty and Community Development*.

Covington, S. (2007). Working with substance abusing mothers: A trauma-informed, gender-responsive approach. *The Source, 16*(1), 1–11.

Cox, R. J. A. (2015, January 16). Where do we go from here? Mass incarceration and the struggle for civil rights. *Economic Policy Institute*. Retrieved from https://www.epi.org/publication/where-do-we-go-from-here-mass-incarceration-and-the-struggle-for-civil-rights/

Crime Victims Research and Treatment Center (CVRTC). (1992). *Rape in America: A report to the nation*. Charleston, SC: Medical University of South Carolina.

Cullen, F. T., & Jonson, C. L. (2011). Rehabilitation and treatment programs. In D. A. Andrews & J. Bonta (Eds.), *The psychology of criminal conduct* (5th ed.). New Providence, NJ: Anderson.

Currie, S. R., Patten, S. B., Williams, J. V., Wang, J., Beck, C. A., El-Guebaly, N., & Maxwell, C. (2005). Comorbidity of major depression with substance use disorders. *Canadian Journal of Psychiatry, 50*(10), 660–666.

Curtin, F., Niveau, G. (1998). Psychosocial profile of Swiss sexual offenders. *Journal of Forensic Sciences, 43*(4), 755–759. doi: 10.1520/JFS14302J.

Cushway, D., & Tyler, P. (1996). Stress in clinical psychologists. *International Journal of Social Psychiatry, 42*(2), 141–149.

Cutajar, M. J., Mullen, P., Ogloff, J., Thomas, S. D., Wells, D. L., & Spataro, J. (2010). Psychopathology in a large cohort of sexually abused children followed up to 43 years. *Child Abuse and Neglect, 34*(11), 813–822.

Cutuli, J. J., George, R. M., Coulton, C., Schretzman, M., Crampton, D., Charvat, B. J., ... & Lee, E. L. (2016). From foster care to juvenile justice: Exploring characteristics of youth in three cities. *Children and youth Services Review, 67*(C), 84–94.

Danielson, K. K., Moffit, T. E., Caspi, A., & Silva, P. A. (1998). Comorbidity between abuse of an adult and DSM III-R mental disorder: Evidence from epidemiological study. *American Journal of Psychiatry, 155*(1), 131–133.

Davidson, J. R. T., & Foa, E. B. (Eds.). (1993) *Posttraumatic stress disorder: DSM-IV and beyond*. American Psychiatric Press: Washington, DC.

DeClue, G., & Zavodny, D. L. (2014). Forensic use of the static-99R: Part 4 risk communication. *Journal of Threat Assessment and Management, 1*(3), 145–161. doi:10.1037/tam0000017

De Jonge, J., & Kompier, M. A. J. (1997). A critical examination of the demand-control-support model from a work psychological perspective. *International Journal of Stress Management, 4*(4), 235–258.

Dekel, R., & Goldblatt, H. (2008). Is there intergenerational transmission of trauma? The case of combat veterans' children. *American Journal of Orthopsychiatry, 78*(3), 281–289. doi:10.1037/a0013955.

Dell, C. A., & Poole, N. (2016). Taking a PAWS to reflect on how the work of a therapy dog supports a trauma-informed approach to prisoner health. *Journal of Forensic Nursing, 11*(3), 167–173.

Dembo, R. (1990). *Prototype screening/triage form*. Retrieved from http://www.emcdda.europa.eu/attachements.cfm/att_4462_EN_itpstf[1].html

DePanfilis, D. (2006). *Child neglect: A guide for prevention, assessment, and intervention*. Child Abuse and Neglect User Manual Series. Retrieved from https://www.childwelfare.gov/pubPDFs/neglect.pdf

Department of Defense (DOD). (2014). *Department of Defense annual report on sexual assault in the military*. Washington, DC: Author.

Department of Justice (DOJ). (2014). Crime in the United States. *Criminal Justice Information Services Division*. Retrieved from https://ucr.fbi.gov/crime-in-the-u.s/2014/crime-in-the-u.s.-2014/tables/table-43

Derogatis, L. R. (1983). *Symptom Checklist 90-Revised administration, scoring, and procedures manual II for the revised version* (2nd ed.). Towson, MD: Clinical Psychometrics Research.

Detert, J. R., Trevino, L. K., & Sweitzer, V. L. (2008). Moral disengagement in ethical decision making: A study of antecedents and outcomes. *Journal of Applied Psychology, 93*(2), 374–391.

Deutsch, C. J. (1985). Self-reported sources of stress among psychotherapists. *Professional Psychology: Research and Practice, 15*(6), 833–845. doi:10.1037//0735-7028.15.6.833

Diclemente, C., Prochaska, J. O., & Gibertini, M. (1985). Self-efficacy and the stages of self-change of smoking. *Cognitive Therapy and Research, 9*(2), 181–200. Doi. 10.1007/BF01204849.

Dietz, P. M., Spitz, A. M., Anda, R. F., Williamson, D. F., McMahon, P. M., Santelli, J. S., ... & Kendrick, J. S. (1999). Unintended pregnancy among adult women exposed to abuse or household dysfunction during their childhood. *Journal of the American Medical Association, 282*(14), 1359–1364.

Dix, D. (1971). *On behalf of the insane poor*. New York, NY: Armo Press.

Dolan, K., & Carr, J. L. (n.d.). *The poor get prison: The alarming spread of the criminalization of poverty*. Washington, DC: Institute for Policy Studies. Retrieved from https://www.ips-dc.org/wp-content/uploads/2015/03/IPS-The-Poor-Get-Prison-Final.pdf

Dollard, M., & Winefield, A. (1998). A test of the demand-control/support model of work stress in correctional officers. *Journal of Occupational Health Psychology, 3*(3), 243–264

Dong, M., Anda, R. F., Dube, S. R., Giles, W. H., & Felitti, V. J. (2003). The relationship of exposure to childhood sexual abuse to other forms of abuse, neglect and household dysfunction during childhood. *Child Abuse and Neglect, 27*(6), 625–639.

Douaihy, A. B., Kelly, T. M., & Sullivan, C. (2013). Medications for substance use disorders. *Social Work in Public Health, 28*(3-4), 264-278. doi:10.1080/19371918.2013.759031

Dougher, M. J. (1996). Behavioral techniques to alter sexual arousal. In B. K. Schwartz & H. R. Cellini (Eds.), *The sex offender: Corrections, treatment and legal practice.* Kingston, NJ: Civic Research Institute. Sage.

Doyle, S. R., & Donovan, D. M. (2009). A validation study of the alcohol dependence scale. *Journal of Studies of Alcohol and Drugs, 70*(5), 689-699.

Dubay, L., & Kenney, G. (2009). The impact of CHIP opn children's insurance coverage: An analysis using the National Survey of America's Families. *Health Services Research, 44*(6), 2040-2059. Doi. 10.111/j.1475-6733.2009.01040.x.

Dube, S. R., Anda, R. F., Felitti, V. J., Chapman, D. P., Williamson, D. F., & Giles, W. H. (2001). Childhood abuse, household dysfunction, and the risk of attempted suicide throughout the life span: Findings from the Adverse Childhood Experiences Study. *Journal of the American Medical Association, 286*(24), 3089-3096.

Dube S. R., Anda R. F., Whitfield C. L., Brown D. W., Felitti V. J., Dong M., & Giles, W. (2005). Long-term consequences of childhood sexual abuse by gender of victim. *American Journal of Preventative Medicine, 27*(5), 430-438.

Ducharme, L. J., Mello, H. L., Roman, P. M., Knudsen, H. K., Johnson, A. J. (2007). Service delivery in substance abuse treatment: Reexamining "comprehensive" care. *Journal of Behavioral Health Services and Research, 34*(2), 121-136.

Duhram v. United States, 214 F.2d 862

Durborow, N., Lizdas, K. C., O'Flaherty, A., & Marjavi, A. (2010). *Compendium of state statutes and policies on domestic violence and health care.* Washington, DC: Family Violence Prevention Fund, U. S. Department of Health and Human Services.

Edward, J., Lovins, L., & Lovins, B. (2010). The role of offender risk assessment: A policy maker guide. *Victims and Offenders, 5*(3), 203-219. doi:10.1080/15564886.2010.485900

Eghigian, G., & Hornstein, G. (Eds.) (2010). *From madness to mental health: Psychiatric treatment in Western civilization.* Piscataway, NJ: Rutgers University Press.

El-Ghoroury, N., Galper, D. I., Sawaqdeh, A., & Bufka, L. F. (2012). Stress, coping, and barriers to wellness among psychology graduate students. *Training and Education in Professional Psychology, 6*(2), 122-134. doi:10.1037/a0028768

Elliot, D. (2007). Gault case changed juvenile law. *National Public Radio.* Retrieved from https://www.npr.org/templates/story/story.php?storyId=10279166

Elliott, D. M. (1992). *Traumatic events survey: Unpublished test.* Los Angeles: CA: University of California, Los Angeles.

Elliott, D. M., & Briere, J. (1992). Sexual abuse trauma among professional women: Validating the trauma symptom checklist-40 (TSC-40). *Child Abuse & Neglect, 16,* 391-398.

Elliott, E., & Vollm, B. (2018). The utility of post-conviction polygraph testing among sexual offenders. *Sexual Abuse, 30*(4). 367-392. doi:10.1177/1079063216667922

Elliott, I. A., Beech, A. R., Mandeville-Norden, R., & Hayes, E. (2009). Psychological profiles of Internet sexual offenders: Comparisons with contact sexual offenders. *Sexual Abuse: A Journal of Research and Treatment, 21*(1), 76-92.

Ennis, C. & Douglas, J. (2007). *The safe approach: Controlling risk for workers in the helping professions.* Enumclaw, WA: Issues Press.

Estelle v. Gamble. (1976). 429 U. S. 97. No. 75-929.

Ewing, J. A. (1984). Detecting alcoholism: The CAGE questionnaire. *Journal of the American Medical Association, 252*(14), 1905-1907.

Family Violence Prevention and Services Act (FVPSA) of 1984 (P.L. 98–457).

Farber, B. A. (1991). *Crisis in education: Stress and burnout in the American teacher.* San Francisco, CA: Jossey Bass Publishers.

Farrell, H. M. (2011). Batterers: A review of violence and risk assessment tools. *Journal of the American Academy of Psychiatric Law, 39*(4), 562–564.

Farrington, D. P., (1995, 2003, 2005). Developmental criminology and risk-focused prevention. In M. Maguire, R. Morgan, & R. Reiner (Eds.), *Oxford handbook of criminology* (3rd ed.) (pp. 657–701). Oxford, UK: Oxford University Press.

Farrington, D. P., Piquero, A., & Jennings, W. G. (2013). *Offending from childhood to late middle age: Recent results from the Cambridge study in delinquent development.* New York, NY: Springer.

Fazel, P. S., Hayes, A. J., Bartellas, K., Clerici, M., & Trestmant, R. (2016). The mental health of prisoners: A review of prevalence, adverse outcomes and interventions. *Lancet Psychiatry, 3*(9), 971–881. doi:10.1016/S2215-0366(16)30142-0

Federal Bureau of Investigation (2017). *2017 hate crime statistics.* Retrieved from https://ucr.fbi.gov/hate-crime/2017

Fedovskiy, K., Higgins, S., & Paranjape, A. (2008). Intimate partner violence: How does it impact major depressive disorder and post-traumatic stress disorder among immigrant Latinas? *Journal of Immigrant and Minority Health, 10*(1), 45–51.

Fernandez, P. A. (2011). Sexual assault: An overview and implications for counseling support. *Australasian Medical Journal, 4*(11), 596–602.

Figley, C. R. (1995). Compassion fatigue as secondary traumatic stress disorder: An overview. In C. R. Figley (Ed.), *Compassion fatigue: Coping with secondary traumatic stress disorder in those who treat the traumatized* (pp. 1–20). New York, NY: Bruner/Mazel.

Fink, L. A., Bernstein, D., Handelsman, L., Foote, J., & Lovejoy, M. (1995). Initial reliability and validity of the Child Trauma Interview: A new multidimensional measure of childhood interpersonal trauma. *American Journal of Psychiatry, 152*(9), 1329–1335.

Finkelhor, D., & Jones, L. M. (2004). Explanations for the decline in child sexual abuse cases. *Juvenile Justice Bulletin.* Washington, DC: U.S. Department of Justice.

Finkelhor, D., Ormrod, R., Turner, H., & Hamby, S. (2005). The victimization or children and youth: A comprehensive, national survey. *Child Maltreatment, 10*(5), 5–25. doi:10.1177/1077559504271287

Focht, J. (n.d.). The cycle of domestic violence. *National Center for Health Research.* Retrieved from http://www.center4research.org/cycle-domestic-violence/

Follette, V. M., Polunsy, M. A., Bechtle, A. E., & Naugle, A. E. (1996). Cumulative trauma: The impact of child and sexual abuse, adult sexual assault, and spouse abuse. *Journal of Traumatic Stress, 9*(1), 25–35. doi:10.1002/jts.2490090104

Forester-Miller, H., & Davis, T. E. (n.d.). Practitioner's guide to ethical decision making. Center for Counseling Practice, Policy, and Research. Retrieved from https://www.counseling.org/docs/default-source/ethics/practioner-39-s-guide-to-ethical-decision-making.pdf?sfvrsn=f9e5482c_10

Fortson, B. L., Klevens, J., Merrick, M. T., Gilbert, L. K., & Alexander, S. P. (2016). *Preventing child abuse and neglect: A technical package for policy, norm, and programmatic activities.* Atlanta, GA: Centers for Disease Control and Prevention. Retrieved from https://www.cdc.gov/violenceprevention/pdf/can-prevention-technical-package.pdf

Fowler, D. (2007). The extent of substance use problems among women partner abuse survivors residing in a domestic violence shelter. *Family and Community Health, 30*(1), 106–108.

Fowler, J. W. (1991). Stages in faith consciousness. *New Directions for Child and Adolescent Development, 1991*(52), 27–45.

Freshman, B. (n.d.). Cultural competency: Best intentions are not good enough. *Diversity and Equality in Health and Care*. Retrieved from http://diversityhealthcare.imedpub.com/cultural-competency--best-in-tentions-are-not-goodenough.php?aid=9096

Fry, J. (2012). Suicide awareness and prevention training in a high security setting. *Mental Health Practice, 15*(6), 25–31.

Gade, C. B. N. (2013). Restorative justice and the South African truth and reconciliation process. *South African Journal of Philosophy, 32*(1), 10–35. Retrieved from http://pure.au.dk/portal/files/53264449/Restorative_Justice_and_the_South_African_Truth_and_Reconciliation_Process.pdf

Garcia-Moreno, C., Guedes, A., & Knerr, W. (2012). Understanding and addressing violence against women. *World Health Organization*. Retrieved from http://apps.who.int/iris/bitstream/handle/10665/77432/who_rhr_12.36_eng.pdf;jsessionid=4948633C7387D3D217C85FEB62FF3DAE?sequence=1

Garfinkel, L. (2010). Improving family involvement for juvenile offenders with emotional/behavioral disorders and related disabilities. *Behavioral Disorders, 36*(1), 52–60. Retrieved from http://www.pacer.org/jj/pdf/bedi-36-01-52.pdf

Garner, B. R., Knight, K., & Simpson, D. (2007). Burnout among corrections-based drug treatment staff: Impact of individual and organizational factors. *International Journal of Offender Therapy and Comparative Criminology, 51*(5), 510–522.

Gates, M. L., Staples-Horne, M., Walker, V., & Turney, A. (2017). Substance use disorders and related health problems in an aging offender population. *Journal of Health Care for the Poor and Underserved, 28*(2), 132–154. Retrieved from https://muse.jhu.edu/article/656967

Gerberding, J. L., Binder, S., Hammond, W. R., & Arias, I. (2003). *Costs of intimate partner violence against women in the United States*. Atlanta, GA: National Center for Injury Prevention, Centers for Disease Control and Prevention.

Gil, E. (2006). *Helping abused and traumatized children: Integration directive and nondirective approaches*. New York, NY: Guilford Press.

Gilligan, C. (1982). *In a different voice*. Cambridge, MA: Harvard University Press.

Gilligan, C. (1987). Gender difference and morality: The empirical base. In E. Kittay & D. Meyers (Eds.), *Women and moral theory* (pp. 19–36). New York, NY: Rowman & Littlefield.

Glassman, L. H., Weierich, M. R., Hooley, J. M., & Nock, M. K. (2007). Child maltreatment, non-suicidal self-injury, and the mediating role of self-criticism. *Behaviour Research and Therapy, 45*(10), 2483–2490.

Glaze, L. E., & Maruschak, L. M. (2010). *Parents in prison and their minor children*. Washington, DC: U.S. Department of Justice.

Goldberg, N., & Meyer, I. (2013). Sexual orientation disparities in history of intimate partner violence: Results from the California Health Interview Survey. *Journal of Interpersonal Violence, 28*(5), 1109–1118.

Gondolf, E. W. (1997a). Patterns of re-assault in batterer programs. *Violence and Victims, 12*(4), 373–387.

Gondolf, E. W. (1997b). Batterer programs: What we know and need to know. *Journal of Interpersonal Violence, 12*(1), 83–98.

Gottfredson, S. D., & Moriarity, L. J. (2006). Statistical risk assessment: Old problems and new applications. *Crime and Delinquency, 52*(1), 178–200. doi:10.1177/0011128705281748

Grady, J., & Reynolds, S. (2001, August 20). *A developmental/holistic approach to the etiology and treatment of arousal in sexually aggressive adolescents*. Presentation for the second annual New Hope Treatment Centers Conference. Charleston, South Carolina.

Graham, J., & Bowling, B. (1995). *Young people and crime, home office research study No. 145*. London, UK: Home Office.

Grau, J, Fagan, J., & Wexler, S. (1984). Restraining orders for battered women: Issues of access and efficacy. *Women and Politics, 4*(3), 13–28.

Graziani, C., Ben-Moshe, L., & Cole, H. E. (2017). Beyond alternatives to incarceration and confinement. *Grassroots Leadership*. Retrieved from https://grassrootsleadership.org/sites/default/files/reports/beyond_alternatives_to_incarceration_and_confinement.pdf

Greenberg, J. (2006). Losing sleep over organizational injustice: Attenuating insomniac reactions to underpayment inequity with supervisory training in interactional justice. *Journal of Applied Psychology, 91*(1), 58–69.

Greenwald, R. (2017). What happens if you're too poor to pay bail? *The Nation*. Retrieved from https://www.thenation.com/article/what-happens-if-youre-too-poor-to-pay-bail/

Griffin, M., Hogan, N., & Lambert, E. (2012). Doing people work among a tough crowd: A further examination of the job characteristics model and correctional staff burnout. *Criminal Justice and Behavior, 39*(9), 1131–1147.

Grob, G. N. (1966). *The state and the mentally ill*. Chapel Hill, NC: University of North Carolina Press.

Grob, G. N. (1973). *Mental institutions in America*. New York, NY: Free Press.

Grob, G. N. (2005). Public policy and mental illness: Jimmy Carter's presidential commission on mental health. *Milbank Quarterly, 83*(3), 425–456.

Groth, A. N., & Birnbaum, H. J. (1979). *Men who rape: The psychology of the offender*. New York: Plenum Press.

Gudjonsson, G. H., Sigurdsson, J. F., & Einarsson, E. (2003). The role of personality in relation to confessions and denials. *Journal of Psychology, Crime & Law, 10*(2), 125–135. doi:10.1080/10683160310001634296

Guilamo-Ramos, V., Dittus, P., Jaccard, J., Johansson, M., Bouris, A., & Acosta N. (2007). Parenting practices among Dominican and Puerto Rican mothers. *Social Work, 52*(1), 17–30.

Hamby, S. (2014). Guess how many domestic violence offenders go to jail? *Psychology Today*. Retrieved from https://www.psychologytoday.com/us/blog/the-web-violence/201410/guess-how-many-domestic-violence-offenders-go-jail

Hansson, A. S., Arnetz, B. B., Anderzen, I. (2006). Risk-factors for stress-related absence among healthcare employees: A biopsychosocial perspective. *Italian Journal of Public Health, 3*, 53–61.

Hargrove, D. S., & Curtin, L. (2012). Rural mental health practitioners: Their own mental health needs. In K. B. Smalley, J. C. Warner, & J. R., Rainer (Eds.), *Rural mental health: Issues, policies, and best practices* (pp. 113–130). New York, NY: Springer.

Harrell, A. V. (1991). *Evaluation of court-ordered treatment for domestic violence*. Washington, DC: Urban Institute.

Harrell A., & Smith, B. (1996). Effects of restraining orders on domestic violence victims. In C. Buzawa & E. Buzawa (Eds.), *Do arrests and restraining orders work?* (pp. 214–242). Thousand Oaks, CA: SAGE.

Hart, B. J., & Klein, A. R. (2013). *Practical implications of current intimate partner violence research for victim advocates and service providers*. Washington, DC: U. S. Department of Justice. Retrieved from https://www.ncjrs.gov/pdffiles1/nij/grants/244348.pdf

Hart, S. D., & Hare, R. D. (1997). Psychopathy: Assessment and association with criminal conduct. In D. M. Stoff, J. Breiling, & J. D. Master (Eds.), *Handbook of antisocial behavior* (pp. 22–35). Hoboken, NJ: Wiley.

Healey, K., Smith, C., & O'Sullivan, C. (1998). *Batterer intervention: Program approaches and criminal justice strategies*. Washington, DC: National Institute of Justice, Office of Justice Programs, U.S. Department of Justice.

Henson, J. S. (2017). When compassion is lost. *Medsurg Nursing, 26*(2), 139–142.

Herman, J. (1992). Complex PTSD: A syndrome in survivors of prolonged and repeated trauma. *Journal of Traumatic Stress, 5*(3), 377–391. doi: 10.1007/BF00977235

Herman, J. (1995, 1997). *Trauma and recovery: The aftermath of violence—from domestic abuse to political terror.* New York, NY: Basic Books.

Herman, J. (2015). *Trauma and recovery.* New York, NY: Basic Books.

Hermann, R., Dorwart, R., Hoover, C., & Brody, J. (1995). Variation in ECT use in the United States. *American Journal of Psychiatry, 152*(6), 869–875.

Herrenkohl, T. I., Hong, S., Klika, J. B., Herrenkohl, R. C., & Russo, M. J. (2013). Developmental impacts of child abuse and neglect related to adult mental health, substance sue, and physical health. *Journal of Family Violence, 28*(2). doi:10.1007/s10896-012-9474-9

Herz, D., Ryan, J. P., & Bilchik, S. (2010). Challenges facing crossover youth: An examination of juvenile-justice decision making and recidivism. *Family Court Review, 48*(2), 305–321. doi:10.1111/j.1744-1617.2010.01312.x

Hildyard, K. L., & Wolfe, D. A. (2002). Child neglect: Developmental issues and outcomes. *Child Abuse and Neglect, 26i*(6–7), 679–695.

Hilton, N. Z., Harris, G. T., Rice, M. E., Lang, C., Cormier, C. A., Lines, K. J. (2004). A brief actuarial assessment for the prediction of wife assault recidivism: The Ontario Domestic Assault Risk Assessment. *Psychological Assessment, 16*(3), 267275. Doi. 10.1037/1040-3590.16.3.267.

Hiltzik, M. (2018). Republicans fund children's health insurance program, but leave their local health centers in the lurch. *Los Angeles Times.* Retrieved from http://www.latimes.com/business/hiltzik/la-fi-hiltzik-community-health-20180123-story.html

Hindelang, M. J. (1976). *Criminal victimization in eight American cities: A descriptive analysis of common theft and assault.* Cambridge, MA: Ballinger.

Hindman, J., & Peters, M. M. (2001). Polygraph testing leads to better understanding adult and juvenile sex offenders. *Federal Probation, 65*(3), 8–15.

History Channel. (2000). *Hooked: Illegal drugs* [Documentary]. United States: Author.

Hobfoll, S. E. (2001). The influence of culture, community, and the nested self in the stress process: Advancing conversation of resources theory. *Applied Psychology: An International Review, 50*(3), 337–421.

Hockenberry, S., & Puzzanchera, C. (2017). Juvenile court statistics 2014. *National Center for Juvenile Justice.* Retrieved from http://www.ncjj.org/pdf/jcsreports/jcs2014.pdf

Hoeve, M., Dubas, J. S., Eichelsheim, V. I., van der Laan, P. H., Smeenk, W., & Gerris, J. R. M. (2009). The relationship between parenting and delinquency: A meta-analysis. *Journal of Abnormal child Psychology, 37*(4), 749–775.

Holman, L. (2017). Treatment settings and treatment planning. In P. Stevens & R. L. Smith (Eds.), *Substance abuse counseling: Theory and practice* (6th ed.) (pp. 143–165). New York, NY: Pearson.

Holman, L. F., Wilkerson, S., Ellmo, F. & Skirius, M. (revise and resubmit, Journal of Creativity in Mental Health). Animal assisted therapy's impact on mental health symptomology among females housed on a mental health unit of a prison.

Holmes, S. T., & Holmes, R. M. (2009). *Sex crimes: Patterns and behavior.* Thousand Oaks, CA: SAGE.

Holtzworth-Munroe, A., & Stuart, G. L. (1994). Typologies of male batterers: Three subtypes and the differences among them. *Psychological Bulletin, 116*(3), 476–497.

Hunter, J. A., Jr., & Goodwin, D. W. (1992). The clinical utility of satiation therapy with juvenile sexual offenders: Variations and efficacy. *Annals of Sex Research, 5*(2), 71–80.

Hurst, T., & Hurst, M. (1997). Gender differences in mediation of severe occupational stress among correctional officers. *American Journal of Criminal Justice, 22*(1), 121–137.

Hyman, S. E. (1997). *Genetics and mental disorders: Report of the National Institute of Mental Health's genetics workgroup*. Retrieved from https://www.nimh.nih.gov/about/advisory-boards-and-groups/namhc/reports/genetics-and-mental-disorders-report-of-the-national-institute-of-mental-healths-genetics-workgroup.shtml

In re gault. (1967). 387 U.S. 1.

In re Winship. (1970). 397 U.S. 358.

Isaacs, C. (2016). *Community Cages: Profitizing community corrections and alternatives to incarceration.* Phoenix, AZ: American Friends Service Committee. Retrieved from https://afscarizona.files.wordpress.com/2016/08/communitycages.pdf

Ivicic, R., & Motta, R. (2017). Variables associated with secondary traumatic stress among mental health professionals. *Traumatology, 23*(2), 196–204.

Jackson, S. (2005). *Do batterer intervention programs work? Two studies.* Washington, DC: National Institute of Justice. Retrieved from http://victimsofcrime.org/docs/Information%20Clearinghouse/Batterer%20Intervention%20Programs%20Where%20Do%20We%20Go%20from%20Here.pdf?sfvrsn=0

Jaggi, L. J., Mezuk, B., Watkins, D. C., & Jackson, J. S. (2016). The relationship between trauma, arrest, and incarceration history among Black Americans: Findings from the national survey of American life. *Society and Mental Health, 6*(3), 187–206. Retrieved from https://www.ncbi.nlm.nih.gov/pmc/articles/PMC5079438/

James, D. J., & Glaze, L. E. (2006). Mental health problems of prison and jail inmates: Bureau of Justice Statistics special report. *Bureau of Justice Statistics Report.* Retrieved from https://www.bjs.gov/content/pub/pdf/mhppji.pdf

James R. K., Meyer, R., & Moore, H. (2006). *Triage assessment checklist for law enforcement (TACKLE) manual and CD.* Pittsburgh, PA: Crisis Intervention and Prevention Solutions.

James, N. (2015). Risk and needs assessment in the criminal justice system. *Congressional Research Service.* Retrieved from https://fas.org/sgp/crs/misc/R44087.pdf

Jansson, B. (1998). *Controversial psychosurgery resulted in a Nobel prize.* Retrieved from https://www.nobelprize.org/nobel_prizes/medicine/laureates/1949/moniz-article.html

Jewkes, R., Garcia-Moren, C. & Sen, P. (2003). In E. G. Krug, L. L. Dahlberg, J. A. Mercy, A. B. Zwi, & R. Lozano (Eds.), *World report on violence and health*, (pp. 147–174). Geneva, Switzerland: World Health Organization.

Johnson, J. (2018). American lobotomy: A rhetorical history. Ann Arbor, MI: University of Michigan Press.

Jonson-Reid, M., & Barth, R. P. (2000a). From maltreatment report to juvenile incarceration: The role of child welfare services. *Child Abuse and Neglect, 24*(4), 505–520. doi:10.1016/S0145-2134(00)00107-1

Judge, T. A., Van Vianen, A. E. M., & De Pater, I. E. (2004). Emotional stability, core self-evaluations and job outcomes: A review of the evidence and an agenda for future research. *Human Performance, 17*(3), 325–346.

Judicial Branch of California. (n.d.). *Succeeding through Achievement and Resilience (STAR) Court.* Retrieved from http://www.courts.ca.gov/27693.htm

Kafka, M. P., & Hennen, J. (2002). A DSM IV axis I comorbidity study of males with paraphilias and paraphilia-related disorders. *Sexual Abuse: A Journal of Research and Treatment, 14*(4), 349–366.

Kafka, M. P., & Prentkey, R. A. (1994). Preliminary observations of DSM II-R axis I comorbidity paraphilias and paraphilia-related disorders. *Journal of Clinical Psychiatry, 55*(11), 481–487.

Kafka, M. P., & Prentkey, R. A. (1998). Attention deficit hyperactivity disorder in males with paraphilias and paraphilia-related disorders: A comorbidity study. *Journal of Clinical Psychiatry, 59*(7), 388–396.

Kaminer, Y., Bukstein, O., & Tarter, R. E. (1991). The Teen-Addiction Severity Index: Rationale and reliability. *International Journal of Addiction, 26*(2), 219–226.

Kann, L., McManus, T., Harris, W. A., Shanklin, S. L., Flint, K., H., Hawkins, J., ... & Zaza, S. (2016). Youth risk behavior surveillance: United States, 2015. *MMWR Surveillance Summaries, 65*(6), 1–174.

Kanno, H., Kim, Y. M., & Constance-Huggins, M. (2016). Risk and protective factors of secondary traumatic stress in social workers responding to the great east Japan earthquake. *International Consortium for Social Development, 38*(3), 64–78.

Kansas v. Crane (2002). 534 U.S. 407, 122 S.Ct. 867, 151 L.Ed.2d 856.

Kansas v. Hendricks (1997). 521. U.S. 346, 356–358. 117 S.Ct. 2072, 138 L.Ed.2d 501.

Kapoor, R., Dike, C., Burns, C., & Carvalho, V. (2013). Cultural competence in correctional mental health. *International Journal of Law and Psychiatry, 36*(3–4), 273–280.

Karakurt, G., Smith, D., & Whiting, J. (2014). Impact of intimate partner violence on women's mental health. *Journal of Family Violence, 29*(7), 693–702.

Karasek, R. A. (1979). Job demands, job decision latitude, and mental strain: Implications for job redesign. *Administrative Science Quarterly, 24*(2), 285–311.

Karasek, R. A. (1982). Coworker and supervisor support as moderators of associations between task characteristics and mental strain. *Journal of Occupational Behavior, 3*(2), 181–200.

Karasek, R. A., & Theorell, T. (1990). *Healthy work: Stress, productivity, and the reconstruction of working life*. New York, NY: Basic Books.

Katz, J. (1988). *Seductions of crime: Moral and sensual attractions in doing evil*. New York, NY: Basic Books.

Kaufman, P. (2010). Prison rape: Research explores prevalence, prevention. *National Institute of Justice*. Retrieved from https://www.nij.gov/journals/259/Pages/prison-rape.aspx

Kavoussi, R., Armstead, P., & Coccaro, E. (1997). The neurobiology of impulsive aggression. *Psychiatry Clinics of North America, 20*(2), 395–403.

Kearney, M. S., & Harris, B. H. (2014, April 28). The unequal burden of crime and incarceration on America's poor. *Brookings*. Retrieved from https://www.brookings.edu/blog/up-front/2014/04/28/the-unequal-burden-of-crime-and-incarceration-on-americas-poor/

Kee, J. A., Johnson, D., & Hunt, P. (2002). Burnout and social support in rural mental health counselors. *Journal of Rural Community Psychology, 5*, 16.

Keeping Children and Families Safe Act of 2003. Pub. L. No. 108–36.

Keiltz, S. (2004). *Specialization of domestic violence case management in courts: A national survey*. Williamsburg, VA: National Institute of Justice, Office of Justice Programs, U.S. Department of Justice. Retrieved from https://www.ncjrs.gov/pdffiles1/nij/199724.pdf

Kennedy, J. F. (1963). *Remarks on signing mental retardation facilitates and community health centers construction bill* (Speech). Washington, DC: John F. Kennedy Presidential Library and Museum.

Kent v. U.S. (1966). 383 U. S. 541.

Kesey, K. (1963). *One flew over the cuckoo's nest*. New York, NY: Putnam.

Kilpatrick, D. G. (2004). What is violence against women? Defining and measuring the problem. *Journal of Interpersonal Violence, 19*(11), 1209–1234. doi:10.1177/0886260504269679

Kim, K., Becker-Cohen, M., & Serakos, M. (2015). The processing and treatment of mentally ill persons in the criminal justice system: A scan of practice and background analysis. *Urban Institute*. Retrieved from https://www.urban.org/sites/default/files/publication/48981/2000173-The-Processing-and-Treatment-of-Mentally-Ill-Persons-in-the-Criminal-Justice-System.pdf

Kimble, M., Neacsiu, A. D., Flack, W. F., & Horner, J. (2010). Risk of unwanted sex for college women: Evidence for a red zone. *Journal of American college Health, 57*(3), 331–338. doi:10.3200/JACH.57.3.331-338

Kirk, D. S., & Sampson, R. J. (2013). Juvenile arrest and collateral educational damage in the transition to adulthood. *Sociology of Education, 86*(1), 36–62. doi:10.1177/0038040712448862

Knight, J. R., Sherritt, L., Shrier, L. A., Harris, S. K., & Chang, G. (2002). Validity of the CRAFFT substance abuse screening test among adolescent clinic patients. *Archives of Pediatrics and Adolescent Medicine, 156*(6), 607–614. doi:10.1001/archpedi.156.6.607

Knudsen, H. K., Ducharme, L. J., & Roman, P. M. (2006). Counselor emotional exhaustion and turnover intention in therapeutic communities. *Journal of Substance Abuse Treatment, 31*(2), 173–180. doi:10.1016/j.jsat.2006.04.003

Kohlberg, L., & Hersh, R. H. (1977). Moral development: A review of the theory. *Theory into Practice, 16*(2), 53–59.

Kohn, M. L., & Schooler, C. (1982). Job conditions and personality: A longitudinal assessment of their reciprocal effects. *American Journal of Sociology, 87*(6), 1257–1286.

Kolivoski, K. M., Shook, J. J., Goodkind, S., & Kim, K. H. (2014). Developmental trajectories and predictors of juvenile detention, placement, and jail among youth with out-of-home child welfare placement. *Journal of the Society for Social Work and Research, 5*(2), 137–160.

Kraus, C., Strohm, K., Hill, A., Habermann, N., Berner, W., & Briken, P. (2007). Selective serotonin reuptake inhibitors (SSRI) in the treatment of paraphilia: A retrospective study. *Forensic Neurology and Psychiatry, 75*(6), 351–356.

Kraus, V. I. (2005). Relationship between self-care and compassion satisfaction, compassion fatigue, and burnout among mental health professionals working with adolescent sex offenders. *Counseling and Clinical Psychology Journal, 2*(2), 81–88.

Kreisman, J. J., & Straus, H. (2010). *I hate you. Don't leave me: Understanding the borderline personality.* New York, NY: Penguin Random House.

Kreisman, J. J., & Straus, H. (2004). *Sometimes I act crazy: Living with borderline personality disorder.* Hoboken, NJ: Wiley.

Kropp, P., Hart, S., & Webster, C. (1999). *Spousal Assault Risk Assessment (SARA) user's manual.* Toronto, ON: Multi-Health Systems, Inc.

Krug, E. G., Dahlberg, L. L., Mercy, J. A., Zwi, A. B., & Lozano, R. (2003). In E. G. Krug, L. L. Dahlberg, J. A. Mercy, A. B. Zwi, & R. Lozano (Eds.), *World report on violence and health,* (pp. 141–181). Geneva, Switzerland: World Health Organization.

Kupfer, D. J. (2015). Anxiety and DSM-5. *Dialogues in Clinical Neuroscience, 17*(3), 245–246. Retrieved from https://www.ncbi.nlm.nih.gov/pmc/articles/PMC4610609/

Kuykendall, S. (Ed.). (2018). *Encyclopedia of Public Health: Principles, People, and Programs.* Santa Barbra, CA: ABC-CLIO, LLC.

Laband, D. N., & Sophocleus, J. P. (1992). *The Quarterly Journal of Economics, 107*(3), 959–983. Doi: 10.2307/2118370.

Labriola, M., Bradley, S., O'Sullivan, C. S., Rempel, M., & Moore, S. (2010). *A national portrait of domestic violence courts.* Washington, DC: U. S. Department of Justice. Retrieved from https://www.ncjrs.gov/pdffiles1/nij/grants/229659.pdf

Lambert, E., Altheimer, I., & Hogan, N. (2010). Exploring the relationship between social support and job burnout among correctional staff: An exploratory study. *Criminal Justice and Behavior, 37*(11), 1217–1236.

Lambert, E., Hogan, N., & Jiang, S. (2010). A preliminary examination of the relationship between organizational structure and emotional burnout among correctional staff. *Howard Journal of Criminal Justice, 49*(2), 125–146.

Lambert, E. G., Barton-Bellessa, S. M., Hogan, N. L. (2015). The consequences of emotional burnout among correctional staff. *Sage Open*. doi:10.1177/2158244015590444

Lambert, E. G., Hogan, N. L., Griffin, M. L., & Kelley, T. (2015). The correctional staff burnout literature. *Criminal Justice Studies, 28*(4), 397–443.

Langenderfer-Magruder, L., Whitfield, D. L., Walls, N. E., Kattari, S. K., & Ramos, D. (2014). Experiences of intimate partner violence and subsequent police reporting among lesbian, gay, bisexual, transgender, and queer adults in Colorado: Comparing rates of cisgender and transgender victimization. *Journal of Interpersonal Violence, 31*(5), 855–871. doi:10.1177/0886260514556767

Lauritsen, J. L. Sampson, R. J., & Laub, J. H. (1991). The link between offending and victimization among adolescents. *Criminology, 29*, 265–292. Doi. 10.1111/j.1745-9125.1991.tb0167.x

Laws, D. R., & O'Donohue, W. *Sexual deviance: Theory, assessment, and treatment.* New York, NY: Guilford Press.

Letvak, S., & Buck, R. (2008). Factors influencing work productivity and intent to stay in nursing. *Nurse Economist, 26*(3), 159–165.

Liberty Healthcare Corporation. (1998). *Treatment of Sexually Violent Persons: Program Description.* Bala Cynwyd, PA: Author.

Lindgren, M. S., & Renck, B. (2008). It is still so deep-seated, the fear: Psychological stress reactions as consequences of intimate partner violence. *Journal of Psychiatric and Mental Health Nursing, 15*(3), 219–228. doi:10.1111/j.1365-2850.2007.01215.x

Linehan, M. M. (1993). *Cognitive-behavioral treatment of borderline personality disorder.* New York, NY: Guilford Press.

Litz, B. T., & Gray, M. J. (2002). Emotional numbing in posttraumatic stress disorder: Current and future directions. *Australian and New Zealand Journal of Psychiatry, 36*(2), 198–204.

Loerzel, R. (2010). *An Illinois history of juvenile court.* Retrieved from https://www.wbez.org/shows/eight-fortyeight/an-illinois-history-of-juvenile-court/68cc998f-033a-45f2-9087-5030bbf342cb

Lubell, K. M., Lofton, T., & Singer, H. H. (2008). *Promoting healthy parenting practices across cultural groups: A CDC research brief.* Atlanta, GA: Centers for Disease Control and Prevention, National Center for Injury Prevention and Control. Retrieved from https://rhyclearinghouse.acf.hhs.gov/library/2008/promoting-healthy-parenting-practices-across-cultural-groups-cdc-research-brief

Luthans, F., Norman, S. M., Avolio, B. J., & Avey, J. B. (2008). The mediating role of psychological capital in the supportive organizational climate-employee performance relationship. *Journal of Organizational Behavior, 29*(2), 219–238.

Lynch, S. M., Heath, N. M., Mathews, K. C., & Cepeda, G. J. (2012). Seeking Safety: An intervention for trauma-exposed incarcerated women? *Journal of Trauma and Dissociation, 13*(1), 88–101. doi:10.1080/15299732.2011.608780

MacDonald, J. M. (1963). The threat to kill. *American Journal of Psychiatry, 120*(2), 125–130. doi:10.1176/aip.120.2.125.

Mairean, C., & Turliuc, M. N. (2013). Predictors of vicarious trauma beliefs among medical staff. *Journal of Loss and Trauma, 18*, 414–428.

Maiter, S., Alaggia, R., & Trocme, N. (2004). Perceptions of child maltreatment by parents from the Indian subcontinent: Challenging myths about culturally based abusive parenting practices. *Child Maltreatment, 9*(3), 309–324.

Marshall, W. L., Laws, D. R., & Barbaree, H. E. (Eds.). (1990). *Handbook of sexual assault: Issues, theories, and treatment of the offender.* New York, NY: Plenum Press.

Martin, K., Giannandrea, P., Rogers, B., & Johnson, J. (1996). Group intervention with pre-recovery patients. *Journal of Substance Abuse Treatment, 13*(1), 33–41. doi:10.1016/0740-5472(95)02045-4

Martin, S. L., Moracco, K. E., Chang, J. C., Council, C. L., & Dulli, L. S. (2008). Substance abuse issues among women in domestic violence programs. *Violence Against Women, 14*(9), 985–997. doi:10.1177/1077801208322103

Maschi, T., Hatcher, S. S., Schwalbe, C. S., & Rosato, N. S. (2008). Mapping the social service pathways of youth to and through the juvenile justice system: A comprehensive review. *Children and Youth Services Review, 30*(12), 1376–1385.

Maslach, C. (1978). The client role in staff burnout. *Journal of Social Issues, 34*(4), 111–124.

Maslach, C. (1982). *Burnout: The cost of caring.* Englewood Cliffs, NJ: Prentice-Hall.

Maslach, C. (1986). Stress, burnout and workaholism. In R. R. Kilburg, P. E. Nathan, & R. W. Thoreson (Eds.), *Professionals in distress, issues, syndromes, and solutions in psychology* (pp. 53–76). Washington, DC: American Psychological Association.

Maslach, C., & Jackson, S. (1981). The measurement of experienced burnout. *Journal of Occupational Behavior, 2*(2), 1–15.

Maslach, C., Jackson, S. E., & Leiter, M. P. (1997). Maslach Burnout Inventory (3rd Ed.). In C. P. Zalaquett, & R. J. Wood (Eds.), *Evaluating stress: A book of resources* (pp. 191–218). Lanham, MD: The Scarecrow Press.

Maslach, C., & Leiter, M. (2008). Early predictors of job burnout and engagement. *Journal of Applied Psychology, 93*(3), 498–512.

Maslow, A. H. (1943). A theory of human motivation. *Psychological Review, 50*(4), 370–396. doi:10.1037/h0054346.

Maslow, A. H. (1968/1999). *Toward a psychology of being* (3rd ed.). Hoboken, NJ: Wiley.

Mathieu, F. (2012). *The compassion fatigue workbook: Creative tools for transforming compassion fatigue and vicarious traumatization.* New York, NY: Taylor & Francis. Doi. 10.4324/9780203803349.

Mazur, R., & Aldrich, L. (2003). What makes a domestic violence court work? Lessons from New York. *Judge's Journal, 42*(2). Retrieved from http://www.courtinnovation.org/sites/default/files/cci-d6-legacy-files/pdf/what_makes_dvcourt_work.pdf

McCann, I. L., & Pearlman, L. A. (1990). Vicarious traumatization: A framework for understanding the psychological effects of working with victims. *Journal of Traumatic Stress, 3*(1), 131–149.

McCann, I. L., & Perlman, L. A. (1993). Vicarious traumatization: The emotional costs of working with survivors. *Treating Abuse Today, 3*(5), 28–31.

McCartin, C. (n.d.). *Family engagement in juvenile justice: JDAI research and policy series.* Retrieved from http://www.mass.gov/eohhs/docs/dys/jdai/family-engagement-brief.pdf

McConnell, T. (2017). The war on women: The collateral consequences of female incarceration. *Lewis & Clark Law Review, 21*(2), 493–524.

McFarlane, J., Malecha, A., & Gist J., Watson, K., Batten, E., Hall, I., & Smith, S. (1994). Protection orders and intimate partner violence: An 18-month study of 150 Black, Hispanic, and White women. *American Journal of Public Health, 94*(4), 613–618.

McKeiver v. Pennsylvania. (1971). 403 U.S. 528.

McNultry, T., Oser, C., Johnson, J. A., Knudsen, H., Roman, P. (2007). Counselor turnover in substance abuse treatment centers: An organizational-level analysis. *Sociological Inquiry, 77*(2), 166–193.

Mee-Lee, D. (Ed.). (1990). *The ASAM criteria: Treatment for addictive, substance-related, and co-occurring conditions* (3rd ed.). Rockville, MD: American Society of Addiction Medicine.

Melendez, W. A., & De Guzman, R. M. (1983). *Burnout: The new academic disease.* Washington, DC: Clearinghouse on Higher Education.

Menard, S. (2012). Age, criminal victimization and offender: Changing relationships from adolescence to middle adulthood. *Victims and Offenders, 7*(3), 227–254. doi:10.1080/15564886.2012.685353

Mennen, F. E., Kim, K., Sang, J., & Trickett, P. K. (2010). Child neglect: Definition and identification of youth's experiences in official reports of maltreatment. *Child Abuse & Neglect, 34*(9), 647–658.

Mertin, P. G., & Mohr, P. B. (2001). A follow-up study of posttraumatic stress disorder, anxiety, and depression in Australian victims of domestic violence. *Violence and Victims, 16*(6), 645–653.

Merton, R. K. (1957). *Social theory and social structure.* New York: The Free Press.

Messinger, A. (2011). Invisible victims: Same-sex IPV in the National Violence against Women Survey. *Journal of Interpersonal Violence, 26*(11), 2228–2243.

Metzner, J. L., & Fellner, J. (2010). Solitary confinement and mental illness in U.S. Prisons: A challenge for medical ethics. *Journal of the American Academy of Psychiatry and the Law, 38*(1), 104–108. Retrieved from http://jaapl.org/content/jaapl/38/1/104.full.pdf

Meyer, R. A. (2001). *Assessment for crisis intervention: A triage assessment model.* Belmont, CA: Thomson Brooks/Cole.

Meyer, R. A., James, R. K., & Moulton, P. (2011). *This is not a fire drill: Crisis intervention and prevention on college campuses.* Hoboken, NJ: Wiley.

Meyer, R. A., & Moore, H. (2006). Crisis in context theory: An ecological model. *Journal of Counseling & Development, 84*(2), 139–147.

Meyer, R. A., Williams, R. C., Ottens, A. J., & Schmidt, A. E. (1992). Three-dimensional crisis assessment model. *Journal of Mental Health Counseling, 14*(2), 137–148.

Meyer, R. M., & Conte, C. (2006). Assessment for crisis intervention. *Journal of Clinical Psychology, 62*(8), 959–970. doi:10.1002/jclp.20282

Middlebrooks, J. S., & Audage, N. C. (2008). The effects of childhood stress on health across the lifespan. *U.S. Department of Health and Human Services, Centers for Disease Control and Prevention.* Retrieved from http://health-equity.lib.umd.edu/932/1/Childhood_Stress.pdf

Miethe, T. D., & Meier, R. F. (1994). *Crime and its social context: Toward an integrated theory of offenders, victims, and situations.* Albany, NY: State University of New York Press.

Milkman, H., & Wanberg, K. (2007). *Cognitive-behavioral treatment: A review and discussion for corrections professionals.* Washington, DC: National Institute of Corrections. Retrieved from https://s3.amazonaws.com/static.nicic.gov/Library/021657.pdf

Miller, B., & Sprang, G. (2017). A components-based practice and supervision model for reducing compassion fatigue by affecting clinician experience. *Traumatology, 23*(2), 153–164.

Miller, G. (1997). Substance Abuse Subtle Screening Inventory. Springville, IN: SASSI Institute.

Miller, L. (1998). Our own medicine: Traumatized psychotherapists and the stresses of doing therapy. *Psychotherapy, 35*(2), 137–146.

Miller, W. R., & Rollnick, S. (2013). *Motivational interviewing: Helping people change* (3rd ed.). New York, NY: Guilford Press.

Mimms, D., Waddell, R., & Holton, J. (2017). Inmate perceptions: The impact of a prison animal training program. *Sociology and Criminology-Open Access, 5*(2), 175. doi:10.4172/2375-4435.1000175

Moffat, K. H. (2010). *Actuarial sentencing: an 'unsettled' proposition*. Paper presented at University at Albany Symposium on Sentencing. Albany, NY.

Moffitt, T. E. (1993). Adolescence-limited and life-course-persistent antisocial behavior: A developmental taxonomy. *Psychological Review, 100*(4), 674–701. Retrieved from https://www.colorado.edu/ibs/jessor/psych7536-805/readings/moffitt-1993_674-701.pdf

Mollmann, M. (2017). *Neither justice nor treatment: Drug courts in the United States.* Physicians for Human Rights.New York: NY. Retrieved from: http://pbpd.org.br/wp-content/uploads/2017/06/PHR_Drug-Courts_Report-1.pdf

Molnar, B. E., Sprang, G., Killian, K. D., Gottfried, R., Emery, V., & Bride, B. E. (2017). Advancing science and practice for vicarious traumatization/secondary traumatic stress: A research agenda. *Traumatology, 23*(2), 129–142.

Monea J., & Thomas, A. (2011). Unintended pregnancy and taxpayer spending. *Perspectives on Sexual and Reproductive Health, 43*(2), 88–93. doi:10.1363/4308811

Moore, J. D., & Smith, D. G. (2005). Legislating Medicaid: Considering Medicaid and its origins. *Health Care Financing Review, 27*(2), 45–52.

Morgan, R. D., Flora, D. B., Kroner, D. G., Mills, J. F., Varghese, F., & Steffan, J. S. (2012). Treating offenders with mental illness: A research synthesis. *Law and Human Behavior, 36*(1), 37–50. doi:10.1037/h0093964

Morrison, D., Payne, R. L., & Wall, T. D. (2003). Is job a viable unit of analysis? A multilevel analysis of demand-control-support models. *Journal of Occupational Health Psychology, 8*(3), 209–219.

Moster, A., Wunk, D. W., & Jeglic, E. L. (2008). Cognitive behavioral therapy interventions with sex offenders. *Journal of Correctional Health Care, 14*(2), 109–121. doi:10.1177/1078345807313874

Motivans, M., Snyder, H. N. (2018). Federal prosecution of human-trafficking cases, 2015. Washington, D. C.: U.S. Department of Justice. Office of Justice Programs. Bureau of Justice Statistics. Retrieved from https://www.bjs.gov/content/pub/pdf/fphtc15.pdf.

Mullen, P. E. (2000). Editorial: Forensic mental health. *British Journal of Psychiatry, 176*(4), 307–311.

Murray, C. J. L., & Lopez, A. D. (Eds.) (1996). *The global burden of disease: A comprehensive assessment of mortality and disability from diseases, injuries and risk factors in 1990 and projected to 2020.* Geneva, Switzerland: World Health Organization.

Najavits, L. (2002). *Seeking safety: A treatment manual for PTSD and substance abuse.* New York, NY: Guilford Press.

Najmi, S., Wegner, D. M., & Nock, M. K. (2007). Thought suppression and self-injurious thoughts and behaviors. *Behaviour Research and Therapy, 45*(8), 1957–1965.

Nathanson, A. M., Shorey, R. C., Tirone, V., & Rhatigan, D. L. (2012). The prevalence of mental health disorders in a community sample of female victims of intimate partner violence. *Partner Abuse, 3*(1), 59–75.

National Alliance on Mental Illness (NAMI). (n.d.). *Juvenile justice.* Retrieved from https://www.nami.org/Learn-More/Mental-Health-Public-Policy/Juvenile-Justice

National Association of Advancement of Colored People (NAACP) (n.d.). *Criminal justice fact sheet.* Retrieved from https://www.naacp.org/criminal-justice-fact-sheet/

National Center for Juvenile Justice. (2012). *Juvenile court statistics 2009.* Retrieved from: http://www.ncjj.org/pdf/jcsreports/jcs2009.pdf

National Center for Transgender Equality. (n.d.). *Issues: Police, jails and prisons.* Retrieved from https://transequality.org/issues/police-jails-prisons

National Child Traumatic Stress Network. (NCTSN) (n.d.). *Complex trauma.* Retrieved from http://www.nctsn.org/trauma-types/complex-trauma

National Children's Advocacy Center. (NCAC) (n.d.). *History*. Retrieved from https://www.nationalcac.org/history/

National Conference of State Legislatures. (2017). *Disproportionality and disparity in child welfare*. Retrieved from http://www.ncsl.org/research/human-services/disproportionality-and-disparity-in-child-welfare.aspx

National Council on Crime and Delinquency. (2006). *The spiral of risk: Health care provision to incarcerated women*. Washington, D.C.: Author.

National Institute of Justice. (n.d.). *Juvenile delinquency prevention*. Retrieved from https://www.crimesolutions.gov/TopicDetails.aspx?ID=62#practice

National Institute of Justice (NIJ). (2010). Measuring intimate partner (domestic) violence. *Office of Justice Programs*. Retrieved from https://www.nij.gov/topics/crime/intimate-partner-violence/pages/measuring.aspx

National Institute on Drug Abuse (NIDA), 2018). *Screening and assessment tools chart*. Retrieved from https://www.drugabuse.gov/nidamed-medical-health-professionals/tool-resources-your-practice/screening-assessment-drug-testing-resources/chart-evidence-based-screening-tools

National LGBTQ Institute on IPV. (2018). *Highlights from the revised FVPSA regulations for advocates and programs serving LGBTQ survivors*. Retrieved from http://lgbtqipv.org/wp-content/uploads/2018/05/FVPSA-Regs-Highlights-LGBTQ-Institute.pdf

Nelson, S. (2009). Care and support needs of male survivors of childhood sexual abuse. *Centre for Research on Families and Relationships, Briefing 44*. Retrieved from https://www.era.lib.ed.ac.uk/bitstream/handle/1842/2973/8058.pdf;sequence=6

Nestler, E. J., Barrot, M., DiLeone, R. J., Eisch, A. J., Gold, S. J., & Monetggia, L. M. (2002). Neurobiology of depression. *Neuron, 34*(1), 13–25.

Neveu, J. P. (2007). Jailed resources: Conservation of resources theory as applied to burnout among prison guards. *Journal of Organizational Behavior, 28*(1), 21–42.

New Hope Charleston, The Waypoint Program. (2001). *Staff member's Guide to Family Matters*. Charleston, SC: Author.

Newhill, C. E. (2003). *Client violence in social work practice: Prevention, intervention, and research*. New York, NY: Guilford Press.

Newman, A., Round, H., Bhattacharya, S., & Roy, A. (2017). Ethical climates in organizations: A review and research agenda. *Business Ethics Quarterly, 27*(4), 475–512.

Nock, M. K., Joiner, T. E., Gordon, K., Lloyd-Richardson, E., & Prinstein, M. J. (2006). Non-suicidal self-injury among adolescents: Diagnostic correlates and relation to suicide attempts. *Psychiatry Research, 144*(1), 65–72.

Nock, M. K., & Kessler, R. C. (2006). Prevalence of and risk factors for suicide attempts versus suicide gestures: Analysis of the National Comorbidity Survey. *Journal of Abnormal Psychology, 115*(3), 616–623.

Nock, M. K., & Prinstein, M. J. (2004). A functional approach to the assessment of self-mutilative behavior. *Journal of Consulting and Clinical Psychology, 72*(5), 885–890.

Nock, M. K., & Prinstein, M. J. (2005). Contextual features and behavioral functions of self-mutilation among adolescents. *Journal of Abnormal Psychology, 114*(1), 140–146.

Oddie, S., & Ousley, L. (2007). Assessing burn-out and occupational stressors in a medium secure service. *British Journal of Forensic Practice, 9*(2), 32–48.

Oddone-Paolucci, E., Genuis, M. L., & Violato, C. (2001). A meta-analysis of published research on the effects of child sexual abuse. *Journal of Psychology, 135*(1), 17–36.

Odgers, C. L., Burnette, M. L., Chauhan, P., Moretti, M. M., & Reppucci, N. D. (2005). Misdiagnosing the problem: Mental health profiles of incarcerated juveniles. *Canadian Journal of Child and Adolescent Psychiatry, 14*(1), 26–29.

Office of Juvenile Justice and Delinquency Prevention (OJJDP). 2016). *Juvenile drug treatment court guidelines.* Washington, DC: U.S. Department of Justice. Retrieved from https://www.ojjdp.gov/pubs/250368.pdf

Offices of the U. S. Attorney's (2018). *United States attorneys' manual* (USAM): *Section 9-8.00 juveniles.* Retrieved from https://www.justice.gov/usam/united-states-attorneys-manual

Ogden, P., Minton, K., & Pain, C. (2006). *Trauma and the body: A sensorimotor approach to psychotherapy.* New York, NY: Norton.

Orleck, A., & Hazirjian, L. G. (Eds.). (2011). *The war on poverty.* Athens, GA: University of Georgia Press.

Parks, A. B. (2013). The effects of family structure on juvenile delinquency. *Electronic Theses and Dissertations.* Paper 2299.

Parry, M. (2006). "I tell what I have seen": The reports of asylum reformer Dorothea Dix. *American Journal of Public Health, 96*(4), 622–625.

Pearlman, L. (2003). *Trauma and attachment belief scale.* Los Angeles, CA: Western Psychological Services.

Pearlman, L., & Mac Ian, P. (1995). Vicarious traumatization: An empirical study of the effects of trauma work on trauma therapists. *Professional Psychology: Research and Practice, 26*(6), 448–454.

Pence, E. (n.d.). Duluth model. Duluth, MN: Domestic Abuse Intervention Programs. Retrieved from https://www.theduluthmodel.org/wp-content/uploads/2017/03/The-Duluth-Model.pdf

Perry, B. D. (1995). Childhood trauma, the neurobiology of adaptation, and the "use-dependent" development of the brain: How states become traits. *Infant Mental Health Journal, 16*(4), 271–291.

Perry, B. D. (1997). Incubated in terror: Neurodevelopmental factors in the "cycle of violence." In J. Osofsky (Ed.), *Children in a violence society* (pp. 124–149). New York, NY: Guilford Press.

Perry, B. D. (1999). Memories of states: How the brain stores and retrieves traumatic experience. In J. Goodwin & R. Attias (Eds.), *Splintered reflections: Images of the body in trauma* (pp. 9–38). New York, NY: Basic Books.

Perry, B. D. (2006). Applying principles of neurodevelopment to clinical work with maltreated and traumatized children: The neurosequential model of therapeutics. In N. B. Webb (Ed.) *Working with traumatized youth in child welfare* (pp. 27–52). New York, NY: Guilford Press.

Perry, B. D. (2009). Examining child maltreatment through a neurodevelopmental lens: Clinical applications of the neurosequential model of therapeutics. *Journal of Loss and Trauma, 14*(4), 240–255.

Perry, B. D. (2014). The cost of caring: Secondary traumatic stress and the impact of working with high-risk children and families. Houston, TX: Child Trauma Academy. Retrieved from https://childtrauma.org/wp-content/uploads/2014/01/Cost_of_Caring_Secondary_Traumatic_Stress_Perry_s.pdf.

Perry, S. W. (2004). *American Indians and crime.* Washington, DC: Bureau of Justice Statistics, Office of Justice Programs, U.S. Department of Justice.

Perry v. Lynaugh. (1989). 492 U.S. 302.

Peters, M., Thomas, D., & Zamberlan, C. (1997). *Boot camps for juvenile offenders.* Washington, DC: Office of Juvenile Justice and Delinquency Prevention. Retrieved from https://www.ncjrs.gov/pdffiles/164258.pdf

Pfeiffer, W., Feuerlein, W., Brenk-Schulte, E. (1991). The motivation of alcohol dependents to undergo treatment. *Drug and Alcohol Dependence, 29*(1) 87–95. https://doi.org/10.1016/0376-8716(91)90025-T

Pickren, W. E., & Schneider, S. F. (2005). *Psychology and the National Institute of Mental Health: A historical analysis of science, practice, and policy.* Washington, DC: American Psychological Association.

Pompili, M., Mancinelli, I., Giardi, P., & Tatarelli, R. (2003). Nursing schizophrenic patients who are at risk of suicide. *Journal of Psychiatric and Mental Health Nursing, 10*(5), 622–624.

Pope, K. S., & Tabachnick, B. G. (1994). Therapists as patients: A national survey of psychologists' experiences, problems, and beliefs. *Professional Psychology Research and Practice, 25*(3), 247–258. Doi. 10.1037/0735-7028.25.3.247.

Ports, K. A., Ford, D. C., Merrick, M. T. (2017). Adverse childhood experiences and sexual victimization in adulthood. *Child Abuse and Neglect, 51*, 313–322. Doi: 10.1016/j.chiabu.2015.08.017.

Positive Psychology Program. (2018, August 21). *Trauma-focused cognitive behavioral ttherapy: How far we've come from Freud*. Retrieved from https://positivepsychologyprogram.com/trauma-focused-cognitive-behavioral-therapy/

Prison Rape Elimination Act (2003). Pub. Law 108–79.

Prochaska, J. O., & DiClemente, C. C. (1982). Transtheoretical therapy: Toward a more integrative model of change. *Psychotherapy: Theory, Research, and Practice, 19*(3), 276–288.

Procter, N., Ayling, B., Croft, L., DeGaris, P., Devine, M., Dimanic, A., et al. (2017). Trauma-informed approaches in forensic mental health: A practical resource for health professionals. University of South Australia, SA Health, Adelaide. Retrieved from http://www.unisa.edu.au/siteassets/episerver-6-files/global/health/sansom/documents/mhsa/trauma-informed-approaches-in-forensic-mental-health-resource.pdf.

Putnam, F. W. (2003). Ten-year research update review: Child sexual abuse. *Journal of the American Academy of Child and Adolescent Psychiatry, 42*(3), 269–278.

Queen v. M'Naghten. (1843). 8 Eng. Rep. 718.

Quinones, S. (2015). *Dreamland: The true tale of America's opiate epidemic*. New York, NY: Bloomsbury Press.

Raffin-Bouchal, S., Venturato, L., Mijovic-Kondejewski, J., & Smith-MacDonald, L. (2017). Compassion fatigue: A meta-narrative review of the healthcare literature. *International Journal of Nursing Studies, 69*, 9–24.

Rainville, G. A., & Smith, S. K., (2003). *Juvenile felony defendants in criminal courts: Bureau of Justice Statistics special report*. Washington, DC: U.S. Department of Justice. Retrieved from https://www.bjs.gov/content/pub/pdf/jfdcc98.pdf

Rand, M. R. (2008). *Criminal victimization*, 2007. Washington, DC: Office of Justice Programs.

Rape, Abuse, and Incest National Network. [RAINN]. (n.d.) Sexual Assault Laws and Court Decisions. Retrieved from https://www.rainn.org/sexual-assault-laws-and-court-decisions.

Rasmussen, L. A. (1999). The trauma outcome process: An integrated model for guiding clinical practice with children with sexually abusive behavior problems. *Journal of Child Sexual Abuse, 8*(4), 3–33.

Rasmussen, L. A. (2001). Integrating cognitive-behavioral and expressive therapy interventions: Applying the trauma outcome process in treating children with sexually abusive behavior problems. *Journal of Child Sexual Abuse, 10*, 1–29.

Rasmussen, L. A. (2004). Differentiating youth who sexually abuse: Applying a multidimensional framework when assessing and treating subtypes. *Journal of Child Sexual Abuse, 13*(3–4), 57–82.

Rasmussen, L. A. (2008). *Challenging traditional paradigms: Applying the trauma outcome process (TOPA) Model in treating sexually abusive youth who have histories of abusive trauma*. Doi. 10.1080/19361521.2012.646645.

Rasmussen, L. A., Burton, J., & Christopherson, B. J. (1992). Precursors to offending and the trauma outcome process in sexually reactive children. *Journal of Child Sexual Abuse, 1*(1), 33–48.

Raymond, N. C., Coleman, E., Ohlerking, F., Christenson, G. A., & Miner, M. (1999). Psychiatric comorbidity in pedophilic sex offenders. *American Journal of Psychiatry, 159*, 786–788.

Refuge Recovery (n.d.). Retrieved from https://refugerecovery.org/

Reinhardt, V., & Rogers, R. (1998). Differences in anxiety between first-time and multiple-time inmates: A multicultural perspective. *Journal of American Academy of Psychiatry and Law, 26*(3), 375–382. Retrieved from https://pdfs.semanticscholar.org/e47c/a2a2095e03b52742c650eb7a414db81be94d.pdf

Renfrew, J. (1997). *Aggression and its causes: A biopsychosocial approach.* New York, NY: Oxford University Press.

Resnick, H. S., Falsetti, S. A., Kilpatrick, D. G., & Freedy, J. R. (1996). Assessment of rape and other civilian trauma-related PTSD: Emphasis on assessment of potentially traumatic events In T. W. Miller (Ed.), *International Universities Press stress and health series. Theory and assessment of stressful life events* (pp. 235–271). Madison, CT: International Universities Press.

Responsibility and Work Opportunity Reconciliation Act of 1996 (PRWORA; P.L. 104–193)

Ringstad, R. (2005, October). Conflict in the workplace: Social workers as victims and perpetrators. *Social Work, 50*(4), 305–313.

Rogers, C. (1957). The necessary and sufficient conditions of therapeutic personality change. *Journal of Consulting and Clinical Psychology, 21*(2), 95–103. doi: 10.1037/h0045367.

Rohland, B. M. (2000). A survey of burnout among mental health center directors in a rural state. *Administration & Policy in Mental Health, 27*(4), 221–237.

Romans, S. E., Martin, J. L., Anderson, J. C., Herbison, G. P., & Mullen, P. E. (1995). Sexual abuse in childhood and deliberate self-harm. *American Journal of Psychiatry, 152*(9), 1336–1342. doi: 10.1176/ajp.152.9.1336.

Roper v. Simmons. (2005). U. S. 125 S. Ct. 1183.

Rosenberg, K. P., & Feder, L. C. (2014). *Behavioral addictions: Criteria, evidence, and treatment.* San Diego, CA: Academic Press.

Roundy, L. M., & Horton, A. L. (1990). Professional and treatment issues for clinicians who intervene with incest perpetrators. In A. L. Horton, B. L. Johnson, L. M. Roundy, & D. Williams (Eds.), *The incest perpetrator* (pp. 164–189). Thousand Oaks: CA: SAGE.

Royner, J. (2016, April). *Policy Brief: Racial Disparities in Youth Commitments and Arrests.* Washington, D. C. The Sentencing Project. Retrieved from https://www.sentencingproject.org/wp-content/uploads/2016/04/Racial-Disparities-in-Youth-Commitments-and-Arrests.pdf.

Rudorfer, M. V., Henry, M. E., Sackheim, H. A. (1997). Electroconvulsive therapy. In A. Tasman, & J. A. Lieberman (Eds.), *Psychiatry* (pp. 1535–1556). Philadelphia, PA: W. B. Saunders.

Rupert, P. A., & Kent, J. S. (2007). Gender and work setting differences in career-sustaining behaviors and burnout among professional psychologists. *Professional Psychology: Research and Practice, 38*(1), 88–96. Doi. 10.1037/0735-7028.38.1.88.

Rupert, P. A., & Morgan, D. J. (2005). Work setting and burnout among professional psychologists. *Professional Psychology: Research and Practice, 36*(5), 544–550. doi:10.1037/0735-7028.36.5.544

Rupert, P. A., Stevanovic, P., & Hunley, H. A. (2009). Work-family conflict and burnout among practicing psychologists. *Professional Psychology: Research and Practice, 40*(1), 54–61. doi:10.1037/a0012538

Russell, M. (1994). New assessment tools for risk drinking during pregnancy: T-ACE, TWEAK, and others. *Alcohol Health and Research World, 18*(1), 55–61.

Ryan, J. P., & Testa, M. F. (2005). Child maltreatment and juvenile delinquency: Investigating the role of placement and placement stability. *Children and Youth Services Review, 27*(3), 227–249. doi:10.1016/j.childyouth.2004.05.007

Sacks, V., Murphey, D., & Moore, K. (2014). Adverse childhood experiences: National and state-level prevalence. *Child trends: Research brief* (Publication #2014-28). Retrieved from https://www.childtrends.org/wp-content/uploads/2014/07/Brief-adverse-childhood-experiences_FINAL.pdf

Sanders, S., Stensland, M., & Juraco, K. (2018). Agency behind bars: Advanced care planning with aging and dying offenders. *Death Studies, 42*(1), 45–51.

Santa Clara County. (2013). *Dually involved youth initiative: Improving outcomes for dually involved youth.* Retrieved from https://rfknrcjj.org/images/PDFs/Santa-Clara-County-Dual-Status-Youth-Initiative-Site-Manual-2013.pdf

Sarteschi, C. M. (2013). Mentally ill offenders involved with the U.S. criminal justice system: A synthesis. *SAGE Open, 1*(11). doi: 10.1177/2158244013497029.

Saunders, J. B., Aasland, O. G., Babor, T. F., De La Fuente, J., & Grant, M. (1993). Development of the Alcohol Use Disorders Identification Test (AUDIT): WHO collaborative project on early detection of persons with harmful alcohol consumption-II. *Addiction, 88*(6), 791–804.

Sauter, S. L., & Murphy, L. R. (1995). The changing face of work and stress. In S. L. Sauter, & L. R. Murphy (Eds.), *Organizational risk factors for job stress* (pp. 1–6). Washington, DC: American Psychological Association.

Sauter, S., Murphy, L., Colligan, M., Swanson, N., Hurrell, J. Jr., Scharf, F. Jr., … & Tisdale, J. (2014). *Stress at work.* Washington, DC: National Institute for Occupational Safety and Health. Retrieved from https://www.cdc.gov/niosh/docs/99-101/pdfs/99-101.pdf

Savicki, V., Cooley, E., & Gjesvold, J. (2003). Harassment as a predictor of job burnout in corrections officers. *Criminal Justice and Behavior, 30*(5), 602–619.

Schaenman, P., Davies, E., Jordan, R., & Chakraborty, R. (2013). *Opportunities for cost savings in corrections without sacrificing service quality: Inmate health care.* Retrieved from https://www.urban.org/sites/default/files/publication/23341/412754-Opportunities-for-Cost-Savings-in-Corrections-Without-Sacrificing-Service-Quality-Inmate-Health-Care.PDF

Schein, E. H. (2010). *Organizational culture and leadership* (4th ed.). San Francisco, CA: Jossey-Bass.

Schiff, M., Chao, S., Huh, K., Bell, E., Choudhry, K., & McKillop, M. (2014). *State prison health care spending: An examination.* Pew Charitable Trusts & the MacArthur Foundation. Retrieved from https://www.pewtrusts.org/~/media/legacy/uploadedfiles/pcs_assets/2014/PCTCorrectionsHealthcareBrief050814pdf.pdf

Schneider, B., Salvaggio, A. N., & Subirates, M. (2002). Climate strength: A new direction for climate research. *Journal of Applied Psychology, 87*(2), 220–229.

Sedlak, A. J., Mettenburg, J., Basena, M., Petta, I., McPherson, K., Greene, A., & Li, S. (2010). *Fourth national incidence study of child abuse and neglect (NIS–4): Report to Congress.* Washington, DC: U.S. Department of Health and Human Services, Administration for Children and Families.

Seedat, S., & Stein, D. J. (2000). Trauma and post-traumatic stress disorder in women: A review. *International Clinical Psychopharmacology, 15*(3), 25–33.

Selye, H. (1950). *The physiology and pathology of exposure to stress: A treatise based on the concepts of the general-adaptation syndrome and the diseases of adaptation.* Montreal, Canada: Acta.

Senter, S., Morgan, R., Serna-McDonald, C., & Bewley, M. (2010). Correctional psychologist burnout, job satisfaction, and life satisfaction. *Psychological Services, 7*(3), 190–201.

Seto, M. C., Cantor, J. M., & Blanchard, R. (2006). Child pornography offenses are a valid diagnostic indicator of pedophilia. *Journal of Abnormal Child Psychology, 115*(3), 610–615.

Seto, M. C., & Eke, A. W. (2005). The future offending of child pornography offenders. *Sexual Abuse: A Journal of Research and Treatment, 17*(2), 201–210.

Sex Offender Management and Planning Initiative. (n.d.). *Executive summary.* Retrieved from https://smart.gov/SOMAPI/exec_summ.html

Shapiro, R. (2010). *The trauma treatment handbook: Protocols across the spectrum.* New York, NY: Norton.

Shapiro, S. L., Brown, K., & Biegel, G. M. (2007). Teaching self-care to caregivers: Effects of mindfulness-based stress reduction on the mental health of therapists in training. *Training and Education in Professional Psychology, 1*(2), 105–115. doi:10.1037/1931-3918.1.2.105

Shook, J. J., Goodkind, S., Herring, D., Pohlig, R. T., Kolivoski, K., & Kim, K. H. (2013). How different are their experiences and outcomes? Comparing aged out and other child welfare involved youth. *Children and Youth Services Review, 35*(1), 11–18. doi:10.1016.j.childyouth.2012.09/017

Shorter, E. (2013). The history of pediatric ECT. In N. Ghaziuddin & G. Walter (Eds.), *Electroconvulsive therapy in children and adolescents.* Oxford, UK: Oxford University Press.

Shufelt, J. L., & Cocozza, J. J. (2006). Research and program brief: Youth with mental health disorders in the juvenile justice system: Results from a multi-state prevalence study. *National Center for Mental Health and Juvenile Justice.* Retrieved from https://www.ncmhjj.com/wp-content/uploads/2015/02/2006_Youth_with_Mental_Health_Disorders_in_the_Juvenile_Justice_System.pdf

Siebert, D. C. (2005). Personal and occupational factors in burnout among practicing social workers: Implications for research, practitioners, and managers. *Journal of Social Service Research, 32*(2), 25–44.

Siegel, D. J. (1999). *The developing mind: How relationships and the brain interact to shape who we are.* New York, NY: Guilford Press.

Sigler, A. (2017). Risk and prevalence of personality disorders in sex offenders. *John Jay College of Criminal Justice.* Retrieved from https://academicworks.cuny.edu/cgi/viewcontent.cgi?article=1007&context=jj_etds

Simmons, R. (2007). Private criminal justice. *Wake Forest Law Review, 42,* 911–990. Retrieved from http://wakeforestlawreview.com/wp-content/uploads/2014/10/Simmons_LawReview_12.07.pdf.

Sindicich, N., Mills, K. L., Barrett, E. L., Indig, D., Sunjic, S., Sannibale, C., … & Najavits, L. M. (2014). Offenders as victims: Post-traumatic stress disorder and substance use disorder among male prisoners. *Journal of Forensic Psychiatry & Psychology, 25*(1), 44–60. doi:10.1080/14789949.2013.877516

Singh, J. P., & Fazel, S. (2010). Forensic risk assessment: A meta-review. *Criminal Justice and Behavior, 37*(9), 965–988.

Sinozich, S., & Langston, L. (2014). *Rape and sexual assault victimization among college-age females, 1995–2013.* Washington, DC: Bureau of Justice Statistics, Office of Justice Programs. U.S. Department of Justice.

Skeem, J. L., Emke-Francis, P., & Louden, J. E. (2006). Probation, mental health, and mandated treatment: A national survey. *Criminal Justice and Behavior, 33*(2), 158–184.

Skeem, J. L., & Monahan, J. (2011). Current directions in violence risk assessment. *University of Virginia Law School Public Law and Legal Theory Research Paper Series,* no. 2011–2013, 8–9.

Skinner, H. A. (1982). The Drug Abuse Screening Test. *Addictive Behavior, 7*(4), 363–371.

Slattery, S. M. (2003). Contributors to secondary traumatic stress and burnout among domestic violence advocates: An ecological approach. *Dissertation Abstracts International, 34*(3), 40–64.

Smith, H. (n.d.). Models for change: Building momentum for juvenile justice reform. Washington, D.C.: Justice Policy Institute Report. http://www.justicepolicy.org/uploads/justicepolicy/documents/models_for_change.pdf

Smith, P. (n.d.). *Chaperone training overview.* Cookeville, TN: PLS Resources. Retrieved from https://patriciasmithlpc.com/wp-content/uploads/2018/06/Chaperone_Letter_to_applicants.pdf

Smith, S. G., Chen, J., Basile, K. C., Gilbert, L. K., Merrick, M. T., Patel, N. Walling, M., & Jain, A. (2017). *The National Intimate Partner and Sexual Violence Survey: 2010–2012 state report.* Washington, DC: National Center for Injury Prevention and Control. Retrieved from https://www.cdc.gov/violenceprevention/pdf/NISVS-StateReportBook.pdf

Snyder, H. N. (2008). *Juvenile arrests 2006.* Washington, DC: Office of Juvenile Justice and Delinquency Prevention.

Snyder, H. N., & Sickmund, M. (2006). *Juvenile offenders and victims: 2006 national report*. Washington, DC: Office of Juvenile Justice and Delinquency Prevention.

Sokol, R. J., Martier, S. S., & Ager, J. W. (1989). The T-ACE questions: Practical prenatal detection of risk-drinking. *American Journal of Obstetrics and Gynecology, 160*(4), 863–870. doi:10.1016/0002-9378(89)90302-5

Sparkes, A. C., & Day, J. (2016). Aging bodies and desistance from crime: Insights from the life stories of offenders. *Journal of Aging Studies, 36*, 47–58.

Spencer, P. C., & Munch, S. (2003). Client violence toward social workers: The role of management in community mental health programs. *Social Work, 48*(4), 532–544.

Spenser, W. (2017). The steep cost of medical co-pays in prison puts health at risk. *Prison Policy Initiative*. Retrieved from https://www.prisonpolicy.org/blog/2017/04/19/copays/

Spielberger, C. D., Vagg, P. R., & Wasala, C. F. (2003). Occupational stress: Job pressures and lack of support. In J. C. Quick & L. E. Tetrick (Eds.), *Handbook of occupational health psychology*, (pp. 185–200). Washington, DC: American Psychological Association.

Spirer, J. (1943). Psychology of irresistible impulse. *Journal of Criminal Law and Criminology, 33*(6), 457–462. Retrieved from https://scholarlycommons.law.northwestern.edu/cgi/viewcontent.cgi?article=3182&context=jclc

Spitzberg, B. H. (2002). The tactical topography of stalking victimization and management. *Trauma, Violence, & Abuse, 3*(4), 261–288.

Staller, K. M., & Nelson-Gardell, D. (2005). A burden in your heart: Lessons of disclosure from female preadolescent and adolescent survivors of sexual abuse. *Child Abuse and Neglect, 29*(12), 1415–1432. Doi: 10.1016/j.chiabu.2005.06.007.

Stanford V. Kentucky. (1989). 492 U. S. 361.

Stargell, N. A. (2017). Therapeutic relationship outcome effectiveness: Implications for counselor educators. *Journal of Counselor Preparation and Supervision, 9*(2). Retrieved from https://repository.wcsu.edu/cgi/viewcontent.cgi?article=1164&context=jcps

Steadman, H. J., & Veysey, B. M. (1997). Providing services for jail inmates with mental disorders. *National Institute of Justice Brief*. Retrieved from http://web.archive.org/web/20150910081408/https://www.ncjrs.gov/pdffiles/162207.pdf

Stern, A M. (2005). *Eugenic nation: Faults and frontiers of a better breeding in modern America*. Berkeley, CA: University of California Press.

Steward, M. (2014). Fathers behind bars: The problem and solution for America's children [Infographic]. *National Fatherhood Initiative*. Retrieved from https://www.fatherhood.org/fatherhood/fathers-behind-bars-the-problem-and-solution-for-americas-children-infographic

Stoltenborgh, M., van Ijzendoorn, H., Euser, E. M., & Bakermans-Kranenburg, M. J. (2011). A global perspective on child sexual abuse: Meta-analysis of prevalence around the world. *Child Maltreatment, 16*(2), 79–101.

Straus, M. A. (1979). Measuring intrafamily conflict and violence: The Conflict Tactics Scales. *Journal of Marriage and the Family, 41*(1), 75–88.

Straus, M. A., (1990). The conflict Tactics Scale and its critics: An evaluation and new data on validity and reliability. In M. A. Straus & R. J. Gelles (Eds.), *Physical violence in American families: risk factors and adaptations to violence* (pp. 49–73). New Brunswick, NJ: Transaction Publishing.

Straus, M. A. (1995). *Manual for the Conflict Tactics Scale*. Durham, NH: Family Research Laboratory.

Streib, V. L. (2005). *The juvenile death penalty today: Death sentences and executions for juvenile crimes*. Ada, OH: Ohio Northern University. Retrieved from https://deathpenaltyinfo.org/documents/StreibJuvDP2005.pdf

Struass, M. A., & Smith, C. (1990). Family patterns of primary prevention of family violence. In M. A. Strauss & R. J. Gelles (Eds.), *Physical violence in American families: Risk factors and adaptations to violence in 8 families* (pp. 507–526). New York, NY: Taylor and Francis.

Stullich, S., Morgan, I., & Schak, O. (2016). *State and local expenditures on corrections and education.* Washington, DC: U.S. Department of Education. Retrieved from https://www2.ed.gov/rschstat/eval/other/expenditures-corrections-education/brief.pdf

Substance Abuse and Mental Health Services Administration (SAMHSA). (n.d.). SAMHSA's efforts on criminal and juvenile justice issues. Retrieved from https://www.samhsa.gov/criminal-juvenile-justice/samhsas-efforts

Substance Abuse and Mental Health Services Administration (SAMHSA). (2005). *Treatment improvement protocols.* Rockville, MD: Office of Applied Studies.

Substance Abuse and Mental Health Services Administration (SAMHSA). (2014). *A treatment improvement protocol: Trauma-informed care in behavioral health services.* Washington, DC: Author.

Suffolk University. (2019). What is restorative justice? *Suffolk University, College of Arts & Sciences, Center for Restorative Justice.* Retrieved from https://www.suffolk.edu/cas/centers-institutes/center-for-restorative-justice/what-is-restorative-justice

Sun, A., Ashley, L., & Dickson, L. (2012). *Behavioral addiction: Screening, assessment, and treatment.* Las Vegas, NV: Central Recovery Press.

Swanson, J. W., Frisman, L. K., Robertson, A. G., Lin, H. J., Tresman, R. L., Shelton, D. A., Parr, K., Buchanan, A., & Swatz, M. A. (2013). Costs of criminal justice involvement among persons with serious mental illness in Connecticut. *Psyciatric Services, 64*(1), 630–637.

Sykes, G. M., & Matza, D. (1957). Techniques of neutralization: A theory of delinquency. *American Sociological Review, 22*(6), 665–670.

Szabo, S., Tache, Y., & Somogyi, A. (2012). The legacy of Hans Selye and the origins of stress research: A retrospective 75 years after his landmark brief "letter" to the editor of *Nature. Stress, 15*(5), 472–478.

Taheri, S. A. (2016). Do crisis intervention teams reduce arrests and improve officer safety? A systematic review and meta-analysis. *Criminal Justice Policy Review, 27*(1), 76–96. doi:10.1177/0887403414556289

Tarasoff v. Regents of the University of Calefonia, 17 Cal. 3d 425, 551 P.2d 334, 131 Cal.Rptr 14.

Teyber, E., & Teyber, F. H. (2017). *Interpersonal process in therapy: An integrative model* (7th ed.). Boston, MA: Cengage.

Theorell, T., & Karasek, R. A. (1996). Current issues relating to psychosocial job strain and cardiovascular disease research. *Journal of Occupational health Psychology, 1*(1), 9–26.

Thériault, A., & Gazzola, N. (2006). What are the sources of feelings of incompetence in experienced therapists? *Counseling Psychology Quarterly, 19,* 313–330.

Thompson, C., & Eldridge, T. E. (2018). "No one to talk you down": Inside federal prisons' dangerous failure to treat inmates with mental-health disorders. *Washington Post.* Retrieved from https://www.washingtonpost.com/news/national/wp/2018/11/21/feature/federal-prisons-were-told-to-improve-inmates-access-to-mental-health-care-theyve-failed-miserably/?noredirect=on&utm_term=.5e4cfd552129

Thompson v. Oklahoma. (1988). 487 U. S. 815.

THORN. (n.d.). *Statistics on child sex trafficking.* Retrieved from https://www.wearethorn.org/child-trafficking-statistics/

Thornberry, T. P. (2005). Explaining multiple patterns of offending across the life course and across generations. *Annals of the American Academy of Political and Social Science, 602*(1), 156–195.

Thornberry, T. P., & Krohn, M. D. (2005). Applying interactional theory to the explanation of continuity and change in antisocial behavior. In D. P. Farrington (Ed.), *Integrated developmental and life-course theories of offending* (pp. 183–209). New Brunswick, NJ: Transaction.

Thornberry, T. P., & Matsuda, M. (2011). *Why do late bloomers wait? An examination of factors that delay the onset of offending.* Paper presented at the Stockholm Criminology Symposium. Stockholm, Sweden.

Timmerman, I. G. H., & Emmelkamp, P. M. G. (2001). The relationship between traumatic experiences, dissociation, and borderline personality pathology among male forensic patients and prisoners. *Journal of Personality Disorders, 15*(2), 136–149.

Ting, L., Jacobsen, J. M., & Sanders, S. (2011). Current levels of perceived stress among mental health social workers who work with suicidal clients. *Social Work, 56*(4), 327–336.

Title XIX of the Social Security Amendments of 1965. Pub. L. 89–97.

Tolan, C. (2017). Making freedom free. *Slate and Fair Punishment Project.* Retrieved from http://www.slate.com/articles/news_and_politics/trials_and_error/2017/03/poor_defendants_get_locked_up_because_they_can_t_afford_cash_bail_here_s.html

Tonry, M. (2014). Legal and ethical issues in the prediction of recidivism. *Federal Sentencing Reporter, 26*(3), 167–176.

Torbet, P., Gable, R., Hurst, H., Montgomery, I., Szymanski, L., & Thomas, D. (1996). *State responses to serious and violent juvenile crime.* Washington, DC: Office of Juvenile Justice and Delinquency Prevention.

Torrey, E. F. (1997). *Out of the shadows: Confronting America's mental illness crisis.* New York, NY: Wiley and Sons.

Torrey, E. F., Kennard, A. D., Eslinger, D., Lamb, R., & Pavle, J. (2010). *More mentally ill persons are in jails and prisons than hospitals: A survey of the states.* Arlington, VA: Treatment Advocacy Center. Retrieved from https://www.treatmentadvocacycenter.org/storage/documents/final_jails_v_hospitals_study.pdf

Torrey, E. F., Zdanowicz, M. T., Kennard, A. D., Lamb, H. R., Eslinger, D. F., Biasottie, M. C., & Fuller, D. A. (2015). *The treatment of persons with mental Illness in prisons and jails: A state survey.* Arlington, VA: Treatment Advocacy Center.

Trevino, L. K., Butterfield, K. D., & McCabe, D. L. (1998). The ethical context in organizations: Influences on employee attitudes and behaviors. *Business Ethics Quarterly, 8*(3), 447–477.

Trimpey, J. (1989). *The small book: A revolutionary alternative for overcoming alcohol and drug dependence.* New York, NY: Random House.

Trippany, R. L., White-Kress, V. E., & Wilcoxon, S. (2004). Preventing vicarious trauma: What counselors should know when working with trauma survivors. *Journal of Counseling and Development, 82*(1), 31–37.

Truman, J. L., Langton, L. (2015). *Criminal victimization, 2014.* Washington, DC: Bureau of Justice Statistics, Office of Justice Programs. U.S. Department of Justice.

Tsai, B. (2000). The trend toward specialized domestic violence courts: Improvements on an effective innovation. *Fordham Law Review, 68*(4), 1285–1327. Retrieved from https://ir.lawnet.fordham.edu/cgi/viewcontent.cgi?article=3628&context=flr

Tully, R. J., Chou, S., & Browne, K. D. (2013). A systematic review on the effectiveness of sex offender risk assessment tools in predicting sexual recidivism of adult male sex offenders. *Clinical Psychology Review, 33*(2), 287–315.

Turgoose, D., Glover, N., Barker, C., & Maddox, L. (2017). Empathy, compassion fatigue, and burnout in police officers working with rape victims. *Traumatology, 23*(2), 205–213.

Ullman, S. E., Najdowski, C. J., & Filipas, H. H. (2009). Child sexual abuse, post-traumatic stress disorder, and substance use: Predictors of revictimization in adult sexual assault survivors. *Journal of child Sexual Abuse, 18,* 367–385.

U. S. Department of Justice. (2007). Crime in the United States. Washington, DC: Author.

U.S. Department of Justice. (2018). *Drug courts*. Retrieved from https://www.ncjrs.gov/pdffiles1/nij/238527.pdf

U.S. Department of Veterans Affairs. (n.d.). PTSD: National Center for PTSD. Self-Harm and Trauma. Retrieved from https://www.ptsd.va.gov/understand/related/self_harm.asp

U.S. v. Comstock. (2010). 560 U.S., 2010 W.L. 1946729 (U.S.)

Vagins D. J., & McCurdy, J. (2006). *Cracks in the system: Twenty years of the unjust federal crack cocaine law*. Washington, DC: American Civil Liberties Union. Retrieved from https://www.aclu.org/files/pdfs/drugpolicy/cracksinsystem_20061025.pdf

van den Heuvel, M., Demerouti, E., Schaufeli, W. B., & Bakker, A. B. (2010). Personal resources and work engagement in the face of change. In J. Houdmont & S. Leka (Eds.), *Contemporary occupational health psychology: Global perspectives on research and practice* (pp. 124–150). Hoboken, N.J.: Wiley.

van der Doef, M., & Maes, S. (1999). The job demand-control (-support) model and psychological well-being: A review of 20 years of empirical research. *Work & Stress, 13*(2), 87–114.

van der Hart, O., Nijenhuis, E. R. S., & Steele, K. (2006). *The haunted self: Structural dissociation and the treatment of chronic traumatization*. New York, NY: Norton.

van der Kolk, B. (2014). *The body keeps the score: Brain, mind, and body in the healing of trauma*. New York, NY: Random House.

van der Kolk, B. A. (1987). *Psychological trauma*. Washington, DC: American Psychiatric Press.

van der Kolk, B. A. (2005). Developmental trauma disorder: Toward a rational diagnosis for children with complex trauma histories. *Psychiatric Annals, 35*(5), 401–408.

van der Kolk, B. A., McFarlane, A. C., & Weisaeth, L. (Eds.). (1996). *Traumatic stress: The effects of overwhelming experience on mind, body, and society*. New York, NY: Guilford Press.

van der Kolk, B. A., Roth, S., Pelcovitz, D., Sunday, S., & Spinazzola, J. (2005). Disorders of extreme stress: The empirical foundation of a complex adaptation to trauma. *Journal of Traumatic Stress, 18*(5), 389–399. Retrieved from http://www.traumacenter.org/products/pdf_files/specialissuecomplextraumaoct2006jts3.pdf

Van Ness, D. W., & Strong, K. H. (2010). *Restorative justice: An introduction to restorative justice* (4th ed.). New Province, NJ: Matthew Bender & Co.

Victor, B., & Cullen, J. B. (1987). A theory and measure of ethical climate in organizations. In W. C. Frederick (Ed.), *Research in corporate social performance and policy,* (pp. 51–71). Greenwich, CT: JAI Press.

Viding, E. (2004). On the nature and nurture of antisocial behavior and violence. *Annals of the New York Academy of Sciences, 1036*(1), 267–277.

Violence Against Women Act (VAWA), Title IV of the Violent Crime Control and Law Enforcement Act (P.L. 103–322).

Vogt, K., Hakanen, J. J., Jenny, G. J., & Bauer, G. F. (2016). Sense of coherence and motivational process of the job-demands-resources model. *Journal of Occupational Health Psychology, 21*(2), 194–207.

Volkow, N. D. (Ed.). (n.d.). *Comorbidity: Addiction and other mental illnesses*. Washington, DC: National Institute on Drug Abuse. Retrieved from https://www.drugabuse.gov/sites/default/files/rrcomorbidity.pdf

von Hentig, H. (1940). Remarks on the interaction of perpetrator and victim. *Journal of Criminal Law and Criminology, 31*(3), 303–309. Retrieved from https://scholarlycommons.law.northwestern.edu/cgi/viewcontent.cgi?article=2969&context=jclc

Walklate, S. (2003). *Understanding criminology: Current theoretical debates* (2nd ed.). Maidenhead, UK: Open University Press.

Walrath, C. M., Ybarra, M. L., Sheenan, A. K., Holden, E. W., & Burns, B. J. (2006). Impact of maltreatment on children served in community mental health programs. *Journal of Emotional and Behavioral Disorders, 14*(3), 143–156.

Wanberg, K. W. (2004). *Adult Substance Use Survey revised.* Arvada, CO: Center for Addiction Research and Evaluation (CARE).

Warshaw, C., Brashler, P., & Gil, J. (2009). Mental health consequences of intimate partner violence. In C. Mitchell & D. Anglin (Eds.), *Intimate partner violence: A health-based perspective* (pp. 147–170). New York, NY: Oxford University Press.

Watson, C. G., Barnett, M., Nikunen, L, Schultz, C., Randolph-Elgin, T., & Mendez, C. M. (1997). Lifetime prevalences of non common psychiatric/personality disorders in female domestic abuse survivors. *Journal of Nervous and Mental Disease, 185*(10), 645–647. doi:10.1097/00005053=199710000-00011

Watts, D., & Morgan, G. (1994). Malignant alienation: Dangers for patients who are hard to like. *British Journal of Psychiatry, 164,*(1), 11–15.

Weathers, F. W., Litz, B. T., Keane, T. M., Palmieri, P. A., Marx, B. P., & Schnurr, P. P. (2013). *The PTSD Checklist for DSM-5* (PCL-5). Retrieved from www.ptsd.va.gov

Weaver, T. L., & Clum, G. A. (1995). Psychological distress associated with interpersonal violence: A meta-analysis. *Clinical Psychology Review, 15*(2), 115–140. doi:10.1016/0272-7358(95)00004-9

Webster, L., & Hacket, R. K. (1999). Burnout and leadership in community mental health systems. *Administration and Policy in Mental Health and mental Health Services Research, 26*(6), 387–399.

Wee, D. F., & Myers, D. (2002). Stress response of mental health workers following disaster: The Oklahoma City bombing. In C. R. Figley (Ed.). *Treating compassion fatigue* (pp. 57–84). New York: NY: Bruner/Mazel.

Weierich, M. R., & Nock, M. K. (2008). Posttraumatic stress symptoms mediate the relation between childhood sexual abuse and nonsuicidal self-injury. *Journal of Consulting and Clinical Psychology, 76*(1), 39–44.

Weigel, M. (2012). Juvenile arrest and collateral educational damage in the transition to adulthood. *Journalist's Resource.* Retrieved from https://journalistsresource.org/studies/society/education/juvenile-arrest-collateral-educational-damage

Westermeyer, J., Yargic, I., & Thuras, P. (2004). Michigan assessment-screening test for alcohol and drugs (MAST/AD): Evaluation in a clinical sample. *American Journal of Addiction, 13*(2), 151–162.

Westman, M., & Eden, D. (1996). The inverted-U relationship between job stress and performance. *Work Stress, 10*(2), 164–173.

Whitaker, T., Weismiller, T., & Clark, E. (2006). Social workers and safety fact sheet. *National Association of Social Workers Center for Workforce Studies.* Retrieved from https://www.socialworkers.org/LinkClick.aspx?fileticket=ESTCCZA4HAE%3D&portalid=0

Whitehead, J. T. (1989). *Burnout in probation and corrections.* New York, NY: Praeger.

Williams, S. (1968). Blach child's pledge. *The Black Panther, 26.* Retrieved from https://herb.ashp.cuny.edu/items/show/1254.

Wilson, A. B., Draineb, J., Hadley, T., Metraux, S., & Evans, A. (2011). Examining the impact of mental illness and substance use on recidivism in a county jail. *International Journal of Law and Psychiatry, 34*(4), 265–268. doi:10.1016/j.ijlp.2011.07/004

Wilson, J., & Lindy, J. (1994). Empathic strain and countertransference. In J. Wilson & J. Lindy (Eds.), *Countertransference in the treatment of PTSD* (pp. 5–30). New York, NY: Guilford Press.

Winfrey, O. (2010, October 20). *Oprah opens up about her abusive childhood* [Video file]. Retrieved from http://www.oprah.com/own-oprahshow/oprah-opens-up-about-her-abusive-childhood-video

Wolff, N., Chugo, M. G., Shi, J., Huening, J., & Frueh, M.C. (2015). Screening for PTSD among incarcerated men: A comparative analysis of computer-administered and orally administered modalities. *Criminal Justice and Behavior, 42*(2), 219–236. doi:10.1177/0093854814551601

Wolff, N., Huening, J., Shi, J., & Frueh, C. (2014). Trauma exposure and posttraumatic stress disorder among incarcerated men. *Journal of Urban Health, 91*(4), 707–719. doi:10.1007/s11524-014-9871-x

Wolff, N., & Shi, J. (2012). Childhood and adult trauma experiences of incarcerated persons and their relationship to adult behavioral health problems and treatment. *International Journal of Environmental Research and Public Policy, 9*(5), 1908–1926. Retrieved from https://www.ncbi.nlm.nih.gov/pmc/articles/PMC3386595/

World Health Organization (WHO) (n.d.). *Child abuse and neglect facts*. Retrieved from http://www.who.int/violence_injury_prevention/violence/world_report/factsheets/en/childabusefacts.pdf

World Health Organization. (1999). *Guidelines for medical and legal care for victims of sexual violence*. Retrieved from https://apps.who.int/iris/bitstream/handle/10665/42788/924154628X.pdf;jsessionid=AD7DE27A6925BC0D12A33F40D6EBFBB3?sequence=1

World Health Organization. (2004). *Managing child abuse: A handbook for medical officers*. Retrieved from https://apps.who.int/iris/bitstream/handle/10665/205458/B0008.pdf

World Health Organization. (2007). *Preventing suicide in jails and prisons*. Geneva, Switzerland: Author.

Wyatt v. Stickney, 344 F.Supp. 387 (M.D. Ala. 1971).

Xanthopoulou, D., Bakker, A. B., Demerouti, E., & Schaufeli, W. B. (2007). The role of personal resources in the job demands-resource model. *International Journal of Stress Management, 14*(2), 121–141.

Xanthopoulou, D., Bakker, A. B., Demerouti, E., & Schaufeli, W. B. (2009). Reciprocal relationships between job resources, personal resources, and work engagement. *Journal of Vocational Behavior, 74*(3), 235–244.

Yampolskaya, S., & Chuang, E. (2012). Effects of mental health disorders on the risk of juvenile justice system involvement and recidivism among children placed in out-of-home care. *American journal of Orthopsychiatry, 82*(4), 585–593.

Zehr, H. (2002). *The little book of restorative justice*. Intercourse, PA: Good Books.

Zehr, H. (2005). *Changing lenses: A new focus for crime and justice* (3rd ed.). Scottdale, PA: Herald Press.

Zeidner, M., Hadar, D., Mattews, G., & Roberts, R. D. (2013). Personal factors related to compassion fatigue in health professionals. *Anxiety, Stress and Coping, 26*(6), 595–609.

Index